A Level Religious Studies for Eduqas

Religion and Ethics

CLARE
LLOYD

OXFORD
UNIVERSITY PRESS

OXFORD
UNIVERSITY PRESS

Great Clarendon Street, Oxford, OX2 6DP, United Kingdom

Oxford University Press is a department of the University of Oxford. It furthers the University's objective of excellence in research, scholarship, and education by publishing worldwide. Oxford is a registered trade mark of Oxford University Press in the UK and in certain other countries

British Library Cataloguing in Publication Data
Data available

978-1-382-02900-1

978-1-382-02901-8 (ebook)

10 9 8 7 6 5 4 3 2

Paper used in the production of this book is a natural, recyclable product made from wood grown in sustainable forests.

The manufacturing process conforms to the environmental regulations of the country of origin.

Printed in China by Shanghai Offset Printing Products Ltd

This resource has been reviewed against WJEC Eduqas' endorsement criteria. As this resource belongs to a third party, there may be occasions where a specification may be updated and that update will not be reflected in the third party resource. Users should always refer to WJEC Eduqas' specification and Sample Assessment Materials to ensure that learners are studying the most up to date course.

It is recommended that teachers use a range of resources to fully prepare their learners for the exam and not rely solely on one textbook or digital resource.

WJEC, nor anyone employed by WJEC has been paid for the endorsement of this resource, nor does WJEC receive any royalties from its sale.

Author thanks: I would like to thank two of my very valuable friends and colleagues who have offered me both moral and practical support as I have faced the challenges involved in writing this book. Thank you to Dr Greg Barker for all your patience and support fielding questions and pointing me in the right direction. Thank you to Richard Gray for your support and good humour as I have stretched myself further than ever before. Both of you have been wonderfully understanding as I have been on this journey. Finally thank you to my wonderful husband Steven Lloyd who has weathered tears and tantrums and without whom this book would not have been written.

The publisher would also like to thank Mark Griffiths, Julie Haigh and David Legrand for their help preparing this book for publication, and James Helling for the index.

Contents

Introduction

Religious Studies is a fascinating subject. Not only does it involve learning facts about other people's opinions, beliefs and practices, but it also raises some very deep and important questions that have excited thinkers for centuries. What does it mean to be a good person? Is there a God? Why is there evil and suffering in the world? If one religion is true, must other religions, therefore, be false? What is the best method of making moral decisions? Is there a truth 'out there' to be discovered? Is there a reason why the universe exists, and why humanity exists? Questions like these really matter for all of us as human beings; this subject is not just a means to getting a good grade, it will draw your attention to some of the most important aspects of human life.

Following a course in Religious Studies will enrich your thinking, and help you to develop your skills in a wide range of ways. It will help you cultivate a questioning disposition, expand your debating skills, and help you write more thoughtfully and persuasively. You will learn to be a better listener and to develop your own opinions using reasoning, so that you can justify your point of view while being open to hearing the views of others. All of these skills will help you in adult life, and are excellent preparation for many degree courses and career choices.

Although you will gain a great deal from Religious Studies, regardless of the exams, you are probably keen to achieve the best grade you can, to reflect your abilities and recognise all you have achieved. This section of this book will give you some guidance about the exams, showing you what to expect and what examiners will be looking for when they read your work.

Features

This book has been written to help you with the Religion and Ethics component of your course.

The first part of each chapter takes you through the AO1 content you need to cover for each theme in the specification. It introduces you to key issues and thinkers, and explains ideas that may be new to you. Throughout the AO1 section, you will see activities that will help you develop your knowledge and understanding. For example:

> ### AO1 activity 3
> Create a knowledge organiser or mind map that summarises Divine Command Theory. You should include:
>
> - what Divine Command Theory is
> - Robert Adams' modification
> - the three listed challenges.
>
> Include examples of divine commands, scholarly quotations, and specialist vocabulary. Do not forget to use colour and pictures to make it more memorable.

The second part of each chapter concentrates on the AO2 skills of analysis and evaluation, inviting you to consider different points of view in relation to the issues and perspectives in the specification. For each discussion question, you are given contrasting points of view with reasons people could give to support them. Scholars that do not appear in the specification are mentioned to help with your evaluation; these scholars will not be named in an exam question. The AO2 activities encourage you to weigh up the different points of view and decide which you find the most convincing. For example:

> ### AO2 activity 1
> Look at the arguments for and against the question 'Is morality whatever God commands?'. Identify which arguments seem to go together as opposite sides of the same point. For each pair, decide which argument you find more convincing, and give two reasons why.

Some of the vocabulary in this course may be unfamiliar to you, and so key words have been identified and defined. For example:

Key term

Divine Command Theory: an ethical theory that believes morality is dependent upon God; moral goodness occurs when moral agents are obedient to God's commands

Definitions are closely based on the official Eduqas glossary (https://www.eduqas.co.uk/umbraco/ surface/blobstorage/download?nodeId=13812) but have sometimes been condensed or split up into smaller entries, and we've added some additional definitions to help you. All the key words are also collected together at the back of the book in the glossary, so you can refer to them throughout the course.

Many areas of the course have connections within and across themes, and within and across components. These connections are highlighted with the 'Synoptic link' feature, so you can revisit different parts of the course and see how ideas are connected. For example:

Synoptic Link

Link to *Chapter 7: Determinism and free will: Determinism* and *Chapter 8: Determinism and free will: free will*. Divine Command Theory assumes that we are free to choose behaviour that is in accordance with the command of God. There is significant debate over the extent to which we are free agents or are predestined by God.

This feature of the book will be particularly useful when you revise.

Quotations from a range of scholars are used in the book to help you clarify your understanding, and to give you opportunities to read scholars' ideas in their own words. If you plan to go on to further study after A Level, it will be useful for you to begin reading passages from scholars' original writings. The quotations in this book stand out from the rest of the text to make them more obvious. For example:

> *If the universe began to exist, and the universe is caused, then the cause of the universe must be a personal being who freely chooses to create the world.*
>
> William Lane Craig,
> *The Kalam Cosmological Argument*

It can help you to demonstrate your knowledge and understanding if you sometimes use quotations from scholars, but you do not need to learn every passage by heart as if you were going to be performing it in a play. An occasional well-chosen short phrase or sentence is plenty for a quotation in an essay; there is no need to quote entire paragraphs.

The Exam support sections at the end of each chapter introduce you to some past paper questions, and give you some guidance about how to tackle them in an exam. There are example paragraphs to demonstrate what good responses could look like, sometimes in comparison with example paragraphs that would not score so highly. These are intended to be used as possible models for your own writing, but they are not 'perfect answers' to be learned or copied. Instead, look at them to see how the writer of the paragraph has tailored their response to meet the assessment objectives. The work has been highlighted in different colours to help you see the different skills displayed. There are also other activities in the Exam support section to help you improve your skills, as well as more questions from past papers to help you practise.

Exam support

How is the course structured?

In this course, you will explore three components: A Study of Religion (where you will focus on one of the six major world religions); Philosophy of Religion; Religion and Ethics.

Each component is worth one-third of the total marks. For A Level, you will study four themes for each component, and for AS Level, you will study fewer themes in less detail.

What will the exams be like?

For A Level, you will sit three papers, one for each component. All of the assessment tasks will be essays; there are no multiple-choice questions, short-answer questions, or coursework tasks.

Sections A and B

Each A Level paper will have two parts: Section A and Section B. Section A contains two questions, usually both from the same theme, and you must choose just one of them to answer. Section B will contain three questions taken from anywhere else in the component, and you must choose one of them. You must answer parts (a) and (b) of the same question; you cannot choose to answer part (a) from one question and part (b) from a different question. When you are choosing which questions to tackle, read the question as a whole, and make sure you are confident about tackling both parts before you begin.

The papers are divided into two sections, to make sure you cover all of the course when you are learning and revising. Sometimes, students realise that they have left their revision too late. They think they can cut down the amount of work they need to do by trying to guess what the questions will be, and then only revise thoroughly for those selected topics. This is a very bad idea, because those students may have chosen to ignore the theme that appears in Section A, and then they will not be able to answer either question in that section. By choosing one compulsory theme for Section A, and not letting you know in advance which theme it will be, the question setters make sure that you cover all the course when you learn and revise. Any theme can be chosen for Section A, including a theme that has appeared in recent past papers.

Timing in the exam

Make sure you allow equal time to answer both questions. Some students make the mistake of allowing too much time to answer the question from Section A, and not enough time to answer the questions from Section B; this can mean their Section B answers are rushed, short or even missing.

At A Level you have 2 hours, or 120 minutes, to answer both questions (unless you have extra time). Plan your time carefully, giving yourself enough time to settle, read the questions carefully, and plan your answers to the questions you choose.

Understanding the Assessment Objectives

At A Level, your work is assessed against two different criteria. It is important to understand what examiners are looking for, so that you can present your knowledge and your skills in a way that helps them reward you. During your course, your teacher will use the same criteria to mark your work and give you feedback so that you can see how to improve.

Assessment Objective 1 (AO1) requires you to demonstrate your knowledge and understanding of the material in the course. You need to show that you understand religious and philosophical ideas and teachings. You need to show an understanding of the contributions that different thinkers have made to the issues in the course, as well as the challenges these contributions present and the views of people who disagree with them. In every question in the exam, for every component, part (a) assesses this knowledge and understanding, using 'Explain', 'Examine', 'Compare', 'Apply' and – if you are sitting an AS examination – 'Outline' to tell you what you need to do.

For high marks in AO1, your work needs to demonstrate knowledge and understanding that is relevant to the specific question. Make sure you read the question carefully so that you can address exactly what it is asking; your response needs to be thorough and accurate. Where possible, you should use examples to clarify your response, and you should support the claims you make with evidence.

If appropriate, you should make reference to sacred texts. Sometimes, it can be appropriate to show that there are links between the issue in the question and issues in other areas of the course. You should demonstrate a good knowledge and understanding of a range of scholarly views, and you should aim to use the specialist terms that theologians and philosophers use confidently and accurately in your writing. AO1 is about demonstrating what you know; you do not need to give your own views in responses to part (a) questions.

The marks for part (a) are worth 40% of the question total at A Level.

Assessment Objective 2 (AO2) requires you to analyse and evaluate the different issues and perspectives in the course. You need to show that you understand why there are different opinions about an issue, and develop an opinion of your own that you can justify with reasoned argument. In part (b) responses, you do not need to give lengthy descriptions and explanations; you should concentrate on analysis and evaluation.

Analysis involves unpacking a claim or an argument to explore its structure; you need to consider the chains of reasoning that have been used to justify a view.

Evaluation involves weighing up an argument or a point of view, deciding whether or not it is persuasive, and making a reasoned judgement. You could conclude that an argument is flawed, or effective, or that an issue is significant, for example. You need to develop your own views, and not just describe the opinions of others.

For high marks in AO2, your response needs to address the question asked specifically. You need to show that you understand the issues raised by the question, and focus your answer on those issues, rather than discussing more generally. There may be opportunities in part (b) to show how the issues in the question have connections with other areas of the course. And, as with AO1, you should use specialist language accurately and with confidence where appropriate.

Thinking for yourself is important here. However, avoid simply giving your own view without making any reference to scholarly thinking. Aim to show which side of the debate you prefer, while at the same time making it clear that you have a good understanding of key thinkers and the contribution each has made to the debate. You should use the ideas of different scholars or different schools of thought in your response; but the emphasis should be on *using* them, and not just on *listing* them. You should show how scholar X's thinking is more persuasive than scholar Y's thinking, or how there are flaws in scholar Z's reasoning that make their argument ineffective, rather than simply saying, 'X said this, but Y said that'.

As you answer the question and analyse scholars' views, you should aim to use reasoning and evidence to support the evaluations you make.

Think of approaching AO2 as you would approach attending a meeting. Your role is not the role of a secretary: you are not there simply to record who says something and what they say, while keeping quiet yourself. You are a participant, so you have a voice. Pay attention to the views of scholars, as you would listen to the other people in the meeting. In part (a) of your answer, you are asked to explain, examine, outline, or compare different ideas that others have put forward. However, part (b) is your own turn to speak: refer to what others have said, and then make it clear what your opinion is: 'I agree with A and B because …, I agree with C, but only up to a point because …, I think D and E are wrong because . . .; and, therefore, I conclude with *this* judgement.' Make sure that your judgements are backed up with reasoning, and are not just asserted as though it is obvious that you are right and your opinion does not need explaining.

When you study this course, you may have strong beliefs of your own, either as a religious believer or as someone who thinks religion is wrong; or you may be undecided about many of the questions that the subject raises. Although Religious Studies courses are intended to help you think about and shape, your own beliefs, in an exam it is your reasoning that is awarded not your beliefs. You should focus on telling the examiner how your reasoning leads to your conclusions; you will not gain marks by telling the examiner about your personal religious or non-religious beliefs.

There are lots of ways you can improve your performance in AO1 and AO2:

- Reading is always important. The course is quite detailed, and you may feel you do not have a lot of time for additional reading; but try, if possible, to read more than just one textbook or resource. Reading will enrich your knowledge and help you to feel more confident about the subject matter. If you read good-quality writing, your own written style will improve, as you will become more familiar with the kind of language professional writers and philosophers use to express what they want to say. When possible, read extracts from philosophers in their own words; some are more accessible than others. Reading and note-taking is a valuable skill to practise if you hope to go on to further study after your A Levels.

- Involving yourself in class discussions is very helpful. You will remember ideas more clearly if you have engaged in debates about them. If you strongly agree or disagree with thinkers, you are more likely to remember their names. Discussion will help you develop your own opinions so that you can articulate them clearly; it will help you find ways to challenge the views of those you disagree with; it will help you respond to challenges and defend your own views against criticism. It will also help you to develop useful skills for later life, as you learn to speak with confidence, listen to others, and work through differences of opinion in a civilised and constructive way.

- For AO2, make a habit of thinking about different ideas when they are presented to you in class, rather than simply writing them down. Ask yourself whether you agree with the idea, or whether you think the scholar or school of thought is wrong, and think about why you agree or disagree.

- This book gives you plenty of activities to help you develop your skills in AO1 and AO2.

Command words

Command words are the words in exam questions that tell you want you need to do, such as 'Explain' or 'Evaluate'.

For AO1 – part (a) – different command words are used. These include:

- **Apply:** This command word requires you to show how a principle, theory, or teaching might be used in relation to an issue or a situation; for example, how Utilitarianism might be applied to animal experimentation for medical research. To gain high marks, you must show how the theory works to decide which actions are right or wrong in the specific moral dilemma mentioned in the question.

- **Compare:** This command word requires you to explain the similarities and differences between two things, perhaps two arguments, two scholars' perspectives, or two theories. To gain high marks, you need to avoid simply describing one and then the other; you should concentrate on drawing out ways in which they are similar and different.

- **Explain:** This command word asks you to write a full and detailed account of a topic. The question will tell you what to explain, and you need to pay careful attention to exactly what you are being asked to do. For example, the question could say 'Explain the significance of …', in which case you need to concentrate on giving reasons why the thing is significant, rather than simply describing the thing. You might be asked to explain how a thinker deals with an issue, or why someone criticises a view.

- **Examine:** This command word asks you to give an account of one or more aspects of something fairly complex. In Religion and Ethics, for example, you might be asked to examine a particular aspect of Aquinas' theory of Natural Law such as his use of reason. Or in Philosophy of Religion, you could be asked to examine selected features of Irenaeus' approach to the problem of evil, such as his ideas about growing into the likeness of God. An 'examine' question asks you to go into depth about a narrower topic, while an 'explain' question asks for a broader range of detail.

- **Outline:** AS questions sometimes use the command word 'outline'. For this, you need to identify the key features of the thing you are describing; try to draw a picture of it in words as if you are teaching the examiner about it.

For AO2 – part (b) – the same command word is always used:

- **Evaluate:** The question might be phrased as follows: *'Here is a statement asserting a position.' Evaluate this view.*

Alternatively, it might say: *Evaluate the view that (followed by a point of view).*

You need to weigh up a variety of arguments and ideas, making reference to scholars where appropriate, and making a reasoned judgement about them. You must include a conclusion, showing what you think of the idea you were asked to evaluate.

Structuring your responses

There is no single right way to structure your answers. Eduqas does not have a formulaic essay template that you should follow. As long as your essays meet the assessment objectives, you can structure them in whatever way you think best.

However, some students struggle to know where to start and how to proceed with presenting material or an argument, and so teachers sometimes offer them essay structures to use. (They might have mnemonics to help you remember them, such as PEREL: Point Explain Response Evaluate Link.) These structures can be useful, in the same way that stabilisers can be useful when learning to ride a bicycle; but not everyone will find them helpful, and there will come a time when you find you write more naturally and fluently without them.

For part (a), you do not need an introduction or a conclusion, because you are not making any judgements that require summing up. However, you do need to organise your material so that it follows an orderly structure. It could make sense to present the material in chronological order, showing what early thinkers said and then how later thinkers developed those ideas. If you are explaining a theory or one thinker's ideas, it may not matter which order you choose to present the different facets of the material. Sometimes the question will require you to explain the thinking of two or three different people, or to give two different arguments, and then it would make sense to explore each in turn, rather than going back and forth between them.

For part (b), you must have a conclusion because you are being asked for your judgement, so you need to say what that judgement is. You could begin your response with your own judgement, or put it at the end, or have a series of mini-conclusions throughout your answer.

One structure that can work quite well for part (b) responses is to set up the points of view that you disagree with, say why you think they are wrong, and then present views you prefer and say why you find them stronger. This is one of the ways people present arguments in everyday life. If your friend is asking for your advice about what to wear to a wedding, you might say: 'Not the red dress: the colour is too shouty and you will look as if you want to be the centre of attention. Not the blue dress either: it is too short for a religious ceremony and the bride's mother is wearing exactly the same colour. I think you should wear the green one: the colour suits you and you have a nice jacket that goes with it in case the weather is cool.' For each of the options, you are giving reasons to support your opinion, resulting in a persuasive argument.

Another structure that can work well is an 'ABCD' approach. In each paragraph, you give an **A**rgument. Then you **B**ack it up with reasons. Next you offer a **C**ounter-argument. And, finally, you **D**ecide which view is stronger. This can be a good approach because you are displaying analysis and evaluation in every paragraph, so if you were to run out of time, you have demonstrated all the AO2 skills despite not finishing. You may find other structures that work well for you; there is no need to pick just one and stick to it rigidly.

Making essay plans

Your essays will be more coherent and more thorough if you plan them before you begin writing. If you are writing an essay for homework, you will have the time to make a more detailed essay plan. In an exam, you will have time only for a few brief notes to remind yourself of the key points you want to make.

Your plan functions like a shopping list. It reminds you of the ingredients you need for your essay, so that you avoid missing out something essential. A good shopping list also organises the ingredients, so all the fruit and vegetables are together, and all the dairy items together and so on; so that, in the shop, you do not waste time going back and forth for individual items, but can make an efficient single circuit of the supermarket and save time. Your essay plan should organise your material in a similar way, so that you know what you want to say first, and where you want to end up, and the route you plan to take between the two. With a good plan in place, you will be able to write a thorough, easy-to-follow essay with more confidence.

As you go through the course, practise making plans for the past paper questions in the Exam support sections of each chapter. When you revise, look at past paper questions on the Eduqas website and practise making plans for them.

In the exam, choose your questions carefully, making sure that you can answer both parts of the questions you choose. Once you have chosen your two questions, write all four plans before beginning to write your first essay. This will help you keep calm, as you will begin writing knowing that you have both questions under control; you will not be worrying about the second question while you are trying to concentrate on the first one.

Using band descriptors and mark schemes

If you look at Eduqas' website (www.eduqas.co.uk), you will find past papers and mark schemes to help you with your learning.

Mark schemes contain what is called 'indicative content'. They show you the kinds of things examiners were expecting candidates to write. They are not a checklist. Examiners do not try to match your response against the mark scheme, nor do they take marks away from you if your response does not include some of the indicative content. Instead, the mark schemes are a useful guide to show you the level of detail required for a top-level response. If you are writing a practice essay, it can be useful to look at the mark scheme for some guidance about what to include, but you do not need to follow it exactly. Examiners will credit relevant material in your essay that does not appear in the mark scheme, and they will award you appropriately if you have taken a different approach, or used different thinkers to demonstrate your skills instead of the ones in the mark scheme, provided they are relevant to the question that was asked.

Band descriptors are used to determine the quality of your answer and show the examiners which marks to give you. The examiner decides whether your answer is 'thorough, accurate and relevant', for example, or 'satisfactory' or 'limited', and awards you the appropriate mark. These band descriptors will help you understand the marks your teacher gives the essays you write during the course, and you can use them to help you improve your work. When your marked essays are returned to you, look at the band descriptors to see what your mark means, and also look at the description in the band above, to see where you need to improve. You may need to make your work more accurate, for example, or make better use of scholarly thought, or be more thorough in your analysis.

Revision

Revision is essential for success in your A Levels. You need to allow plenty of time for it. The February half term before your exams is a good time to start organising your notes and recapping the work you did at the start of the course. You can also do things throughout the course to help you prepare for your revision:

- Make a regular habit of revisiting your notes and reading the material you have covered, rather than leaving all your revision to the end of the course.
- Try making flash cards with key bullet points whenever you finish a unit of study. The process of picking out the key points and making the cards is very useful for embedding the content in your memory and developing your understanding.
- Try setting yourself quick quiz questions as you finish each unit of study. Writing the questions will help you remember the key information, and you could put the questions aside so that you can test yourself when you come to revise.

Remember to revise for AO2 as well as for AO1. When you are revising for AO1, you will be noting and memorising the content you have covered. For AO2, rehearse the arguments you will put forward when you are asked for your view on an issue. Many students concentrate their revision too heavily on AO1 and forget to revise for AO2; but if you were a lawyer defending a client, you would not go into court without an idea of what you were going to say in the client's defence; you would have rehearsed your argument carefully. You can do the same for AO2, reminding yourself of the reasons why you reached your current opinion as you do your revision.

Imagine you have not completed your Religious Studies homework for the second time in a week; you forgot because you were socialising with friends. Your tutor is well known for having a fierce temper and has already given you one warning. Do you lie to your tutor to get out of trouble, or do you tell the truth? How do you make your decision?

Moral decisions are choices that you make based on ideas that you have about what is right and what is wrong. This chapter explores ethical thought, the rules and principles that guide those decisions.

There are many scholarly ideas about the basis for morality. Some scholars feel that morality and religion are very closely linked, and that it is necessary to consult religious experts in order to discover what is right and what is wrong. Others claim that morality has nothing to do with religion at all and that the basis for deciding 'goodness' comes from something more worldly, such as personal desire.

In this chapter you will consider three ethical approaches: Divine Command Theory, Virtue Theory and Ethical Egoism. Divine Command Theory understands the basis of morality to be found in religion or God. Virtue Theory considers morality to have either a philosophical and a religious foundation, or both. Ethical Egoism sees morality as being a responsibility to ourselves alone, rather than any obligation to religion or other people.

Where do you think morality comes from?

How do we know what is good?

This section of the chapter will enhance your **knowledge** and **understanding** of the topic and help you develop your AO1 skills.

Divine Command Theory

Divine Command Theory is an ethical approach that is also known as theological voluntarism. This approach says that morality is directed by God's commands. For theological voluntarists, morality has a supernatural basis, so what is 'good' is necessarily linked to the existence of a divine being. This means that whatever God commands is morally right, and whatever God forbids is morally wrong.

God as the origin and regulator of morality

Divine Command Theory assumes that God, the creator and sustainer of the universe, exists and is concerned with human action. **Theists** who support Divine Command Theory argue that all moral requirements come from God who has created all things. They believe that God is the originator of morality: if things are good it is because God wills them, and if they are bad it is because God forbids them. Essentially, for theological voluntarists, there is a single moral obligation to obey God. All other commands, such as those that forbid theft or lying, should be obeyed because God commands them.

This approach requires a belief that we have free will to choose behaviours that are contrary to God's command, but that we should choose to avoid these behaviours if we are to be morally virtuous. We can see examples of such commands in scripture. For example, in Exodus 20 God commanded the Hebrews that they should not lie or steal, and in Matthew 22 Jesus commands that people should love God and their neighbour.

> *You shall not murder.*
> *You shall not commit adultery.*
> *You shall not steal.* "
>
> Exodus 20:13–15, *Holy Bible (NIV)*

> *Jesus replied, '"Love the Lord your God with all your heart and with all your soul and with all your mind." This is the first and greatest commandment. And the second is like it: "Love your neighbour as yourself." All the Law and Prophets hang on these two commandments.'* "
>
> Matthew 22:37–40, *Holy Bible (NIV)*

Key terms

Divine Command Theory: an ethical theory that believes morality is dependent upon God; moral goodness occurs when moral agents are obedient to God's commands

theists: people who believe in a personal, creator God who can and does interact with humanity; Christians, Muslims and Jews are theists

Synoptic link

Link to *Chapter 7: Determinism and free will: Determinism* and *Chapter 8: Determinism and free will: free will*. Divine Command Theory assumes that we are free to choose behaviour that is in accordance with the command of God. There is significant debate over the extent to which we are free agents or are predestined by God.

Right and wrong as objective truths based on God's will or command

Divine Command Theory is a successful account of morality in the sense that it bypasses the problems associated with morality being subjective. According to Divine Command Theory, morality is not just a point of view, a matter of opinion, or a social custom. It is an objective, impartial law that is not dependent upon any limited human perspective; it is the result of a transcendent decree. It also answers the question of 'why' we should do anything moral, by giving the reason that there will be divine punishment if the decrees are ignored or divine reward if they are obeyed.

Divine Command Theory says that goodness is whatever God commands.

Moral goodness is achieved by complying with divine command

Divine Command Theory states two things:

1. What God commands is the same as that which is good (a **meta-ethical** claim).
2. We ought to obey anything that God commands (a **normative** claim).

A meta-ethical approach to ethics is concerned with the definitions of moral terms like 'good' or 'evil'. It says that 'goodness' is defined as 'what God commands'.

A normative approach to ethics is concerned with formulating actual rules for human behaviour. This approach says that we should obey whatever God commands. So, moral 'oughts' or obligations should be performed by us because God has commanded them.

Therefore, to be a morally good person, people should obey God's commands. Intellectually it is unreasonable to act contrary to any command from God.

Divine command as a requirement of God's omnipotence

Descriptions of the character of God include moral perfection and **omnipotence**. Even atheist theological voluntarist scholars agree that if such a being exists then it would require obedience, because all of the being's commands would be morally perfect. It is logically coherent to say that an all-powerful creator God would have created the standard of morality for humanity and it must, therefore, be obeyed.

Divine command as an objective metaphysical foundation for morality

In summary, the basis of all moral action is found in anything that God commands, which is beyond the ordinary workings of the **empirical** world or individual desires. Whatever God commands is objectively good and not subject to personal preferences or options. To be a good person only requires you to comply with God's will.

Challenges

The Euthyphro dilemma and the arbitrariness problem

One of the most famous challenges to the Divine Command Theory is known as the **Euthyphro dilemma**. This challenge is based on the writings of the ancient Greek scholar, Plato. Plato wrote in dialogues, which are conversations between characters, like a play. In his dialogue called *Euthyphro*, Plato uses the conversation between the characters Euthyphro and Socrates to discuss the nature of goodness.

In *Euthyphro*, both characters are waiting outside a courthouse. Socrates is awaiting prosecution, having been accused by the state of corrupting the young. Euthyphro is there because he has accused his father of murdering a labourer who worked for him. Socrates is surprised and asks Euthyphro if he is certain that he is doing the right thing. Euthyphro is sure because he knows that the gods hate murder. Euthyphro summarises his position by saying:

> *Piety, then, is that which is dear to the gods, and impiety is that which is not dear to them.* 🙶
>
> Plato, *The Republic and Other Works*

Socrates challenges Euthyphro by asking him to define 'piety' further, and to explain how we are to know that his statement is true. He asks:

> *The point which I should first wish to understand is whether the pious or holy is beloved by the gods because it is holy, or holy because it is beloved of the gods?* 🙶
>
> Plato, *The Republic and Other Works*

This statement is the crux of the problem with Divine Command Theory. There are two options:

1. Good is commanded by God *because* it is good.
2. Good is commanded by God *therefore* it is good.

These two options are sometimes known as the two 'horns' of the Euthyphro dilemma.

The first horn of the Euthyphro dilemma suggests that 'good' is a separate entity from God and God's will. Theists are now left with the problem that when God is good, God is living up to an external and independent standard. This means that humanity has no need of God to achieve goodness, and can

Key terms

empirical: based on, and verifiable, using our five senses; empirical knowledge comes from things that can be experienced or observed

Euthyphro dilemma: a dilemma originally found in Plato's dialogue *Euthyphro*, asking if goodness is dependent on, or independent of, God

AO1 activity 1

Miracle Workers is a television series set in Heaven. Sanjay works for God, and in Season 1 Episode 2, God asks him to punish a famous unbeliever. Should Sanjay obey God's command or not? Why?

Plato (c. 428–348 BCE)

instead look directly to the independent standard. This is an unacceptable approach for theists because if we ask the question 'Why should I tell the truth?', the answer is not 'because God wills it' but 'because truthfulness is a good thing'; what is good is independent of God.

The second horn of the Euthyphro dilemma is called the **arbitrariness problem**. It suggests that goodness is caused by God's approval. This means that God could command anything and it would be called 'good' simply because God commanded it. Goodness becomes entirely arbitrary. If God commanded murder, Euthyphro would be forced to support his father's actions.

The pluralism objection

Another challenge to the Divine Command Theory is the **pluralism objection**, which points out that there are lots of different religions. As a result, there are numerous understandings of what divinity is, and different conceptions of what humanity has been commanded to do by the divine. Some of these concepts contradict each other. For example, classical theism holds that there is one **omnipotent** God. Polytheism holds that there are many deities. Some might argue that the commands that are found in the Old and New Testaments can even be seen to be in conflict with each other. These conflicting commands cannot all be good, and therefore how are religious believers to know which commands to follow?

Since there is no objective way of knowing which commands from the divine are correct, believers must decide for themselves through a process of deliberation and reasoning. This is no different from the process that a non-believer would go through, and so it seems that there is no advantage for the Divine Command Theorist since obedience to commands is insufficient to do what is good.

Key terms

arbitrariness problem: the criticism of Divine Command Theory that morality must be determined by a whim of God if it is based upon God's commands

pluralism objection: an objection to Divine Command Theory that refers to the contradictory nature of God's commands as claimed by different religions

omnipotent: all-powerful

AO1 activity 2

a) Can you find any examples of divine commands that appear to conflict? Start by looking at the Ten Commandments in Exodus 20. Can you find any divine commands elsewhere in the Bible or in other world religions that directly conflict with these commands? (Consider Genesis 22:1–2 or Hosea 3:1 if you are struggling.)

b) If there are no commands that directly conflict, does the pluralism objection fail? Why or why not?

Robert Adams' Modified Divine Command Theory

American philosopher Robert Merrihew Adams acknowledges the difficulties posed by the Divine Command Theory, and proposes a modified Divine Command Theory in response. The gravest objection that Adams sees arising from Divine Command Theory is the arbitrariness problem. He feels that there are three possible solutions to the arbitrariness problem, two of which are as follows:

1. It is logically impossible for God to command cruelty for its own sake, and so it is senseless to debate it.
2. God could command cruelty for its own sake and, if God commanded it, we would be obliged to obey. (God just does not do so.)

Adams does not find either of these two solutions acceptable. Firstly, he sees no logical reason why it is impossible for God to command cruelty for its own sake. For it to be impossible, God's nature would have to be subject to an external standard of right and wrong, so that it would be wrong for God to command such cruelty. It is unacceptable in Christian thinking for God to be subject to any external standard.

Secondly, it is abhorrent in Christian theology to assume that God could ever command cruelty because, while it is logically consistent, it does not reflect the Christian understanding of the nature of God. If God were to command cruelty, Adams finds it difficult to agree that we should obey, but to say that we should not obey abandons the Divine Command Theory.

Robert Adams, born 1937

Divine Command based on God's omnibenevolence

This leaves us with a third solution. Divine Command Theory claims that the statement 'Cruelty is wrong' means the same as the statement 'Cruelty is against God's command'. Adams agrees but says that this is only true if we assume God has a benevolent (loving) character. If God did command cruelty then God would not have a kind and loving character, and therefore it may be acceptable to disobey God.

However, Adams is careful because he does not want to risk abandoning Divine Command Theory by claiming that we should disobey God if God commands cruelty. Adams deliberately makes no claims about whether we should or should not obey if God commands cruelty because the concept of 'wrong' would become meaningless if God did. The concept of 'wrong' would no longer mean the same thing if God commanded it. This means that the Divine Command Theory must be developed to say:

> *… by 'X is ethically wrong' I mean 'X is contrary to the commands of a loving God' … and by 'X is ethically permitted' I mean 'X is in accord with the commands of a loving God'* **"**
>
> Robert Adams, 'A Modified Divine Command Theory of Ethical Wrongness'

The Modified Divine Command Theory says that it is logically possible that God could command cruelty for its own sake, but it is unthinkable that God would do so because God is a loving God. An advantage of Adams' position is that the content of moral judgements is not arbitrary. Moral commands arise from the very nature of God and so they cannot contain any random content. A being who commands cruelty for its own sake is not a loving God, and therefore these commands need not be obeyed.

AO1 activity 3

Create a knowledge organiser or mind map that summarises Divine Command Theory. You should include:

- what Divine Command Theory is
- Robert Adams' modification
- the three listed challenges.

Include examples of divine commands, scholarly quotations, and specialist vocabulary. Do not forget to use colour and pictures to make it more memorable.

Virtue Theory

Virtue Theory, also known as Virtue Ethics, is an ancient way of looking at ethics, and it experienced a revival during the twentieth century. This theory is considered an alternative to the usual normative approaches to ethics, which focus on the worth of particular actions. Virtue comes from the Greek word *arete*, which can be translated as 'virtue' or 'excellence'. Virtue Theory focuses on the moral agent who is doing the acting, rather than considering the actions they perform. Many different ethical theories acknowledge virtue, but Virtue Theory concentrates on virtues as the main or most important thing for ethical action. This philosophical approach to ethics does not require a religious belief, however it does have characteristics that are compatible with, or evident within, religious teaching.

An ethical system based on defining personal qualities or a person's character

There are several different versions of Virtue Theory, and all focus on dispositions or personal qualities that enable a person to feel, choose, and act in a certain way. A virtuous person has developed a habit of character that enables them to act virtuously, with little or no struggle, in any situation. For example, a virtuous person may possess an honest character. This means that when faced with a challenge in which lying might be an option, they would tell the truth easily because they recognise its value, and can balance it with tact or discretion. Virtue Theory plays down or even denies the importance of rules or principles because morality is understood in terms of inner traits that are valuable for their own sake.

Aristotle's moral virtues

Aristotle was an ancient thinker whose ethical writing focused on the importance of virtue in moral decision making. He was by no means the first or the only ethical thinker to develop a form of Virtue Ethics, but his writing on virtue has been very influential.

Eudaimonia: the goal of life

The aim or purpose of Virtue Theory is to achieve **eudaimonia**. This is often translated as human flourishing or living well. Eudaimonia is an experience of life achieved by virtuous living, and not by living a life that focuses on your own enjoyment, nor by living a life focusing on public service and helping others. It is a journey travelled over the course of a whole lifetime, rather than a goal reached after performing individual good deeds.

> *One swallow does not make a summer; neither does one day. Similarly, neither can one day, or a brief space of time, make a man blessed and happy.*
>
> Aristotle, *Ethics*

> **Key terms**
>
> **Virtue Theory:** a broad term for a range of moral theories that focus on the role of character and virtue rather than specific actions; also known as Virtue Ethics
>
> **arete:** (Greek) excellence, goodness, or virtue
>
> **eudaimonia:** human flourishing or living well (sometimes translated as happiness)

To achieve eudaimonia, an individual must exercise certain values to become virtuous. Eudaimonia is achieved by a person fulfilling their function in life. Just as an excellent harpist plays the harp well after dedication and practice, an excellent human lives a life of reason in accordance with virtue only after devoting themselves to practising this way of life.

> *But the virtues we do acquire by first exercising them, just as happens in the arts. Anything that we must learn to do we learn by the actual doing of it: people become builders by building and instrumentalists by playing instruments.*
>
> Aristotle, *Ethics*

Only adult humans can achieve eudaimonia. Animals cannot reason, and while a child may behave well, children lack an important quality. Aristotle distinguished between intellectual and moral virtues, and believed that **phronesis** was an intellectual virtue only available to adults. Phronesis is the ability to use practical wisdom, an understanding that comes with life experience, to work out how to be virtuous in any given situation. A child may well grow up to be a virtuous person if they have had the right upbringing, guidance, and examples to follow, but until they have phronesis, are able to think for themselves and use the other intellectual virtues to perfect how they act, they cannot be considered virtuous.

The five intellectual virtues and the twelve moral virtues

Aristotle identified five intellectual virtues in total. These are achieved through education, and help a person to come to an understanding of truth.

science (episteme)	the capability of demonstrating the logical truth of a fact
art (techne)	the ability to use reason to plan and produce in a particular situation
prudence (phronesis)	using practical wisdom or prudence to work out how to be virtuous in a given situation
intuition (nous)	the ability to grasp the first principles of truth
wisdom (sophia)	the most finished or perfected form of knowledge

Aristotle established a list of 12 **moral virtues**. He saw these dispositions or personal qualities as falling on a spectrum, with the ideal as the mean in the middle, and the two vices of excess and deficiency on either side. With too much of one quality, a person possesses the vice of excess, and with too little, a person possesses the vice of deficiency.

Aristotle (384–322 BCE)

Key terms

phronesis: using practical wisdom or prudence to work out how to be virtuous in a given situation

moral virtues: Aristotle established 12 moral virtues that need to be developed by identifying and practising the mean between the two vices of deficiency and excess

Excess	Mean	Deficiency
rashness	courage	cowardice
licentiousness (unrestrained behaviour)	temperance	insensibility (not caring or being reactive)
prodigality (being lavish or wasteful)	liberality (being generous)	illiberality (being mean or stingy)
vulgarity (uncontrolled spending)	magnificence (spending a suitable amount)	pettiness (stingy or lacking generosity)
vanity (acting for praise, fame or approval)	magnanimity (acting with kindness and generosity)	pusillanimity (being a pushover)
ambition	proper ambition	unambitiousness
irascibility (easily angered)	patience	lack of spirit
boastfulness	truthfulness	understatement
buffoonery	wittiness	boorishness
obsequiousness (fawning, being eager to obey)	friendliness	cantankerousness (being irritable and complaining)
shyness	modesty	shamelessness
envy	righteous indignation	malicious enjoyment

Aristotle admits that it is easier said than done. Finding the middle or moderate line to tread between the two vices is difficult, and depends upon the situation. The mean can be closer to a vice in some circumstances and not so much in others. Aristotle compares a professional wrestler, who must consume a large quantity of food to be healthy, with a student who has only just started to train and requires much less food for good health. Only an adult with life experience and intellectual virtue can understand the complexity of moral situations, apply phronesis, and understand the mean response.

> *It is easy to miss the target and difficult to hit it.*
>
> Aristotle, *Ethics*

Aristotle noted that there are some people who find it more challenging than others to be virtuous. Those who live in a state of vice have no desire to achieve excellence. Other people do try, and these he calls 'incontinent'. They make resolutions and may even understand what is best, but they give in easily to temptation or act according to whim rather than reason. Some people, the 'continent', calculate successfully and know the mean path to follow. They experience temptation and struggles, but they can resist and control their desires. The ideal person is virtuous, without struggle or temptation. They have no difficulty in seeing the best course of action and following it. They live a life of excellence and virtue.

Jesus' teachings on virtue

While the Virtue Theory approach to ethics does not require religious faith, there is an element of compatibility or correlation between Virtue Theory and religious belief. The depiction of Jesus in the letters of Paul and Matthew's gospel can be read as containing teachings that share concerns with Virtue Theory, but it should be noted that neither writer intentionally worked from a virtue framework nor developed any kind of explicit, systematic Virtue Theory.

AO1 activity 4

In *Divergent*, a series of novels written by Veronica Roth, society is divided into five groups, or 'factions', based on their predominant characteristic: selfless, peaceful, honest, brave, and intelligent. Rare individuals who possess more than one of these characteristics become factionless and are removed from society. Can you identify any problems for society if, for example, it contained only completely honest people who possessed none of the other characteristics? Would there be problems for any of the other groups?

In 1 Corinthians 13:13, Paul lists faith, hope, and love as the most important personal qualities. These virtues have been given by God, and have been used by several other thinkers since, notably Thomas Aquinas, who is covered in Chapter 3. Elsewhere, Paul lists other virtues or 'fruits' that Christians are expected to demonstrate as a result of their relationship with God.

> But the fruit of the Spirit is love, joy, peace, patience, kindness, generosity, faithfulness, gentleness and self-control. Against such things there is no law.
>
> Galatians 5:22–23, *Holy Bible (NIV)*

Jesus, as presented in the gospels, is seen supporting both love and the law. However, his moral teaching does not concern these things exclusively. In the book of Matthew, Jesus is concerned with features of morality that look similar to the morality of Virtue Theory.

The most obvious use of Virtue Theory in Matthew's depiction of Jesus is his concern with features of a person's character that inspire human behaviour rather than specific laws or acts. One of the most famous collections of Jesus' sayings is called the Sermon on the Mount. This sermon is unlikely to have been preached on one occasion; it is more likely that Matthew collected several of Jesus' sermons together. One section of the sermon has become known as the **Beatitudes**. Here, Jesus lists dispositions or personal characteristics that receive God's blessing and are paired with a reward that people should expect to receive in heaven if they perfect them; they do not describe specific actions. There is disagreement among scholars over how many Beatitudes there are, with numbers ranging from eight to ten. Most scholars agree that there are eight; the ninth, which is often discounted, is directed personally at the hearer.

There is some discussion among scholars regarding whether the spiritual rewards are received in the present or in the future. The Beatitudes indicate that the state of being blessed could be in the present or in the future, after death. Blessedness may refer to an untroubled mental state or an ability to cope with the trials of life. The kingdom of heaven may be experienced here and now, on Earth, as the disciples perfect their character and live flourishing lives.

Later in the Sermon on the Mount, Jesus continues to teach about personal qualities rather than actions. He warns

Key term

Beatitudes: blessedness; the complete happiness that comes from being blessed by God; the blessings recounted by Jesus in the Sermon on the Mount

> Blessed are the poor in spirit,
>   for theirs is the kingdom of heaven.
> Blessed are those who mourn,
>   for they will be comforted.
> Blessed are the meek,
>   for they will inherit the Earth.
> Blessed are those who hunger and thirst for
>   righteousness,
>   for they will be filled.
> Blessed are the merciful,
>   for they will receive mercy.
> Blessed are the pure in heart,
>   for they will see God.
> Blessed are the peacemakers
>   for they will be called children of God.
> Blessed are those who are persecuted because of
>   righteousness, for theirs is the kingdom of heaven.
> Blessed are you when people insult you, persecute you and falsely say all kinds of evil against you because of me. Rejoice and be glad, because great is your reward in heaven, for in the same way they persecuted the prophets who were before you.
>
> Matthew 5:3–12, *Holy Bible (NIV)*

against anger and lust rather than focusing on murder and adultery. He does not suggest that these kinds of actions are ever acceptable or unimportant, but he moves away from the law-centred ethics of the Pharisees. The Pharisees were concerned with no more and no less than obedience to exact legal commands, an approach that ignores the personal qualities that make a person good. The Pharisees are depicted as avoiding going beyond the law's requirements to help another person and being very quick to point the finger at those who did not succeed at sticking to the law, regardless of their situation. In contrast, the quotation below implies that Jesus' teachings on virtue are concerned with moral excellence. He expects his followers to aim for moral perfection.

> Be perfect, therefore, as your heavenly Father is perfect. 99
>
> Matthew 5:48, *Holy Bible (NIV)*

Jesus does not ignore the fact that his followers make mistakes and are less than perfect in their faith and actions, but he stands ready to forgive those whose dispositions are worthy. He holds up key figures, such as prophets of the Old Testament like Abraham, as examples of virtuous people to follow, and he acts as a role model himself. Jesus' teachings also recognise that morality is not only an individual concern. He fosters a close relationship with his followers and emphasises qualities – such as friendship, justice, and generosity – that depend upon social connections with other people.

AO1 activity 5
Read the whole of the Sermon on the Mount (Matthew 5:1–7:29) and create a list of all the dispositions or personal qualities that Jesus is presented as advocating in the sermon.

Challenges

Virtues are not a practical guide to moral behaviour

Virtue Theory is less practical than other ethical approaches. This is because it is difficult for a person who is not already virtuous to understand what is required to become moral, because there are no clear rules to follow. Aristotle's Virtue Theory requires children to be educated in the intellectual virtues and brought up to recognise the virtuous mean by witnessing virtuous behaviour in society. However, people who have not received this upbringing have no way to correctly understand what is required of them.

Virtue Theory also assumes that the virtuous person knows what is moral. However, it is not always obvious what a person should do in any given situation. Virtue Theory does not prioritise the acts or the consequences of those acts when discerning what it means to be moral. Instead, people are judged by their adherence to virtues, such as generosity or honesty. But this does not help at all because an honest action could also be cruel, and a generous action could also be self-serving, and cruel and self-serving actions are not virtuous.

For a teenager who becomes pregnant after being raped or a soldier who is threatened at gunpoint by a civilian, there may not be an example of a virtuous person whose behaviour they can copy, and no rule book they can follow so that they know what they should do to behave morally in the moment. Virtue Theory is, therefore, an impractical approach to ethical behaviour. If an ordinary person is unable to use it to discover how to become moral, it becomes necessary to ask what purpose it serves.

The issue of Cultural Relativism

An additional problem with Virtue Theory is that different cultures appear to consider different sets of personal qualities as virtuous. This means that different people from different cultures will admire different behavioural responses to a situation. For example, in some cultures it was considered virtuous for a new widow to perform sati (to throw herself on to her husband's funeral pyre to die with him). In contrast, Queen Victoria's widowhood was considered virtuous because she lived the rest of her life in mourning, wearing black clothes and a white lace widow's cap. Virtue Theory does not provide us with a method for deciding on a universal list of acceptable or desirable virtues. Cultural Relativism means that different cultures identify different behaviours as 'right' or 'wrong' relative to the culture in which those behaviours are experienced.

Virtues can be used for immoral acts

Virtue Theory can lead to immorality in certain circumstances. For instance, there may be times when virtues conflict, and yet there is no method to help a moral agent know which virtue to choose. In some situations, a person's honesty might cause pain to another person, whereas kindness would mean someone had to lie. Alternatively, being charitable might lead someone to feel that they should kill a person who is in extreme suffering, but justice might cause them to preserve life even when the person whose life they are preserving no longer wants to live. Virtue Theory does not offer guidance to help a person decide which is the best course of action.

In addition, Virtue Theory can lead directly to immorality. For example, courage is a virtue that was highlighted by Aristotle. However, while a fire fighter might require courage to step into a burning building, some might try to argue it also takes courage for someone to enter a place of worship with a gun and shoot the worshippers. One might argue that such an act demonstrates an excess of courage, which is called rashness. However, if the act is planned and reasoned then it is not rash, yet we would still describe it as immoral. Virtue Theory does not offer any clarity to guide a moral agent along a virtuous path.

Ethical Egoism

Ethical Egoism is a normative ethical theory which says that each person ought only to pursue their own self-interest. This means that a person's only duty is to themselves and not to another person. There is no moral duty for a person to put their needs to one side for the sake of others or to obey particular rules, and a person's only duty is to themself. This is a non-religious ethical theory which does not acknowledge God, or another divinity, as a source of moral authority; instead it defines morality in terms of self-interest.

AO1 activity 6

In the film *The Hunger Games*, based on the novel by Susanne Collins, Katniss sees a sworn rival, Cato, fall from the Cornucopia and get savaged by wild beasts. He is alive and conscious but dying. Katniss has a bow and arrow. In the film, she shoots him quickly to end his suffering. In the book, she listens to his torment over many hours before finally choosing to end his misery. What would a virtuous person do? How do you know?

Key term

Ethical Egoism: an ethical theory that claims moral agents should do what is in their own self-interest; an action is morally right if it maximises one's self-interest

An ethical theory based on self-interest and not altruism

In 2017, Jamel Dunn's body was recovered from a lake in Florida where he had drowned. Later, it was discovered that some teenagers had uploaded a video to social media which showed him drowning while they mocked him. The teenagers were not prosecuted: although they did nothing to help Jamel and did not raise the alarm, they were in no way involved in his death.

It is assumed that all people have a responsibility towards other people and that moral choices should be made on that basis. The example of Jamel Dunn raises important questions about whether anyone has a moral obligation or duty to help someone else who is in need. Performing an act that helps other people, especially if it is at a cost to yourself, is known as **altruism**.

The egoist philosopher, Ayn Rand, regarded altruism as destructive because it treats an individual's life as a disposable commodity. She argued that a person has only one life, but altruism demands that they sacrifice this life for the good of others, either by literally dying for them, or more often, by sacrificing their own well-being or needs for another person. This attitude devalues the individual person. She saw the supporters of altruism as 'parasites [and] moochers' who treat other people as sacrificial animals for their own needs or desires. Therefore, egoism is the only way to ensure your life is valued and taken seriously, and the teenagers had no obligation to help Jamel because helping him could have put their own lives at risk.

Egoism says that the only obligation a person has is to look after their own interests. However, this does not mean that we should avoid helping others. Sometimes helping others will be a side effect of something we do in our own interest. There is no problem with this, but what makes an action morally right is that we are motivated by personal interest.

Psychological Egoism

Psychological Egoism is a descriptive theory that states not how we should act but how we do actually act. This theory claims that people performing altruistic acts, even at great personal cost, are not being selfless at all but are acting to benefit themselves. For example, during the global Covid-19 pandemic of 2020 and beyond, Captain Sir Tom Moore walked 100 laps of his garden by his 100th birthday, and in doing so, raised over £32 million for the National Health Service (NHS), to help it in its fight against the virus. His actions were met with acclaim and considered altruistic by many.

However, Psychological Egoism argues that acts such as these are not altruistic at all. They are all motivated by self-interest. For example, psychological egoists might say that Captain Moore acted from a sense of satisfaction: he kept busy and reached a personal goal.

Ethical Egoism says that actions performed in accordance with our own desires are morally correct. So, when Captain Moore or any other person acts in a way that satisfies their own interests, they do nothing wrong. In

> ### Key terms
>
> **altruism:** actions that are motivated by a desire for the well-being of another person, even at one's own personal cost
>
> **Psychological Egoism:** a descriptive theory that proposes that people naturally act out of self-interest

Captain Sir Tom Moore: egoist or altruist?

fact, if Psychological Egoism is correct then it makes no sense to say that we 'ought' to behave in any other way. If our capacity to do 'good' is only motivated by self-interest, then we can only be obligated to act in our own interest and not in the interest of others.

The idea that we are motivated by self-interest was proposed by Plato, through the character Glaucon in Book II of *The Republic*. Glaucon tells the Myth of Gyges, about a shepherd who finds a ring that makes him invisible. His invisibility makes him undetectable to everyone and he gains access to the royal palace, seduces the queen, kills the king, and seizes the throne. Glaucon proposes that if there were two rings, one given to a virtuous person and the other to a criminal, both would act in their own self-interest and neither would do what convention dictates is right.

> *No man would keep his hands off what was not his own when he could safely take what he likes out of the market or go into houses and lie with any one at his pleasure, or kill or release from prison whom he would and in all respects be like a God among men.*
>
> Plato, *The Republic and Other Works*

Concentrating on long-term self-interests rather than short-term self-interests

Ethical Egoism argues that we should act in our own self-interest, but this is not necessarily the same thing as **hedonism**. Hedonism involves seeking pleasure in the moment. This might sometimes be in a person's self-interest, but not necessarily. For example, a person may get pleasure from binge drinking on a night out. However, it is not necessarily in their self-interest to do this as it may be self-destructive, putting their health or safety at risk.

> **Key term**
>
> **hedonism:** valuing or seeking pleasure as the highest good

Self-interest is also more than simple selfishness. To act in self-interest is to act in a way that benefits the self, while recognising that others will do the same. For example, I might eat an apple because I am hungry. This act would not be regarded as selfish; I am just attending to my needs. I recognise that others might be hungry too and I acknowledge that they may also eat apples if they wish. To act selfishly would be to clear all the apples from the shelves in the shop so that no one else but me could eat them. To act altruistically would be to buy all the apples and give them to others while I remained hungry.

Ethical Egoism argues that a person may need to weigh their short-term self-interest against their long-term self-interest. This means that when making a moral decision, a person should balance the pleasure or benefit that they receive in the present with the consequences they will experience in the future. For example, a student who skips their ethics lesson to enjoy an extra hour with their friend acts in their short-term self-interest by doing something they know they will enjoy. However, if they were acting in their long-term self-interest, they would attend the lesson so that they did not miss anything important and did not have to catch up later or be confused during the next lesson.

Following rules can be in an egoist's long-term self-interest. To abide by rules that forbid us from harming others is helpful in the long-term because it means other people are less likely to harm us. The Golden Rule of treating others as you would like to be treated yourself is also motivated by long-term self-interest: cooperating and being kind to others will benefit you in the long-term when other people cooperate with you and are kind to you.

Max Stirner

Max Stirner, the author of *The Ego and Its Own*, was very hostile towards religion. He felt that religion involves the subjugation of the individual when they should be self-ruling. While religions like Christianity seem to promise freedom, they do not really mean it. They actually require an individual to be constrained or shackled by duty or obligation to their faith. Stirner believed that the freedom promised by religion is a '**spook**' or an illusion. Religious people think they are free because they can inwardly choose to believe or not believe, but they are not free from faith, the law, or a sense of obligation to others.

> *You have been set free from sin and have become slaves to righteousness.* **"**
>
> Romans 6:18, *Holy Bible (NIV)*

Is self-interest the root cause of every human action even if it appears altruistic?

Initially, Stirner appears to suggest that the reason people obey God and commandments (including those of the state) is for personal gain. This implies that he agrees with Psychological Egoism that all acts are performed out of self-interest. He argues that we would reject God's commands if it became clear they would cause us harm. However, he goes on to imply that Psychological Egoism should, in fact, be rejected. He gives the example of Shakespeare's *Romeo and Juliet*. Juliet sacrificed her love for Romeo out of respect for her family's wishes. Stirner recognises that some would argue she acted out of self-interest; that she preferred following the wishes of her family to Romeo. However, Stirner goes on to reject this argument, because Juliet knew that her own desires were left unsatisfied. She subjected herself to a higher power and she was therefore constrained, and forced to act in a particular way rather than being able to act in her own self-interest. He argues that those who are unselfish and acting in accordance with obligations to others are weak. They do not belong to themselves. Like Gyges, Stirner argues that if we can free ourselves from the 'spooks' of duty and obligation, we will be free to act in our own self-interest.

Stirner says that religion gives people cheated egoism, promising them freedom – to say or believe what they wish, for example – but instead requiring them to satisfy something other than themselves. They set aside their true wishes and become fettered to obligation, but they do not know that they are not in control.

Key term

spook: an illusion or an abstract idea that people treat as reality

Max Stirner (1806–1856)

> *Of what use is it to sheep that no one abridges their freedom of speech? They stick to bleating. Give one who is inwardly a Mohammedan, a Jew or a Christian, permission to speak what he likes: he will yet utter only narrow-minded stuff.*
>
> Max Stirner, *The Ego and His Own*. Note that, today, the term 'Mohammedan' is considered archaic and offensive; the appropriate term is 'Muslim'.

Rejection of egoism for material gain

Stirner recognises that there are many things other than religion that can act as 'spooks', controlling and subjugating people so that they do not act in their own self-interest. He gives an example of a person who sacrifices everything to pursue material riches. While this person seems to act in their own self-interest, they have actually become enslaved to something that is not compatible with true egoism: material possessions. Egoism is less about self-interest and more about self-rule. If a person is a slave to other things, then they do not have true autonomy. Stirner calls this ***eigenheit*** ('ownness'). It involves being in complete control of one's own decisions and choices rather than being controlled by something else, including our appetites. Stirner values ownness or self-rule as the most important good, which is superior to everything else and is completely incompatible with any obligation to anyone or anything else.

> **Key term**
>
> ***eigenheit:*** (German) ownness; Max Stirner's word for complete moral control over one's own decisions

Union of Egoists

We are taught by society that we are all equals, but the result of this teaching is that we are depersonalised. It sets on us certain obligations that we are chained to and must obey because we are told we are all the same, we are all human. Religious believers do the same when they create a 'community of worship'.

> *Now you are the body of Christ, and each one of you is a part of it.*
>
> 1 Corinthians 12:27, *Holy Bible (NIV)*

'I' becomes abstract and lost. Nationality or equality is a 'spook' or a ghostly illusion. These things are not real because they deny the unique individual 'I'. Obedience to the state is of no interest to the egoist because it involves subjugation of the individual.

For example, Stirner points out that Socrates was foolish and not praiseworthy because, despite appearing to oppose Athenian government, he accepted the verdict when he was tried by the state for corrupting the young, and cooperated with his execution. He was deluded in thinking that he was a mere member of 'the people'. Socrates subordinated himself to the law and recognised, in the people, his judgement. He submitted to might and was treated as virtuous for submitting, but he should have been his own person and understood that he was the only one fit to judge his own actions.

> **Synoptic link**
>
> Link to *Chapter 8: Determinism and free will: free will*. Stirner's work was influenced by the work of existentialists such as Sartre. Look at Sartre's exploration of bad faith, when people act because they feel a sense of duty or obligation.

However, Stirner argues that there are benefits for individuals of forming temporary relationships and working in an alliance while remaining independent and self-determining. People can form a 'Union of Egoists' without losing their autonomy. For example, going for a drink with a friend, not out of obligation or duty but just because it will be enjoyable, is this kind of union. There is no loyalty or obligation, just self-serving enjoyment in and of the moment. A Union of Egoists is a purely functional association that only occurs because it can achieve a goal for the self. It will disband as soon as an individual's goal has been met. There is no duty involved, no higher value in the partnership and no obligation to other members of the union. The moment any principles become binding, it is a dead union. No organisation or party matters; individuality is all that is important.

> *In the very act of joining them and entering their circle one forms a union with them that lasts as long as party and I pursue one and the same goal … The party has nothing binding (obligatory) for me, and I do not have respect for it; if it no longer pleases me, I become its foe.*
>
> Max Stirner, *The Ego and His Own*

AO1 activity 8

Choose three things you have done today; for example: going to an ethics lesson. Identify which, if any, spooks may have affected your decision to do what you did; for example, your belief in your parent's authority over you or honouring a contract between yourself and the college or school you attend. Can you think of one thing you did today that was 'self-ruled'?

Challenges

Destruction of a community ethos

Ethical Egoism seems to be an unacceptable method of making moral decisions. If, for example, a friend asks you for advice, egoism demands that you give advice that is in your best interest, not the best interest of your friend. But when a friend asks for advice, you are motivated to help them because you feel concern for them. If it were not for feelings of concern for others, human beings would not help each other. When a person gives money to charity, they do not do so because it is in their own interest to give away their money. They do it because they do not want others to suffer. Altruism says we should actively seek the advancement of the good of others. This means we should help other people and work together as a community to improve things for everyone. If we decide only to act in our own self-interest, we would all act as individuals and there would be little reason to work together, and little reason to try to improve things for the whole community.

Stirner seems to associate belonging to a group with subordination: belonging to a nation, a community, even a family, is something to be treated with suspicion. Yet, he does not consider the positive consequences of belonging. For example, we gain security and contentment from being part of a group. Stirner rejects even democratic societies where the rules are established by the community itself. He sees it all as a threat to an individual's self-rule. He sees no obligation to keep promises or care for others because doing so is a constraint that is incompatible with self-rule. This leads to a destruction of community spirit, where telling the truth, helping each other, and keeping promises are no longer valuable, leading to a breakdown of trust and a lack of mutual regard for other members of society.

Social injustices could occur as individuals put their own interests first

At the start of the Covid-19 pandemic, many people rushed to the shops to stockpile resources, such as tinned food, bread, and toilet rolls. The consequences of this were empty shelves, months of shortages and some families having to go without the basics.

Ethical Egoism appears to allow any behaviour that puts the interests of the self before the interests of others. This means that people are morally justified in performing acts that many other ethical theories would consider completely unacceptable. The act of stockpiling food during a time of national crisis prioritised the needs of the individual and caused social injustice because those who did not have the means to stockpile were forced to go without.

Ethical Egoism means that individuals will cooperate only with those who serve their own self-interest. If a Union of Egoists can form a big enough cooperative, it can arrange society in a way that most benefits it, regardless of the effect it might have on other people. If a Union of Egoists is interested in promoting white interests, this will be to the detriment of Black people; if a Union of Egoists serves the interests of men, then women are left disadvantaged; and so on. If it is a moral duty for individuals to put themselves before others, there is no reason for anyone to work to protect the interests of the poor, the weak, or the vulnerable, and anyone who is in a minority group is at risk of becoming a victim of social injustice.

A form of bigotry

Racism, sexism, nationalism, antisemitism, and Islamophobia are all ways of dividing society into groups and arguing that one group's interests are worth more than another group's interests. Ethical Egoism divides society into two groups: 'me' and 'them', with 'me' taking priority.

Usually, ethical theories that prioritise one group of people over another run into moral problems. The division of people into groups tends to be arbitrary and unsupported by testable differences that justify better resources for one group over another. While some might try to argue that another group is stupid, greedy, or lazy, such stereotypes cannot be justified by scientific evidence. There is no justifiable reason why, for example, people with different skin tones should be treated differently or why people belonging to one religion should be treated differently from people belonging to a different religion or no religion at all, but egoists make the same type of arbitrary distinctions by unjustifiably prioritising the self over others. This can lead to bigotry, as a Union of Egoists puts itself before others and, in doing so, develops prejudices against those who do not belong to the union.

Egoism divides people into arbitrary groups: 'them' and 'us'.

AO1 activity 9

a) Imagine that you are an ethical egoist who has borrowed £1000 from a friend. Your friend has now asked for their money back. Give three reasons why you would return the money and three reasons why you would not.

b) Look at your list of reasons. Would Stirner consider them to be egoistic or influenced by 'spooks'?

This section of the chapter will enhance your ability to **analyse** and **evaluate** the topic and help you develop your AO2 skills. For each question, think about the different positions you might take, and decide which you find most persuasive and why. It is not enough to memorise a list of 'for and against' points; you need to develop an argument.

Is morality whatever God commands?

This is a meta-ethical question. It is asking us to consider what is meant by 'morality'. We should consider how morality can be defined and how we know what morality is.

The view that morality is whatever God commands

God is omnipotent. Therefore morality can logically be whatever God commands because God has an unlimited level of power. Philip L. Quinn argues that God's moral commands can be clearly seen in scripture, which is divine revelation and therefore a moral authority. For example, Exodus 20 contains the Ten Commandments, and in Matthew 22:37–39, Jesus commands his followers to love God and their neighbours. The Bible, which is God's word, is revealed to humanity as the absolute standard of morality and Jesus, as the Son of God, can and does command God's will.

God is **omnibenevolent** and therefore what God commands is the absolute standard of morality because God is all loving. Morality can logically be whatever God commands because God is omnipotent and omnibenevolent. God only commands things that are good, and never commands cruelty for its own sake because it is not in God's nature to do so. Thomas Aquinas denies that any command God gives would ever be evil. For example, in Genesis 22:1–2, God does not command Abraham to murder his son Isaac. It cannot be murder because God, the author of life and death, commands what Isaac, along with the rest of humanity, deserves as a result of original sin. Therefore, Isaac's death is what he is due by the command of God, and so it cannot be murder. Aquinas argues the same for Exodus 11:2, where God appears to command the Hebrews to steal from the Egyptians, but the Israelites only took what God commanded was their due, and so it was not theft.

Robert Merrihew Adams' modified version of the Divine Command Theory shows that God's character is reflected in God's commands. This means that the very definition of 'God' is of an omnipotent, omnibenevolent being. Therefore, any being that commanded evil would not be 'God', and so there would be no obligation to obey. Morality is rooted in the unchanging omnibenevolent nature of God, and is not arbitrary or cruel.

> **Synoptic link**
>
> Link to *Chapter 2: Ethical thought (part 2)*. Read the introduction to find out a little more about what is meant by 'meta-ethics'.

> **Key term**
>
> **omnibenevolent:** all-loving, perfectly good

In the fourteenth century, William of Ockham argued that God is the ultimate standard of morality, and that God's will establishes right and wrong. It is possible for God to command evil, but this will not happen. God is completely free; there are no constraints, external or internal, to what God can command.

> *… hatred, theft, adultery and the like may involve evil according to the common law … God can perform them without involving any evil. And they can be performed meritoriously by someone on Earth if they should fall under a divine command.*
>
> William of Ockham, *Opera Theologica V*

The view that morality is not whatever God commands

To claim that God's commands are moral because they appear in scripture is a circular argument that says morality is what God commands because God commands morality. There is nothing outside this circle that confirms God's commands are good or that God is an authority, and there is no way to check how good or bad God's commands are without going back to look at scripture. Jeremy Bentham adds to this challenge by arguing that Divine Command Theory is of no practical use. He also argues that scripture does not provide enough detail to command moral behaviour anyway. In support of Bentham, we can observe that scripture does not tell us what to do about stem cell research or online behaviour. People need a practical method, like Utilitarianism, to work out what is right or wrong before they can know what God commands. It is not enough to be told that God commands morality if Divine Command Theory provides humanity with no way of checking whether an action is commanded by God or not.

Thomas Aquinas rejected the view that morality is simply whatever God commands. It is unacceptable to view God's commands as arbitrary or as independent standards. For Aquinas, God's omnipotence means God can do all things that are logically possible and not things that are impossible. God cannot make a square circle because it is a contradiction in terms. Similarly, God cannot command evil because it is against God's nature to command evil.

Plato's challenge to Divine Command Theory, framed in the Euthyphro dilemma, shows it is illogical to argue that morality is what God commands. Either God is living up to an external standard of morality or God can command anything and we would still call it good. There is no solution to the dilemma because belief in God and God's goodness is a matter of faith, and nothing can demonstrate God's character one way or the other.

Morality cannot be whatever God commands because scripture seems to paint a picture of an arbitrary and partisan God who commands a father to sacrifice his only son (Genesis 22:1–10), condones daughters drugging their father so they can become pregnant through incest (Genesis 19:30–38), and instructs a man to abandon a slave, and the child he fathered with her, when his wife later becomes pregnant (Genesis 21: 8–14). No other standard of morality would ever see these as good acts. Ralph Cudworth argues that to accept Divine Command Theory means that there is nothing we can imagine that is so grossly wicked, foully unjust or dishonest that it could not become righteous if it were commanded by God.

AO2 activity 1

Look at the arguments for and against the question 'Is morality whatever God commands?'. Identify which arguments seem to go together as opposite sides of the same point. For each pair, decide which argument you find more convincing, and give two reasons why.

Is being a good person better than just doing good deeds?

This question involves weighing the extent to which an action is more or less important than the character of the person performing the action. For example, is it more or less important to obey the law than to act virtuously?

The view that being a good person is better than doing good deeds

Being a good person is a better than doing good deeds because it involves perfecting personal qualities to such an extent that you then know what to do in any given situation. A good person can focus on human flourishing in a way that those who are focused on doing things cannot. For example, in the parable of the Good Samaritan in Luke 10:25–37, the experts in the law rigidly obeyed purity regulations and ensured they were not rendered unclean by touching a dead or dying body by the roadside. They did nothing that violated a legal code; yet, when they walked by on the other side, they failed to be compassionate people, which is the purpose of moral behaviour.

Attempts to codify ethics, so that people know which deeds are good and which deeds are not good, eventually lead to immoral acts. For example, laws about abortion or killing either result in a minority being sacrificed for the good of the majority (as in the case of Utilitarianism) or they force people to obey rigid laws that lack basic compassion (as can be seen in Divine Command Theory or Natural Law). It is more important that people develop a strong moral character so that they can think through the diverse and complicated situations they might find themselves in. Julia Annas adds that virtue does not dispose of moral laws but encourages us to reflect on them to uncover their inadequacies, enabling us to develop into the people we are really striving to be.

Becoming a good person sometimes involves making mistakes. Deed-focused ethics condemns wrong actions, but Virtue Ethics recognises that making a mistake does not necessarily make a person evil. Someone can

Synoptic link

Link to *Chapter 6: Teleological ethics: Utilitarianism*. Notice that Utilitarianism argues that good moral choices create the greatest happiness for the greatest number of people.

Link to *Chapter 3: Deontological ethics: Aquinas' Natural Law*. Notice that Natural Law involves a set of absolute moral rules that are applied universally.

make a decision based upon the best information available to them at the time, and if that decision turns out to be a mistake, it is not necessarily an indication of immoral character. Virtue allows people to base their moral decisions on specific circumstances, and these are not always straightforward. N.F. Gier points out that generous people do not cease to be virtuous just because they fail to donate to a particular charity. Becoming a good person is a journey, and mistakes can be teaching moments rather than opportunities for condemnation.

The view that doing good deeds is better than being a good person

Good deeds are more important that moral virtue because deeds directly affect other people. Deeds are the things people have to live with and must accept responsibility for, and so it is vital that there is specific and useful guidance to help people know that they are acting morally. For example, moral theories that measure the consequences of actions are superior to Virtue Theory, because they are based on the real-life situations and produce clear, enforceable rules, rather than an abstract ideal of what it means to be a good person.

Doing good deeds is a more effective route to morality because there is no way to codify virtue and so people are left with a degree of uncertainty about what being a good person means. At best, virtue can be a useful supplement to a more concrete form of ethics, like Natural Law or Divine Command Theory, so that people are able to perfect their actions. However, this reduced version of Virtue Ethics requires practical reason to take a back seat to fixed laws or codes, so there is less personal responsibility. Virtue, in this context, is more about developing personal qualities that help a person obey the law than developing personal qualities that mark them out as a good person.

Robert Louden argues that it is more important to focus on deeds than character because it is necessary for people to identify actions that are so harmful and destructive that they make it impossible for anything good to be achieved. There are certain actions, like rape and torture, that must be governed by rules because they are simply intolerable, and Virtue Ethics does not help us construct a list of these actions.

The view that moral agents must be good people to do good deeds

Julia Annas points out that virtue is a disposition towards certain kinds of behaviour that is exercised when reasoned choices are made. It is impossible to be a good person without doing good deeds because there is no way to observe that a person is good unless they do something. However, it is clear that deeds alone are insufficient for demonstrating morality because circumstances and character are also important factors in moral decision making. Practical reasoning is an essential part of deciding whether or not an action is good and should be performed, and so both deeds and character are part of moral decision making.

Elizabeth Anscombe has noted that guidance and rules on how to do good deeds can be found in virtues, using what Louden calls 'V-rules' such as 'be honest', 'be chaste', or 'be just'. These V-rules are derived from any list of virtues, and make it possible to do ethics without resorting to terms like 'good', 'bad', 'right', or 'wrong' as they simply and more factually describe the actions that should be performed by the virtuous person.

Virtue Theory has human flourishing, rather than obedience to God or self-rule, as its goal. Human flourishing is a holistic idea that allows moral agents to choose actions based upon how they will bring about excellence in human characteristics. Rather than mindless obedience to rules, virtuous moral agents must use reason or phronesis to work out which deeds will enable further flourishing. Aristotle himself argued that everyone seeks not what is traditional but what is good. Therefore, moral people aspire to be better and use their reason to work out exactly how to do it. Deeds are the result of virtue, so deeds and virtue cannot be separated from each other.

> ### AO2 activity 2
> What do you think?
> Do you think it is more important to be a good person or to do good deeds? Do you think that good action and good character go hand in hand? Formulate a judgement of your own and support it with at least one reason or example.

Is Virtue Theory useful when faced with a moral dilemma?

This question relates to how practical Virtue Theory is when applied to real-life situations. It relates to whether or not the theory gives moral agents guidance or help in making real-life moral decisions.

The view that Virtue Theory is useful when faced with a moral dilemma

Ethics is complex. While other ethical theories try to reduce ethics down to a set of rules or principles for good moral action, Virtue Theory recognises that practical reason only operates in concrete moral contexts as they arise. This approach cannot be codified, but this is the reality of practical ethics. It is more useful to look to virtuous people as examples of how to behave, as part of the process of developing as a person of virtue, rather than to reach for a package of prefabricated rules that will often be inappropriate in the circumstances.

Law and morality are not the same thing. Law constructs rules for people to follow, and this is not the job of morality. Morality concerns itself with personal inner qualities that cannot be governed, and encourages self-improvement and reasoned deliberation. Virtue Ethics is useful in considering how to think about moral dilemmas and what it means to be a good person. It helps people carefully consider whether rules and laws should be followed or abandoned.

Elizabeth Anscombe analyses the ethical problems faced by other secular ethical theories, theories that condemn individual actions as 'wrong' without any foundation for doing so. She argues that, unless there is belief in a God or another objective source of 'good', there is no reason to understand specific actions as being inherently good or bad. Virtue Ethics allows people to practically assess what is courageous or just in particular circumstances, without the restriction of labelling an act 'good' or 'bad'. This is a practical approach, and one that encourages human flourishing rather than reducing actions to those that meet a rigid set of rules regardless of the situation.

Virtue Theory fosters moral autonomy – individual freedom to choose moral actions for oneself – because it is determined by right reason and right desire. Intellectual virtues such as phronesis can be taught so that an individual has the skill to be able to respond to the complex moral situations in which they find themselves. This is beneficial because other ethical theories do not always have ready-made rules that can be applied to every single new dilemma that arises. In addition, the motivation for moral action in Virtue Theory is eudaimonia, something that everyone desires for its own sake.

The view that Virtue Theory it is not useful when faced with a moral dilemma

Robert Louden claims that writing on virtue has a 'misty antiquarian air'. What is being advocated is not spelled out, and so no one knows what kind of behaviour is acceptable. People require moral 'oughts' so they know what they ought to do. Attempts by Anscombe to establish V-rules are not helpful: 'be honest' is just another way of saying 'lying is wrong', and it is equally as difficult to apply to all real-life situations.

There is no guidance to help us recognise who is morally virtuous and who is not, so it is difficult to determine whose example we should follow as Virtue Theory suggests. One way we could judge people's true moral characters is by looking at their external moral conduct (their actions). However, this suggests that people should know what conduct is right and what conduct is wrong, but we do not because there are no rules. Also, whether a person is morally virtuous or not may not be easy to identify by looking at their actions alone, and we cannot see inside them and look at their internal qualities. Consequently, the concept of virtue in moral behaviour is of little use.

Virtue is not useful because it is simply an illusion. The virtuous person is either weak, acting in bad faith and not accepting responsibility for their own well-being, or doing exactly what they want to do and not acting out of virtue at all. Egoists like Rand and Stirner would argue that the only useful way to act is according to one's own self-interest, and this is a person's only real moral requirement.

In our pluralistic world, there is little agreement about which qualities define a good character; different cultures consider different virtues important. While one culture might value a person who keeps their behaviour modest and self-effacing, another culture might value a forthright, assertive character who speaks up and pushes themself forward. With a lack of agreement about what makes someone a virtuous person, it becomes necessary to make rules that govern behaviour.

Does Ethical Egoism inevitably lead to moral evil?

The use of the word 'inevitably' is at the heart of this question. If Ethical Egoism inevitably leads to moral evil, it means that moral evil is unavoidable for egoists. However, is it possible to argue that Ethical Egoism *could* lead to moral evil but that moral evil is not inevitable?

The view that Ethical Egoism does inevitably lead to moral evil

The concepts of good and evil usually involve some consideration of how we treat other beings. Ethical Egoism says that there is no imperative to consider how others are treated at all; therefore, it is inevitable that moral evil will result because there is nothing to prevent a person from harming another if it benefits them to do so. There is not even a guarantee that some kind of common good will be upheld by a Union of Egoists because there is no obligation to keep agreements made between individuals, and no way of regulating behaviour if everyone acts in their own self-interest.

Ayn Rand shows that Egoism leads to moral evil because she demonstrates the inevitable bigotry that results if everyone acts out of self-interest. She describes altruists as 'parasites' and 'moochers', suggesting that anyone who advocates acting on behalf of others is feeding off the good will of other people and treating them as 'sacrificial animals'. This kind of imagery is what leads to people to withhold humanitarian aid or deny basic human dignities to people who are in need of help and support.

There is no moral code in Ethical Egoism that prevents someone from doing anything they want. For example, I can set fire to a building for my own entertainment, even if it kills or harms those inside because the welfare of others is no concern of mine. In the Myth of Gyges, Plato's character Glaucon suggests that even the most virtuous person will do evil if they can avoid detection, which is in direct conflict with the moral requirement for us to attempt to live peacefully and cooperatively with others. To kill someone may be in someone's best interests if, for instance, they stand to inherit a lot of money, but it is not in the best interests of the person they kill, and there is nothing in Ethical Egoism prevents them from carrying out murder.

AO2 activity 3

Look at the arguments for and against the question 'Is Virtue Theory useful when faced with a moral dilemma?'. Make a list of the scholars who have been mentioned, and note down the main points they make. This will help you remember them when you are evaluating in an essay.

The view that Ethical Egoism does not inevitably lead to moral evil

Ethical Egoism defines moral evil as any act that is contrary to one's own self-interest or self-rule. Therefore, Ethical Egoism does not allow for the existence of moral evil because it advocates acting only in self-interest, never with any regard for laws, obligations, or commitments to another.

Ethical Egoism is not the same as selfishness or pleasure. To live in a way that benefits the self inevitably requires some consideration of, or cooperation with, other people. It is vital that we trade fairly, keep our word, and respect the lives and property of those around us if we want to fulfil our own self-interest with no restriction on our ability to self-rule. If we consistently fail to respect the interests of others, then we will not be tolerated in society and this would not be in our own self-interest. Adam Smith goes so far as to point out that the success of society depends upon us acting in our own self-interest. For example, if a business can act to benefit itself, without moral or legal controls that restrict it actions in the hope of protecting individuals, then it will flourish and benefit the community as a whole. This means that Ethical Egoism would lead to a greater good.

Laws can operate alongside Ethical Egoism. There is no advantage to me in performing acts that are against law if I am likely to be caught and punished. I cannot harm another person or damage their property because society will not tolerate it. While Ethical Egoism allows us to do these things in principle, it would not be beneficial to us to do them in practice. Therefore, acts that harm other people are not an inevitable result of Ethical Egoism.

The view that Ethical Egoism may lead to moral evil

Ethical Egoism does not make moral evil inevitable because it creates no rules or obligations to treat anyone in any particular way at all. Therefore, moral evil resulting from egoistic action is allowed, and perhaps even facilitated, but not caused by Ethical Egoism; consequently, is not inevitable.

Ethical Egoism allows people to act in their own self-interest, but this does not mean that people should act selfishly. Ethical Egoism allows selfish behaviour but it does not require it. Kurt Baier points out that egoism requires us to act rationally to ensure our own self-interest, and there is nothing rational about going out of one's way to harm others unless it actively benefits us to do so. This means that moral evil may be done in the pursuance of our own interests, but it is not inevitable. Moral evil that occurs as a result of our pursuing one's own interests is incidental rather than intentional.

It is often true that what is in one person's interest is also in the interest of others. While a moral agent should not purposefully act in the interest of others according to Ethical Egoism, there is nothing to prevent an individual's interests from coinciding with the interests of others. Stirner's Union of Egoists actively encourages people to group together when it is in their common interest to do so, provided all understand that they have

AO2 activity 4

Near the end of *The Hobbit* by J.R.R. Tolkien, Bilbo Baggins uses a stolen ring that makes him invisible to betray his friends and ransom their most treasured possession, the Arkenstone. Bilbo had stolen the stone from his friends for himself, but he gave it to their enemies to prevent a war, fearful that his friends will discover his theft. Does Bilbo act selfishly or altruistically? What would you do if you had a ring that would make you undetectable? What relevance do you think this might have to the behaviour that people display online?

no obligation to each other. Therefore, moral evil is not inherent in Ethical Egoism, even if it sometimes occurs.

Are all moral actions motivated by self-interest?

This question concerns the descriptive theory of Psychological Egoism and whether we consistently act in our own self-interest when we do good deeds. It is not about whether or not we should act in our own self-interest when we do good deeds.

The view that all moral actions are motivated by self-interest

James Rachels points out that regardless of whether a person gives to charity or keeps their money for themselves, they are doing what they want to do if they act freely. Therefore, both giving and not giving are motivated by self-interest. A person may want to give to charity because they want the positive feelings that come with giving, or they may want to avoid the negative feelings that come with not giving. Alternatively, they might have a sense of duty that is fulfilled by the act of giving. It does not matter what a person's motivation is; so long as an action is freely performed, it is done for the self.

Self-interested and selfless actions both produce feelings of pleasure. The purpose of the action is to achieve pleasure for the self and not to bring about good for others. The good for others is not the ultimate goal; the ultimate goal is the pleasure that it causes. Rachels tells a story about Abraham Lincoln, who stopped his train to help a sow whose piglets were stranded in mud. Lincoln described the act as the 'essence of selfishness' because the thought of the pigs would have bothered him all day had he not helped. Therefore, even though the action appeared selfless, it was ultimately motivated by self-interest.

Self-interest is at the heart of moral actions, even when they are commanded by religion. Religious morality promises divine rewards for moral actions, and divine punishment for immoral actions. This appeals to an individual's long-term self-interest, inspiring them to act in a way that outwardly benefits society rather than the individual while inwardly benefitting their own self-interest. The moral actions that result are not fundamentally altruistic because people perform them believing that they will be rewarded by God for their sacrifice.

The view that some moral actions are motivated by self-interest

We clearly do not always act in our own self-interest; people indulge in all manner of activities that do not benefit them. For example, people smoke and drink for short-term pleasure even though they know tobacco and alcohol are harmful in the long term. People also do things that bring them no pleasure at all, simply because they have a sense that they ought to do them. For example, they may postpone a long-anticipated night out to help a friend who is in distress, even though they wish they could be elsewhere.

Actions can also have more than one motive. It is not the case that we must be motivated either by self-interest or by altruism. There is no inconsistency in wanting everyone, including oneself, to be well-off and happy. Our interests do not always conflict with the interests of others, although sometimes they might. This means that we can be considerate and kind to another person even if we put ourselves first because our actions have no positive or negative effects for them.

Psychological Egoism rests on the assumption that all moral actions are motivated by self-interest, and then interprets all actions according to that assumption. The hypothesis that all people act out of self-interest is not falsifiable, and so it is meaningless. Actions that appear to be contrary to this hypothesis are reinterpreted so that they fit, but there is no reasonable justification for doing this because some moral actions may be motivated by self-interest, while others are not.

The view that moral actions are not motivated by self-interest

There are evidently people in the world who act in ways that help others despite the fact that they do not really want to do the action. We do sometimes act out of obligation rather than desire: I might not want to keep a promise, it might not benefit me to do so, but I feel I should, and so I do. This is why a moral agent sometimes experiences an inner conflict, because their sense of obligation conflicts with their desires. Stirner recognises this, even though he argues that it should not be the case.

Rachels points out that even if we do want to perform a charitable action, it does not mean that we are selfish or that our action cannot be considered altruistic. It is the very fact that we want to do something for someone else, even if it risks our own well-being, that makes our action selfless. Rachels asks what else could unselfishness be if it is not wanting to do something to help someone else? It is the thing that is desired, not the fact that we desire it, that determines whether an act is in a person's own self-interest. A person who acts because they desire the well-being of someone else is not motivated by self-interest even if they gain satisfaction from what they do.

If a person is truly selfish, they are not bothered by the predicaments of others. If a moral agent gains pleasure or peace of mind from an act, it shows they are concerned with the welfare of others, and this makes them selfless or altruistic. Stirner would point out that such a person is motivated by the 'spooks' of duty or obligation rather than pure interest for others. But, either way, moral actions are not motivated by self-interest. Hume argues that it is ridiculous to suggest that people whose self-love gives them concern for others are in any way the same as people whose self-love gives them no regard for anything other than their own pleasure.

Synoptic link

Link to *A Level Religious Studies for Eduqas: Philosophy of Religion, Chapter 7 Religious language (part one)*. It is useful to be aware that falsifiability – how we set about proving a proposition to be false – is a scientific principle that people like Antony Flew argued should be applied to statements, including ethical statements, to see if they contain factual content.

AO2 activity 5

Design an experiment that could be used to find out if all moral actions are motivated by self-interest, or if some moral actions are motivated by something different. What kinds of observations would you have to make to distinguish self-interested acts from altruistic acts?

Which is the superior ethical theory: Divine Command Theory, Virtue Theory or Ethical Egoism?

This question asks you to weigh up and make a reasoned judgement about which ethical theory is superior. You need to begin by deciding what makes an ethical theory superior; for example, is it the most practical, the most compassionate, or the most logically consistent ethical theory?

The view that Divine Command Theory is superior

Ethical Egoism is ultimately useless as an ethical moral theory because it cannot be universalised. A requirement of logic is that we are consistent in our evaluations, but I cannot say that it is acceptable for me to steal your wallet and then complain when you steal mine. Divine Command Theory is superior because it provides universal moral laws that cannot be changed on a whim.

Virtue Theory gives no clear guidance on what a person should do in any given moral situation. To be told that one must follow the example of a virtuous person, like Socrates, is not enough to help a person make a wide range of complex decisions. Divine Command Theory makes clear and distinct rules that are authoritative because they come directly from God.

Divine Command Theory is superior because it is simple to follow. It is easy to know what God commands because we can look to scripture or any other source of moral authority provided by God and find clear instructions that tell us how to behave. Such commands are absolute and unbending, so the moral agent can feel a sense of moral certainty when they act.

The view that Virtue Theory is superior

If everyone acted in self-interest, as Ethical Egoism suggests, then society would collapse. Stirner may have advocated the Union of Egoists, but he also claimed that there is nothing holding an individual to an agreement with the union if that agreement ceases to be in the individual's self-interest. Virtue Theory is superior because it considers the flourishing of society alongside the flourishing of the individual, at the same time as maintaining the flexibility required to enable a moral agent to respond to the specific circumstances they are experiencing. The virtues relate to how an individual acts as a member of the wider community.

Anscombe points out that Divine Command Theory fails because it is dependent on a God that may not exist. Other secular theories have no foundation for their understanding of good or evil because they have done away with God's authority. Virtue Ethics has, however, replaced ideas of 'good' and 'evil' with a series of virtues, including 'honesty' and 'courage'. This approach is logically consistent, and therefore superior to both Divine Command Theory and other secular ethical approaches.

Virtue Theory is superior because it has as its goal the one thing we know all human beings yearn for: well-being or flourishing (eudaimonia). Aristotle described it as the ultimate goal of all action, subordinate to no other goal. Virtue Theory is superior because it does not require religious belief, and is based upon something genuinely desirable to all.

The view that Ethical Egoism is superior

Divine Command Theory removes people's ability to self-rule; they are subjugated to the will of a divine being, having been misled into believing they are acting freely. This makes Ethical Egoism superior because it openly advocates the freedom and moral autonomy of the individual, rather than fooling people into slavish adherence to duty or obligation. Ethical Egoism, therefore, avoids the trap of acting in bad faith. To act in bad faith is to lie to ourselves, pretending that we are under an obligation to a God or a higher power, when in fact we are free to choose our own actions.

Virtue Theory appears to remove the sense of moral obligation or 'ought' because it does away with absolute rules. However, it just replaces one set of rules with another (such as Anscombe's V-rules). It requires people to be honest, just, and compassionate when they have no obligation to be any of these things. Like Divine Command Theory, Virtue Theory requires a slavish adherence to specific ideals about excellence, whereas Ethical Egoism removes all of this, and allows people complete freedom to act in their own self-interest.

Ethical Egoism is the superior ethical theory because it is more honest than Divine Command Theory and Virtue Theory. It acknowledges the real reason why people want to perform actions, and it allows people to live genuine, flourishing lives that they have constructed for themselves, rather than forcing them to live up to a standard that has been created for them and forced upon them. Rand saw the achievement of happiness for ourselves as being our 'highest purpose'.

> ### Synoptic link
>
> Link to *Chapter 8: Determinism and free will: free will*. Take a look at Sartre's concept of 'bad faith', which challenges people who act as though they are restricted in their actions when in fact they are free.

AO2 activity 6

Rank the nine arguments about which ethical theory is superior in order from 1 to 9, with 1 being the best argument. Give one reason why you think the argument in first place is at the top and one reason why you think the argument in ninth place is at the bottom. What is it about each argument that you find convincing or unconvincing?

Practising AO1 questions

AO1 questions begin with one of a range of possible command words (see pages 8–9 for more detail). The following past paper questions all begin with the word 'Explain'. 'Explain' questions require you to cover the broad topic area in the question in as much detail as possible. You do not need to consider the quality of the theory or offer any views about it.

Read the question below and the two example paragraphs written in response before completing the activity on page 42.

> *Explain Virtue Theory with reference to Aristotle.*
>
> (Eduqas A Level Religious Studies, Summer 2019,
> Component 3: Religion and Ethics, Question 2a)

Example 1

Virtue Theory[2] is an approach to ethics that focuses on the virtues of a moral agent. Virtue Theory[2] does not set out rules or laws[1] that describe good or bad acts. Instead, there is a list of habits[7] that should be perfected[1] so that the person can make moral decisions. This approach is evident in the teachings of Jesus, including the Beatitudes[4]. He mentioned that 'blessed are the meek' because they will 'inherit the Earth' and 'blessed are the merciful' because 'they will be shown mercy'[4]. There are many lists of different virtues that a moral agent might display. Jesus' virtues of meekness and mercy involve being compassionate to other people and putting them first.[1] Other lists of virtues might include[3] faith, hope, love or patience, kindness, gentleness, and self-control[4]. A virtuous person will be virtuous rather than just blindly following laws or rules without thinking. All of this requires that a moral agent is an adult who can weigh up all the circumstances[1] and understand that virtuous actions will not necessarily look the same in every situation. A child cannot understand why you do not just blindly follow the rules and they will not know all the different things that need to be taken into consideration when making a difficult decision.

Areas for development

1 The paragraph shows mainly accurate and relevant knowledge and understanding, but while the material on Jesus is accurate and awardable, it is not required.

2 This paragraph addresses some of the demands of the question, but it does not directly reference Aristotle.

3 There is satisfactory use of evidence, with references to the lists of biblical virtues.

4 There is accurate reference to sacred texts, but much more than the question requires is included here.

5 This paragraph does not include any connections with other areas of study. It is not essential for a response to include connections, but including a connection that arises naturally will make your answer stronger.

6 There is no reference to scholarly views. This essay should specifically reference the scholarly views of Aristotle.

7 There is some accurate use of specialist language in context.

Example 2: an improved response

Virtue Theory[2] is an approach to ethics that focuses on the character of a moral agent rather than the specific actions the agent performs[1]. Virtue Theory[2] emphasises the personal qualities[1] an individual may develop, and does not set out rules or laws that describe good or bad acts. Instead, there are a list of habits[7] that should be perfected[1] so that the individual becomes capable of making moral decisions and achieving moral excellence[7]. This approach is evident in the teachings of Jesus, including the Beatitudes[4]. However, the secular Greek thinker, Aristotle[2], developed a list of twelve virtues[1] that form a 'mean'[7] or an average falling between two vices: excess and deficiency[1]. For example, the virtue of courage[7] falls between the excess of rashness[7] and the deficiency of cowardice[7]. A truly virtuous person will demonstrate the mean, the more moderate approach to life, rather than rushing headlong into events or running away and not getting involved. For instance, if a child were trapped in a burning building, a moderate person would not run in without formulating a plan, such as calling the fire brigade or establishing how to get the child out. Nor would they walk past and hope that someone else would deal with the problem.[3] All of this requires that a moral agent is an adult who has been educated[1] in the skill of phronesis or practical wisdom[7] because being good is difficult. Aristotle[2] acknowledged that 'it is easy to miss the target and difficult to hit it'[6]. A person must be able to weigh up all the circumstances in each situation[1] because virtuous actions will not necessarily look the same in each situation. Aristotle[2] gave the example of a wrestler who eats a moderate diet for their body type and lifestyle. Their moderate diet will look very different from the moderate diet of someone who leads a more sedentary lifestyle[3]. Moderation looks different in different situations and a child will not be capable of understanding the complexities involved in this.

What went well

1. The paragraph contains thorough, accurate, and relevant knowledge and understanding.

2. This response answers the specific question asked.

3. There is excellent use of evidence and examples.

4. There is relevant and accurate reference to sacred texts where appropriate.

5. There is not always an opportunity to make connections with other areas of study, and it is better not to force connections that do not arise naturally. Those studying Buddhism could demonstrate awareness of the similarities with the Eightfold Path.

6. Scholarly views are used accurately and appropriately.

7. There is thorough and accurate use of specialist language in context.

Activity

a) Read Example 1 on page 41 and the areas for development. Identify one thing you could do to make this paragraph better.

b) Read Example 2 and what went well, above. Make a list of at least three things you can find that make it better than Example 1.

AO1 practice question 1

Now it is your turn. Have a go at answering the following question. There are some points to remember below to help you if you are not sure how to start.

Explain how Robert Adams modified Divine Command Theory.

(Eduqas A Level Religious Studies, Summer 2019, Component 3: Religion and Ethics, Question 1a)

Points to remember

- Remember that to explain Adams' modification of the Divine Command Theory, you will first need to explain the classical presentation of the Divine Command Theory before it was modified.
- You will need to show why Adams needed to make the modification, so you should talk about the Euthyphro dilemma with particular reference to the arbitrariness problem.
- The focus of this question is Robert Adams. Therefore, your response should spend as much time as possible giving details of Adams' modification to the Divine Command Theory and how he attempted to resolve the issues with Divine Command Theory.

AO1 practice question 2

Now try this question by yourself.

Explain Ethical Egoism with reference to Max Stirner.

(Eduqas A Level Religious Studies, Autumn 2020, Component 3: Religion and Ethics, Question 4a)

Practising AO2 questions

When writing a response to an AO2 question, you must remember that you are being examined on your ability to analyse and evaluate effectively. Analysis involves a detailed examination of something, and you should pick apart the concept to look for its strengths and weaknesses. Evaluation involves judging the quality or importance of the concept. You are expected to analyse and evaluate throughout the whole of your response; you are not expected to include long passages explaining knowledge and understanding.

Read the past paper question below and the example paragraphs written in response before completing the activity on page 46.

'All so called moral actions are ultimately selfish.'
Evaluate this view.

(Eduqas AS Level Religious Studies, Summer 2019, Component 3: An Introduction to Religion and Ethics, Question 3b)

Example 1

The idea that all moral actions are ultimately selfish[2] suggests that even if we perform an action that seems to benefit another person, our motives are focused on how the action benefits ourselves[1]. For example, when someone gives money or food and drink to a homeless person, they may do it because it gives them a sense of satisfaction or social recognition when they post about what they have done on social media.[3] If they did not get something out of it, they would not do it. It is easy to see evidence[6] that we only do things that are selfish[2] because we can see, in day-to-day life, that[1] people make choices that benefit themselves or those closest to them and disregard the needs of others. During the pandemic, people panic-bought toilet rolls and tinned food, emptying the shelves and causing shortages, which meant that other people went without.[3] When someone does a 'good deed'[6] they are only doing it because it makes them feel good or because someone will like them more if they do it. The moment there is no reward they revert to being unkind[6], and if no one can identify them, they are more likely to be deliberately unkind for their own entertainment or to get attention, for example online[3].

Areas for development

1 There is some valid analysis and evaluation of some of the issues raised by the question.

2 This paragraph focuses on the question throughout, but only raises a limited number of issues related to the question, and only partially addresses them.

3 There is use of detailed evidence, examples, and reasoning to support arguments, but they are rather repetitive and focused on only one aspect of the question.

4 Reference to the views of scholars would be expected somewhere in a full answer; there are none in this paragraph.

5 No reference to any connections with other areas of study have been included. This aspect is not essential in a high-quality response, but is credited if used effectively and appropriately.

6 There is some use of basic specialist language and vocabulary.

Example 2: an improved response

The idea that all moral actions are ultimately selfish[2] is the view of psychological egoism. It is, therefore, necessary to consider[1] whether psychological egoism[6] is factually correct. The statement suggests that even if we perform an action that seems to benefit another person, our motives are focused on how the action benefits ourselves. This view is consistent with what we witness[1] in day-to-day life. Even when it looks like someone is acting kindly, they are only doing what they want to do. For example, when someone gives money or food and drink to a homeless person, they may do it because it gives them a sense of satisfaction or social recognition when they post about what they have done on social media.[3] If they did not get any positive feelings, they would not do it. However[1], this is a very cynical view of the world. Many people perform acts that benefit others for reasons other than self-satisfaction[2]. Max Stirner[4] recognised this because he noticed that people are deceived or controlled by the 'spooks'[6] of religion or obligation[6]. They are giving to charity because they feel a sense of duty, not because they are altruistic[6]. Stirner pointed to scripture to back up his point: having supposedly been set free, people have actually been made 'slaves of righteousness'. However[1], this viewpoint is also extremely cynical. It still argues that it is impossible to perform an act simply because we care about the wellbeing of others. This is not borne out by real life.[1] There are plenty of examples of people helping others even when there is a personal cost. Those who give blood or donate organs to strangers[3] do not do so because they enjoy the experience but because they care about the wellbeing of others. Therefore[1], it is unlikely that all moral actions are selfish[2] because any resulting sense of satisfaction is just further evidence that some people care for others and so are not selfish[2] at all.

What went well

1 Confident analysis and evaluation appears throughout, with consideration of different viewpoints.

2 This paragraph focuses on the issues raised by the question throughout.

3 There is extensive use of evidence, examples, and reasoning to support arguments.

4 There is appropriate reference to scholarly views.

5 While there is no natural opportunity for a connection to be made in this paragraph, the student could, later, make reference to Sartre's concept of bad faith to show that moral duty is a lie and agents can act with complete freedom.

6 There is thorough use of specialist language in context.

Activity

a) Read Example 1 on page 44. Identify the argument(s) the student has mentioned in support of the statement in the question. Can you find evidence in the response that supports the argument(s)? Can you find any counter-argument(s) and supporting evidence in the response?

b) Read Example 2 on page 45 and do the same:

- Identify the argument(s) and evidence in support of the statement in the question.
- Identify any counter-argument(s) and supporting evidence.

c) Compare your findings. How do the two responses compare?

AO2 practice question 1

Now it is your turn. Have a go at answering the following question. There are some points to remember underneath to help you if you are not sure how to start.

'Morality is whatever God commands it to be'
Evaluate this view.

(Eduqas A Level Religious Studies, Summer 2019,
Component 3: Religion and Ethics, Question 1b)

Points to remember

- Remember that normative ethics considers what a moral agent should do. Meta-ethics is more concerned with the meaning of moral terms and how we can know what is good. This statement is meta-ethical.
- Give plenty of examples throughout the essay, to back up your arguments and illustrate your ideas. You can use examples from scripture or anecdotes from real life.
- Try and include scholarly quotations, teachings or arguments wherever possible, but make sure you weigh up their quality or effectiveness; do not just describe them.

AO2 practice question 2

Now try this question by yourself.

'Virtue Theory is impractical when faced with a moral dilemma.' Evaluate this view.

(Eduqas AS Level Religious Studies, Summer 2017,
Component 3: An Introduction to Religion and Ethics, Question 4b)

Mark schemes for all exam questions can be found at www.eduqas.co.uk and www.wjec.co.uk.

Your friend shares a viral video of rioters smashing vehicles at a rally against changes to policing laws that affect people's right to protest. Your friend comments that the actions of the rioters were morally wrong. You agree that the violent actions broke the law, but you also say that the protesters were morally right. Your friend argues that law and morality are the same thing, but you are not so sure! What are you and your friend doing when you use value-laden words like 'moral', 'immoral', 'good', 'right', 'bad' and 'wrong'? What exactly is a moral value, and how can we know one when we see one?

This chapter explores meta ethics. This is a branch of moral philosophy that considers the language of ethics and the fundamental nature and existence of moral values. It is important because when we have ethical debates, we need to be clear about what our words mean so that we understand exactly what each participant is trying to say and where we agree or disagree.

Meta ethics is different from normative ethics, which focuses on the construction of systems of morality such as Virtue Theory (see Chapter 1). It also differs from applied ethics, which considers how to use systems of morality in real situations, such as abortion or euthanasia (see Chapter 3).

In this chapter, you will consider the three meta-ethical approaches of Naturalism, Intuitionism and Emotivism. Naturalism finds the meaning of ethical terms in concrete empirical evidence; it means that we should be able to find sensory evidence for the meaning of ethical language in the world around us. In contrast, Intuitionism considers ethical language to be objective and knowable, but indefinable in relation to any other idea; it claims that we just have an instinctive understanding of ethical language. Finally, Emotivism sees ethical language as being no more than an expression of emotion that aims to persuade others to feel the same.

How do you think we can know what ethical words mean?

How do we know what ethical words mean?

This section of the chapter will enhance your knowledge and understanding of the topic and help you develop your AO1 skills.

Meta-ethical approaches: Naturalism

The term '**Naturalism**', in the context of **meta ethics**, was coined by G.E. Moore in 1903. He was a critic of the naturalist approach, but he described it as a method that defined value terms like 'good' by replacing them with a property of a natural object. This means that naturalists use the natural sciences or psychology to explain morality in the same way that science explains any other natural phenomena. Some naturalists, like J.S. Mill for example, define 'good' as an action that brings about maximum happiness. Others might define 'good' as that which achieves the purpose for which it was designed or that which is most natural.

> *Whether good be defined as yellow or green or blue, as loud or soft, as round or square, as sweet or bitter, as productive of life or productive of pleasure, as willed or desired or felt: whichever of these or of any other object in the world, good may be held to mean, the theory, which holds it to mean them, will be a naturalistic theory.*
>
> G.E. Moore, *Principia Ethica*

Objective moral laws exist independently of human beings, and moral terms can be understood by analysing the natural world

Naturalists are **empiricists**. They argue that **objective** moral facts exist, and that they are real and knowable. These moral facts are objectively true, independent of the perceptions of the human mind. They have the same kinds of qualities as other natural facts, and so moral claims can be understood using the same empirical methods that can be applied to other phenomena in the natural world.

Ethical naturalists claim that ethical terms are definable using non-ethical natural terms, such as 'happiness' and 'according to purpose'. They also claim that ethical conclusions, such as 'murder is wrong', can be understood by observing non-ethical, scientific properties. For example, the claim that 'good' is the same as happiness and helping is 'good' can be investigated empirically by going out into the world and observing whether helping people brings about happiness.

Ethical statements are cognitivist and can be verified or falsified

While there are many different forms of Naturalism, all naturalists agree that moral language is **cognitive**. This means that the meaning of moral claims can

Key terms

Naturalism: an ethical theory which argues that objective moral principles can be derived from empirical, naturalistic facts; also known as Ethical Naturalism or Naturalistic Ethics

meta ethics: a branch of ethics that is concerned with the meaning of ethical terms, the nature of moral statements and the foundations of moral principles

empiricist: someone who states that knowledge can only be found through experience of the material world

objective: a truth or reality that is independent from the mind of the individual who perceives it

cognitive: connected with thinking or mental processes relating to knowledge; a cognitive statement is a statement that can be known to be true or false

Synoptic link

Link to *Chapter 6: Teleological ethics: Utilitarianism*. Utilitarianism is a normative expression of Naturalism because it starts from the assumption that good can be defined in terms of something we can see in the world: happiness.

be understood and therefore investigated for truth or falsity. It is clearly insufficient to base morality on opinion or convention because there is a risk that morality will become arbitrary and unreliable. Moral claims must, instead, be measurable by some kind of independent standard if they are to be judged as good or bad. Terms like 'good' or 'right' must be treated in the same way as other descriptive claims about the world. They must be analysed for truth or falsity just like any other natural phenomena.

Some naturalists have defined 'good' as meaning the same as 'bringing about happiness'.

Naturalists argue that moral facts can be identified by observing the natural world, and these observations inform our ability to make value judgements and use value terms accurately. For example, a societal convention can be described as 'good' if it is shown to contribute to happiness, or if it is shown to be consistent with a familiar feature of the natural world that is observable. Naturalism is usually consistent with **moral realism**, which means that moral facts exist and they are objective, existing independently of the human mind. Today, science is concerned only with the kinds of facts that can be verified through observation and experimentation, and scientists argue that these are the only kinds of facts that are to be believed. Therefore, naturalists argue that moral facts must be the same as scientific fact.

> **Key term**
>
> **moral realism:** ethical statements can be shown to have an objective reality or be objectively true; they are not just a matter of opinion or feelings

Verified moral statements are objective truths and universal

All of this means that if a moral statement, such as 'helping someone is good', can be verified then it is objectively true and applies to everyone in all situations. Naturalism, therefore, allows for the creation of absolute moral laws or principles.

However, Naturalism does not require all naturalists to be absolutists. An empirically verified moral fact is true, just like other fact. However, a naturalist who takes a relativist position can argue that although we know 'good' and 'happiness' are the same thing, how we achieve happiness is relative; it depends on the situation.

AO1 activity 1

Look at the following scenarios:

a) A child is starving with no access to food.

b) A person falls and is having difficulty getting up.

c) A person cannot reach the gun on a high shelf.

d) A cat is struggling to catch a mouse.

How can you find out whether it is good to help the beings in each of these scenarios?
What do you think 'good' means if you agree that helping is 'good'?
Can you see any problems with this definition?

F.H. Bradley: ethical sentences express propositions

F.H. Bradley's 1876 work *Ethical Studies* is a series of essays that, he argued, should be read in the order in which they are presented. Bradley's intention was to write and then critique a number of different approaches to ethics, saying in his own preface that he believed many of the fundamental ideas that were current in England at the time were confused or false.

In Bradley's fifth essay, 'My **Station** and its Duties', he presents a meta-ethical approach that has features of Naturalism. However, this essay is not the end of *Ethical Studies*, and Bradley later proceeds to analyse the weaknesses of his own approach and dismiss it in favour of other ideas.

In 'My Station and its Duties', Bradley begins by discussing the goal of moral behaviour. He is not satisfied with approaches that emphasise hedonistic Utilitarianism, and that claim individual happiness is the only goal or ideal of moral behaviour. However, he is also not content with Kant's idea that the goal of moral behaviour is to do our duty for the sake of doing our duty. Bradley claims that this is an empty formula containing no real ethical content.

For Bradley, the goal of moral behaviour is **self-realisation**. This is coming to an understanding of the individual self as part of a societal whole, identifying one's role in society and the duties that are associated with that role. Self-realisation is a unique synthesis of the notion of individual happiness and the sense of duty drawn from Kantian ethics.

This end, or goal, is what Bradley called the '**concrete universal**'. He describes this as self-realisation, duty, and happiness in one. It is a universal goal that has a fixed imperative, and is the realisation of the self as intrinsically part of the whole of society. Ethical statements express **propositions** about each person's integral place in society as inseparable from the communities in which they live. A person's station in society, and the duties their station requires of them, are observable in society, just like any other propositions about the world.

Objective features of the world make propositions true or false

Bradley writes that every community, be it a family, a society, or a state, consists of individual people. Without the individuals, there would be no community. These individuals and communities are verifiable facts. But each individual only has their character because of these communities. A child inherits a genetic predisposition towards certain characteristics from their parents at conception, and is not a *tabula rasa* at birth. Once born, a child is continually influenced, taught, and affected by the interactions with the communities that surround them.

> ## Key terms
>
> **station:** our place within society; the role that we play in society
>
> **self-realisation:** identifying one's place in society and the role or function that one plays in society, and the duties associated with that role
>
> **concrete universal:** the realisation of the self as an integrated part of the society that has constructed it
>
> **proposition:** a statement or proposal that requires proof or demonstration
>
> ***tabula rasa:*** (Latin) blank slate; the idea that at birth there is no part of our character that is predetermined or fixed

> *The icy chains of universal custom are hardening themselves around his cradled life.* **99**
>
> F.H. Bradley, *Ethical Studies*

A person's self-consciousness is, therefore, moulded by interaction with others in the community and cannot be separated from the community. Facts, like the family a person is born into, the profession a person has, and the society and state they live in, dictate the duties a person has. To see oneself as separate from such organism is a delusion. If a person turns against the community, they turn against themselves. Therefore, to be moral is to behave in accordance with the moral traditions of one's country and education. A good act is relative to the place that a person is in, what their function is, and all that comes from their station in society.

Synoptic link

Link to *Chapter 7: Determinism and free will: Determinism* and *Chapter 8: Determinism and free will: free will*. There is discussion to be had here about the extent to which human beings are free to choose their actions, or are constrained or determined by upbringing and genetics.

> *A man's life with its moral duties is in the main filled up by his station in that system of wholes which the state is, and that this, partly by its laws and institutions, and still more by its spirit, gives him the life which he does live and ought to live.* **99**
>
> F.H. Bradley, *Ethical Studies*

The concrete universal is objective. We can verify the existence and working of a community using empirical methods to arrive at moral facts. It is also governed by our station rather than our personal whims. While someone can choose their station to some degree, they must accept the duties that come with it because these are not negotiable. Our duty is clear and at work for the good of the whole community, much like an organ is always at work for the good of the whole body and the whole body is at work for the organs. Different societies have different stations and different duties associated with them, depending on how they are set up, so morality is always relative to the society it is in. However, to be moral we must desire our station and its duties, and apply the moral system of the society we live in in all situations.

Meta-ethical statements can be seen in scientific terms

Bradley appeals to scientific principles to argue that morality is linked to our station and duties. He rejects the idea that there is an objective moral law that exists independently of humans and he also rejects the notion of moral individualism, whereby each person makes their own morality.

History, politics, science, and philosophy, according to Bradley, all discredit the individualistic idea that societies are just collections of individuals that are held together because of some social contract. He claims that there is evidence from all sides to show that human nature and the emergence and structure of societies mean that human beings are created by, and intrinsically part of, their communities, both past and present.

Bradley points to evolutionary principles to support his argument. Through the process of evolution, humanity has moved from primitive, animalistic forms to become more sophisticated. Moral norms or ideals have gradually changed and advanced as humanity has evolved. The morality that we have at present is the result of all the stages of development we have been through so far, so it is not an objective, fixed standard; it is relative to our society at this time. Bradley points out that if morality was a fixed standard, given to humanity from heaven, then early humans would have had no way to understand it anyway!

However, morality is not a result of the invention of individuals or random chance either. Morality exists because of the evolutionary process, and is a product of the society that we are part of; it is far greater than any one individual. If morality were random and unrelated to previous events, it would also be empty and meaningless. 'My Station and its Duties' recognises that the individual and society are intrinsically linked to each other, and exist only because of the work and suffering that took place during earlier stages of development it has been built upon. Morality has not come about by chance. Each version of morality that has existed is appropriate for the stage of development that produced it.

Francis Herbert Bradley (1846–1924)

AO1 activity 2

a) Make a list of all the things that have caused you (or someone you know well, including a character from film or television) to become the person you (or they) are today. Divide your list into two sections: *Physical influences* and *Psychological influences*. Consider influences from both the past and the present.

b) Do you think it is logically possible to view yourself as an individual who exists independently of the communities you are part of?

Challenges

Hume's Law

At the end of Section 1 of Book 3 of his 1739 *Treatise of Human Nature*, David Hume includes a paragraph that has become known as **Hume's Law**. He challenges the idea that the same philosophical reasoning processes used in **Moral Rationalism** can be used in Moral Naturalism to establish normative statements about how a person should behave.

For example, if I argue:

Premise 1: Voldemort killed Snape.

Premise 2: Killing Snape ended his life.

Premise 3: Killing Snape caused him pain and suffering.

Premise 4: Killing Snape brought pain to others who knew him.

Conclusion: Therefore, Voldemort ought not to have killed Snape.

The conclusion is a statement containing the word 'ought'. This is an evaluative claim that gives a prescription for moral behaviour. However, when looking back through the premises that precede the conclusion, there is no evaluative information there at all. All the premises are factual

> **Key terms**
>
> **Hume's Law:** Hume argued that there is a significant difference between descriptive statements (what is) and prescriptive statements (what one ought to do), so you cannot derive what should be done from what is the case; also known as 'Hume's Guillotine'
>
> **Moral Rationalism (Ethical Rationalism):** the meta-ethical view that moral principles are knowable through a process of philosophical reasoning

statements or 'is' claims. In rationalism, it is illegitimate for a conclusion to contain information that was not present in the premises. This means that an argument cannot logically move from descriptive statements to prescriptive statements.

This idea is summed up as 'an "ought" cannot be derived from an "is"'. Hume himself says:

> In every system of morality, which I have hitherto met with, I have always remark'd, that the author proceeds for some time in the ordinary way of reasoning, and establishes the being of a God, or makes observations concerning human affairs; when of a sudden I am supriz'd to find, that instead of the usual copulations of propositions, is, and is not, I meet with no proposition that connected with an ought, or an ought not. This change is imperceptible; but is, however, of the last consequence.
>
> David Hume, *Treatise of Human Nature: Book Three*

This is a challenge to Naturalism because it shows that the transition from statements that describe facts about the world, such as those that describe natural phenomena or the function of society, do not enable us to deduce moral statements that give a rational conclusion about how we should behave. This argument is sometimes called 'Hume's Guillotine' because it severs the false connection that has been made between descriptive 'is' statements and the 'ought' statements that prescribe behaviour.

Moore's Naturalistic Fallacy

The scholar G.E. Moore challenged Naturalism, and presented a different approach to meta ethics that we will consider shortly. Moore argued that 'good' cannot be defined because ethical facts are not the same as natural ones. The '**fallacy**' that naturalists commit is treating them as the same kind of thing. For example, utilitarians define 'good' as meaning 'what brings about pleasure or happiness'. Pleasure or happiness are natural properties, but to decide that something is good because it is pleasant commits the **Naturalistic Fallacy**.

This argument has similarities with Hume's Law. It points out that facts about the natural world do not support claims about moral terms.

> **Key terms**
>
> **fallacy:** a false or mistaken idea
>
> **Naturalistic Fallacy:** an argument associated with G.E. Moore which states that moral facts cannot be reduced to natural properties

> But if he confuses 'good', which is not in the same sense a natural object, with any natural object whatever, then there is a reason for calling that a naturalistic fallacy.
>
> G.E. Moore, *Principia Ethica*

Different Naturalists attempt to define good in different ways. They define it as pleasure or that which people desire (or, in Bradley's case, the duties which our station demands). There is no way of proving empirically that any one definition is accurate. In addition, while we might be able to agree that things which cause us pleasure have goodness as a quality, we cannot agree that good *is* pleasure. The two words are not referring to exactly the same thing. Such a definition would present us with a **tautology**. This means that it would be the same as saying 'good' is 'good' or 'pleasure' is 'pleasure'. It would tell us nothing about the meaning of the term 'good'.

> *When they say, 'pleasure is good', we cannot believe that they merely mean 'pleasure is pleasure' and nothing more than that.* 99
>
> G.E. Moore, *Principia Ethica*

Moore argues that, in fact, 'good' and other moral terms like it are indefinable. They are not natural properties and cannot be defined with reference to natural properties. Naturalists express propositions about good as though they are natural properties, and this is committing the Naturalistic Fallacy.

> *If I am asked 'what is good?' my answer is that good is good, and that is the end of the matter. Or if I am asked 'How is good to be defined?' my answer is that it cannot be defined, and that is all I have to say about it.* 99
>
> G.E. Moore, *Principia Ethica*

Moore argues that 'good' cannot be defined as a natural property, such as pleasure, or any other synthetic idea, such as station in society, because these are not what the word means. Definitions of this type are possible when the subject being defined is something complex, like for example, a horse. To define a horse is possible because it is a complex item: we can point to its hooves and its four legs among other things. However, 'good' is something simple; it is not composed of any parts. Moore compares it with the colour yellow, also a simple concept. The colour yellow cannot be defined in the sense that you cannot explain it to another person who does not already know what yellow is. Even if we describe yellow in scientific terms, describing the effect of light on the eye, we do not explain our perception of yellow. The most one can do is point to things that have a quality of being yellow. But this does not define what yellow is; it merely demonstrates that some items share the feature of being yellow among the other features they also possess.

The Open Question Argument

The **Open Question Argument** is a challenge to Naturalism devised by Moore, and it is closely relates to his Naturalistic Fallacy. There are some questions that are closed questions; a closed question is a question about which there is no doubt that the answer is 'yes' or 'no'. For example, the question 'Is a bachelor an unmarried man?' is a closed question because there can be no doubt that the answer is 'yes'. Anyone who tries to dig deeper by asking, 'But, is an unmarried man a bachelor?' simply does not understand the meaning of the words.

There are also some questions that are open, because the answer is not that simple, and even a reasonable and well-educated person can feel the need to raise questions. Moore argued that any attempt

Key terms

tautology: repeating an idea within a statement, maybe with different words, but giving no new information about the idea

Open Question Argument: an argument associated with G.E. Moore and his Naturalistic Fallacy; terms like 'good' cannot be defined according to natural qualities because any attempt to do so results in an open question

to define goodness according to natural properties leaves us with an open question. As we have seen, naturalists claim that ethical words like 'good' can be defined in natural terms. So those naturalists who define 'good' as 'that which maximises pleasure' treat the question 'Is good the same as that which maximises pleasure?' as a closed question. However, Moore says they are mistaken. It is still reasonable for someone to witness an action that maximises pleasure and ask, 'But, is that good?'. The most a naturalist can do is give examples of things that have goodness as part of their nature; they cannot define goodness because it cannot be defined.

AO1 activity 3

Do you agree with Moore that 'good' is indefinable? Make a list of five things that you would usually describe as 'good' (they can be physical objects or they can be natural phenomena like pleasure). When you have drawn up your list, consider the following:

a) Are any of things the same as 'good', or do they just have a 'good' quality about them?

b) Write five sentences. Each sentence should contain the name of a thing on your list. Substitute the word 'good' for the name of the thing in each sentence. Do the sentences still make sense?

c) Do you know anything more about what 'good' is now that you have identified these five good things?

Meta-ethical approaches: Intuitionism

As we have seen, Naturalism argues that moral terms can be objectively defined using empirical evidence from the natural world. G.E. Moore raised fundamental challenges to this approach: the Naturalistic Fallacy and the Open Question Argument. However, while Moore and others objected to Naturalism, this did not mean that they rejected a cognitive understanding of ethical language. Moore is classed as an intuitionist (although he rejected the label himself). **Intuitionism**, also called Ethical Non-Naturalism, is a cognitive theory that accepts there are moral truths that can be known objectively but through a different process than the process described by Naturalism.

Objective moral laws exist independently of human beings

Intuitionism can be approached in different ways, but common to all intuitionists is the claim that moral truths are known to be true or false immediately, through intuition. This is not the same as an individual having a feeling or an opinion about a moral issue. Instead, it means that some part of an ethical statement or judgement must exist independently of human beings, and be objectively knowable through non-sensory intuition because it refers to a **non-natural property** that is *sui generis* and, therefore, completely different from any other kind of property.

Key terms

Intuitionism: an ethical theory which argues that intuition forms the foundation of ethical knowledge; also known as Ethical Non-Naturalism

non-natural property: a term Moore uses to refer to an ethical property that is not discoverable by empirical investigation

sui generis: (Latin) of its own kind; unique; in a class of its own

Moral truths can be discovered using our minds in an intuitive way

Intuitionists argue that moral truths can be understood directly by intuition without using rational processes such as **induction** or **deduction**. Moral facts or properties are self-justifying; they do not need to be, and cannot be, supported by empirical or rational evidence.

Moore argues that there are two questions that must be answered by moral philosophy:

1. What is intrinsically good/valuable?
2. What kinds of actions ought I to perform?

For Moore, the first question is answered directly through intuition, and it is incapable of proof. The second question does require proof. It is understood through our knowledge of the good, combined with an analysis of the consequences of our actions.

For all intuitionists, intuition is essentially an immediate apprehension or understanding of **self-evident** propositions. Intuitionists hold that moral truths present themselves to the mind as true, and that these truths cannot be justified with evidence or argument. Such truths are considered incapable of proof; it is not simply that no proof has been found. This is not the same as holding a belief because the values that are intuited are known to be objective truths.

Intuitive ability is innate and the same for all moral agents

In Chapter 5 of *Principia Ethica*, Moore says that while 'good' is self-evident and indefinable, it is still clear that we can disagree over ethics. A self-evident proposition is not the same as an obvious truth. An obvious truth tends to be relative to whoever is viewing it. Therefore, what is obvious to me might not be so obvious to you. A self-evident truth is one that is objective and does not need evidence to prove it because it provides the evidence within itself.

Utilitarians argue that pleasure alone is the sole good, whereas Moore claims that it is self-evident that this is not the case (although he also points out that there is nothing anyone can do to prove that such a claim is untrue). Moore says that the reason there is disagreement is because ethicists have been trying to answer different questions or failing to identify the real ethical questions in the first place. He argues that the whole world would agree if they could clearly understand the question that is actually being debated. This is because everyone has an innate awareness of the objective, self-evident truth of what 'goodness' is, which is revealed through intuition.

Key terms

induction: reasoning in which the premises of an argument lead towards one possible conclusion

deduction: reasoning in which the premises of an argument, if correct, lead to one possible conclusion

self-evident: containing within itself the evidence or justification for itself; no external proof is required

Synoptic link

Link to *A Level Religious Studies for Eduqas: Philosophy of Religion, Chapter 1: Arguments for the existence of God: inductive* and *Chapter 2: Arguments for the existence of God: deductive*. The logic that is used in philosophy to prove things like the existence of God is inappropriate for moral reasoning, according to Intuitionism. This is because the process of moving from premises to a conclusion involves deriving an 'ought' from an 'is' if the conclusion is a moral one.

Synoptic link

Link to *Chapter 6: Teleological ethics: Utilitarianism*. Moore challenges naturalist expressions of Utilitarianism. However, he argues that once a person has recognised the good through intuition (it cannot simply be defined as pleasure) then one can find out how to behave by establishing which actions will produce the maximum number of goods. This could be seen as an intuitionist expression of Utilitarianism.

Intuition needs a mature mind so it is not infallible

Moore makes clear, in his preface to *Principia Ethica*, that he is not suggesting that a proposition is true just because it is immediately understood through intuition. He recognised that just as it is possible to understand a true proposition, it is equally possible to understand a false one.

> *Still less do I imply (as most intuitionists have done) that any intuition whatever is true because we cognise it in a particular way or by the exercise of any particular faculty: I hold, on the contrary, that in every way in which it is possible to cognise a true proposition, it is also possible to cognise a false one.*
>
> G.E. Moore, *Principia Ethica*

Intuitionism claims that moral truths present themselves to the mind as true without the need for reason.

As we will see later, H.A. Prichard argued that to know a moral duty, the moral agent must understand the situation fully. They need to first fully consider the details of the action, and then second, understand the relationship between their action and the other people involved. For example, I need to understand that by telling a story, I might hurt the feelings of the person I am talking about or to. Once a moral agent has fully understood the situation, intuition will show them what their moral duty is. However, if they have not got all the information they need, their intuition will be wrong and they will experience error or doubt. Therefore, it is important to collect all the facts before an intuition takes place.

However, if all the facts of the act are completely stated, there is no need to give a reason or proof for one's moral duty; it is self-evident.

Intuition allows for objective moral values

Moore held that there are things that are inherently good or valuable, independent of the existence of humanity. We can know what is good through intuition, not through any process of reasoning. When trying to discover what is good, we should try to imagine good things existing in isolation from everything else. Moore was concerned to guard against two errors in judgement. Firstly, we must guard against considering something to be good only because it is instrumental in achieving something else. For example, it would be an error to assume that giving someone some flowers is good simply because it makes them happy. For something to be intrinsically good, it must be good independent of anything else at all. Secondly, we must guard against assuming there is just one feature that makes something good. For example, to assume that happiness alone is the sole good, because it is the thing that all good actions have in common, is an error of judgement. To Moore, it is obvious that there are many goods. For him, the two most obvious were human interaction and aesthetic appreciation. These two things Moore considered to be good purely for their own sake and not for the pursuance of something else.

> *By far the most valuable things which we know or can imagine, are certain states of consciousness, which may be roughly described as the pleasures of human intercourse and the enjoyment of beautiful objects.* 99
>
> G.E. Moore, *Principia Ethica*

Having identified what is intrinsically good through intuition, it is possible to use empirical investigation to weigh up the possible consequences of our actions to ensure that the most good is achieved through our actions. This is how we reach an answer to the question 'What kinds of actions ought I perform?'.

> *The best idea we can construct will be that state of things which contains the greatest number of things having positive value, and which contains nothing evil or indifferent – provided that the present of none of these goods, or the absence of things evil or indifferent, seems to diminish the value of the whole.* 99
>
> G.E. Moore, *Principia Ethica*

H.A. Prichard: 'ought to do' has no definition

Prichard's form of Intuitionism claims that what we can intuit is our sense of duty, obligation, or 'ought'. Based on Hume's argument that we cannot derive an 'ought' from an 'is', Prichard argued that no study of how the world 'is', carried out using scientific or empiricist methods, can tell us how we 'ought' to behave. Even if we could establish a universal objective good, we cannot logically claim that we 'ought' to do it.

> *An 'ought' if it is to be derived at all, can only be derived from another 'ought'.* 99
>
> H.A. Prichard, 'Does Moral Philosophy Rest on a Mistake?'

In his 1912 article, 'Does Moral Philosophy Rest on a Mistake?', Prichard claims that the sense of obligation to perform a particular action is **underivative** and immediate. It is not possible to use reason to work out what we ought to do by working out what is good. The belief that we must attempt to find reasons or prove that we ought to perform certain acts, is the mistake Prichard is referring to in the title of his article.

> *The sense of obligation to do, or of the rightness of, an action of a particular kind is absolutely underivative or immediate.* 99
>
> H.A. Prichard, 'Does Moral Philosophy Rest on a Mistake?'

Prichard recognised that we sometimes have doubts about our moral duty or obligations. Maybe, we are aware that performing a particular action is not going to be particularly beneficial for us. For example, I might have felt it was my duty to tell the truth in the past, but if telling the truth is only going to lead to bad things for me now, I might wonder if it really is my duty to tell the truth after all!

AO1 activity 4

Imagine you are standing before a burning building and the fire engine is an hour away. You discover that your best friend, a beloved family member, a renowned scientist on the verge of a cure for cancer, and a new-born baby are trapped inside. You cannot save everyone, but you decide to try and help. Who do you try and save first? Do you think you can know, through intuition, whether you have a duty to save one person rather than another?

Key term

underivative: original, not having been brought about by, or based upon, other things

Harold Arthur Prichard (1871–1947)

This is when we seek reassurance, looking for some kind of proof that something really is our duty. If the reason I 'ought' to tell the truth is that it benefits me, I will at some stage believe that I should no longer tell the truth because it does not benefit me anymore. Even if an act does benefit us, this does not explain why we 'ought' to do it. There is no rational link between the action and a moral 'ought'. Just because an act makes my life better, does not mean I am obligated to do it.

Alternatively, we might be tempted to look for some kind of proof that something really is our duty in the act itself or its consequences. For example, I could be tempted to say that telling the truth will lead to a more trusting society or that it will bring more happiness to other people. However, there is also no link between the inherent goodness of an action and our duty. Again, even if the act is good or somehow leads to good, there is no link between this fact and the sense that I 'ought' to do it.

Two ways of thinking (general and moral)

An obligation is an action we are required to do in a particular situation, involving a relationship between the moral agent and other people or themselves. Prichard gives the example of repaying a debt. This involves the action of returning money, and the relationship between the moral agent and the person who previously lent them money. It is important that the moral agent engages in what Prichard called **general thinking** to ensure that they are aware of the full story and have understood what Prichard called the **preliminaries**, the facts that will help an intuition to be formed. It is not enough for the moral agent to know that the person who loaned them money wants it back. It is also necessary for the moral agent to know that this is money that should be returned to the person who loaned it to them. General thinking is the thinking that is usually required in matters of philosophy and science. It is the process that enables a person to use reasoning to discover what is true. However, general thinking will not bring a person to conclude that they have a duty to act in a certain way. Through general thinking, a person can come to realise the whole picture, the actions, and relationships involved in the situation, but this is all.

Moral thinking is the recognition of an obligation that arises in the **unreflective consciousness**. It is not derived from facts about the world. It is intuitive knowledge about which we are certain when we are faced with it, which cannot be derived from empirical evidence and reasoning. Without the application of moral thinking, we would always have reason to doubt our moral duty. Having engaged in general thinking, a moral agent will appreciate their obligation immediately and directly within their moral thinking.

> *We do not come to appreciate an obligation by an argument,* ❞
> *i.e. by a process of non-moral thinking.*
>
> H.A. Prichard, 'Does Moral Philosophy Rest on a Mistake?'

Key terms

general thinking: using empirical evidence and reasoning to determine the facts and relationships involved in a situation

preliminaries: the initial facts about a situation that will help an intuition to be formed

moral thinking: coming to an intuitive understanding of our obligations

unreflective consciousness: an awareness in the mind of our moral obligations, which is independent of general thinking

Recognise what we 'ought to do' by intuition

Prichard says that if, for some reason, we come to doubt that we ought to repay the debt we owe, there is no sense in resorting to general reasoning to prove whether or not we really have a duty to repay the debt. An understanding of the duty can only be found by actually being in a situation that gives rise to the feeling of the obligation or, if our imagination is good enough, by imagining ourselves in the situation and letting our intuition take over. According to Prichard, there is nothing else available in moral philosophy to bring us to an understanding of our duty. The principle that someone ought to repay their debts is self evident. No reasoning can be given in support of the principle because it contains, within itself, its own reason.

> *Suppose we come genuinely to doubt whether we ought, for example, to pay our debts … The only remedy lies in actually getting into a situation which occasions the obligation, or – if our imagination be strong enough – in imagining ourselves in that situation, and then letting our moral capacities of thinking do their work.*
>
> H.A. Prichard, 'Does Moral Philosophy Rest on a Mistake?'

Challenges

There is no proof that moral intuition exists

The difficulty with Intuitionism is that there is little support for the approach beyond the feeling or sensation of having a duty or knowing goodness. This means that there is no way of verifying or falsifying an intuitive claim. In fact, the whole theory of Intuitionism rests upon this very point: that one cannot prove the 'good' through empirical investigation. This means we cannot know that what is intuited is the same for each person. This is a very unreliable and unphilosophical approach to ethical language.

J. Dancy points out that if intuitionists are trying to show that there are moral facts, it is difficult to understand where we can find these moral facts in the world that is described by physics and biology. J.L. Mackie, in his response to Intuitionism, referred to as his 'Argument from Queerness', agrees that if moral properties are facts, then why are they not analysable in the same way as natural properties are analysable. Intuitionism provides us with a very strange kind of understanding of a property or fact, unlike anything else in the universe.

> *The suggestion that moral judgements are made, or moral problems solved by just sitting down and having an ethical intuition is a travesty of actual moral thinking.*
>
> J.L. Mackie, *Inventing Right and Wrong*

AO1 activity 5

You have considered two scholarly intuitionist approaches. To help you to remember them, divide a large sheet of paper into two sections. In each section, pinpoint the main ideas of each scholar and the specialist vocabulary they use to describe their approach to Intuitionism. To help with your revision, include a 'lift the flap' feature with the specialist vocabulary on the outside of the flap and the definition underneath.

Synoptic link

Link to *A Level Religious Studies for Eduqas: Philosophy of Religion*, Chapter 7: Religious language (part one). According to logical positivists, meaningful claims must be capable of verification (known as the 'verification principle'). This means that if they are not analytic (true by definition) then they must be synthetic (true in reference to the empirical world) or they cannot be philosophically analysable and are therefore meaningless.

Mackie also argued that if intuitionists claim there are moral facts, how do we come to know them? The claim that they are known by intuition seems to suggest that we have some kind of sixth sense or moral faculty that reveals moral truth to us in the same way that our eyes reveal truths about the world. This led G.J. Warnock to claim that intuitionists offer nothing more than a sense of bewilderment dressed up to look like an answer!

Dancy points out that Intuitionism seems to be a way to try and award oneself some kind of moral authority that enables us to accuse anyone who disagrees with us of 'moral blindness', as we have intuited the truth and they have not. However, without any real account of how such knowledge is gained, the idea is simply mysterious or even vacuous.

Intuitive 'truths' can differ widely

Moore and Prichard do not agree over what it is that is intuited or how we come by our intuition. Moore intuits the 'good', whereas Prichard intuits a moral duty to perform certain actions. Each of these scholars argued that what is known through intuition is different. Moore takes a **consequentialist** approach to his application of moral intuitions, arguing that the goodness or badness of a moral action is based on its outcome, whereas Prichard is more **deontological** when he suggests that there are clear duties that govern how a person 'ought' to behave.

We should not underestimate the extent to which we are influenced by the society we live in. What one society intuits to be a duty may not be intuited by another to be a duty, and different societies have understood different duties or 'goods' at different times in history. There is no reason why what is seen by these scholars as intuition, might not be just the unconscious acceptance of the norms of the society that they live in.

Scholars like A.J. Ayer and C.L. Stevenson have been led, by these challenges, to develop Intuitionism further. They argue that moral statements, far from being cognitive, are actually **non-cognitive**, meaning that we cannot 'know' any true moral facts at all. The best we can do is understand moral statements as expressions of emotion, or maybe belief, but never any kind of objective, factual knowledge.

There is no obvious way to resolve conflicting intuitions

Without a firm basis for moral judgements, such as empirical evidence, there is no way for us to choose between different intuitions, and it seems unclear how the differences between scholars can be resolved. If two people have different intuitions about a moral case, how do we choose between the intuitions? Ordinarily, we might resort to approaches like deductive or inductive reasoning to prove the truth of a proposition. However, in the case of Intuitionism, Hume's Law means that these approaches have been dismissed as inaccurate ways of understanding moral truths or values.

Prichard's system attempts to explain that errors in intuition are actually failures in gathering all the facts of a situation prior to intuition taking

Key terms

consequentialist: a theory that judges the goodness or badness of a moral action based on its outcome

deontological: from the Greek, *déon*, for duty; deontological ethical theories are normative ethical theories that focus on duty and rules that govern how a person 'ought' to behave

non-cognitive: a proposition that is not concerned with facts about the world and cannot, therefore, be known as true or false

Synoptic link

Link to *A Level Religious Studies for Eduqas: Philosophy of Religion*, Chapter 4: Challenges to religious belief: religious belief as a product of the human mind. According to Freud, our sense of morality resides in our superego, which is formulated by our upbringing and the norms of the society that we live in.

place. Therefore, a conflict between two intuitions is based on poor general reasoning, and we should return to the situation to find out more about it. However, intuition itself cannot be verified, and no amount of fact gathering will ever prove which intuition is correct. The best we can hope for is that gathering more facts will lead to renewed intuitions that might agree with each other.

Meta-ethical approaches: Emotivism

So far, we have considered two quite different understandings of moral language. Both Naturalism and Intuitionism take a cognitivist position, holding that there is something knowable in ethical statements or propositions, but they disagree over the meaning of language.

Emotivism, which is also known as ethical non-cognitivism, takes a different approach. Key thinkers like A.J. Ayer and C.L. Stevenson claimed that ethical statements are not making factual claims about the world. There are multiple ways in which humans use language: they report facts but they also give commands, express feelings, exclaim, and ask questions. It is nonsense to ask if all language is true or false because sometimes language is not used in a way that can be described like this. Ethical statements, such as moral judgements, are not the kind of language that is supposed to report facts, and so Naturalism and Intuitionism are mistaken when they treat ethical language as though it is factual.

Objective moral laws do not exist

Emotivism considers that moral statements have two elements. For example, let us examine the moral statement, 'Stealing is wrong'. Firstly, this statement is expressing a feeling that the speaker has about stealing. They feel something negative when they think about stealing and they are expressing that feeling. Secondly, the statement is attempting to evoke a response in the hearer. It is trying to encourage the hearer not to steal, so it has an aspect to it that is persuasive.

Emotional expressions and attempts to persuade people to a particular point of view are not the kinds of statements that we can judge to be true or false. They are not propositions or facts about the world. Therefore, a moral judgement does not report an objective moral fact or law that applies to the world. It expresses the feelings of the speaker, and prescribes behaviour for the hearer. Consequently, objective moral laws cannot exist.

Emotivism is a non-cognitivist theory: moral terms express personal emotional attitudes and not propositions

Emotivism is, therefore, a non-cognitivist theory. If moral judgements simply express the agent's inner feelings, there is nothing within the statement that can be said to be known or knowable.

It is important at this stage to note that there is a difference between reporting a feeling and expressing a feeling. Look at the following statements:

● I like Marmite on toast.
● Marmite, woo hoo!

The first statement is a proposition that reports a feeling. It is, potentially, something you can call true or false. The second statement is an expression of feeling. It is not a proposition and it is not something that it would make sense to call true or false.

According to Emotivism, moral language is not fact-stating language. It is not designed to convey information and its only purpose is to influence others. So, if someone says, 'Going into a shop without a face mask is wrong,' the speaker is simply expressing a negative feeling about failing to wear a face mask, and is trying to encourage you to wear a face mask when you go into a shop. The statement is not a proposition that makes a factual claim. Therefore, moral statements cannot be cognitive because there is nothing in them that can be judged to be true or false.

Ethical terms are just expressions of personal approval (hurrah) or disapproval (boo)

Since moral judgements are non-propositional expressions of feeling rather than the presentation of a fact, they are more like an exclamation than something reporting information. As a result, Emotivism has been given the popular nickname 'The boo/hurrah theory'. This is because proponents of Emotivism argue that statements like 'Murder is wrong' give no more information than 'Murder, boo!'. This account of moral language adequately accounts for the apparent connection between a statement of moral judgement and the behaviour of the person making the statement. People who emote that murder or failure to wear face masks in shops are wrong behaviours, would be expected to resist both murder and not wearing a face mask in a shop because they have negative feelings about these behaviours. It would be inconsistent to see them adopting these behaviours because of their distaste for them.

Emotivism explains why people disagree about morality

When two people disagree over moral issues, they are usually disagreeing about matters of fact. When engaged in a moral dispute, participants will debate things like intentions, the situation, or the possible consequences of different responses to the situation. All of these things are factual matters and, when arguing, a moral agent may well bring them up to try and demonstrate that their opponent has forgotten or misunderstood important facts when coming to a moral judgement. When two people are from similar backgrounds or have, we assume, similar values, we would expect that, once they have agreed on such facts, they would come to a similar moral judgement and the argument would be resolved.

However, sometimes in moral debate, it is possible to come across two people who agree on the facts of the case yet still come to different moral judgements. For example, during the American Presidential Elections in 2020, it was possible to find individuals who agreed about the details of the behaviour of the various candidates yet disagreed over whether voting for them was the right thing to do. This is because people on opposing sides can hold different values. While people on one side might feel hostility towards acts like lying, and would want other people and particularly their President to avoid lying too, people on the other side might not share these negative feelings. At this point, it is common to see individuals resorting to insults rather than facts as they point out the distorted morality of their opponent! Moral argument fails when people try to deal with matters of value rather than facts because what they disagree about is not factual and cannot be verified. Moral arguments can only take place when people presume the same values (such as how people ought to treat women or the importance of telling the truth) because, once factual details are resolved, one person can presume to convince another person of own moral view.

Ethical judgements are simply expressions of emotion.

A.J. Ayer: ethical statements are neither verifiable nor analytic

In Chapter 6 of his 1936 book, *Language, Truth and Logic*, A.J. Ayer attempts to give an account of ethical statements that is consistent with the empiricist principles that he expresses elsewhere in the book. Ayer describes four main classes of ethical statement:

1. Definitions of ethical terms or judgements about the legitimacy of definitions: this is the work of meta ethics and, for Ayer, is the only kind of ethical philosophy possible.
2. The phenomena of moral experience and their causes: this is the business of psychology or sociology rather than ethics. This is descriptive ethics, which accounts for the behaviour that we can witness in people or societies but makes no judgement about its worth.
3. Exhortations to moral virtue: these are commands designed to provoke people into action. Such exhortations are not propositions; they make no claims and so they are not appropriate subjects for philosophy or science.
4. Ethical judgements: Ayer feels it is unclear what these kinds of statements are. However, as normative judgements, they are not definitions and so they are not the subject of any kind of philosophy.

Ayer claimed that the work of philosophy is not to make ethical pronouncements, but to analyse and categorise ethical terms. Ethical pronouncements are not tautologies, nor can they be checked against empirical evidence. Therefore, they do not make any kind of factual claims.

AO1 activity 7

Take a look at the comments section under a news story on the internet. You will usually find a debate concerning the rightness or wrongness of the behaviour of the people in the story. Find examples of the following:

- a statement that attempts to persuade
- a statement that expresses emotion
- statements of fact (or statements that could be verified)
- someone resorting to insults when values are not shared.

Ethical terms are made to express joy or pain (emotion)

Ethical naturalists attempt to translate ethical terms into statements of empirical fact. For example, utilitarians define 'good' as 'that which produces the most happiness'. Subjectivists define 'good' as 'that which a group generally approves of'. These approaches try to define 'good' in a way that can be analysed empirically and Ayer felt that, if they were correct, moral statements would be no different from any other kind of statement, and would be verifiable.

However, Ayer argued that both Utilitarianism and Subjectivism are wrong. This is because there is nothing self-contradictory in saying that an action that makes me happy is still a bad action or that an action that my society approves of is still a bad action. The definitions that these approaches give of 'good' and 'bad' are not consistent with language conventions because ethical statements are not the same as ordinary empirical statements.

Ayer also dismisses Intuitionism because it treats ethical judgements as propositions but still maintains they are unverifiable. Intuitionism assumes that all will intuit the same truth, but in reality, people feel very differently about morality. Intuitionism gives no method for deciding between conflicting intuitions, and so is worthless as a way to test the validity of moral propositions.

Ayer agrees with the intuitionists that fundamental ethical concepts are unanalysable since there is no criteria by which they can be tested for validity. However, he argues that this is because they are **pseudo-concepts**. The fact that ethical-sounding words are used, does not add anything to the actual content of a statement.

> It is as if I had said, 'You stole that money,' in a peculiar tone of horror, or written it with the addition of some special exclamation marks. The tone or the exclamation marks, adds nothing to the literal meaning of the sentence.
>
> A.J. Ayer, *Language, Truth and Logic*

Even if we make a more general statement, such as 'Stealing is wrong', there is no more factual meaning.

Nothing in the statements above about stealing can be considered true or false, and therefore, the statements have no objective validity. Consequently, an argument between two moral agents is not based in fact. Agents on both sides of the debate are simply emoting, and neither are asserting real propositions. This applies to all ethical terminology: 'good', 'bad', 'right', 'wrong', 'value', and so on. Sometimes these terms appear in sentences that do contain empirical facts but, regardless, the function of a statement of ethical judgement is purely emotive. For example, two people may argue about whether abortion is right. They may argue about the facts of abortion, the consequences of it, the circumstances in which it takes place, and the motivations of the people involved. However, the judgement about the rightness or wrongness of abortion is unverifiable in the same way that a cry of joy, a cry of pain, or a word of command cannot be verified.

Synoptic link

Link to *A Level Religious Studies for Eduqas: Philosophy of Religion, Chapter 7: Religious language (part one)*. The logical positivists distinguish between meaningful statements that are analytic or synthetic in nature, and meaningless statements that cannot be shown to be true or false.

Key term

pseudo-concept: having the appearance of a concept but falsely categorised as a concept

Ethical judgements are expressed to be persuasive

Ayer admits that there is a further function to ethical judgements, and that is to arouse the same kinds of feelings in others and affect their actions. Therefore, the statement, 'It is your duty to tell the truth' is both an expression of a feeling about truth-telling and a command to 'tell the truth'. Statements also have different levels of persuasive intensity depending on the terms used, with 'It is good to tell the truth' little more than a suggestion that the hearer is advised to follow. In this way, the meaning of 'good' is different from the meaning of 'duty' or 'ought' because it provokes a different level of response.

Emotivism is not Subjectivism

Ayer takes pains to point out that Emotivism is different from Subjectivism for two reasons.

A.J. Ayer (1910–1989)

1. Subjectivists understand ethical statements as non-empirical propositions *about* how one is feeling. However, Ayer counters that if the statements were propositions, they could be proven true or false. However, it is impossible to challenge or prove an utterance that makes no proposition at all. A statement that makes feeling noises is not the same thing as stating that one has feelings. Ayer admits that statements *about* feelings and statements *of* feeling sometimes look similar. If I moan 'I am bored', I show boredom and state a proposition about it at the same time. But I can also show boredom with a sigh, without ever stating a single proposition about it. Emotivists say that ethical statements are akin to that sigh.

2. The main objection to Subjectivism is that the goodness or badness of an action is not determined by what a person feels: I can hate lying and decide it might still be good to lie on occasion. However, Emotivism escapes this challenge. It denies that ethical judgements have validity, and so it does not try to suggest that feelings are enough to base an ethical judgement upon.

> *For the orthodox subjectivist does not deny, as we do, that the sentences of a moraliser express genuine propositions. All he denies is that they express propositions of a unique non-empirical character. His own view is that they express propositions about the speaker's feelings.* **"**
>
> A.J. Ayer, *Language, Truth and Logic*

In addition to this, Subjectivism finds itself having to treat ethical propositions as infallible since they report an internal state and therefore cannot be proven wrong. For instance, if 'stealing is bad' simply means 'I don't like stealing', then no one can ever argue that I am wrong because I am reporting my own feelings, and no one can challenge that fact. However, Emotivism claims that such utterances make no claims at all.

Furthermore, subjectivists cannot explain how there could ever be a moral disagreement if moral statements simply report a person's emotional state. For instance, if Rami says lying is wrong (meaning that he dislikes lying) and Farid says that lying is right (meaning that he likes lying), there is no contradiction to be found. They can agree that their emotional response is correctly reported and there is no argument to be had.

AO1 activity 8

Identify how Ayer would account for each of the following moral statements. The first one is done for you.

a) Murder is wrong. *Murder. Boo! Don't murder.*

b) It is your duty to tell the truth.

c) It is good to love your neighbour.

d) Courage is a moral virtue.

e) Do the right thing.

f) You ought to tell the police.

g) Generosity is a moral value.

h) I think that you did a bad thing.

Challenges

No basic moral principles can be established

James Rachels accused Emotivism of being too **reductionist**, causing moral debate to become no more than hot air. It makes it impossible for anyone to make moral judgements about issues like genocide, child abuse, or rape. Whether I tell a lie or steal is reduced to nothing more than my subjective feeling, which cannot be investigated, supported, or proven.

> **Key term**
>
> **reductionist:** an attempt to explain something complex in an over-simplified way

Emotivism makes the claim that all moral judgements can be reduced to emitting a feeling noise. R.W. Hepburn pointed out that this view omits a large amount of subject matter, and disregards the fact that a moral agent who does not know the answer to a moral question will use reasoning and thought to come to a moral conclusion. Emotivists think that moral judgements are no more than the reaction we have when we stub our toe! Rachels said this misses the fact that a statement such as 'Lovely, tea!' needs no reasoning behind it and does not need to be proved to be true or false, but a statement such as 'Murder is wrong' is more than just an expression of feelings; it is based on significant reasoning, evidence, and thought.

Hume pointed out that if we examine a 'bad act' like lying or murder, we cannot find any matter of fact that corresponds to this 'badness'. This means that moral values have no objective status because we cannot find evidence for them in the world. They are, after all, different from empirical objects like tables or chairs.

Ethical debate becomes a pointless activity

Moral language sounds very much like something that employs reason and rational thought. However, emotivists say that this is a confusion. We say things like, 'I know that stealing is wrong', or 'I believe that helping people is good', but if they are no more than an outburst of emotion, then such statements are false or meaningless, and therefore there is little purpose to them.

If Emotivism is correct, then when people have an ethical discussion, they are potentially doing two things. Firstly, they are emoting in the sense that they are expressing feelings about an issue but making no factual claims.

This means that an ethical debate is no more than a set of people making emotional noises at each other, and it becomes empty and without purpose. Secondly, as emotivists like C.L. Stevenson argued, they could also be trying to persuade their listener to their point of view. John Rafferty, in a 2006 article for the journal *Dialogue*, compared this to advertising or the kind of marketing language employed by charity workers or lawyers. And, if the language of ethics is used for dynamic impact upon the audience, ethical debate becomes centred on manipulating an audience to feel the same way as us, rather than establishing truth. This makes ethical debate superficial at best, and meaningless at worst.

Emotivism reduces moral language to emotional manipulation or a pointless shouting match.

There is no universal agreement that some actions are wrong

By abandoning objective morality altogether, Emotivism does not give us a way to resolve moral disagreements. Morality is not based on facts and there is no way of establishing whether an act is wrong or a goal is valid. Emotivism characterises moral debate as a form of noise-making in which opponents do nothing more than attempt to persuade by emoting louder or longer than each other. But this approach does not explain why anyone should ever change their mind about moral issues, and does not establish why people do come to moral judgements.

Stevenson argued that a statement about a fact which a speaker considers likely to alter someone's attitude is a 'reason' for or against an ethical judgement. But this position ignores the fact that such a statement must surely be at least relevant to the argument. Following Stevenson's logic, I could make completely irrelevant observations about a person to persuade you that they are immoral, and if the statements appealed to your prejudices and consequently convinced you, they would be 'reasons' for your judgement. For example, Rachels pointed out that someone could try and persuade you of a person's immorality by pointing out their ethnic background. This does not distinguish between invalid moral judgements made from irrelevant, arbitrary and – in this case – racist data and valid moral judgements made in the light of reasoning and supportive evidence. Emotivism does not allow for 'correct reasoning', and therefore does not allow for universal moral agreement on ethical terms.

AO1 activity 9

Look at the following statements:

- Lovely, tea!
- Rape is wrong.
- Ow! My Toe!
- It is usually right to be honest.
- We ought to allow euthanasia in some extreme cases.

a) Do you think it is appropriate to say that any of these statements are true or false?

b) Is there a way that people could reach an agreement over the meaning of any of these statements?

This section of the chapter will enhance your ability to analyse and evaluate the topic and help you develop your AO2 skills. For each question, think about the different positions you might take, and decide which you find most persuasive and why. It is not enough to memorise a list of 'for and against' points; you need to develop an argument.

Are ethical and non-ethical statements the same?

The issue here is the phrase 'the same'. The question requires you to consider the extent to which ethical and non-ethical statements share certain qualities.

The view that ethical and non-ethical statements are the same

'Goodness' and other ethical terms can be defined using non-ethical terms. Utilitarians argue that 'goodness' can be defined as 'happiness' or 'pleasure', and in his essay 'My Station and its Duties', Bradley suggested that 'goodness' can be defined in terms of the role and position of an individual in society. Therefore, ethical statements can be observed and verified in the world in the same way as non-ethical statements can be observed and verified.

Naturalists argue that ethical and non-ethical statements are the same because it is possible to find evidence from the world to support their truth or falsity, just as we can find evidence from the world to support the truth or otherwise of scientific statements. Ethical judgements are based upon facts that are available through sensory evidence. So, to come to the judgement that murder is wrong, I can observe the facts of a murder: that it is the taking of a life, that it causes physical and psychological suffering to the people involved, and that it causes people within a society to feel afraid or unsafe. I can then use reason to deduce the conclusion that murder is wrong and should be avoided.

Rachels pointed out that even if it is not possible to use the scientific method to establish the truth or falsity of an ethical statement, it is not reasonable to dismiss moral judgements as cognitively meaningless or simply emotive utterances. Rachels argued that many moral judgements are extremely complex, and while we might not be able to find 'proof' to support the objective value of immigration policy or capital punishment, there are also complex scientific theories that are not supported by 'proof'. For example, it is simple enough to establish the boiling point of water, but in the arena of quantum physics there is a great deal of uncertainty, and many ideas are supported by theoretical reasoning and not concrete empirical evidence.

N.L. Sturgeon presents the view that ethical statements and non-ethical statements can be investigated in the same way. However, he points out that this view depends upon how you define a natural property and how you think such properties should be investigated. It is reasonable to say that any statement that reports a social convention or a feeling could be considered to be reporting facts about the world, because social conventions and feelings are natural facts just as physical objects are facts. Therefore, a statement such as, 'It is good to be generous' can be investigated for its natural properties. It might be that one society agrees with the statement and another does not, but the truth or falsity of the statement, even if it is relative to society, is something that can be discovered in the natural world.

The view that ethical and non-ethical statements are not the same

There are many kinds of non-ethical statements, and it is easy to see that few of them bear a resemblance to ethical statements. Non-ethical statements may include factual reporting, as we find in science, but they also include giving commands, telling jokes, expressing feelings, and exclaiming. They come in the form of poetry, prose, lists, reports, and so on, and ethical statements are clearly not the same as all these forms of communication. Yet, ethical statements do have similarities with some non-ethical statements, for instance, descriptive ethical statements do report facts, and normative ethical statements give commands. However, emotivists show that ethical statements also have a strong emotional element to them. While Emotivism may be simplistic in suggesting that emitting emotion is the sole expression behind ethical statements, it highlights a significant difference in their character.

Hume pointed out, in *Treatise of Human Nature*, that when we look at an example of an ethical statement, such as 'murder is wrong', we can see that while we might be able to look at the objective facts surrounding a murder – such as the knife, the body, the pool of blood, and so on – we cannot observe the part that is 'wrong'. Ethical statements contain a part that is not observable and, furthermore, several of these objective facts would be true of a completely different scenario, such as the scene in an operating theatre. Therefore, ethical and non-ethical statements are not the same, because ethical statements cannot be supported simply by observation.

Ethical statements are very different from non-ethical statements. It is clear, from Moore's *Principia Ethica*, that while we use words like 'good' or 'bad' as though they are the same as non-ethical language, we cannot define them in the same way as non-ethical language, and attempts to do so do not bring us to a deeper understanding of the concepts they represent. Moore's Naturalistic Fallacy and Open Question Argument demonstrate that, while a description of something like a horse involves descriptions of lots of different observable parts, 'good' is a simple concept that is not composed of parts.

Therefore, non-ethical and ethical language are quite different because ethical values cannot be defined and are known purely by intuition.

In his 1977 book *Ethics: Inventing Right and Wrong*, J.L. Mackie argued that there are no objective values or natural moral facts. He calls this view 'moral scepticism' because he regards moral terms such as 'good', 'bad', 'right', and 'wrong' as inappropriate descriptions of the natural world. He argues that moral facts do not exist, so it is not the purpose of ethical language to make factual statements. Instead, moral language is about expressing favourable or unfavourable attitudes or prescriptions. Mackie does not deny that actions can be kind or cruel. What he denies is whether there is any value or disvalue to being kind or being cruel. There is no way to demonstrate objectively that cruelty should be condemned. His 'Argument from Queerness' shows that ethical statements are very different to non-ethical statements because they are utterly different from anything else in the universe.

To what extent are ethical statements not objective?

This question asks about the 'extent' to which ethical statements are not objective, therefore this question is open to an answer that may be more complex than simply whether ethical statements are or are not objective. There might be a middle position, where ethical statements can be considered objectively true or false but with some conditions. While the question presents a non-cognitive position, you should be prepared to draw on any of the meta-ethical positions that you have studied so far.

The view that ethical statements are not objective

Sturgeon suggested that there is no certainty that anyone can gain ethical knowledge simply by making the process look scientific. You can only make objective statements about the world when the procedure for producing the knowledge on which the statements are based is reliable. The procedures for producing factual statements about the world using science methods are reliable because they are based upon basic assumptions, such as the laws of cause and effect, which are known to be true; and ethical statements will only be reliable if the background assumptions or beliefs that they are based upon are approximately true. It is not enough to say that an ethical statement is based upon empirical evidence, because it is necessary to have followed a reliable process when creating the statement, even though no such process exists.

Roy Jackson argues that it seems very unphilosophical to claim that moral agents can have intuitions that are objectively true if they do not originate from God or some other metaphysical or external phenomenon. Sturgeon agreed that ethical statements are not really talking about anything concrete if there is no objective basis for, or source of, morality and so

AO2 activity 1
Look through the arguments for and against the proposition that ethical and non-ethical statements are the same, and rank them in order of how convincing you find them, with 1 being the most convincing and 5 being the least convincing. Then take the top arguments from each side of the debate and decide which one you agree with most. Explain why you find your chosen argument more persuasive than the others.

theories like Naturalism or Intuitionism, which try to claim that ethical statements are objective but deny any divine source for them, must be wrong. Although, of course, if morality is based on the existence of some divine standard, we are still brought back to the Euthyphro dilemma: is 'good' good because God commands or because it is good in itself?

J.L. Mackie pointed out that for Naturalism to produce objective ethical statements, it has to be able provide prescriptions for behaviour that give moral agents a reason for moral action that is not simply based on their own personal desires. But there is no evidence that facts like these exist. Therefore, moral statements are not objective statements about ethical facts. Instead, Mackie argued that morality is created by society or institutions. Moral statements are not objective and so morality is not obligatory.

Emotivists argue that where morality is concerned, there are no facts, and no one is right or wrong. Morality is little more than an expression of someone's feelings about a moral issue. Hume said, in *Treatise on Human Nature*, that moral statements are not objectively factual and are 'the object of feeling, not reason'. Reason can inform us of facts about the world, but it cannot ever tell us what we 'ought' to do. And, because moral statements guide an agent's moral conduct by reflecting sentiment or emotions, they are not objective.

The view that ethical statements are objective

Naturalism claims that there are objective features of the world that we can observe to determine the truth or falsity of ethical statements, as we observe the natural world to determine the truth of a scientific statement. We can understand the truth of a statement like 'murder is wrong' by looking at the physical act of murder, assessing its consequences for the individual and the impact upon society, and determining that we ought not to murder someone. This position assumes that moral facts are the same as any other facts about the natural world, and recognises the causal relationship between our actions and the world in which we live. For example, we can establish that we ought to eat if we want to survive and be healthy by considering the consequences that happen if we do not. Similarly, our moral choices are intrinsically connected to the world we live in.

F.H. Bradley recognised that our place in society plays a central part in our moral behaviour. We are products of the society we live in. We live and act within society, and the values we hold are inherited through centuries of cultural evolution. Moral statements are, therefore, objective in the sense that they are the product of cause and effect operating upon culture and society in the same way as cause and effect operates on any other part of the natural world. Our role in society and the duties we have are observable and, therefore, ethical statements about our behaviour are objective in reporting what is expected of us.

Prichard adopted a deontological approach by arguing that you can intuit an ought in a situation in the same way you can intuit mathematical truths.

Thus, we can know our duty objectively through intuition. Roy Jackson says that this is a weak analogy to demonstrate the truth of Intuitionism because we do not just know mathematics, we have to learn it, and usually there is a consensus among mathematicians as to the correct answer. However, if we must learn about moral rules by studying morality in the same way that we learn mathematics by studying it, this seems to suggest a similar approach to Naturalism, and implies that there can be objective ethical statements. Jackson also goes on to argue that there can be considered a general consensus about ethical statements among those philosophers who take the same naturalist stance to ethics and assume that Naturalism is the correct approach.

Subjectivism allows for people to make statements such as 'murder is wrong', and even though they are statements of moral feelings, they are infallible. Such statements cannot be wrong because they report moral facts. This is not the same as Emotivism, because the statements are not simply an expulsion of moral feelings. Subjectivism allows a person to report their moral stance and so, if a person says 'abortion is wrong', they mean that they feel negatively about abortion and they are objectively correct in reporting what they feel. The same person can also acknowledge that an opponent is correctly reporting a moral fact when they say 'abortion is right' and mean that they agree with abortion. Both statements can be infallibly correct and objectively true.

The view that ethical statements may be partially objective

It is worth remembering that there are several different types of ethical statements. While it might be difficult to hold the view that normative statements are objective, descriptive ethical statements certainly can be. While Ayer believed that descriptive ethical statements are more suitable for the fields of anthropology and psychology, they can give factual descriptions that show exactly what people believe and how they behave. Ayer also argued that the only valid field of moral philosophy is meta ethics. Meta ethics makes statements about the validity of ethical language, so even Ayer cannot dismiss meta-ethical statements as not objective. The objectivity of an ethical statement may, therefore, depend on what type of ethical statement it is.

Ayer described ethical statements as having two aspects. The first aspect is an emotional utterance; the second is a prescription for moral behaviour. Ayer argued that there is nothing factual to verify in either instance. However, we could counter argue that an emotional utterance counts as evidence of a person's feelings. Further evidence of that feeling is in the efforts that a moral agent makes to encourage or dissuade others of that behaviour. We may then say that a moral statement has some objective meaning because it demonstrates the feeling that a moral agent has towards an ethical action.

AO2 activity 2
Summarise, in a 'tweet' of 140 characters, the strongest argument you have read regarding whether or not ethical statements are objective.

Are moral terms intuitive?

This question is specifically asking you to consider the merit of Intuitionism. Again, for successful analysis to take place, it is important that you do not focus entirely on Intuitionism and draw upon all the material that you have covered in this chapter on meta ethics.

The view that moral terms are intuitive

Intuitionism by-passes the rational difficulty presented by Hume's Law. Intuitionists do not commit the rational error of moving from a descriptive statement to a prescriptive statement without appropriate reasoning or evidence. Prichard allowed that we can sense our moral obligation and do not need to support it with reason, and this is difficult to counter since the whole point is that we cannot offer empirical evidence to support or reject moral obligations that we intuitively know to be true.

Intuitionism still takes a realist position, meaning that statement can be true or false. While intuitionists like W.D. Ross recognised that moral intuition is not perfect, they do recognise the reality of what people are doing when they say that an action is 'wrong' or 'right'. When people make statements of this sort, it is rarely as a result of lengthy moral deliberation but more a gut reaction based upon certain values that they already hold. A person who argues that abortion is wrong may not have weighed the pros and cons, but may have instinctively rejected it based upon the value they place on what they consider to be human life.

Maybe we do just know what is meant by 'right' and 'wrong', but the reason we have this knowledge is because the learning we have participated in during our lifetime has become part of our subconscious. Freud says that our superego contains the restrictions we have learned from society, and these are essentially subconscious. Therefore, we have been influenced by our upbringing, the society we live in, and our experience of the world, but our expression of these ideas appears in the form of intuition. This approach suggests that, while moral terms appear as intuitions, they are not objectively true because they are based on knowledge that we have gained by learning from our society.

J. Dancy says that Intuitionism in mathematics can be compared with Intuitionism in ethics. Numbers are abstract concepts, as are terms like 'good' or 'wrong'. We are aware of these concepts because we operate reason or judgement, but we do not enter into any kind of causal relationship with them. We can be led to recognise the properties of things that are not causal. Therefore, moral terms may be intuitively known.

The view that moral terms are not intuitive

Peter Vardy argues that Intuitionism does not show that there is a difference between statements about belief (such as 'I believe that it is right to give to charity') and statements about the objective rightness or wrongness of an action (such as 'It is right to give to charity'). Intuitionists simply appeal to intuition to argue that a moral statement is of the second type, but there does not seem to be a reason why this claim is more convincing than any other approach to ethics, such as Naturalism. Usually, when someone attempts to make a factual claim about the world, we expect them to justify their position by giving reasoning or evidence, and the same should be true of a claim about morality, even if the evidence is drawn from conventions in society.

Intuitionists do not appear to agree about which moral principles are supposed to be self-evident. Moore argued that the 'goods' we can know through intuition are many, and include human interactions and the appreciation of beautiful things. He took a **teleological** approach, in that he felt we can use reason to work out which actions will maximise the enjoyment of these kinds of things. In contrast, Prichard identified duties that he felt can be intuitively known and that we are obliged to perform. If there is no agreement between those who are considered knowledgeable and well-educated on these matters, it is hard to see what it is that we can reliably intuit.

There is no way to verify intuitions that are sensed by moral agents. They are essentially infallible because they are intuited. However, Moore implied that not everything one intuits is necessarily a moral truth, and Prichard implied that we need a full understanding of the whole problem before an intuition is possible. There is, as a result, a risk that moral 'truths' can only be deduced by the elite, by a highly-educated few, rather than by ordinary people. This suggests not only that education and training (which, even today, are not available to everyone) are required to intuit moral truths, but also that intuition is a skill to be learned rather than a true intuition. This means that we know the meaning of moral terms through experience and practice, and not from actual intuition at all.

The difficulties with Intuitionism have given rise to Emotivism. Ultimately, if we cannot choose between intuitions how can we know that an intuition is any more meaningful than a simple feeling? Scholars like Mackie and Ayer have pointed out that there is no difference between an intuited moral statements and an emotional outburst, and so an emotional outburst is the most that a moral statement can amount to. This shows that ethical statements cannot be a kind of infallible intuition that produces knowledge because they contain nothing that can be confirmed as factually meaningful.

> ### Key term
>
> **teleological:** from the Greek, *telos*; to do with end goals or outcomes

> ### AO2 activity 3
> Identify the two weakest arguments about whether or not moral terms are intuitive. Write down three reasons why you think each argument is weak.

To what extent are moral terms just expressions of our emotions?

This question focuses on the main premise of the emotivists, and asks you to consider how far moral language is simply an expression of emotion. You could argue that moral terms are just expressions of our emotions and nothing more, or that moral terms have nothing to do with expressing emotion. Alternatively, you could argue that emotions play a limited part in moral language.

The view that moral terms are just expressions of our emotions

Hume's Law argues that Naturalism is fundamentally flawed when it attempts to derive moral 'oughts' from statements that describe the world. This error of reasoning means that moral terms cannot be expressions of facts about the world, but if they are not expressions of facts about the world, then what are they? If we are to claim moral terms represent real things, we are forced to believe that we know them from a source other than the natural world. However, if we reject intuition or the divine as the source, it is attractive to believe that moral terms are either a report of an emotional state (Subjectivism) or an expression of a feeling (Emotivism).

Emotivism denies that there is such a thing as a moral fact. Moral terms do not relate to anything real in the world, and are not derived from a divine being. The theory is attractive because it is based upon the observation that facts can be derived from sensory evidence. Since there is no sensory evidence to support moral claims about right and wrong, it is reasonable to conclude that there are no moral facts. The theory is consistent with modern scientific understanding about knowledge and truth. It also accounts for the many different understandings of right and wrong that can be found around the globe. Finally, Rafferty suggests that it explains why people are reluctant to change their minds in the face of empirical data about a moral issue, because moral views are not derived from factual information but arise from an emotional response to a situation.

Rachels said that the idea that moral terms are just expressions of our emotions successfully bypasses the problems that have been found with other theories, such as Subjectivism. Subjectivism cannot account for moral disagreements because there is nothing to disagree about if moral terms simply report the feelings of a moral agent. If I report that I feel badly about using nuclear weapons and you report that you feel good about using nuclear weapons, we are not disagreeing because we can acknowledge that we do both feel these things at the same time. Emotivism accounts for the emotion involved in moral debate: we are trying to persuade each other to hold the same feelings and our feelings are in conflict; we cannot both have our own way and so we disagree.

Ayer's Emotivism shows that it is more rational, and therefore more philosophical, to view moral terms as expressions of emotion. He agreed with Hume that ethical terms are not propositions because they cannot be demonstrated to be true or false, and he rejected the 'mysterious intuition' that claims moral terms are factual yet not verifiable. Ayer thought that intuition was 'worthless' as a test of the validity of a moral claim. But there is no need for any kind of test if moral terms are just emotive utterances, because they are not statements that need to be judged as true or false. Just as my exclamation of 'Ow!' when I fall over does not need to be verified, my exclamation that 'Murder is wrong!' is an expression of my feelings when presented with facts about someone who has been killed. Emotivism accepts that there is no relevant test to be done, and accounts for it.

The view that moral terms are not just expressions of our emotions

Rafferty points out that, when a person makes a moral judgement, they often express it in the language of facts. Statements such as 'I believe that murder is wrong', 'I know that courage is a virtue', or 'It is true that abortion is morally allowable' are more than just outbursts of emotion. They are supported by reasoning and evidence, and are grounded in empirical facts gathered from observing the natural world. By abandoning moral realism altogether, emotivists make moral discourse into meaningless noise. While this is a meta-ethical issue rather than a normative issue, the implications of the emotivist position mean that it is impossible to meaningfully condemn acts like child torture or rape because statements of moral indignation are no more than personal emotional utterances.

Emotivism does not account for moral discussions that occur between people who hold the same moral view. When we have ethical discussions, we do not merely try and shout loudly enough to persuade others of an alternative view. Sometimes ethical discussion can be an exploration of moral issues or a quest for deeper understanding. In addition, Emotivism does not account for personal deliberation, when we are clearly not trying to persuade ourselves to take a particular moral stance and are not merely expressing our own emotions to ourselves. Rachels pointed out that it would seem that Emotivism does not account for the deliberation that takes place when someone is employing reason to consider a moral position, and yet this is what ethicists engage in all the time.

Rachels went on to argue that Emotivism fails to acknowledge any connection between a moral judgement and the reasoning given to support it. Reasoning is dismissed as something that is used to affect the emotions of the hearer, to cause a change in heart. This means that it does not really matter if there is no connection between the reason and the judgement. Stevenson allowed any argument provided it had the desired effect, but this means I could argue that abortion is wrong because a major supporter of abortion is an atheist or a woman, and this argument would be acceptable if it played on the hearer's prejudices and changed their mind. This must be rejected because these kinds of arguments are irrational, false, and could lead to discriminatory conclusions. There is a connection between reasons and judgement in a moral argument; moral arguments contain content that can be deliberated and are not merely emotional.

Emotions may play a limited role in the use of moral terms

Emotivism is very reductionist in its approach to ethical language, and consequently fails to recognise the complexity of what moral agents are trying to do when they use moral terms. It can certainly be demonstrated that moral terms express emotion and that they aim to persuade, but they express so much more. Moral terms are also the product of reasoning; they are an expression of cultural norms, an indication of an individual's state of mind, a response to a specific set of circumstances and environmental factors, and a description of past reactions to moral problems. Elizabeth Anscombe illustrated the idea that there are multiple uses of language with the example of a shopping list. It both instructs the user what to buy (prescribes action) and acts as a record of what was bought (describes action). Ethical terms can be used to express emotions, but they also can be used for other purposes too.

Even Ayer did not suggest that there was nothing more to moral language than simply an emotional utterance (although this was the main thrust of his argument). While the argument is more fully developed in the work of Stevenson, Ayer acknowledged that part of what is happening when someone makes an ethical judgement is that they are persuading or recommending moral behaviour to others. This means that moral terms are not purely expressions of our emotions and they are not philosophically meaningless. They have a function, and that function can be understood.

AO2 activity 4

Scour the news for a recent debate on a moral issue, such as abortion, euthanasia, or capital punishment; or an issue that is unrelated to this course, such as mask wearing or protests. Read the article and, if it is online, take a glance at the comments as well. Now consider the following:

Do you think that the views expressed are a result of legitimate reasoning, or are they just expressions of an emotion? Give three reasons to back up your view.

Which is the superior theory: Naturalism, Intuitionism or Emotivism?

Clearly this question requires you to draw on knowledge from all three meta-ethical theories. You will need to weigh up the strengths and weaknesses of each in relation to the others to form a judgement.

The view that Naturalism is superior

Naturalism is the superior theory because ethical statements are understood in relation to natural phenomena that can be verified or falsified. Ethical terms can be supported with scientific evidence that is universally available, and can be used to investigate other facts about the world. It is an attractive theory because it means ethical terms are cognitive and meaningful in a way that should be agreeable to everyone and it does not depend upon any divine understanding of the world.

Naturalism is a more practical way of analysing ethical language because it gives rise to meaningful normative statements that can be applied in real situations. For example, the ethical statement 'Good acts are those that produce maximum happiness' means that we can analyse the world for behaviour that maximises happiness, and can produce normative statements such as 'Stealing is wrong' on the basis that stealing reduces happiness. This statement can then be used by someone weighing up whether or not to steal. It means that Naturalism is much more useable than Intuitionism, which relies on vague notions of special kinds of 'knowledge' that are undefinable, or Emotivism, which reduces ethical statements to feeling-induced grunting.

Charles R. Pigden argues that Naturalism still works despite the challenge from Hume's Law. Hume argued that an 'is' statement cannot logically lead you to an 'ought' statement. This is a logical fact about philosophical arguments which says that a conclusion must only contain information that is available within the premises. However, Pigden points out that it is not necessary to abandon Naturalism and resort to Intuitionism to overcome Hume's is/ought distinction. Naturalists must simply make sure they use premises to come to valid conclusions. He used a joke by A.N. Prior to illustrate his argument. It would be ridiculous to say that there is no such thing as a proposition about hedgehogs or to propose a 'fact/hedgehog distinction' just because you cannot get a hedgehog conclusion from hedgehog-free premises! 'English people drink tea' does not lead us to conclude that English people are hedgehogs. Clearly, this is an invalid argument. But valid arguments about hedgehogs can still exist. Similarly, Naturalism can be successful if you do not commit this kind of faulty logic. Provided a naturalist identifies appropriate facts that lead to a logical conclusion, there is no need to resort to *sui generis* moral properties like intuition to solve the problem of Hume's Law.

The view that Intuitionism is superior

Moore's Intuitionism is superior because it drills down to the real nature of ethical terminology and the mistakes that are made by moral philosophers. He does not suggest that we cannot identify anything that is 'good', after all he considers friendship and appreciation of beauty to be good, but these things do not *define* 'good'. The goodness of these things is the indefinable quality that cannot be limited by trying to conflate it with something that is a natural phenomenon. This identifies the quality of 'good' in a way that Naturalism does not. Naturalism is such a limited way of looking at the world because it assumes everything is the same, with the same kinds of qualities, and does not allow that there could be things in the world that are not analysable in the same way.

Intuitionism is the more superior theory because it recognises the limitations of Naturalism without letting go of the cognitivist approach to ethical statements. While Emotivism consigns all ethical language to emotional noises that cannot contain factual information, Intuitionism allows ethical statements to be factual but not limited by the rules of the verification principle. It is the superior theory because it allows for moral statements to be immediately true or false, and allows for actions to be objectively praised or condemned.

Prichard has a superior approach to Intuitionism. He maintained that moral facts can be known through intuition, but also acknowledged that there are a great many things to know that are important to how one should behave. Moral facts are related to non-moral facts because we must find out the details of a moral case before we can intuit a moral principle, but moral facts are not the same as non-moral facts because they exist even though physics does not say much about them.

The view that Emotivism is superior

Mackie pointed out that there are no moral facts and no natural moral facts but, he argues, it is not the function of ethical language to state such facts anyway. The function of ethical language is to express feelings towards things or prescribe feelings in others. This ties into a naturalistic world view in the sense that meaningful language is that which can be verified by empirical evidence, and can be universally understood, but recognises that ethical language is not of this kind.

Scholars like R.M. Hare, who developed the Emotivist approach to become Prescriptivism, argued that moral judgements are different from natural facts because they do not describe facts about the world; they prescribe how the world should be. They are like orders. This is a more appropriate description of ethical judgements than the cognitivist theories of Naturalism and Intuitionism, because statements like 'Murder is wrong' cannot reflect anything about the world as it stands. There is no 'wrong' that can be identified and pinpointed through natural investigation, and so such statements are really saying 'I will not murder, and neither should you'.

Emotivism is superior because it holds up against the criticisms levelled at Subjectivism, in that it allows for propositions about people's emotions to become infallible and does not account for moral disagreements. Emotivism does not rely upon a divine being or vague notions of a moral faculty that just knows moral truths. It is founded in an empirical understanding of the world and observation of the ways in which moral language is used, and while it may not be popular because it removes objectivity from ethics, it does not have to be popular to be true.

To what extent do different meta-ethical theories encourage moral debate?

Once again, knowledge of all three meta-ethical theories is useful when answering this question. By asking you about the 'extent' to which *different* meta-ethical theories encourage debate, this question is asking you not only to explore whether one of the theories is better than the others at encouraging debate, but also to examine whether any of the theories discourage moral debate.

AO2 activity 5

It always helps, when faced with an essay question, to know what you really think before you begin to write.

To help you work out what you really think, copy and complete the following sentences:

a) The hardest argument for me to understand was … because …

b) The most surprising argument was … because …

c) The argument I felt the most convinced by was … because …

d) The most irritating argument was … because …

e) An argument I would like to add is …

The view that meta-ethical theories do encourage moral debate

Meta-ethical theories such as Naturalism do encourage moral debate because they require moral agents to engage with data in the empirical world and evaluate physical evidence in support of propositions. The weight of the evidence presented can be evaluated, and the extent to which moral propositions can be considered true, both of which are essential for moral debate.

Meta ethics asks us to consider whether there are moral truths or properties, the difference between moral and ordinary concerns, and what ethical terms might mean or relate to. Meta-ethical theories all encourage moral debate, and David Copp suggests that meta ethics actually engages with morality rather than simply describing it. The debates cover a wide range of questions: Are there such things as moral facts? If there are, where they come from (from scripture or from the natural world)? How we know them (through evidence, intuition, or divine command)? And what exactly do moral judgements do (describe facts, reflect feelings, or promote a change in behaviour)? These debates have a bearing upon the authority of moral language, and therefore upon human behaviour.

The emotivist approach to meta-ethics has given moral debate a new lease of life because it challenges the idea of objective moral facts, and proposes that there can be no factual content within ethical statements. This prevents anyone from having any kind of moral knowledge, and means that it is impossible to praise or condemn moral and immoral actions no matter how wonderful or abhorrent they are. The implications of this approach for normative ethics are far reaching, because it means that there is no longer any reason to obey moral commands. If moral commands are indeed arbitrary, the debates about Moral Relativism and the use of punishment for immoral behaviour become essential.

When considered from a meta-ethical perspective, Divine Command Theory has encouraged centuries of debate over the nature of God's commands with the Euthyphro dilemma and Adams' subsequent development. Modern scholars, such as Adams and Julian Baggini (who argues that Adams simply restates the argument and asks whether God's nature is good because being good is what God is, or whether God is good because God has all the properties of goodness), show that it is still of contemporary relevance.

The view that meta-ethical theories do not encourage moral debate

Naturalism can discourage moral debate because it argues there are objective moral facts that can be known and that we can, therefore, objectively know what is right or wrong. This suggests that moral debate is unnecessary because once a moral truth has been discovered, it need not be challenged. This approach can encourage a normative moral absolutism that, once accepted, discourages moral debate.

Intuitionism does not encourage moral debate because it simply states that we know about moral theories through intuition. Moore himself was unwilling to debate the definition of moral terms:

> *If I am asked 'How is good to be defined?' my answer is that it cannot be defined, and that is all I have to say about it.*
>
> G.E. Moore, *Principia Ethica*

There is no opportunity to engage in moral debate if someone who argues a different point is simply told they are wrong and there is nothing more to be said.

Theories such as Emotivism can be accused of shutting down moral debate. This is because the reductionist idea that moral statements are devoid of factual content means they hold no value for philosophers to discuss. In addition, Ayer reduced the content of moral discourse down to only that which is meta-ethical, meaning that it is no longer possible to have a meaningful moral debate about the rightness or wrongness of moral actions. Ayer even dismissed discussion outside of the meta-ethical realm as being the subject matter for psychology and sociology rather than moral philosophy.

As a meta-ethical theory, Divine Command Theory does not encourage moral debate because, once it is established that what is good is what God commands, all that follows is understanding that God's commands are absolute, unchanging, and universally good. This approach dismisses evidence from the natural world and individual intuition, as well as circumstances that might be presented as evidence of a contrary position. There is no question that God's commands can be anything other than good because they are not open to falsification.

AO2 activity 6

Draw an outline of your hand.

a) On the thumb, write down which argument is most convincing.
b) On the index finger, write down something you feel needs to be pointed out.
c) On the middle finger, write down the worst argument you have read.
d) On the ring finger, write down something from the debate that you think is important.
e) On the little finger, write down a small point or example you want to add.
f) On the palm, write your judgement: Have Naturalism, Intuitionism, and Emotivism encouraged moral debate?

Practising AO1 questions

AO1 questions begin with one of a range of possible command words (see pages 8–9 for more detail). The question below begins with the word 'Compare'. 'Compare' questions require you to show the similarities and differences between the theories in the question; you do not need to consider the quality of the theories or offer any views about them. It is a good idea to compare aspects of both theories side by side, rather than describing each theory in turn; this allows you to draw out the similarities and differences more easily.

Read the past paper question and the example paragraph written in response before completing the activity on page 84.

> *Compare the meta-ethical approaches of Intuitionism and Emotivism.*
>
> (WJEC A Level Religious Studies, Summer 2018, A2 Unit 4: Religion and Ethics, Question 1)

Example

Intuitionism and Emotivism[7] are both[2] non-naturalist[7] approaches[2] to meta-ethics[7]. They both[2] deny the idea that moral facts can be derived from[1] non-moral[7] features of the world and support[1] Hume's[6] Guillotine[7], that an 'ought cannot be derived from an is'[1]. This similarity is important, because[2] it rejects the approach of some utilitarians, like[3] J.S. Mill[6], who argue that what is 'good' is what brings about the greatest happiness and so we know what moral acts we should perform by looking at the world and identifying what would bring about the most happiness[3]. Both intuitionists and emotivists[2] reject this definition of goodness and the way in which it leads to moral 'oughts' that can be known. This is the 'mistake' that[1] Prichard[6] identified in his essay: there can be no definition of what we[3] 'ought to do'[7] and any attempt to justify moral judgements using data from the natural world is in error[3]. Similarly[2], Ayer[6] argued that fundamental ethical concepts[7] are not[3] analysable[7] because there is no criterion by which they can be judged accurately as true or false[3].

What went well

1 The paragraph shows thorough, accurate, and relevant knowledge about both meta-ethical approaches and the similarities between them.

2 This paragraph addresses the specific demands of the question by clearly showing similarities between Intuitionism and Emotivism. The student should continue the essay by exploring the differences between the two approaches in subsequent paragraphs.

3 There is detailed use of evidence and examples, with the paragraph including Utilitarianism as an example of the kind of idea that both approaches would reject, and examples of ideas from Intuitionism and Emotivism.

4 You should include references to sacred texts where an opportunity arises naturally, but this should not be forced. It is acceptable for this to be absent if it is not appropriate to the question.

5 Connections with other areas studied should be included only where appropriate; connections should not be forced.

6 There is extensive use of scholarly views, with Hume, Mill, Prichard, and Ayer all referenced.

7 There is thorough and accurate use of specialist language in context.

Activity

a) Read the example paragraph on page 83 and note down at least three similarities between Intuitionism and Emotivism that are mentioned.

b) The example paragraph is strong with many key features from the band descriptors confidently displayed. However, it is only one paragraph and more needs to be added to complete the answer. Write a second paragraph looking at some key differences between the two meta-ethical approaches.

AO1 practice question 1

Now it is your turn. Have a go at answering the following question. There are some points to remember underneath to help you if you are not sure how to start.

Explain the meta-ethical approach of Naturalism.

(Eduqas A Level Religious Studies, Sample Assessment Materials, Component 3: Religion and Ethics, Question 3a)

Points to remember

- Remember to concentrate on explaining the meta-ethical focus of Naturalism: how we may come to know the meaning of ethical propositions by analysing the natural world in a scientific way.
- Use key vocabulary that relates to Naturalism, such as 'cognitivist', 'objective', and 'moral realism'.
- Give examples of scholarly views, such as F.H. Bradley's presentation of a naturalist approach in 'My Station and its Duties'.

AO1 practice question 2

Now try this question by yourself.

Explain the meta-ethical approach of Emotivism, including reference to A.J. Ayer.

(Eduqas A Level Religious Studies, Summer 2018, Component 3: Religion and Ethics, Question 3a)

Practising AO2 questions

When writing a response to an AO2 question, you must remember that you are being examined on your ability to analyse and evaluate effectively. Analysis involves a detailed examination of something and you should pick apart the concept to look for the strengths and the weaknesses. Evaluation involves judging the quality or importance of the concept. You are expected to analyse and evaluate throughout the whole of your response; you are not expected to include long passages explaining of knowledge and understanding.

Read the past paper question below and the example paragraphs written in response before completing the activity on page 86.

> *'Moral terms are nothing more than expressions of human emotions.' Evaluate this view.*
>
> (WJEC A Level Religious Studies, Summer 2019, A2 Unit 4: Religion and Ethics, Question 3)

Example 1

The idea that moral terms are nothing more than expressions of human[2] emotions is the view of emotivists[6] like A.J. Ayer[4], who claimed that statements like 'Stealing is wrong'[3] contain no factual information, much like the statement, 'Stealing – boo!'[3]. He claimed, 'I am simply evincing my moral disapproval of it'[4]. A.J. Ayer[4] claimed that moral statements are nothing more than[2] pseudo-concepts[6], which means they are dressed up to look like facts but are actually nothing more than expressions of human emotions[1]. He said that, 'It is as if I had written "Stealing money!!" – where the shape and thickness of the exclamation marks show, by a suitable convention, that a special sort of moral disapproval is the feeling which is being expressed'[4]. By this he means that there are no facts conveyed by the statement 'Stealing is wrong'[3] because the term 'wrong'[3] is not a fact that can be verified[6] with scientific evidence, and does not correspond with an object within the world. The other thing that Ayer[4] pointed out was that moral statements are intended to be[2] persuasive[6]; their function is not only to express an emotion, but to convince others to share that emotional response too. Thus, moral terms are nothing more than expressions of human emotion[2] and do not contain factual data[6] or information.

Areas for development

1 There is little valid analysis and evaluation of the issues raised by the question. The student has chosen to write in an AO1 style in answer to an AO2 question, and has simply described Ayer's views rather than developing relevant arguments and counter arguments.

2 The paragraph focuses on the subject of the question throughout, but it does not engage in any evaluation of the issues.

3 The paragraph contains evidence and examples of ethical language, but these support the knowledge that is explained rather than any arguments.

4 There are plenty of references to A.J. Ayer's scholarly views. However, the paragraph is one-sided and no alternative view is offered.

5 Connections with other areas studied – from religion, philosophy or ethics – should be included only where appropriate; connections should not be forced.

6 There is plenty of use of specialist language in context.

Example 2: an improved response

The idea that moral terms are nothing more than expressions of human[2] emotions is the view of emotivists[6] like A.J. Ayer[4], who claimed that statements like 'Stealing is wrong'[3] contain no factual information, much like the statement, 'Stealing – boo!'[3]. He claimed, 'I am simply evincing my moral disapproval of it'[4]. This is an attractive evaluation of the worth of moral statements[1] because it is based on a scientific view of the world that claims facts are only those things that can be[3] verified[6] or[3] falsified[6] with[3] empirical[6] evidence, such as 'This is a tree' or 'Bob stole that cake'[3]. It is true that there is no object in the world we can point to as a 'wrong' and no quality that we can identify as 'good' that all moral acts possess.[1] The passion that moral debate tends to evoke[3] is also consistent with the idea that moral judgements are[1] emotional responses to an action[2]. However[1], even Ayer[4] himself did not dismiss moral statements as 'nothing more'[2] than this. He acknowledged that we can know that moral statements are[1] persuasive[6] or advisory and can be used to affect the feelings of others. This approach was explored more fully by[1] C.L. Stevenson[4], who developed models to show that[1] 'This is good' means 'I approve of this; do so as well'[4]. While this argument does show that moral terms are more than simply expressions of human emotions[2], it does not demonstrate that they contain anything more than[1] pseudo-facts[6] and, in terms of their content, it seems convincing[1] that they are nothing more than expressions of human emotion[2].

What went well

1 Confident analysis and evaluation appears throughout the paragraph, with different viewpoints for and against the statement in the question considered.

2 This paragraph contains regular reference to the wording of the question throughout.

3 There is extensive use of evidence, examples of ethical language, and reasoning to support the arguments in this paragraph.

4 There is appropriate reference to scholarly views.

5 Connections with other areas studied – from religion, philosophy or ethics – should be included only where appropriate; connections should not be forced.

6 There is thorough use of specialist language in context.

Activity

a) Read Example 1 on page 85 and identify one thing you would do to improve the evaluation in this paragraph.

b) Read Example 2 above. The evaluation is much stronger. Make a list of at least two arguments that agree with the statement in the question, and at least two arguments that disagree with the statement in the question.

AO2 practice question 1

Now it is your turn. Have a go at answering the following question. There are some points to remember underneath to help you if you are not sure how to start.

> *'The Naturalistic Fallacy illustrates that ethical language can never be objective.' Evaluate this view.*
>
> (Eduqas A Level Religious Studies, Sample Assessment Materials, Component 3: Religion and Ethics, Question 3b)

Points to remember

- This question focuses on G.E. Moore's Naturalistic Fallacy. Remember to give arguments on both sides of the debate. For example, you can point out that the Naturalistic Fallacy rejects Naturalism, but that Moore still felt that there was an objective 'good'.
- Give plenty of examples to back up your arguments throughout the essay, and ensure that you include examples of ethical language alongside examples of non-ethical language.
- When you use scholarly quotations and examples, try and embed them into your sentences or explain what they mean to show your understanding. Try and keep quotations short and to the point. It is more important that you have good-quality arguments than learn lengthy quotations.

AO2 practice question 2

Now try this question by yourself.

> *'Intuitionism is the best way to understand moral language.' Evaluate this view.*
>
> (WJEC A Level Religious Studies, Sample Assessment Material, A2 Unit 4: Religion and Ethics, Question 3)

Mark schemes for all exam questions can be found at www.eduqas.co.uk and www.wjec.co.uk.

3 Deontological ethics: Aquinas' Natural Law

In 1996, 66-year-old Bob Dent from Northern Australia was the first of four people to legally end their lives with the help of a doctor before the act that allowed it was overturned. Northern Australia had briefly become the first place in the world to legalise voluntary euthanasia. Dent was terminally ill and close to the end of his life. He had suffered from prostate cancer for five years, was bedridden, required 24-hour care and was in constant pain.

Dent wrote a letter arguing that no one should have a right to demand that he stay alive against his own wishes. He argued that he should have the right to use voluntary euthanasia if and when he wanted to. He was helped to die by Dr Philip Nitschke, who followed all the safeguarding rules put in place by the act. He asked Dent three times if he understood what would happen and then set up the 'Deliverance Machine', which Dent activated himself to administer a drug that ended his life.

Is it right to keep someone alive even if there is no hope of recovery? Do we have a moral duty to preserve a human life, no matter what the situation? Is failure to keep someone alive the same as murder? It is the work of normative ethical theories to come up with a system, or criteria, for moral behaviour which enables a moral agent to formulate moral rules that help them answer these kinds of questions.

In this theme, you will consider the key features of Aquinas' Natural Law – including his laws, precepts, virtues, and goods – and how Aquinas' Natural Law can be applied to real-world examples of ethical problems, such as abortion and voluntary euthanasia.

How does Aquinas' Natural Law say we should behave?

AO1

This section of the chapter will enhance your knowledge and understanding of the topic and help you develop your AO1 skills.

Thomas Aquinas' Natural Law: laws and precepts as the basis of morality

Aquinas' Natural Law is often viewed as a deontological ethical theory; it is a normative ethical theory that focuses on duty and rules that govern how a person 'ought' to behave. It is often presented as the only, or the most significant, interpretation of Natural Law. However, while it is the approach that has been adopted by the Catholic Church, Natural Law did not begin and end with Aquinas. It is based on the work of the ancient Greek scholar Aristotle, and has been developed by later scholars (see Chapter 4).

Aristotle argued that there is something in human nature that distinguishes humans from the rest of the world. His Natural Law involved an understanding of the nature of human beings as rational creatures. The difficulty with this is that human reasoning can make errors and become corrupt. Therefore, gradually, Natural Law concerned itself with a narrower understanding of right or sane reason. The Roman lawyer Cicero said:

> *True law is right reason in agreement with nature; it is of universal application, unchanging and everlasting; it summons to duty by its commands, and averts from wrong doing by its prohibitions.* 99
>
> Cicero, *De Re Publica III xxii*

Aquinas' four levels of law

Aquinas set out his interpretation of Natural Law in *Summa Theologica*, which he wrote between 1265 and 1274. He wished to show that while there are several different forms of law, they do not conflict with each other. He understood there to be a hierarchy of **four levels of law** and, like other medieval scholars, he believed that at the heart of nature there is an unchanging Eternal Law. According to Aquinas, no one can know Eternal Law completely. Humanity can only discern a partial reflection of Eternal Law through the other three levels of law he identified: Divine Law, Natural Law and Human Law. However, Eternal Law is best understood as being reflected in the physical laws of nature intrinsic to God's created order, and it cannot be violated. Eternal Law is God's created plan that directs the whole of creation towards it final purpose. The laws of physics, such as gravity and the laws of motion, may be understood as a reflection of God's Eternal Law.

> **Key term**
>
> **four levels of law:** Aquinas believed there was a hierarchy of law, with four levels: Eternal Law, Divine Law, Natural Law, and Human Law

> *So then no one can know the eternal law, as it is in itself, except the blessed who see God in [God's] Essence. But every rational creature knows it in its reflection, greater or less. For every knowledge of truth is a kind of reflection and participation of the eternal law which is the unchangeable truth.* 99
>
> Thomas Aquinas, *Summa Theologica*

Divine Law is the laws given to humanity through God's **special revelation**. These laws are mostly found in scripture, or sometimes through the direct intervention of the Holy Spirit. They develop Eternal Law but never conflict with it, because God will not command anything that is logically impossible or against God's nature. **Inerrant** Divine Law directs human action in a way that Human Law never can. For example, humans can create laws that govern which acts we should and should not perform, but Human Law cannot govern our intentions or our innermost thoughts as Divine Law can, by instructing us against jealousy or lust. Divine Law has authority; it is never wrong and directs humanity towards a God-given purpose that exists outside of the natural world: to achieve eternal happiness in union with God after death in the **beatific vision**.

> *that no evil might remain unforbidden and unpunished, it was necessary for the Divine law to supervene whereby all sins are forbidden.* ""
>
> Thomas Aquinas, *Summa Theologica*

The third level of law is Natural Law. Natural Law is the first principle or starting point for working out what is good or evil using ***recta ratio*** or 'right reason'. All creatures have a purpose which is inherent in their nature, but humanity is different because they were created ***imago dei*** (in the image of God). This means that humans are free, rational, self-conscious beings. Humans are not free to choose for themselves what is good and what is evil, as Natural Law is still subject to the force of Eternal Law and actions can be good or evil in themselves. However, humans are free to decide whether they direct themselves towards their true created purpose or turn away from God.

> *Natural Law is nothing else than the rational creature's participation of the eternal law.* ""
>
> Thomas Aquinas, *Summa Theologica*

The fourth and final level of law is Human Law. People are part of many different groups and communities. Divine Law is made for the community of humans in relation to God, whereas Human Law is made for civil communities. While Eternal Law does not change and does not comment on individual cases, Human Law adapts as society changes, and it can be applied to individual cases. Human Law is not, however, inerrant. Human Law can conflict with Eternal Law, and when this happens, they are 'wrong'. 'Good' human laws align with Eternal Law and are discoverable through human reason.

Natural Law is derived from rational thought

Aquinas' work is a fusion of Aristotelian philosophy and theology. In line with Aristotle, Aquinas held that a moral life is lived according to reason. Natural beings can work out how they should behave. Natural Law dictates correct behaviour in accordance with God's created purpose for humanity. It is a law that acknowledges human nature as rational, and it is therefore more than a list of rules to obey. It requires humans to make use of conscience. Conscience, for Aquinas, is not the voice of God or an intuition

Key terms

special revelation: the knowledge that God reveals directly to humanity through supernatural means (e.g. via the Bible)

inerrant: without error; cannot be wrong

beatific vision: a right relationship or fellowship with God that is sought through reason in this life and fully achieved in eternal life with God in heaven after death

***recta ratio*:** (Latin) right reason

***imago dei*:** (Latin) in the image of God

AO1 activity 1

Create a diagram to demonstrate the relationship between Aquinas' four levels of law. Colour code it, and ensure that each level of law is labelled with at least three key features that distinguish it from the other levels of law.

in the mind that makes a person feel guilty when they have acted poorly; it is the process of right reason.

Aquinas and other medieval theologians understood conscience to be made up of two parts:

1. Synderesis: This is a special habit of intellect that provides the first moral principles. It gives a person the interest in performing acts that are in accordance with their human nature as rational beings created by God for a purpose.

> *Synderesis is said to incite to good, and to murmur at evil, inasmuch as through first principles we proceed to discover, and judge of what we have discovered. It is therefore clear that synderesis is not a power, but a natural habit.*
>
> Thomas Aquinas, *Summa Theologica*

2. Conscientia: This is the ability to make the correct moral judgements about the correct way to act in a particular situation.

Conscience is therefore required so that a moral agent can understand what is good according to the created order and then apply reason to establish how to achieve the good in a particular situation.

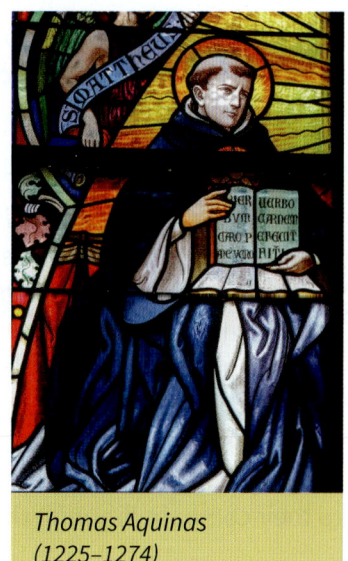

Thomas Aquinas (1225–1274)

Natural Law is based on a belief in a divine creator

While there is no requirement to believe in God or follow religious practices to apply reason, belief in God is central to Aquinas' Natural Law. For Aquinas, all human beings are rational creatures who can apply reason for themselves. However, everything in existence was created by God, who is both the origin and purpose of all human beings. Aquinas held that human beings were made by God for fellowship with God. Morality is not based on divine commands but, instead, is found within our human nature as rational beings created *imago dei*. Therefore, to act in accordance with human nature is to use God-given rational abilities to understand what is good and behave accordingly. The highest good is the beatific vision. This is the knowledge of, and fellowship with, God which can be sought through reason and is ultimately perfected in the next life.

Natural Law is a form of moral absolutism and a theory with both deontological and teleological aspects

Modern belief about Natural Law is that it is a set of fixed, unalterable rules that are applied to human conduct regardless of the circumstances. Natural Law is a deontological theory, in the sense that the goodness of an action is based on some quality of the action itself, and therefore it is an agent's duty to perform them. There are objective, real foundations for moral behaviour that govern how a person 'ought' to behave. Natural Law is also **absolutist**, in that there are **precepts** or goods that must not be broken (as we shall learn shortly).

> ### Key terms
>
> **absolutist:** the belief that there are universal moral principles or acts that are intrinsically right or wrong
>
> **precepts:** guiding principles, rules, or commands

> *A precept of law has compulsory power. Hence that on which the compulsion of the law is brought to bear, falls directly under the precept of the law.* **99**
>
> Thomas Aquinas, *Summa Theologica*

It is also possible to emphasise Natural Law's teleological nature. Teleological theories establish the goodness of an action by considering its goal or purpose rather than any characteristic of the action itself. Aquinas' understanding of Natural Law relies on a strong sense of purpose: the goal of moral behaviour in Natural Law is to achieve the beatific vision. Part of the reasoning process involves the use of conscientia, working out how to be good and fulfil human purpose in individual situations rather than obeying a fixed list of rules. Moral acts are judged as good or bad in relation to their compatibility with the *telos* of achieving the beatific vision.

However, although Natural Law has teleological elements, it is not a consequentialist theory. This is because it does not decide what action is good based upon changeable and unpredictable outcomes alone. Instead, Natural Law looks at the unique circumstances of a moral dilemma and works out the good action based upon knowledge of what is objectively and absolutely good according to the God-given purpose of humanity.

The five primary precepts

Aquinas believed that the purpose of moral behaviour is to do good and avoid evil in accordance with humanity's natural tendency or desire. He called this the **synderesis rule**. The synderesis rule underpins all the subsequent precepts of Natural Law, and is important to establish a right relationship with God and gain eternal life with God in heaven.

> *'Good is that which all things seek after.' Hence the first precept of law that 'good is to be done and pursued, and evil is to be avoided.' All other precepts of the Natural Law are based upon this.* **99**
>
> Thomas Aquinas, *Summa Theologica*

The synderesis rule is very general, and tells humanity very little about how they are supposed to behave. So, Aquinas identified five other main precepts or goods that have become known as the **five primary precepts**. These are goals or ends to which Aquinas said humanity has a natural inclination; they can be understood by reason to be good, and their opposites can be understood by reason to be evil. Aquinas divided the precepts into three types, some of which applied to all living things, some to all creatures, and others to humanity alone.

The five primary precepts can be summarised as follows:

	Primary precept	Type of precept
1	self-preservation or preservation of life	All living things are naturally inclined towards this good.
2	reproduction through sexual intercourse	All creatures are naturally inclined towards these goods.
3	education of offspring	
4	worship and know the truth about God	Human beings alone are naturally inclined towards these goods because they are specific to their nature as rational beings.
5	live peacefully and cooperatively in society	

Every substance seeks the preservation of its own being, according to its nature: any by reason of this inclination, whatever is a means of preserving human life, and of warding off its obstacles, belongs to the Natural Law. Secondly ... sexual intercourse, education of offspring and so forth. Thirdly ... man has a natural inclination to know the truth about God and to live in society.

Thomas Aquinas, *Summa Theologica*

These primary precepts are self-evident, although a person must have an educated mind to perceive and understand them. The primary precepts are the underlying first principles of Natural Law, from which all moral behaviour can be derived. It is the duty of all humans to ensure that these precepts are followed to gain a right relationship with God and gain eternal life with God in heaven.

The secondary precepts

It is necessary for a human being to apply reason to know exactly what to do in any given situation. The primary precepts are universal and inviolable; they must not be broken. They contain the truth without fail. However, they are general, not specific, and they do not tell us exactly what to do when faced with a moral dilemma. Therefore, a person facing a moral dilemma must use their knowledge of the primary precepts to establish secondary precepts that describe exactly how they should behave. Aquinas did not specify what these secondary precepts are, because they depend upon the situation.

Aquinas argued that a person must have an educated mind to perceive and understand the precepts.

Secondary precepts are still laws or rules, but they have the potential to change according to the needs of society and the specifics of a situation. For example, it is a primary precept that a couple should reproduce and educate their children; this is an unchanging law. However, how to educate their children may look different in different situations, depending on how their society approaches education. Those who have access to free full-time state education may send their children to school, whereas other societies may need to educate their children at home or within the family to ensure that they are given the knowledge and skills necessary to live a successful and moral life.

Aquinas said that reason is the same for all humans and, therefore, there is a right way of reasoning and an absolute set of primary precepts that cannot be violated. However, he also acknowledged that practical reason busies itself with details that have to be worked out and that are sometimes subject to change. Aquinas gave the example that, in general, goods in the care of another person should be returned to their rightful owner. But, he argued, this is in some cases unreasonable because it could violate a primary precept, such as the preservation of life. While the primary precepts cannot be changed, the secondary precepts can be flexible in certain situations.

> *Goods entrusted to another should be restored to their owner. Now this is true for the majority of cases: but it may happen in a particular case that it would be injurious, and therefore unreasonable, to resort goods held in trust: for instance, if they are claimed for the purpose of fighting against one's country.*
>
> Thomas Aquinas, *Summa Theologica*

It is vital to remember that the primary precepts are inviolable. Therefore, secondary precepts that violate a primary precept cannot be formulated. For example, the primary precept to preserve life cannot, under any circumstances, allow a secondary precept that requires one person to kill another person. It is the role of reason to work out the best course of action in a situation: one that does not violate the general purpose of human life to do good and avoid evil to achieve fellowship with God and gain eternal life in heaven.

A good example, showing how secondary precepts can be formed, is sexual intercourse. The primary precept to reproduce through sexual intercourse tells us that the *telos*, or purpose, of sex is reproduction. Therefore, any act that prevents reproduction through sexual intercourse is an act that does not aim towards the good. Consequently, secondary precepts that forbid a range of acts – including artificial methods of contraception, masturbation and same-sex sexual acts – can be formed.

It is important to keep both the primary and secondary precepts in order to achieve the beatific vision – a right relationship or fellowship with God and ultimately eternal life with God in heaven after death.

Aquinas' Natural Law: the role of virtues and goods in supporting moral behaviour

The bulk of Aquinas' writing on ethics in his best-known work, *Summa Theologica*, was not about rules or precepts for moral behaviour at all. Influenced by Aristotle, Aquinas, in common with other medieval scholars, felt that it was vital to be the kind of person who could fulfil God's created purpose. Blindly following lists of rules and regulations is not enough. It is necessary to refine your character so that you can easily make good choices and really desire to become more like God. Virtues are stable dispositions that a person acquires after years of practice, enabling them to act in a

Aquinas believed that it is a natural human inclination to seek knowledge and truth.

AO1 activity 3

Consider the five primary precepts. For each primary precept, provide two secondary precepts that could be established to indicate how a person should behave. For example, for the primary precept of 'preservation of life', two secondary precepts could be 'do not kill' and 'do not perform euthanasia'.

Make sure that none of your secondary precepts violate any of the other primary precepts.

particular way. This is more than simple self-discipline; it is perfection of a person's character.

> *Human virtue is a habit perfecting man in view of his doing good deeds.*
>
> Thomas Aquinas, *Summa Theologica*

The three revealed virtues

In 1 Corinthians 13:13, Paul lists what have become known as the **three revealed virtues** or the three theological virtues.

> *And now these three remain: faith, hope, and love. But the greatest of these is love.*
>
> 1 Corinthians 13:13, *Holy Bible (NIV)*

These three character traits – faith, hope, and love – are called 'revealed virtues' by Aquinas for three reasons. Firstly, they are **theocentric**, focused upon God and directed towards God. Secondly, they are given to humanity by God and cannot be achieved without God. Finally, they are made known to humans through the scriptures and cannot be discovered through reason.

Faith

The act of faith, according to Aquinas, is to believe in God despite our inability to see God or perceive empirical evidence of God. It is a free and deliberate act of the intellect. Faith, for Aquinas, was defined by the words of Paul in Hebrews:

> *Now faith is confidence in what we hope for and assurance about what we do not see.*
>
> Hebrews 11:1, *Holy Bible (NIV)*

Hope

Aquinas said that God is the focus of the virtue of hope. Hope involves looking forward to eternal life with God in heaven after death (the beatific vision). All good actions are aiming for this goal, which Aquinas describes as an infinite goal that requires an infinite power. God is both the object of hope and the being on whom humans depend for it to be realised.

Love

Love or charity is described by Aquinas as wishing good for other people without concern for the self. Aquinas pointed out that we only 'love' things like horses or wine because of what they can bring us, rather than what we can bring them (he saw animals as being given by God for the benefit of humanity). However, the love described by Paul in 1 Corinthians, and now Aquinas, is wishing the best for others, and it mirrors the love between God and humanity. Love is the greatest virtue; it is the love of God and of other people with no desire for anything in return.

Key terms

three revealed virtues: the three virtues of faith, hope and charity, revealed or disclosed through Scripture in 1 Corinthians 13

theocentric: focused on God as the central or ultimate concern

Synoptic link

Link to *Chapter 5: Teleological ethics: Situation Ethics*. Joseph Fletcher also uses 1 Corinthians 13:13 to establish Situation Ethics, quite a different normative ethical theory.

AO1 activity 4

Look up 1 Corinthians 13 in the New Testament, and read the whole chapter. What is love like according to Paul?

The virtue of love can be shown through actions that benefit others, for example through charitable work.

The four cardinal virtues

The four **cardinal virtues** – prudence, justice, fortitude, and temperance – were familiar to medieval thinkers. While Aquinas uses Aristotle as his source, they predate even Aristotle. The virtues are not simply gifted from God. They are discoverable through reason and must be practised to become part of human character.

Cardo is Latin for 'hinge' and so these cardinal virtues are known as hinge virtues. Aquinas saw them as essential for right reasoning. Without them, our reason, contaminated as it is by **original sin**, is likely to be wrong or corrupted. Therefore, these virtues must be practised and cultivated so that a person may reason correctly.

Prudence

Prudence is wisdom or *prudentia*. It is the ability to make reasoned judgements that direct human acts towards their proper ends or goals. It is practical insight into what should be done in any situation. Prudence needs practice to develop. It requires teaching, experience, and time, alongside a knowledge of what is universally good, to be able to weigh up all the features of a situation and make the right decision.

> *Now prudence is an intellectual virtue … therefore prudence is in us, not by nature, but by teaching and experience.* 99
>
> Thomas Aquinas, *Summa Theologica*

Justice

Justice is fairness or equality. This virtue is about the constant, lasting will to ensure that everyone has what they are due. Justice requires action to be taken to ensure all people are treated fairly, but the virtue also concerns the continual desire to work to ensure this happens. Aquinas is interested in justice on several different levels, such as in the running and ruling of society and between private individuals. Justice ensures that there is a fair share of resources for everyone, that private property is used by owners in a way that does not conflict with everyone being treated fairly, and that people buy, sell, and loan in a fair way. Justice also requires that balance is restored when someone has committed a crime, ensuring appropriate restoration is made when someone has suffered injury or loss of property. Justice also includes ensuring that God, the creator, is worshipped by the creatures God brought into being.

Fortitude

Fortitude is courage. It is the strength of character required to do what reason dictates a person should do. This is vital for a virtuous person. Humans are easily distracted by things that give them pleasure and often do not want to do what reason dictates. A virtuous person will have the strength of mind or patience to battle against their own weaknesses and follow right reason, even when it is difficult. Fortitude is what helps a person resist temptation and conform to reason, even when it is not easy.

AO1 activity 5

Write down each of Aquinas' quotations in this chapter so far on separate index cards. Then write down, on the other side, what the quotation is about in one or two words. Turn all the cards quotation side down, and mix them up. Now select a card and recite or write down the correct quotation without looking at the reverse of the card. Turn the card over to check if you got it right.

Temperance

Temperance is moderation. It is the caution that a person requires to make a considered, thoughtful choice. Temperance is caused by reason and is essential for a virtuous person. Reason applies this moderation to human actions and feelings; it draws people away from temptation rather than gives them the strength to endure it.

Internal and external acts

An action can be intrinsically good or evil. Whether an action is intrinsically good (or evil) is not decided by weighing up the possible consequences of an action. However, an act that is genuinely good should still produce positive effects in the circumstance in which it is performed. Aquinas recognised that a moral action contains two distinctive aspects: interior (internal) and exterior (external) actions. The **external act** is the outward action that the moral agent performs, and it can be intrinsically good or evil. Yet, the external act is not the whole story because no moral act can occur without an intention. Intention is the **internal act**.

> *In a voluntary action, there is a two-fold action, viz. the interior action of the will and the external action: and each of these actions has its object. The end is properly the object of the interior act of the will: while the object of the external action, is that on which the action is brought to bear.*
>
> Thomas Aquinas, *Summa Theologica*

An external act may be intrinsically good, but may be performed with an evil intention. For example, doing charity work so that we can boast about it on social media to signal our virtue is not doing it with a good intention. If an externally good act is done with a bad intention, then the action – consisting of both elements, the external act and the internal act (the intention) – is rendered evil.

> *The giving of alms for vainglory is said to be evil.*
>
> Thomas Aquinas, *Summa Theologica*

Our internal act, our intention, is the motivation or desire that the external act stems from, and it informs the whole action. It is not possible to justify doing an evil action with a 'good intention'. The end does not justify the means. The intention is important because it is part of the action. The good intention should always be to aim towards God. However, intention is not everything; in order for a human action to be morally good, both the internal and the external acts must be good.

> *But if the will be good from its intention of the end, this is not enough to make the external action good.*
>
> Thomas Aquinas, *Summa Theologica*

For Aquinas, intention is not the be all and end all of moral action. Certain actions are inherently or inevitably wrong, regardless of intention, circumstance, and consequence. But our intentions matter, along with a range of other things too. Human external acts can be considered alongside the circumstances, the goal of the act, the intention, and whether it is proportional. A bad intention can sometimes be enough to corrupt a good act, but no good intention can ever make an evil act good. What matters is that both the internal and the external acts are good.

The principle of double effect

The **principle of double effect** is an important part of our understanding of internal and external acts. Double effect is sometimes, incorrectly, seen as a loophole that enables people to get away with doing something that would otherwise be seen as evil. However, this is not Aquinas' point.

Aquinas recognised that sometimes we come across situations where moral precepts conflict. For example, if someone is violently attacked by another person, the primary precepts require them to defend themselves to preserve their own life. However, if in self-defence, they kill their attacker, they have violated the primary precept to preserve life. Aquinas recognised that we need to manage this kind of conflict. It is not rational to allow people to kill, but it is also not rational to submit to attack when the nature of creatures is to strive to survive.

The principle of double effect says that the internal act behind our external actions is the deciding factor in what constitutes a good act or an evil act in cases where there is a double effect. In the example outlined in the previous paragraph, the person being attacked intended to save their own life. They did not intend to kill. Therefore, we can judge the act according to the intended external act.

> **Key term**
>
> **principle of double effect:** a principle to manage situations where precepts conflict; where one action will produce two effects, one of which violates a precept, the action that was intended will be judged

> **Synoptic link**
>
> Link to *Chapter 4: Deontological ethics: Finnis' Natural Law and Proportionalism*. The principle of double effect is key in understanding Proportionalism and its application to capital punishment and immigration.

> *Accordingly, the act of self-defence may have two effects, one is the saving of one's life, the other is the slaying of the aggressor. Therefore, since one's intention is to save one's own life, is not unlawful, seeing that it is natural to everything to keep itself in being as far as possible.*
>
> Thomas Aquinas, *Summa Theologica*

However, Aquinas goes on to say that such an action would be rendered unlawful if were out of all proportion to the intended purpose. So, if a person uses more than necessary violence in self-defence, it is not excusable.

Real and apparent goods

Aquinas had a positive view of humanity, and saw human beings as inclined towards God by nature, believing that humans will not naturally perform an action that they know to be evil. However, it was also clear to him that humans do very evil things. Aquinas felt this was due to an error in reasoning: if a person does something morally wrong, they do it because they mistakenly think that they are doing something good.

For Aquinas, there is an ideal human nature that we all have the potential to live up to. However, when we make a moral decision that focuses too much on trying to achieve good consequences (like pleasure), we may not recognise the evil that comes along with it. An action like this is an **apparent good**. It seems good to our disordered, fallen reasoning, but it is not actually good at all. We have applied reason wrongly and acted against our true potential. Aquinas would call this apparent good a sin.

A **real good** is an act that helps a moral agent achieve God's created purpose for them. It is in accordance with right reason and enables a moral agent to fulfil their potential.

> *Evil may be sought accidentally, so far as it accompanies a good, as appears in each of the appetites. … the fornicator has merely pleasure for his object, and the deformity of sin is only an accompaniment.* 99
>
> Thomas Aquinas, *Summa Theologica*

Aquinas' Natural Law: application of the theory

The main purpose of this section of the specification is to show how Natural Law can be put into practice in real ethical situations. There is no need for you to develop an in-depth understanding of abortion and voluntary euthanasia and the arguments for and against each of them, but there is a need for you to understand some of the issues raised by abortion and voluntary euthanasia before looking at how the theory of Natural Law applies to them.

Abortion: what is the debate?

Abortion is generally defined as a medical procedure to end a pregnancy. The procedure can take place in a number of different ways depending upon the stage of the pregnancy. In the UK, the law permits an abortion to take place up to 24 weeks of pregnancy. It can also occur at any time before birth in cases where continuing with the pregnancy would result in the death of, or grave and permanent injury to, the person who is pregnant, or there is substantial risk that the child will be born with a severe disability. In these cases, abortion can occur at any time before birth.

Abortion has not always been legal, and in some countries it is still prohibited. Today, in the UK it can legally be sought for a wide variety of reasons that are often very traumatic for everyone who is involved. The Catholic Church recognised this in 1995 in Pope John Paul II's Papal encyclical *Evangelium Vitae*.

Key terms

apparent good: Aquinas viewed an apparent good as an act that seems to be in accordance with right reason but is not; instead it moves us further away from the ideal human nature that God had planned for us

real good: Aquinas viewed a real good as an act that is in accordance with right reason, which helps us become nearer to the ideal human nature that God had planned for us

AO1 activity 6

Take a look at some recent news stories about people who are reported to have committed crimes or done something wrong. What do you think their 'apparent good' might have been? Do you agree with Aquinas that people will not naturally choose something that they know is evil or wrong?

> *The decision to have an abortion is often tragic and painful for the mother, insofar as the decision to rid herself of the fruit of conception is not made for purely selfish reasons or out of convenience, but out of a desire to protect certain important values such as her own health or a decent standard of living for the other members of the family. Sometimes it is feared that the child to be born would live in such conditions that it would be better if the birth did not take place.*
>
> Pope John Paul II, *Evangelium Vitae*

Abortion is controversial because there is debate about what is actually being ended when a pregnancy is terminated. Is the **pre-embryo**, **embryo**, or **foetus** a life or a potential life? Is abortion the killing of a human being or the removal of a cluster of cells? Clearly, abortion is ending the development of something that would, provided there are no barriers, otherwise become a human being. However, when someone seeks an abortion, they do so for many complex and important reasons relating to their life and health, as well as the developing life. It is therefore vital to decide whether the developing life has any moral significance in and of itself that would make abortion wrong.

What does Aquinas say about the moral significance of the unborn?

The reason that the question of whether the moral status of the pre-embryo, embryo or foetus is important is because we need to establish whether it would ordinarily be acceptable to end their life. Most of us do not have any moral difficulty with ending the development of a plant if it benefits us to do so. Many do not struggle with ending the development of an animal for the benefit of human beings, and those who do often accept it if the animal is suffering when ending its life humanely might be the right thing to do. However, most people have great difficulty with the idea of killing a person to benefit someone else, and the moral issue of voluntary euthanasia is a debate we will look at later in the chapter. So, what is different about human beings?

Natural Law says that human life is different from any other kind of life. Human beings were created *imago dei*, with purpose, sentience, intelligence, and free will. Therefore, human life is sacred; it is special and should be preserved. It is therefore important to determine whether a pre-embryo, embryo or foetus can be called human life. If they are, then we must hold that abortion is wrong because they are created by God, in God's image, for a purpose, and to end their life is a sin. If Natural Law were not to consider them a human life, there would be less moral difficulty in abortion.

It cannot be denied that a pre-embryo is human material. From conception, it contains all the DNA necessary to become a recognisable human being. It does not look like or even function as a human yet, but it does have all the ingredients present to enable a human being to develop. Some would argue that it is clearly human, but it is not a person. A person is a being of consciousness and rationality. Yet, this definition of 'person' is highly problematic, not least because a new-born baby, to some extent, lacks both while other creatures may possess both. So, when does the pre-embryo become a human being or a person?

Key terms

pre-embryo: a fertilised egg in the first 14 days of development, before implantation in the uterus

embryo: a new organism in an early stage of development, between the second and eighth week after fertilisation

foetus: an unborn young, beyond the eighth week after fertilisation

The Catholic Church holds that human life begins at conception. This is the point at which the genetic material that will enable a human to develop is present. However, many point out that since a pre-embryo does not have the features of consciousness or rationality, it is wrong to claim that it is a human being or a person. This has led others to suggest that a person comes into being at later stages of development; for example, when a heartbeat is detected, when pain can be felt, or even as late as birth. All these stages are rather arbitrary and come with difficulties, which will not be discussed here.

Another approach is to claim that a person comes into being at **ensoulment**. Christians argue that a human being consists of both the physical body and a separate **metaphysical** soul. Ensoulment is the point at which God places the soul into the body, creating a human life. If human life or personhood begins at ensoulment then if we can know when ensoulment takes place, this may help us decide whether it is acceptable to perform an abortion.

Although Aquinas did not comment on the rights and wrongs of abortion, he did have something to say about ensoulment. Aquinas' understanding was based on his limited biological knowledge about how life forms in the womb, which by today's standards is considered scientifically inaccurate. In his *Commentary on the Sentences of Peter Lombard*, Aquinas argued that ensoulment occurs at 40 days from conception (about 5 weeks) for boys and at 90 days (about 12 weeks) for girls. He also drew on Exodus 21:22 to argue, in *Summa Theologica*, that if you hit someone who is pregnant and they miscarry the baby as a direct result, you are only guilty of murder if the foetus is animated. In other words, if ensoulment has taken place.

> *He that strikes a woman with child does something unlawful: wherefore if there results the death either of the woman or of the animated foetus, he will not be excused from homicide, especially seeing that death is the natural result of such a blow.* **99**
>
> Thomas Aquinas, *Summa Theologica*

Aquinas, following Aristotle, taught that prior to the moment of ensoulment, the foetus has at first a **nutritive** soul and then a **sensitive** soul before being given an intellectual soul at ensoulment. Therefore, while Aquinas did not state this outright, it is possible for us to draw the conclusion that the foetus is not fully a human being before ensoulment.

The implications of this could be that, prior to ensoulment, abortion is not a moral dilemma. It could take place in the same way that the development or life of a plant or animal is cut short to benefit humanity or for its own benefit. In practice, this is a difficult position to take because many do not know that they are pregnant in the early stages of pregnancy. However, it could pave the way for abortions to take place very early in pregnancy.

This interpretation is clearly and vehemently rejected as incorrect by the Catholic Church's understanding of Aquinas' Natural Law. They teach that human life begins from conception and, therefore, abortion is always completely wrong and sinful.

Key terms

ensoulment: the dualist idea that a body is animated with a distinct and separate soul at a particular moment in time

metaphysical: relating to existence or knowledge that are non-physical, supernatural and beyond purely sensory description, such as love, truth, and God

nutritive: relating to nutrition or nourishment; characteristic of all living things

sensitive: concerning the senses and features of a being that are shared with all animals, such as feeling and movement

> *Some people try to justify abortion by claiming that the result of conception, at least up to a certain number of days, cannot yet be considered a personal human life. But in facts, 'from the time that the ovum is fertilised, a life is begun which is neither that of the father nor the mother; it is rather the life of a new human being with its own growth … Right from fertilisation the adventure of a human life begins.*
>
> Pope John Paul II, *Evangelium Vitae*

What does Natural Law say about abortion?

Let us assume that the Catholic understanding of when life begins is correct. Natural Law says that killing is evil. The primary precepts state clearly that it is good to defend life and to reproduce. Therefore, since these precepts are absolute, any action that violates these good things is a sin.

However, it is not as simple as this. Sometimes moral questions can be challenging. Primary precepts conflict when protecting the life of the foetus places the life of person who is pregnant in danger. There is also added complexity when someone gets pregnant as the result of rape or when they are very young. In these situations, many people argue that abortion is legitimate because an individual's life plan and freedoms will be compromised by the actions of another if the pregnancy continues.

Double effect

In some cases, where primary precepts conflict, it is possible to apply the principle of double effect. There are two things that should be taken into consideration: the internal act or intention in an action, and the proportion of good that is achieved when weighed against the evil that is created. An intention to end the life of a human being is always wrong. The evil consequence cannot be part of the essence of any moral action, which means that it is not acceptable to do evil so that good may come. So, it is never acceptable to intend to kill a human being for the sake of a greater good, and the death of a person cannot be essential to the good end that is intended.

In general, abortion does not meet the requirements of double effect. If we accept that abortion is both the killing of a person and the frustration of the primary precept to reproduce, then abortion is always forbidden because it can contain nothing good. However, it is not always that simple. There are circumstances in which double effect does come into play.

For example, when someone suffers an ectopic pregnancy, the fertilised egg implants outside the uterus, usually in one of the fallopian tubes. The fallopian tubes are very narrow and, if the embryo continues to develop in a fallopian tube, it will rupture and result in the likely death of both the embryo and the person who is pregnant. An ectopic pregnancy can sometimes be treated by removing the developing embryo, either chemically or surgically, or by removing a section of the fallopian tube. This will also result in the death of the embryo as well as cause a loss of reproductive capacity on one side of the body.

Synoptic link

Link to *Chapter 4: Deontological ethics: Finnis' Natural Law and Proportionalism.* Take a look at John Finnis' seven basic goods to see the kinds of goods that could be understood to be compromised or challenged if someone is pregnant against their will.

We have already established that abortion is unacceptable, so no action that intends to abort the embryo is acceptable. However, if the intention is to save the life of the person who is pregnant, then some actions are permissible. Removing the embryo would be a deliberate killing, and an example of doing evil so that good may come, which is forbidden. However, removing the affected fallopian tube would be surgery to save a life, with the unintended side effect of terminating the embryo. The evil in the action is accidental and not essential to the action. If, by some miracle, the embryo happened to survive, no further action to end its life would be taken and everything possible to ensure its survival could be done. Just like Aquinas' example of killing in self-defence, this action would be morally acceptable because the killing is accidental and not intended.

The same could be said if someone is suffering cancer of the uterus. In this instance, the uterus could be removed and the abortion would be a side effect. However, if there is not an immediate risk of death, it might not be proportionate to remove the uterus, killing the embryo and ending reproductive capacity. It may be more appropriate to consider other treatments until the child is born.

It is important to note that none of this reasoning involves permitting abortion; abortion is still forbidden. What it is doing is saying that an abortion that occurs as an accident, when a different goal is intended, is not blameworthy.

An abortion for the purpose of helping someone in distress or supporting someone's right to choose what happens to their body is an example of doing evil so that good may come. Aquinas and the Catholic Church do not deny that it is good for people to have autonomy over their own bodies or that evil is involved when someone is raped and becomes pregnant, an event that is distressing and terrible. However, they believe that there is no justification for doing evil, for example in performing an abortion so that the good of bodily autonomy can be achieved.

> *Why not say – as some slanderously claim that we say – 'Let us do evil that good may result'? Their condemnation is just!* 99
>
> Romans 3:8, *Holy Bible (NIV)*

Natural Law rejects the consequentialist approach that says no action is intrinsically good or bad and only the consequences of an action matter. Abortion in these circumstances is an apparent good which is never acceptable. An individual's rights are important, but they do not justify deliberate evil.

> *Though it is true that sometimes it is lawful to tolerate a lesser moral evil in order to avoid a greater evil or in order to promote a greater good, it is never lawful, even for the gravest reasons, to do evil that good may come of it – in other words, to intend directly something which of its very nature contradicts the moral order.* 99
>
> Pope Paul VI, *Humanae Vitae*

The interpretation of Natural Law by the Catholic Church is that abortion is always, universally, a sin, regardless of the situation or the consequences, and there can never be a situation in which a direct abortion can ever be intentionally performed.

> *I declare that direct abortion, that is, abortion willed as an end or as a means, always constitutes a grave moral disorder, since it is the deliberate killing of an innocent human being.*
>
> Pope John Paul II, *Evangelium Vitae*

Voluntary euthanasia: what is the debate?

The word 'euthanasia' is a compound of the two Greek words *eu* and *thanatos*, meaning 'a good death'. It is sometimes referred to as 'mercy killing'. Euthanasia is the act of deliberately ending a person's life to relieve suffering, but there are a number of different ways or circumstances in which this might be achieved.

- Voluntary euthanasia: this is when someone expresses a wish to die and clearly asks for help to do so. It involves a doctor performing the act that directly causes death.
- Assisted dying: this is when a terminally ill adult who has mental capacity asks a doctor to prescribe them life-ending medication. They take the medication themselves.
- Non-treatment decision: this is when doctors decide to withdraw medical treatment or life support because they do not think the patient is going to get better or because the patient asks them to through, for example, a living will or an Advance Decision to Refuse Treatment (ADRT).

Euthanasia is illegal in the UK and in most other countries around the globe. However, there are countries where euthanasia is being decriminalised, and in clinics like Dignitas in Switzerland, doctors can legally give patients the means to take medication and end their own lives early.

There are several areas of debate around euthanasia that relate to Natural Law. Firstly, there is an apparent conflict that arises between the sanctity of human life and the quality of human life. Many argue that human life is sacred, and is therefore to be preserved at all costs. Others feel that if life sinks below a certain quality and there is no hope for improvement or long-term survival, it is kinder to allow someone to die. Certainly, most people agree that when an animal's quality of life is poor, it is kinder to allow it to die or even hasten its death to end its suffering, but to allow this for humans is much more controversial.

A second area of debate concerns the issue of rights. It is generally accepted that human beings have a right to life, but some argue that a right to life does not mean the same thing as a requirement to live. Life is not something someone should be forced to do and a person should be allowed the right to choose the manner and timing of their death so that

AO1 activity 7

Look up the encyclical *Evangelium Vitae* online and read the Catholic Church's position on the issue of abortion. Try and pick out as many points as you can that relate to Aquinas' Natural Law.

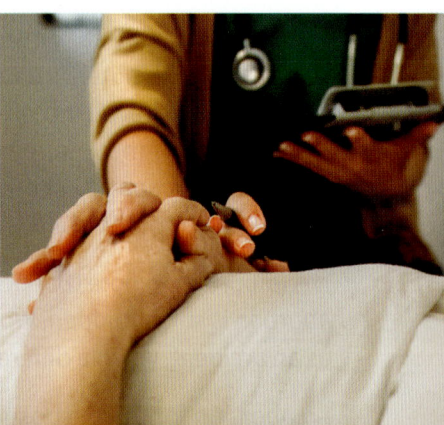

Applied ethical issues, such as abortion and voluntary euthanasia, are complex and highly emotive.

they can die with dignity. Many counter this with a slippery slope argument, expressing the fear that granting people the right to choose voluntary euthanasia would pave the way for abuse, where people who could live better-quality lives are allowed to or even encouraged to die so as not to be a drain on family or resources.

A third area of debate is the distinction between actions and omissions. This is of significance in Natural Law. To give someone medication for the express purpose of hastening their death is an action a person should be held responsible for, even if they were asked to do what they did by the person who dies. This is voluntary euthanasia and following Natural Law, it is an intentional killing.

Not providing medical treatment or life support to someone who is terminally ill is an omission. It allows nature to take its course; it does not preserve human life but it does not intentionally take human life either. This is legal and is referred to as a non-treatment decision. The question is whether a person is morally responsible for a death they could have prevented in the short term but did not. The debate concerns whether or not the death is intended or simply foreseen.

A fourth, and closely related, area of debate is the issue of ordinary and extraordinary means of survival. Ordinarily, to survive, a person needs to be able to take in nutrition, hydration, and oxygen. However, when a person is sick, they may need help to achieve these things and they may also need significant help in other ways. Extraordinary means of survival are those that are beyond what would usually be required. For example, surgery and medication are extraordinary means of survival. Historically, it was considered suicide if someone refused food or water but not if they refused painful or dangerous surgery. However, now that food, water, and oxygen can be given via machinery, the lines between ordinary and extraordinary treatment are blurred.

What does Aquinas say about voluntary euthanasia?

Aquinas does not talk about euthanasia directly. However, he does address when it might be permissible to kill. For example, in self-defence, in a just war, or in some cases by capital punishment. Aquinas cites Exodus 20:13: 'You shall not murder,' and considers killing a **mortal sin** that applies to killing oneself as well as others. He gives three reasons why it is unlawful to kill oneself:

1. Suicide goes against nature and charity, because naturally all things strive to live and to care for themselves.
2. Every human is part of a community and suicide harms the community as well as the self.
3. Life is a gift from God, and it is up to God when it should end. To kill the self to escape suffering in this life or hasten the journey to a better afterlife is an attempt to avoid a lesser evil by performing a greater one.

> **Key term**
>
> **mortal sin:** a grave sin that involves deliberately and knowingly turning away from God and his grace; a mortal sin requires repentance before death or there will be punishment in the afterlife

> *It is not lawful for man to take his own life that he may pass to a happier life, nor that he may escape any unhappiness whatsoever of the present life, because the ultimate and more fearsome evil of this life is death … Therefore, to bring death upon oneself in order to escape the other afflictions of this life, is to adopt a greater evil in order to avoid a lesser.*
>
> Thomas Aquinas, *Summa Theologica*

Aquinas had no difficulty with plants or animals being killed, on the basis that they are not rational and have no fellowship with humans. However, in these cases, the living beings under consideration cannot express any wishes regarding their death. In the instance of voluntary euthanasia, a person expresses a wish to be helped to die.

Advocates for assisted dying argue that a terminally ill person who requests for assistance to die should have their wishes respected. However, Aquinas pointed out that the person who dies by suicide because they are in some form of intolerable suffering does not really desire the evil of death. Instead, what they want is the good of escaping from their current evil. Even if they think that death is desirable, because it is final rest or peace, they are in error because they have mistaken an apparent good for a real good.

What does Natural Law say about voluntary euthanasia?

The Roman Catholic Church produced an official *Declaration on Euthanasia* in 1980, and defined euthanasia as:

> *An action or an omission which of itself or by intention causes death, in order that all suffering may in this way be eliminated.*
>
> Sacred Congregation for the Doctrine of the Faith, *Declaration on Euthanasia*

In this document, the Catholic Church recognises that people have a right to die with a minimum of pain and that, while suffering can have spiritual value in Christian thinking as an opportunity to learn and grow closer to God, this cannot be made a requirement. Painkilling drugs are clearly acceptable, because it is unreasonable to expect people to be heroic in their suffering unless they wish it. However, the Catholic Church raises concerns about painkilling drugs that cause unconsciousness because this removes the opportunity for a person to continue to uphold the primary precepts by maintaining their relationship with God and family members so as to prepare themselves properly for the afterlife. Drugs may not be used, even at a person's own request, to intentionally bring about an early death.

Christianity teaches that human life is sacred and should not be taken deliberately. This is the case even if a person chooses to end their own life. The primary precepts confirm that self-preservation and the preservation of life are absolute goods that we have a duty to uphold. To take a human life is to usurp God's right to give and take life.

> **Synoptic link**
>
> Link to *A Level Religious Studies for Eduqas: Philosophy of Religion*, Chapter 3: Challenges to religious belief: the problem of evil and suffering. In Christian explanations of evil and suffering, it is argued that there is a purpose behind human suffering. For example, it could be a punishment for sin, or an aid to spiritual growth and development.

> *The council therefore condemned crimes against life 'such as any type of murder, genocide, abortion, euthanasia or wilful suicide'.*
>
> Sacred Congregation for the Doctrine of the Faith, *Declaration on Euthanasia*

Euthanasia is quite different from murder and genocide, in that a person may take a life out of mercy rather than from hatred or anger. Yet, the Catholic Church's position on euthanasia seems clear: it is a sin and it cannot be allowed under any circumstances. However, as we have seen already, euthanasia is more complex than this. When a person is terminally ill and requires extraordinary means to keep them alive, it seems unreasonable to treat their refusal of these means or a request for someone to remove them in the same way as murder. And the Catholic Church does recognise that, sometimes, these means might be inappropriate or disproportionate. For example, performing a lengthy, painful operation upon a terminally ill person whose quality of life or length of life will not be significantly improved as a result seems unreasonable.

This interpretation of Aquinas' Natural Law says that, in general, doctors should not be forced to use extraordinary means, such as resuscitation equipment, to prolong the life of a terminally ill person. A doctor omitting to do something is not morally responsible for their patient's death, and a person who asks a doctor to withhold treatment has not died by suicide. Instead, it is an acceptance of the human condition. However, the Catholic Church would object to a doctor who acted to remove feeding tubes from a person to hasten their death, even at their own request and if they are terminally ill. This is because they consider clinically-provided nutrition to be food and food is an ordinary means of survival, part of the requirements of nature, and it is an act of killing to withdraw it.

> *Nothing and no one can in any way permit the killing of an innocent human being, whether a foetus or an embryo, an infant or an adult, an old person, or one suffering from an incurable disease, or a person who is dying. Furthermore, no one is permitted to ask for this act of killing, either for himself or herself or for another person entrusted to his or her care, nor can he or she consent to it, either explicitly or implicitly. Nor can any authority legitimately recommend or permit such an action.*
>
> Sacred Congregation for the Doctrine of the Faith, *Declaration on Euthanasia*

Those who advocate for assisted dying argue that, just as it is inappropriate to continue to treat a terminally ill person who does not want to be treated, it is inappropriate to refuse the request of a terminally ill person who asks for their death to be hastened. The Catholic Church would reject this approach as unacceptable.

Double effect

> *Nothing hinders one act from having two effects, only one of which is intended, while the other is beside the intention.*
>
> Thomas Aquinas, *Summa Theologica*

As we know, Aquinas' principle of double effect helps us to decide how to act when primary precepts conflict. A person can act morally in the full knowledge that what they are doing will have two effects, provided that the effect that is in violation of Natural Law is accidental or unintentional. There is nothing inherent in killing that brings about the law of double effect. However, when presented with a person who is suffering and in pain, it is good to work to be compassionate and prevent unnecessary suffering. Medical advances are such that pain can often be managed and a terminally ill person can be kept comfortable. However, sometimes this is not so easily done, and medication always has side effects.

Following Natural Law, a doctor who deliberately administers medication that they know will kill their patient does something sinful. It is a mortal sin for a doctor to do anything that violates life. However, a doctor can, for example, stop a patient's heart under surgical conditions to fix a problem and then restart it. This act does not violate Natural Law, even though it results in temporary 'death', because it is an action done to improve the patient's life.

In the case of a sick or dying person who is suffering, strong painkillers can be used to reduce pain. However, the use of strong painkillers, especially in high doses, does come with risks. It is possible that a doctor may administer medication with the internal act of treating a patient's pain, but the knowledge that the doses will shorten the patient's life. Provided that the doctor does not actively intend to kill, double effect means that morally the doctor is blameless.

However, this all must be balanced proportionally. Administering high doses of strong painkillers would not be acceptable if a person has simply stubbed their toe! Treatment should be in proportion to the benefits that the patient receives. Giving high doses of strong painkillers to a patient who is close to death to avoid excessive pain can be justified. However, giving the same treatment to a patient who requests such pain relief but could live for months or years with a different pain management regime is not morally justified.

Yet, dying because you are given high doses of strong painkillers by your doctor, when you are close to death and in excessive pain, is not, strictly speaking, an accident. Doctors are trained to know what will happen when they administer pain relief and, consequently, such a death is planned. In 2011, Dr Nigel Cox was convicted of the attempted murder of 70-year-old Lillian Boyes. Boyes suffered from rheumatoid arthritis to such a degree that she could not bear to be touched. She and her family begged Cox to end her life so she could be spared from the pain. He estimated she did not have long to live and administered a lethal dose of potassium chloride. This was clearly a planned event and, even though Cox intended to relieve his patient's pain, he also knew the dose would kill her.

The key is the dose he administered. If it was proportionate to the amount of pain that Boyes was in – only the minimum required to treat the pain that she suffered – and it had the secondary effect of killing her, then Cox's internal act to relieve pain is the act that he can be judged upon. If he gave her a higher dose than was necessary to relieve her pain, to ensure that she died, his action cannot be defended using the law of double effect and, according to Natural Law, is morally indefensible.

The Catholic Church teaches that suffering in life can help a person to identify with the sufferings of Christ and draw closer to God.

AO1 activity 8

Look up the stories of Valentina Maureira and Tony Nicklinson online. Explain how Natural Law would respond to Valentia and Tony's actions and requests.

This section of the chapter will enhance your ability to analyse and evaluate the topic and help you develop your AO2 skills. For each question, think about the different positions you might take, and decide which you find most persuasive and why. It is not enough to memorise a list of 'for and against' points; you need to develop an argument.

How far should Human Law be influenced by Aquinas' Natural Law?

This question is asking whether Aquinas' Natural Law should have an impact upon the laws that are made by and for society. It is relevant here to consider the role of religion in law-making, particularly in an increasingly secular society and in a society that contains many people from non-Christian, religious backgrounds.

The view that Human Law should be influenced by Aquinas' Natural Law

Aquinas was a prolific writer and drew from a great many non-Christian philosophers, as well as Christian, Jewish, and Islamic thinkers from across the globe at a time when there were no libraries, let alone the internet! To read so much, draw so many connections between different works and write over 60 titles is extraordinary. His Natural Law is informed by a great many intellectual and philosophical traditions, and is therefore representative of, and relevant to, a wide range of people from different backgrounds. It seems reasonable to suggest that Human Law can be influenced by Aquinas' Natural Law because it reflects such as wide range of intellectual thought.

Aquinas says in *Summa Theologica* that Human Law is framed for humans who are not perfect. Human Law does not forbid every single vice; it focuses on the worst vices, the ones everyone should abstain from because they harm others. Human laws that forbid murder, theft and so on are designed to protect people from the worst excesses of human nature and keep society together. Therefore, Human Law should be based on Natural Law, because Natural Law provides the reasoned basis for the practical goal of ensuring the continuance of society and the protection of its members. Natural Law can support Human Law by gradually leading people to virtue by showing them the path to perfection and ensuring that human laws are real goods.

F.C. Copleston pointed out that Aquinas felt that Human Law was necessary to ensure the good of everyone. It needs to be present to organise and coordinate the natural tendency of humans, who are social beings who tend towards living in groups. However, Human Law risks being arbitrary or partisan if it is left alone to do as it pleases. Natural Law can provide a structure for human laws that allows society to flourish as it responds to people's specific needs, making sure that human laws are good and in accordance with reason and nature.

Aquinas was not a totalitarian; he did not believe in the absolute power of the state. He believed that, ultimately, God – not the state – rules over humanity, and that the Catholic Church acts on behalf of God, so has more authority than the state. One of the functions of Human Law is, therefore, to establish how to fulfil Natural Law. So, while it is a precept of Natural Law that we should not kill, Human Law decides what individual acts constitute killing. Human Law should always be compatible with Natural Law to prevent a state passing legislation that is immoral. Copleston said this means that the individual is not bound to obey human laws if they are unjust. If Human Law is influenced by Natural Law, then laws should be authoritative and based in reason and this conflict should not arise.

The view that Human Law should not be influenced by Aquinas' Natural Law

It can be argued that Aquinas' Natural Law only really appeals to respectable middle-aged members of society. Bertrand Russell made this criticism about Aristotle's Virtue Theory, but it applies to Natural Law too. Russell said it is used by middle-aged people who want to repress the exuberance of young people. Aquinas' emphasis on education in practical reasoning and the importance of long experience and emotional balance certainly supports this criticism. Natural Law is only accessible to a minority of the population, most of whom are older people.

Peter Jackson argues that Natural Law fails to give enough consideration to the doctrine of the fall. Aquinas said that while our perception is impaired by sin, we can still discern God's intentions for us through reason. However, Jackson argues that sin has so damaged our perception that it is impossible for humans to see anything reliably at all. We should, instead, rely on scripture and divine revelation for our salvation and our laws.

Aquinas has been accused of not valuing the individual within society, of focusing on each member of society as potentially disposable if they do not wish to achieve the same common goals as everyone else. He refers to Matthew 5:30, which says that if a hand causes you to sin, you should cut it off. He understands this to mean that those who damage the good of society should be removed. This is dangerous, because it does not allow people to express themselves as individuals or set their own life goals. It is not a constructive way of people working together to create a society that works well for all; it is more a dictatorship.

UK society is increasingly non-Christian and, more specifically, is no longer predominantly Catholic. This means that basing human laws on the thinking of a Catholic medieval theologian and philosopher is to formulate laws and rules that have little relevance to the lives of the majority of the

AO2 activity 1

a) What dangers can you foresee for society if all UK laws were based on Aquinas' Natural Law?

b) Can you see any benefits for UK society if Aquinas' Natural Law influences law making?

c) If you have identified both dangers and benefits for UK society if Aquinas' Natural Law influences law making, can you see a way to minimise the dangers?

members of society today. It does not seem to be sensible to allow the religious minority to dictate which laws are appropriate to a non-religious majority or to those who are from faiths other than Christianity.

To what extent does the absolutist and deontological nature of Aquinas' Natural Law work in contemporary society?

There are two areas to be aware of with a question like this. Firstly, it states that Natural Law is absolutist and deontological. It is saying that Natural Law is focused on fixed laws that people have a duty to obey regardless of circumstances or culture. Secondly, it is asking if this kind of approach is appropriate for a society that Aquinas was unfamiliar with at his time of writing. In addition, by asking you about 'extent', this question requires you to be open to the possibility that there might be a middle position whereby Aquinas' Natural Law contains some features that work for contemporary society and others that do not.

The view that the absolutist and deontological nature of Aquinas' Natural Law does work in contemporary society

Timothy Renick points out that although Aquinas' Natural Law is deontological, it is more flexible than many people think. The primary precepts are absolute and very general, but the more specific secondary precepts are arrived at by looking at the context of a situation. Aquinas said that secondary precepts may change according to circumstances. The more you descend into the detail, the more that this is the case. This has led to an approach to Natural Law called Proportionalism, which we will consider in the next chapter.

Aquinas has been a strong influence on modern society. Reason is now considered to be very important in making moral decisions, which was not the case in the hundred years before Aquinas, when Peter Abelard was forced to watch his own books being burned for suggesting that reason could illuminate Christian thinking. Modern society questions authority, acknowledges human rights, and considers whether or not war is just. All of these things have come from Aquinas' understanding of Natural Law as duty arrived at via reason.

Natural Law is a practical alternative to moral scepticism, which is the view that there is no explanation of moral duties or rules to be found. Moral sceptics argue that there are no right answers to moral questions, that any idea of morality is only a convention or a tradition, and is not based upon any objective truth or knowledge of right and wrong. However, Natural Law offers a real, universally accessible foundation for solving moral problems. Using Natural Law, answers to moral problems are not only discoverable through reference to a divine command; they can be understood through the application of reason, something that is available to everyone.

While it is true that people do differ in what they understand to be morally good or bad, this does not disprove Aquinas' theory. Copleston commented that there can be an unchanging moral law and, at the same time, different opinions about its content or different insights as to how it can be explained in different situations. Just because people have different ideas does not mean that Relativism (the view that there are no universal norms, but that an action should be judged right or wrong depending on the situation) is true. Aquinas would have recognised differences in opinion but would have argued that everyone is still aware of the most fundamental moral principles in their general form, such as preserving life and cooperating with others. We disagree more about the specifics of how to do these things than we do about whether or not these principles are correct.

The view that the absolutist and deontological nature of Aquinas' Natural Law does not work in contemporary society

Aquinas is a product of his culture and time. He was an Italian medieval monk who was writing at a time when society was very hierarchical and when culture, society, and government were dominated by men and by the Catholic Church. Aquinas' understanding of what constitutes a natural order of society was determined by his environment and he did not conceive of any other kind of societal structure.

Aquinas claimed that there was an unchanging moral law, but evidence from history suggests that this is not the case. Reinhold Niebuhr pointed out that Natural Law is a reflection of the society in Aquinas' era. Renick gives the example that Aquinas regarded it as natural that men should be in authority over women, who were less capable of reason. Today, such attitudes are considered immoral and discriminatory. Aquinas' moral standards were a product of his time, and moral standards are subject to change.

Natural Law is very general and, consequently, not helpful as a practical moral guide. Aquinas himself set down very few practical laws or rules in his writings. However, the flexibility this brings is not an advantage. Stephen Buckle argues that Natural Law avoids the problem of fixed, unbending rules by creating another problem. Increasing the flexibility of Natural Law with situation-based secondary precepts means there is little connection between the general principles and actual practical rules. It means that the answer to the question 'How should I behave?' is not at all straightforward.

Aquinas was out of step with contemporary society. He viewed women as receptacles for child rearing and of little further use to men. While this was fairly typical for his time, in contemporary society, laws that disadvantage and denigrate women in this way are unjust and do not work. Renick points out that in *Summa Theologica*, Aquinas sees women as helpers in the projects men undertake rather than equal partners in life. His absolutist stance would then give little room for an evolving understanding of a woman's role in society.

> ### AO2 activity 2
> Summarise each argument about the extent to which the absolutist and deontological nature of Aquinas' Natural Law works in contemporary society on a separate index card, and arrange into two piles: persuasive and not persuasive. Which pile is larger and what does that lead you to conclude? Choose one argument from each pile and, on the back of the index card, write down three reasons why you assigned it to that pile.

What are the strengths and weaknesses of Aquinas' Natural Law?

Strengths and weaknesses questions may ask you to consider whether the strengths outweigh the weaknesses or vice versa, in which case it is important to be able to weigh up the effectiveness of each argument and not just list a range of arguments.

The strengths of Aquinas' Natural Law

Natural Law places a high value on human life, and is rooted in observations of what people are like and how they interact with their surroundings. Natural Law has a close connection with science, in that it is rational and based upon empirical evidence. It requires an understanding of biology, medicine, psychology, and sociology to discover what is natural. This makes it very appealing as a moral theory that is in keeping with the values of the modern world.

Natural Law is a flexible theory that arrives at specific rules from general, fixed precepts while considering the complexity of moral decision making. Consequences or situations are not ignored completely but are recognised as relevant to moral decision making without being the only ruling factor. This means that it can be flexible while still acknowledging that some actions are intrinsically good or evil.

Natural Law's basis in reason means that everyone can potentially participate in moral decision making, regardless of their religious beliefs. It recognises the worth and contribution of all people, including non-believers or those of other faiths, making Natural Law applicable in the modern world. Aquinas himself recognised the value of the work of Aristotle, a non-Christian, and argued that everyone is capable of reason.

Aquinas' Natural Law allows for the authority of God without falling prey to the same problem as Divine Command Theory of potentially allowing God's commands to be arbitrary. Aquinas' Natural Law does not allow moral truth to be dictated by a changeable society or the whims of a divine being who is separate from the world. Instead, Natural Law is based upon reason and philosophical investigation. Moral laws must be rational to be considered good, and Divine Law provides checks and balances to ensure that human reason is not flawed.

The weaknesses of Aquinas' Natural Law

The primary precept of reproduction through sexual intercourse is absolute. Yet Aquinas was a celibate monk. Aquinas suggests that the whole race need not reproduce; that the precept applies to the community rather than the individual. Yet, his condemnation of same-sex sexual acts, because it does not lead to reproduction, seems irrational if this is the case. Also, Aquinas only allows monks or priests, who are attending to divine concerns, to avoid the precept and it is hard to see how this exception furthers the community as a whole. Furthermore, it is unclear how anyone is to know when a precept applies to an individual and when it applies to a community.

Some scholars question whether Aquinas' Natural Law gives enough space to God's grace. By placing such an emphasis on the importance of reason, it relies too heavily upon human reasoning and good behaviour rather than trust and faith in God for redemption and salvation. While Aquinas did believe that divine revelation is superior to reason and that God is the goal of human behaviour, the role of reason in this thinking was partly why, for the first 200 or so years after his writings were published, they were treated with suspicion by the Catholic Church.

Natural Law allows for moral laws that lack compassion for the individual to be devised. In particular, it disadvantages women by controlling their bodies and focusing on women as receptacles for child bearing rather than as valuable people in their own right. While Aquinas attempted, to some degree, to lessen the impact of this (for example, he forbade killing women struggling in labour so the dying child could be delivered and baptised before its death), he was still a product of his time: a monk who appeared to view women as little more than the way that the human species reproduces.

Aquinas' Natural Law is too optimistic about the natural tendency of human beings to do good and avoid evil. There is clear evidence that human beings are selfish, greedy, and destructive. There is also evidence that human beings do things they know full well are morally evil, because they want something that they think is better for themselves. It is too generous to suggest that this is simply a mistake in reasoning. In fact, psychological egoism takes the opposite view: when people do things for the benefit of others, they are actually just suiting themselves. This may be more realistic.

AO2 activity 3

a) Choose the argument about the strengths and weaknesses of Natural Law that you find weakest (the one you disagree with most strongly) and describe what you think is its biggest problem.

b) Suggest a solution that could improve the argument or make it more convincing.

For example, you may think that the weakest argument against Natural Law is that Aquinas is too optimistic about the natural tendency of humans to do good. You might think this is because it is inaccurate to classify the whole human race as naturally selfish because of the actions of part of the population.
A possible solution could be to adjust your criticism of the argument by acknowledging that, while some human beings may desire good over evil, this is not true of all humans. Instead of seeing the argument as inaccurate because it classifies all humans as naturally selfish, you could argue that humans are all different and so it is not possible to generalise about the moral nature of the whole human race as Aquinas does.

Does Aquinas' Natural Law promote injustice?

This question asks you to consider whether Natural Law requires or requests people to do unjust actions. There are more than two conclusions possible here. We can argue that Natural Law does positively require people to perform unjust actions, that it does not, or that it leaves the path clear for injustice without actively promoting it.

The view that Aquinas' Natural Law does promote injustice

By being so absolute in its interpretation of Natural Law, it appears that the Catholic Church has failed to see the human person in a moral dilemma, complete with their relationship to society and other people. For example, it can be argued that the teachings of the Catholic Church on artificial contraception are at odds with human freedom to choose whether or not to have children. It does not allow a person to use artificial contraception to promote the welfare of an individual, a family or society as a whole, and so it is actively unjust.

Natural Law has been used to perpetuate injustice for centuries. Renick points out that Aquinas did not view women as the intellectual equals of men and they were, therefore, subject to the authority of men, incapable as they were of moral reasoning. He was writing at a time when women were excluded from formal education and intellectual pursuits, and it is unreasonable for Aquinas to suggest they are incapable of reason when they were not given the opportunities to demonstrate otherwise. Furthermore, later in the USA, Natural Law was used by some people to suggest that, since Black people were uneducated and enslaved, it was against Natural Law to abolish the enslavement of peoples. The assumption that because things are a certain way, they should always be that way, is an error of thinking inherent in Natural Law and one that can lead to huge injustice.

The view that Aquinas' Natural Law does not promote injustice

Aquinas' Natural Law makes it clear that certain actions are plain wrong and allows action to be taken to prevent them, allowing the Catholic Church to respond to modern moral dilemmas and speak out clearly against injustice. In 1965, the Second Vatican Council produced *Gaudium et Spes* (*The Church in the Modern World*), which is an analysis of modern society and culture. It emphasised the importance of the Church taking an active role in responding to modern problems such as social inequality, where some live in squalor while others live in luxury. Natural Law allows the Catholic Church to recognise what the world has to say, pay attention to other disciplines (such as science or economics) to inform its views, and ultimately make a judgement about whether something is good or evil rather than sitting on the fence.

Aquinas quoted Aristotle in saying that a law that is not just seems to be no law at all. An unjust law, for Aquinas, is an act of violence, and does not bind people to obey it unless there is a very good reason why they should; for example to keep society from falling apart. If a law goes against Divine Law, it is better to obey God rather than a human law. Therefore, Aquinas' Natural Law does not promote injustice, it strives against it and allows a person to break a law rather than perform an unjust action.

The view that Aquinas' Natural Law allows injustice

Aquinas says, in *Summa Theologica*, that a law should benefit the common good and should not be framed for private benefit. So, human laws should take people into account because the community is made up of many people. Such an approach should prevent the law from being abused by those in power for their own benefit. This shows that Natural Law does not promote injustice by benefiting the few and leaving the many at their mercy.

While it is true that Aquinas formed primary precepts which he declared were immutable and universal, he also kept the specifics of how to apply these precepts quite vague, on the basis that how they should be applied depends on the situation. However, it has been a common practice to treat Natural Law as inflexible, with the precepts determining what people ought to do in all situations and with no acknowledgement that circumstances change, and this can lead to injustice. For example, the Catholic Church has presented rules as absolute norms when they should be culturally and historically relative. Things like ownership of property and freedom of the individual need to be understood in the context of the society, and change as society changes.

While Aquinas' Natural Law does not promote injustice, its focus on laws rather than the needs of people means it paves the way for injustice to be done. The law that requires us not to kill means that someone who is pregnant cannot have an abortion, even if they have been raped, even if they are seriously ill, or even if their child will suffer if it is born. This puts women in a position that men will never have to suffer, and means that there is inequality built into laws based on Natural Law. This is an 'armchair' argument in that those who promote it pretend to be authoritative from the comfortable position of never having to experience such difficulties first hand. In the case of voluntary euthanasia, such 'armchair' arguments require people to suffer for their own edification rather than choosing for themselves when to die, even when their suffering has been caused by the actions of others. Yet, the same Natural Law allows killing in war, killing in capital punishment, and killing in self-defence, meaning that exceptions can be made when it suits the law maker.

AO2 activity 4
Find the central message in each argument about whether or not Natural Law promotes injustice. Summarise each argument in one line that contains the main point and a reminder of one example that illustrates the main point.

How effective is Aquinas' Natural Law in dealing with ethical issues?

This question involves thinking about what it means for an ethical theory to be 'effective'. An ethical theory could be called 'effective' if it can make accurate or reliable moral decisions, if it can do so quickly, if it can be used by everyone regardless of age or circumstance, or if it can be adapted to be used in new moral scenarios that arise.

The view that Aquinas' Natural Law is effective in dealing with ethical issues

Natural Law is surprisingly adaptable for a deontological theory. It can be adapted to be used in new moral scenarios because, while Aquinas did not write about abortion or euthanasia, his system of ethics can easily be applied to establish that both of these actions can be classed as killing. Because they violate the primary precepts, a conclusion can be reached that they are wrong. Natural Law can address more complex situations, where the primary precepts are in conflict, to ensure as much good as possible can be done, even when evil is unavoidable.

Natural Law can be used to make reliable decisions because it is based on primary precepts that are clear, fixed, and inviolable. This means that, unlike relativist theories such as Utilitarianism or Situation Ethics, it is possible to be confident in a moral decision because it is based on clear rules as opposed to a whim or a feeling. Not all decisions made by Natural Law will be popular, but they can be known with certainty to be accurate.

Natural Law can be used by the religious and non-religious alike. Aristotle did not believe in a personal God, and Natural Law theorists can use reason without resorting to revelation to discover moral laws. Aquinas himself recognised this and, although he felt that Aristotle's Natural Law was incomplete as it was not rooted in God's authority, he did acknowledge the capacity of an educated person to use *recta ratio* to discover what is good.

> *He does not need a new light added to his natural light, in order to know the truth in all things.* "
>
> Thomas Aquinas, *Summa Theologica*

Natural Law seems to be effective in dealing with ethical issues because it has been used, not only by the Catholic Church to make moral decisions for centuries, but also by modern governments in numerous scenarios. Aquinas' Natural Law is used when talking about whether or not a war is just, the double effect is applied in ethical scenarios where the lesser of two evils must be chosen, and Natural Law is the basis of the Universal Declaration of Human Rights.

The view that Aquinas' Natural Law is not effective in dealing with ethical issues

At every stage, Aquinas makes assumptions that can be challenged. For example, when discussing reproduction, Aquinas assumes all couples are monogamous. He assumes that the primary purpose of genital organs is reproduction. However, if, as he acknowledged, they also have the secondary purpose of pleasure, then one could argue that masturbation, foreplay and same-sex sexual acts are also acceptable. Yet, Aquinas did not accept this. We can, therefore, challenge his decision about which purpose is superior and, therefore, what is good.

Aquinas fails to take account of a human as a whole person and not a collection of parts. When he quotes from Matthew 5, claiming that a hand can be removed if it causes a person to sin, he considers the function of the hand in isolation and fails to account for its relationship to the rest of the body and to the mind. But the removal or use of a body part has a close relationship with the psychological well-being of a person. When it comes to sex, Aquinas has been accused of only considering the role of the genitals in reproduction and not placing enough value on the importance of sexual pleasure as a contributor to a person's mental well-being.

Aquinas' Natural Law has been used as a basis for positive rules that encourage respect for all people, but it has also been used to justify terrible behaviour, including discrimination against women and the enslavement of peoples to name just two examples. It has been used to vilify gay and bi people and those whose marriages have ended in divorce. Aquinas himself used Natural Law to argue in favour of capital punishment in extreme cases, to protect society, appearing to suggest that one individual could be sacrificed for the good of the whole. It seems, then, that Natural Law is not so reliable in making accurate moral decisions.

Natural Law was not supposed to be used by women. Aquinas did not feel that women were naturally intelligent enough to be able to use right reason. This suggests that it is not useable by 50 per cent of the population. Aquinas also believed that it was necessary for someone to be of significant age and experience to reason correctly. This suggests that the young and those who have had whatever Aquinas felt was an insufficient education cannot reason correctly. Ultimately, one wonders who can use Natural Law. It seems to be an elitist method of decision making, designed for the few who fit the criteria.

> ### AO2 activity 5
> Atheist thinkers have accused religion of limiting scientific progress. Natural Law should, theoretically, encourage science with its emphasis on rationality and empirical evidence. Can you think of any ways that Natural Law could be accused of limiting the progress of science and medicine rather than encouraging it? (Hint: consider some of the methods that scientists might need to use to treat illness and disease or discover more about how human cells work.)

To what extent is Aquinas' Natural Law meaningless without a belief in a creator God?

This question is asking you to consider whether the concept of Natural Law makes any rational sense or can have any impact on real life if God does not exist. It suggests that Natural Law relies on God's authority to be usable.

The view that Natural Law is completely meaningless without a belief in a creator God

Non-believers will find it difficult to use Natural Law because the aim or end of moral acts is different for Christians and non-Christians. The purpose of human existence is, after all, different if there is no God and if life after death is not true. Furthermore, why should someone obey Natural Law if there is no God to implant reason in humans; Natural Law is meaningless because it is no different from any other subjective moral theory.

While Aquinas did entertain the idea that there might be other ends for humanity, such as pleasure or scientific knowledge, he dismissed them all. He argued that if pleasure is the main purpose of human life, then we are no different from animals. And he pointed out that scientific knowledge cannot be the main purpose because it is not available to all humans because not everyone has the capacity to understand such things. For Aquinas, the beatific vision is the only possible universal aim for the whole of humanity. However, God as a purpose is an unproven assumption that Aquinas makes.

Hugo Grotius constructed a more secular interpretation of Natural Law as a body of rights. His interpretation showed that, without God, there is no adequate sense of obligation in Natural Law. If moral duties depend upon people freely accepting and adopting them, then people are equally free to reject them when they do not suit them. Without God, there is no reason why a person should not reject such rights and, if everyone rejected them, society would collapse because it depends upon us accepting and participating in the rules and regulations that it has constructed.

Aquinas did believe that reason could be used without the need to look at God's revelation or wait for some kind of divine miracle. However, for Aquinas, reason was a gift from God that we would not have access to unless God created it in us. Natural Law revolves around the existence of God as our source and our purpose. God is the creator who gave us the gift of reason in the first place and God's Divine Law supersedes and supports any reasoning that humans might do. Human reason can be wrong, but God is inerrant.

The view that Natural Law is still meaningful without a belief in a creator God

Aquinas was not the only advocate of Natural Law. Aristotle was not a Christian and did not believe in a personal God, but advocated Natural Law. Grotius claimed that the foundations of Natural Law are valid even if there is no God. Every human, after all, has the capacity for reason. As you will see in the next chapter, John Finnis elaborated upon Aquinas' Natural Law in a way that suggests that belief in the specifics of Catholicism is unnecessary and that 'religion' can be interpreted more broadly.

Copleston said that even Aquinas himself did not think that it is impossible to have knowledge of the good without revelation from God. Even if a philosopher does not know about the beatific vision, they are perfectly capable of seeing that some actions are more likely to lead to human perfection and that other actions are incompatible with it. Aquinas did not dismiss Aristotle as wrong or a pagan who cannot know morality. He simply acknowledged that Aristotle's concerns were with imperfect, incomplete, temporal happiness rather than that of the eternal. Therefore Natural Law is still meaningful, even without belief in God.

Aquinas distinguished between Natural Law and Eternal Law, suggesting that Natural Law is autonomous and does not require belief in God. The focus is on right reason as a human faculty that all possess. Grotius suggested that, as a result, Natural Law has a degree of validity even if you deny God's existence.

Murray Rothbard pointed out that the Enlightenment produced Newton's laws, which enhanced our understanding of the world as a set of interacting natural laws. Just as science has demonstrated that the natural world can be explained without reference to God as it has progressed, there is no reason why our understanding of human beings cannot be seen in the same light. Morality can surely be explained with reference to reason that follows from the nature of humanity, without the need to refer to a God at all. Aquinas suggested that God was unnecessary to an understanding of the precepts, and we can just take this one step further.

The view that Natural Law is meaningless regardless of a belief in a creator God

Natural Law commits the Naturalistic Fallacy of deriving ethical conclusions from empirical or synthetic descriptive statements. Aristotle was essentially a biologist, and it is difficult to understand how we can grasp what we ought to do from a biological description about how things operate.

The view that Natural Law becomes meaningless when you add belief in a creator God

Natural Law is the exercise of reason based upon an understanding of the nature of the world. Alan Suggate points out that to add God to Natural Law is to add a metaphysical concept. It is very difficult to understand how rational ethical principles or the empirical world have any relationship with talk of a metaphysical being such as God.

AO2 activity 6

Do you agree that God as an aim of humanity is still an unproven assumption? Look at your work from the philosophy paper on inductive arguments for the existence of God. Has Aquinas proven the existence of God already? If so, what do you think this means for the question 'To what extent is Aquinas' Natural Law meaningless without a belief in a creator God?'

Exam support

Practising AO1 questions

AO1 questions may begin with a range of possible command words (see pages 8–9 for more detail). The question below begins with the word 'Apply', and you should be prepared to show that you can use the features of Natural Law to make decisions about abortion. This question does not need you to consider the quality of the theory or offer any views about it. You should also avoid simply describing Natural Law or going into significant detail about what abortion is, how it is performed or any history of the laws surrounding it. Instead, you should show that you can reach a conclusion about the morality of abortion by following the process of reasoning set down by Natural Law.

Read the past paper question below and the example paragraph written in response before completing the activity on page 122.

> *Apply Aquinas' Natural Law to the issue of abortion.*
>
> (Eduqas AS Level Religious Studies, Summer 2019, Component 3: An Introduction to Religion and Ethics, Question 4a)

Example

Abortion can be defined as the ending of a pregnancy[1], before the foetus[7] is ready to be born, through medical intervention. Aquinas' Natural Law[6] is a normative ethical theory[7] that understands God as the highest good[1], or telos[7], for all human behaviour. Aquinas[6] believed in the primary precepts[7], these are general principles[1] that give an overview of acceptable moral behaviour. They are preserve life, live cooperatively in society, worship God, educate children and reproduce[1]. These primary precepts give rise to secondary precepts[7] that can be known through reason and can be deduced from looking at the particular situation[1] in front of us. Therefore, when looking[2] at an example[3] like abortion, we can deduce that[2] an abortion would not preserve life[1] and[2] would not allow someone to reproduce[1]. Therefore[2], abortion would be considered wrong[1] according to Natural Law and the[2] secondary precept[1] would be that[2] we must not perform an abortion[1].

Areas for development

1 The answer shows a knowledge of what abortion is and what Natural Law is. However, it is only in the last sentence that it does what the question asks and applies Natural Law to abortion.

2 The answer does not immediately address the demands of the question. Although it talks about the correct material, it is a while before it actually applies the ethical theory to the practical dilemma.

3 The example of abortion is used at the paragraph end. However, it is a very general example and the student could apply Natural Law to abortion in more depth.

4 This answer does not refer to sacred texts. It may not be appropriate to do so in this paragraph, but it is possible in the full response for the student to refer to commands against killing from the Bible.

5 This answer does not make any specific connections with other areas of study. It may not be appropriate to do so here, and connections should not be forced.

6 There is no need to refer to a wide range of scholars in an answer to this question. However, in the full answer, the student could quote Aquinas talking about ensoulment, which is relevant to a discussion about whether a foetus is a person. It would also be relevant to talk about the Catholic Church's interpretation of Natural Law.

7 There is accurate and appropriate use of specialist vocabulary in context.

Activity

a) Read the example paragraph on page 121 and identify one way in which it:

- successfully applies Natural Law to demonstrate the moral status of abortion
- fails to properly apply Natural Law to demonstrate the moral status of abortion.

b) Improve the paragraph by rewriting it to remove the weaknesses you have identified.

AO1 practice question 1

Now it is your turn. Have a go at answering the following question. There are some points to remember underneath to help you if you are not sure how to start.

> *Examine the precepts and goods within Aquinas' Natural Law.*
>
> (Eduqas AS Level Religious Studies, Summer 2017, Component 3: An Introduction to Religion and Ethics, Question 5a)

Points to remember

- Remember to concentrate on the precepts and goods rather than being distracted by explaining other areas of Natural Law, such as the principle of double effect.
- Use vocabulary that relates to Natural Law specifically, such as 'beatific vision' and 'real and apparent goods'.
- Give examples of Aquinas' teachings and how they have been interpreted by the Catholic Church. You could also include examples of how precepts and goods might work in practice by referencing abortion, euthanasia, or sex.

AO1 practice question 2

Now try this question by yourself.

> *Examine both the deontological and teleological features of Aquinas' Natural Law.*
>
> (Eduqas A Level Religious Studies, Summer 2018, Component 3: Religion and Ethics, Question 4a)

Practising AO2 questions

When writing a response to an AO2 question, you must remember that you are being examined on your ability to analyse and evaluate effectively. Analysis involves a detailed examination of something and you should pick apart the concept to look for the strengths and the weaknesses. Evaluation involves judging the quality or importance of the concept. You are expected to analyse and evaluate throughout the whole of your response; you are not expected to include long passages explaining knowledge and understanding.

Read the past paper question below and the example paragraphs written in response before completing the activity on page 125.

> *'Natural Law has more strengths than weaknesses.' Evaluate this view.*
>
> (WJEC AS Level Religious Studies, Summer 2019, AS Unit 2: An Introduction to Religion and Ethics and the Philosophy of Religion, Question 1b)

Example 1

Natural Law has more weaknesses than strengths[2] because it is too[1] absolutist[6] to be helpful[1] to people in complex moral situations that must be faced in today's world. It makes assumptions[1] about God's existence, rather than being based on something that is more concrete, like happiness in this world. It gives people an excuse to treat others badly[1]; for example, it has been used to justify things like discrimination against women and even enslavement[3]. The strengths[2] of Natural Law are that it is more flexible[1] than it seems at first because the secondary precepts[6] allow rules to be based on the situation. It was used as the basis for[1] the Universal Declaration of Human Rights[3] and Aquinas[4] did think that love and charity[6] were important when making moral decisions. It values human life[1] very highly and it uses reason[1] to work out the rules instead of relying on commands from God. Aquinas[4] also based his work on the thinking of Aristotle[4], who says that an unjust law is no law at all[4], and so it seems that you don't have to obey rules[1] that are unfair according to Aquinas[4].

Areas for development

1 There is some valid analysis of the issues raised by the question, but inconsistent evaluation. However, the student has adopted an AO1 approach to the question, listing the strengths and weaknesses rather than analysing them and considering the power of each argument.

2 This answer focuses on the subject area of the question throughout, but it does not engage in any evaluation of the issues.

3 There is some support for the views given (the student has used examples to show the strengths and weaknesses of Natural Law), but they are quite generalised.

4 The views of scholars are mentioned but only briefly, and more evaluation of scholarly arguments would be expected throughout the response or later in the full answer.

5 No connections have been made with other approaches. While this area should not be forced, students could be awarded for making comparisons with more or less effective approaches.

6 There is some accurate use of specialist language in context.

Example 2: an improved response

Natural Law has more weaknesses than strengths[2] because it is too[1] absolutist[6] to be helpful[1] to people in complex moral situations that must be faced in today's world. The primary precepts[6] leave no room for exceptions in extreme circumstances and, as a result, a young rape victim can be forced to have a baby they cannot care for and a terminally-ill person can be forced to go through prolonged suffering[3] because[1] the deontological[6] rules are more important than the people, and there is only one way of using recta ratio[6]. On the other hand[1], scholars like Renick[4] like to point out that a strength[2] of Natural Law is that it is more flexible than it seems at first[1], and it is true that the secondary precepts[6] allow moral decisions to be made according to the situation. For instance,[3] Aquinas[4] never wrote about abortion or euthanasia, yet we can apply his theory to new scenarios such as these[4]. However[1], Aquinas himself said that 'a precept of law has compulsory power'[4]. This means that[1] while there might be a chance to create laws that apply to specific circumstances, there can be no exceptions to the primary precepts[1], even when suffering is severe. Consequently, the strength[2] Renick[4] highlights is not a strength[2] at all. Therefore, this argument showing[1] the weakness[2] of Natural Law is more compelling because the appearance of flexibility is an illusion[1] and so Natural Law has more weaknesses than strengths[2].

What went well

1 Confident analysis and evaluation appear throughout the paragraph with consideration of different viewpoints both for and against the statement in the question. Judgements concerning the arguments raised are supported with reasoning at the end of the paragraph.

2 This answer contains regular reference to the wording of the question throughout.

3 There is detailed use of evidence, with examples of ethical dilemmas used to give the arguments force.

4 There is appropriate reference to scholarly views.

5 No clear connections are made with other elements of study, but the student could go on to make them in the rest of the answer if appropriate. For example, they could argue that a stronger, more adaptable or compassionate approach might be the proportionalist understanding of Natural Law.

6 There is thorough use of specialist language in context.

Activity

a) Read Example 1 on page 123 and identify three things in the paragraph that show poor evaluation technique.

b) Read Example 2 on page 124. This time, the evaluation is much more effective. Make a list of at least three things that you think the student did that makes the paragraph better.

AO2 practice question 1

Now it is your turn. Have a go at answering the following question. There are some points to remember underneath to help you if you are not sure how to start.

'Following Natural Law results in injustice.' Evaluate this view.

(Eduqas AS Level Religious Studies, Summer 2017, Component 3: An Introduction to Religion and Ethics, Question 5b)

Points to remember

- This question focuses on the idea of justice or fair treatment within Natural Law. Remember to give arguments on both sides of the debate. For example, you can point out that justice is one of the cardinal virtues and so of great importance to Aquinas, but that modern interpretations of justice (such as equal rights for all, including women and members of the LGBTQ+ community) are rather different from Aquinas' views.
- Give plenty of examples throughout your essay, to illustrate your ideas and back up your arguments.
- Use the ideas of scholars, including Aristotle, Copleston and Russell, and weigh up whether or not you think their ideas are persuasive.

AO2 practice question 2

Now try this question by yourself.

'Natural Law is meaningless without belief in a creator God.' Evaluate this view.

(Eduqas A Level Religious Studies, Summer 2018, Component 3: Religion and Ethics, Question 4b)

Mark schemes for all exam questions can be found at www.eduqas.co.uk and www.wjec.co.uk.

4 Deontological ethics: John Finnis' Natural Law and Proportionalism

What ingredients do you think make for a great life? Happiness? Money? Friends? Freedom to do what you want? Something different? Sadly, many of us feel that our 'shopping list' for a great life is not fulfilled in the way we would like it to be. There can be lots of reasons for this. Sometimes, we do not get the opportunities we need or an accident happens, which stalls our progress. Someone might get in the way of our goals as they seek a great life for themselves. Or, when we get the thing that we think will make our lives great, it does not turn out as well as we thought. How do we deal with this? To what lengths can we go to achieve the fulfilling life we want to live? In this chapter, you will consider two different, more modern, approaches to Natural Law.

John Finnis is a Catholic and an Emeritus Professor of Jurisprudence at Oxford University. He has developed a version of Natural Law that focuses on the ingredients of a flourishing life discussed by Aristotle, and considers how practical reason and authority can coordinate all of our actions so that our individual plans for a great life do not conflict.

Bernard Hoose is a Catholic Scholar who described a Catholic development of Aquinas' Natural Law known as Proportionalism. This approach allows moral agents to make exceptions, in extreme circumstances, to even the most absolute sounding rules.

Both these versions of Natural Law continue to argue that there are moral rules and that people have a moral duty to pursue what is good, but they attempt to find ways for human beings to make the best moral choices, from a wide range of options, so that they can live their best lives.

What do we need to live a flourishing life?

AO1

This section of the chapter will enhance your **knowledge** and **understanding** of the topic and help you develop your AO1 skills.

John Finnis' development of Natural Law

John Finnis sees Natural Law as an eternal and objective set of practical principles that are true regardless of individual opinion. Developed from the work of Plato, Aristotle, and Aquinas, Finnis' Natural Law sets out practical criteria to help a person to distinguish between reasonable and unreasonable actions, and to live a flourishing life by doing what is good and avoiding what is evil.

Finnis is not only concerned with personal morality. The principles of Natural Law also apply to wider society, to politics, and to jurisprudence (the philosophy of law). They give authority to the laws that humans make and the administration of justice within the community.

John Finnis (born 1940)

Development of the seven basic human goods

Finnis talks of **basic human goods**, which he also calls basic values or basic aspects of human well-being. The goods are 'basic' because they cannot be reduced to any other form of good. One basic good is not objectively more important than another, and the goods are good for everybody.

The basic goods give context and direction to reasoning, and can be used in many ways to formulate practical principles. They are not goals a person tries to achieve; they are to be participated in through projects, commitments, or actions. The goods are never complete; they take shape in different ways throughout a person's life. This means the basic goods are not as restrictive as laws or rules; instead they are a framework that allows a moral agent to choose from a range of possible moral options.

Finnis argues that the basic goods are self-evident. They are not deduced by looking at facts about the world or from the knowledge that everyone desires them. They are obvious because anyone who has experience of trying to establish facts or make judgements can see that to deny them is unreasonable.

> *They are objective; their validity is not a matter or convention, nor is it relative to anybody's individual purposes ... and to deny them is as straightforwardly unreasonable as anything can be. In all these respects, the principles of theoretical rationality are self-evident.* **99**
>
> John Finnis, *Natural Law and Natural Rights*

Finnis details seven basic goods: life, knowledge, play, aesthetic experience, friendship, practical reasonableness, and religion.

> ### Key term
>
> **basic human good:** Finnis' Natural Law identifies seven basic human goods as the basis for morality: life, knowledge, friendship, play, aesthetic experience, practical reasonableness, and religion

Life

Finnis' first basic good, life, includes everything that enables a human being to make decisions about their own existence freely. So, it includes physical and mental health, and freedom from pain and injury. Operating on a patient to save their life, growing food and looking both ways before you cross the road are all concerned with pursuing this basic good. The basic good of life includes and begins with reproduction.

> The term 'life' here signifies every aspect of the vitality (vita, life) which puts a human being in good shape for self-determination.
>
> John Finnis, *Natural Law and Natural Rights*

Knowledge

Finnis draws a distinction between **speculative knowledge** – theoretical intellectual knowledge that is sought for its own sake out of concern for what is true and a desire to avoid ignorance and error – and **instrumental knowledge**, knowledge that is sought to achieve a further objective like money, popularity, or power. The value of speculative knowledge is obvious to Finnis. It makes sense that people seek it, because it is intrinsically good and desirable for its own sake. It can be pursued in a wide variety of ways, such as by studying science or philosophy, and by reading detective stories and newspapers. Such actions are applied by humans to whatever form of knowledge gathering they choose to interest themselves, and so there is diversity in the method that is used but one basic good.

> **Key terms**
>
> **speculative knowledge:** theoretical, intellectual knowledge that seeks truth
>
> **instrumental knowledge:** knowledge that is sought to achieve a further objective, such as money or popularity

> Is it not the case that knowledge is really a good, an aspect of authentic human flourishing, and that the principle which expresses its value formulates a real (intelligent) reason for action?
>
> John Finnis, *Natural Law and Natural Rights*

Play

Play is the performance of actions for their own sake and for enjoyment. It can be *ad hoc* or planned, social or solitary, intellectual or physical. It has its own value, and can help to bring a sense of meaning and purpose to life beyond work or mere existence. It can also be part of any human activity, even in an apparently serious context.

Aesthetic experience

Aesthetic experience may sometimes be an aspect of play, but it can also be found and enjoyed separately from play. It may not require any particular human action, and can be an external or an internal experience. It can simply be an appreciation of beauty in nature, but it is often to be found in a person's own creative work or the creative work of others.

Friendship

Finnis' fifth basic good of friendship or sociability can be the ability to live alongside others peacefully, or it can be an in-depth relationship with another person. This good involves acting for the sake of the friend and respecting their purpose and well-being, rather than using them as an instrument to one's own ends.

Practical reasonableness

Practical reasonableness is being able to use one's intelligence to shape one's own character, lifestyle, and actions. It is active rather than passive because it aims to perform actions that change the state of the world. Finnis describes it as authentic and reasonable self-determination. To participate in this basic good is to work out how to participate in the others by guiding one's choice of commitments and projects. It is a vital part of turning the basic goods into practical principles for action, and is governed by nine requirements that we will consider later in the chapter.

Religion

Religion, for Finnis, is more than simply falling into line with the teachings and practices of the Catholic Church. It involves an attempt to make sense of the world by grappling with the big questions, such as the origins of cosmic order, the nature of human freedom, and the source of reason. Finnis argues that even the atheist must grapple with these issues to some extent. Seeking the source of order and meaning beyond humanity is religious and, thus, participation in this basic good.

> *Does not even Sartre, taking as his point de départ that God does not exist (and therefore that 'everything is permitted'), none the less appreciate that he is 'responsible' … And is this not a recognition (however residual) of, and concern about, an order of things 'beyond' each and every one of us?*
>
> John Finnis, *Natural Law and Natural Rights*

Synoptic link

Link to *Chapter 8: Determinism and free will: free will*. Look at Sartre's existentialist philosophical Libertarianism, his argument that there is no God and we are, thus, free beings able to create our own morality.

The role of basic goods

While he acknowledges that individuals will disagree over the number of basic goods that exist, Finnis holds that any other apparent forms of good are simply ways of pursuing one of these seven basic goods.

A basic good is a value to be participated in, not a rule to be followed. Each value is objectively, universally, and intrinsically good. But none of them are exclusively good, nor are all people required to pursue them all at all times and in all places. They are '**pre-moral**'; they are not yet moral principles that dictate what ought to happen. It is through the process of practical reasoning that a basic good is formulated into a principle. So, for example, from the basic good of knowledge, we can reason that it is a practical principle to avoid muddle and confusion. This practical principle is not a rule, but it gives structure and focus to moral decision making.

Key term

pre-moral: prior to the formulation of a moral code or law

Unlike Utilitarianism, the point of all of this is not simply to experience pleasure. Finnis says that it is an error to try to find something more basic than the goods, such as pleasure, that would provide a reason for participating in them. According to the scholar Robert Nozick, given the choice of plugging into a pleasure machine or living a real life, everyone would choose real life, even though it can be hard. This is because we want to act within reality, not just feel sensations. We want to live, authentically and freely, in the real world through real participation in these values.

The purpose of life is human flourishing through practically reasoned decisions and free actions that lead to participation in the basic goods.

There are many human behaviours that do not correspond to a basic good, such as taking more than one's fair share or being cruel to others. These urges often begin with the pursuit of a basic good, but they go awry. For example, greed may have started as a tendency towards sustaining life, but a person has become locked into the habit of considering only their own life and failing to consider sustaining the lives of others.

All seven basic goods are equally fundamental, self-evident, and irreducibly basic. Therefore, there is no hierarchy of goods. While certain events and situations might shift a person's focus and bring one of the goods to the forefront of their minds, ultimately no good is more important than any other. When a speeding truck is hurtling towards you, life is a priority in that moment, but it is not fundamentally more vital than any other good.

The distinction between theoretical and practical reason

Finnis makes an important distinction between **practical reason** and **theoretical reason**. This distinction is based on a consideration of Hume's Law which says that an 'ought' cannot be derived from an 'is'.

Theoretical reason is concerned with matters of fact and the workings of the world. While it cannot be used to prove or establish the basic goods, to use theoretical reason to be well-informed, intelligent, and consistent is self-evidently good, and therefore theoretical reason is the knowledge that Finnis declares a basic good.

Practical reason begins with the self-evident knowledge of the basic goods that it is unreasonable to deny, and then focuses on how to participate in them. In this way, practical reason considers which commitments or projects a person should choose, and helps them decide how to carry them out. To work out if an action is practically reasonable, a person must have experience, intelligence, and a desire for practical reason.

Finnis states that Natural Law is not challenged by Hume's Law because, while he agrees that theoretical reasoning ('is' statements about the world) cannot be used to deduce moral imperatives ('ought' statements about how we should behave), he argues that practical reasoning does not do this. Instead, it uses self-evident principles about what is good and then seeks to understand how to practically participate in them.

Nine Requirements of Practical Reason

The basic goods do not acquire moral force until they are put into practice through projects or actions. How they are participated in is the focus of practical reasonableness.

The **Nine Requirements of Practical Reason** concern what a person must do, think, and be in order to participate in the basic good of practical

Key terms

practical reason: a specific form of reasoning that we use to determine what 'ought' to be done; can be contrasted with theoretical reason

theoretical reason: reasoning that concerns factual, descriptive matters; can be contrasted with practical reason

Nine Requirements of Practical Reason: nine principles developed by Finnis that create the optimum conditions to attain the basic goods

Synoptic link

Link to *Chapter 2: Ethical thought (part two)*. Remind yourself of Hume's objection to Ethical Naturalism. He argued that ethical (ought) statements cannot be reached via factual or descriptive (is) statements about the world.

reasonableness. They demonstrate the 'Natural Law method' of working out moral behaviour from the basic goods. To fail to live up to any of the requirements is unreasonable.

> *As with each of the basic forms of good, each of these requirements is fundamental, underived, irreducible … Each of these requirements concerns what one must do, or think, or be if one is to participate in the basic value of practical reasonableness.*
>
> John Finnis, *Natural Law and Natural Rights*

A coherent plan of life (view life as a whole)

The first of the Nine Requirements of Practical Reason is to have a coherent plan for life. It is unreasonable to drift through life following whims and desires. It is also equally unreasonable to be so focused on one goal that life becomes a rigid obedience to rules or life as a whole is abandoned. There is no one way to live a good life, and the basic goods themselves are not goals. We participate in them, so life should be viewed as a coherent whole where the projects we take part in are harmonised so that they all contribute to a whole life plan that enables us to participate in the basic goods.

> *It is unreasonable to live merely from moment to moment, following immediate cravings of just drifting.*
>
> John Finnis, *Natural Law and Natural Rights*

No arbitrary preferences among values (goods)

Secondly, we must have no arbitrary preferences among values. All seven basic goods are objectively and equally good, therefore none of them should be ignored or exaggerated. Finnis says that parents or politicians who require children to conform to their own standards of excellence in academia act as unreasonably as those who deny that knowledge is a basic good. Circumstances sometimes dictate that we must focus on one good: if I am drowning then I must focus on the basic good of life rather than play. Yet this is relative to my situation. In actual fact, play, life, and knowledge are equally, objectively, and intrinsically good, and so our life plan should make reasonable allowance for participation in all seven basic goods, even if there are times when some take the forefront of our concern.

> *It is one thing to have little capacity and even no 'taste' for scholarship, or friendship, or physical heroism, or sanctity; it is quite another thing, and stupid or arbitrary, to think or speak or act as if these were not real forms of good.*
>
> John Finnis, *Natural Law and Natural Rights*

No arbitrary preferences among persons (basic goods apply equally to all)

This third of the Nine Requirements of Practical Reason is sometimes expressed as the **Golden Rule**: to treat others as you would like to be treated. The basic human goods are to be participated in by all human beings. I may be more interested in my own well-being or in the well-being

> **Key term**
>
> **Golden Rule:** the principle of treating others as you would like to be treated, which appears in one form or another in most religions and cultures

of people I love, and this is reasonable. But it is not reasonable to deny that the basic goods are of concern to everyone, or to claim that I am in any way more important or special than other people; they apply equally to all.

Detachment (do not become obsessed with a particular project) and commitment (use effort to improve)

The fourth requirement of detachment and the fifth requirement of commitment are complementary according to Finnis, who sees them as vital to adopting a coherent plan of life and achieving balance.

The importance of participating in all the basic goods means that we should not become obsessed with one project to such an extent that we persist with it regardless of whether it allows participation in the goods. Obsession with a project can lead to fanaticism (an extreme or uncritical devotion), therefore we must remain detached in our view of our projects and be prepared to revise plans that are ineffective or take up new projects when one is completed or fails.

It is equally important to be committed to a project, to see it through and not abandon it carelessly if we are going to achieve any goal at all in life. The two requirements of detachment and commitment enable a balance to be struck between fanaticism and apathy, indifference and disinterest, so that we can apply effort to participate creatively in the basic goods.

The (limited) relevance of consequences: efficiency within reason (plan your actions to do the most good)

Efficiency within reason means that we must think practically and consider the consequences of our actions, but only within the confines of what is reasonable. Finnis has already established that it is unreasonable to reject any of the basic goods, so when we plan our moral actions, we must choose the most efficient action to allow participation in those goods and not frustrate them. For example, when we are forced to choose, it is more efficient and reasonable to choose an action that preserves life rather than property. We should, in other words, carry out a cost/benefit analysis to work out how to practically achieve our reasonable objectives.

But weighing up possible consequences is not the only thing to consider when making moral decisions. It is irrational, according to Finnis, to prioritise consequences to the extent that we prefer one good or one person over another. Utilitarianism does this, and therefore according to Finnis, it should be rejected as arbitrary. There is no one central or superior requirement in ethical action, good cannot be weighed or measured, and there are many ways that humans can flourish. So, actions should be chosen for how efficient they are in enabling participation in the goods, not simply in what the consequences are, and they should never be chosen because the consequences are somehow 'justified' by means that are unreasonable.

> [The nine requirements] require that cost–benefit analysis be contained within a framework that excludes any project involving certain intentional killings, frauds, manipulations of personality, etc.
>
> John Finnis, *Natural Law and Natural Rights*

Respect for every basic value in every act (never harm a basic good)

The seventh requirement means that we should not choose to perform an action which intrinsically damages or hinders participation in one or more of the basic goods; we should never harm a basic good. Moral acts always promote or protect basic goods. When I choose a project, I necessarily limit my ability to pursue another one, but I should avoid choosing a project that actively damages a good. For example, Finnis chose to be a philosopher and so limited his ability to save lives as a doctor, but this choice does not directly damage the good of life. However, if Finnis were to kill one person to save ten others, then his action would damage participation in the good of life as part of the essential nature of the action. There might be positive consequences but they are not certain, while the negative consequences are certain and directly damage a good. This requirement is essential to ensure that no human right can ever be overridden for the sake of a desired outcome. Therefore, every basic value must be respected in every moral act, and may never be directly damaged through any act.

> *For most practical purposes this seventh requirement can be summarised as: Do not choose directly against a basic value.* **"**
>
> John Finnis, *Natural Law and Natural Rights*

The requirements of the common good (foster the common good in the community)

The eighth requirement concerns the requirements of the common good. Most of our concrete moral responsibilities and duties have their basis in this requirement. This is favouring and fostering good for everyone in our communities. This is not the same as the greatest good for the greatest number. Instead, this requirement is one of cooperation, collaboration, and coordination with others in our communities.

Following one's conscience (act in your own conscience and authority)

Finally, practical reason involves following one's conscience. We should not do something we think should not be done. Like Aquinas, Finnis claims that practical judgements required by reason are judgements of conscience. Conscience is the mechanism for producing correct judgements, and is an aspect of what it means to be human. It is possible to be misled by conscience, if we have had an unstable upbringing or character, but conscience will be correct if we strive to be reasonable and understand the ways that the basic goods can be participated in. The fact that we can be misled demonstrates why we need a capable authority, ruler, or government to give us guidance. However, if conscience reasons that something is required, it is unreasonable to act against it, even if it can sometimes, unwittingly, be wrong.

The common good

The common good involves coordination, collaboration, and cooperation with other people according to the requirements of practical reason. Since

AO1 activity 2

Write a list of the Nine Requirements of Practical Reason, evenly spaced out down the left side of your page. Close your notes and set a timer for nine minutes. Write as much as you can about all Nine Requirements in nine minutes. When your time is up, check your work against your notes and add any important points you missed in a different colour.

everyone is entitled to participate in all seven basic goods at any time and in any way they choose, everyone's projects are equally important. This means we need some degree of organisation so that everyone is free to pursue their projects without interfering with anyone else's.

Being part of a community is a sharing of life, action, and interest. It is a unifying relationship between human beings that best enables human flourishing. For example, if a class of students wish to learn about ethics, they need to cooperate with each other. They must agree on the roles of teacher and student, on a common arrival time, on places to sit, and on behaviours that limit disruption. Even if they do not care about the progress of others in the class, if members of the class are competing for a prize, for example, they must work together to learn or at the very least agree not to interfere with each other's learning. For this to happen, it is vital that each person understands that all seven basic goods apply equally to everyone and not just themselves.

The need for authority

For Finnis, law and ethics are part of the same process. Law claims the authority to regulate human behaviour within a community, using rules that have legal force for the community, to enable the community to thrive. Law should be impartial in its dealings with people and basic goods in accordance with practical reason.

There are two reasons why authority is necessary and useful in a community. Firstly, because there are sometimes members of a community who are uncooperative or unreasonable in their dealings with others, and authority provides a mechanism for dealing with this challenging behaviour. Secondly, even when people are reasonable and committed to the common good, there are so many life plans that nothing at all can be achieved without some method of coordinating life plans and resolving the inevitable problems that arise when life plans come into conflict.

It is inevitable that there will be conflict within a community hosting multiple life plans, such as during the Covid-19 pandemic when members of society disagreed over how it should be managed.

> *Intelligence, dedication, skill and commitment thus multiply the problems of co-ordination, by giving the group more possible orientations, commitments, projects, 'priorities' and procedures to choose from.*
>
> John Finnis, *Natural Law and Natural Rights*

For instance, decisions need to be made about how children are to be educated or how natural resources are to be used. There may be more than one possible solution, but until a choice is made and acted upon, nothing can be achieved. Either there must be unanimity in the decision making, which is impractical in a complex world containing so many people, or there needs to be an authority to make decisions in a timely manner. Individuals should have autonomy and be free to make decisions for themselves, but there needs to be some degree of coordination for the common good.

While authorities do sometimes make errors, this is not a reason for there to be no authority. Practical reason calls for a cooperative life, and a governing power is necessary to administer justice and restore balance when someone commits a crime. There may be a need to persuade people, with threats or even force, to behave in a specific way if they deliberately resist authority and act against the common good. However, individual autonomy is the common good of practical reasonableness; therefore, a law should not dictate how one participates in the basic goods. It should allow fairness and justice so that everyone can participate freely in the goods.

AO1 activity 3

There are often conflicts between the rights of two parties, where it is impossible for the parties themselves to reach agreement. For example, in 2019 and beyond, there have been global protests against the handling of the Covid-19 pandemic by ruling authorities. There was a conflict between the rights of citizens to pursue their life plans without restrictions and the rights of members of society to be protected from a dangerous virus.

Look at a range of news stories to find more current examples of conflicting rights or life plans. How has a legal authority acted to resolve the conflicts?

Bernard Hoose's overview of the proportionalist debate

Bernard Hoose wrote *Proportionalism: the American debate and its European roots* in 1987; it gives an historical account of the proportionalist debate in America and Europe as it stood at the end of the 1980s. **Proportionalism** is not a distinct ethical theory. It is a modern development, that is debated within Catholicism, which emphasises certain aspects of Aquinas' Natural Law. How Proportionalism is understood varies significantly between scholars, but generally, proportionalists insist that proportionate reason is central to moral decision making. They claim that they are developing something that has always been part of the Catholic tradition, but which has been downplayed in the past in favour of other factors. Therefore, proportionalists are sometimes called **revisionists** because they suggest that Catholic understanding of Aquinas' Natural Law needs to be revised.

The roots of Proportionalism are found within Aquinas' principle of double effect, sometimes known as the law of **commensurate** or proportionate reason, but there is no real agreement between proportionalists about how it is to be applied. Therefore, the debate that Hoose was writing about is the debate among proportionalists, as well as between traditional Catholic approaches to Natural Law and the proportionalist understanding of Natural Law. It concerns a correct understanding of key vocabulary, how Thomas Aquinas is to be correctly understood, and how or when proportionate reason is to be correctly applied.

Key terms

Proportionalism: a twentieth-century development of Natural Law, centred around a debate about proportionate reason as identified by Aquinas in the principle of double effect

revisionists: another name for proportionalists, who are concerned with a revision of the traditional understanding of Natural Law

commensurate: measuring or weighing up in relation to something else

> *Over the centuries, proportionate reason has played a central role in a number of principles employed in Catholic moral theology, as, for example, the* principle of double effect, *the* **principle of the lesser of two evils**, *and, in more recent times, the* **principle of totality**. 99
>
> Bernard Hoose, *Proportionalism: the American debate and its European roots*

Key terms

principle of the lesser of two evils: a principle that allows a moral agent to choose the lesser evil of two evil options when there is no other choice available

principle of totality: the principle that parts are ordered for the good of the whole; e.g. organs are useful for the whole body, but have no moral significance outside of the body

licit: permissible or legal

The debate is said to have begun in Europe, with a young German student called Peter Knauer, who, in 1965, wrote an article concerning a revision of the interpretation of Aquinas' principle of double effect. Knauer argued that evil may be permitted as an aspect rather than an effect of an action, provided it was not the main purpose of the act and was justified by a proportionate reason. For example, sometimes to achieve good health in a patient, a doctor must cause harm by performing an operation. If the good health is the intended aspect of the act and the act is in proportion to the illness that the person is suffering, then such an act would not be considered evil, even though there is also an evil effect of cutting into someone. This means that evil can be part of the action rather than a separate, secondary effect.

In *Summa Theologica*, Aquinas uses the example of killing in self-defence to explain the principle of double effect. He points out that nothing hinders one act from having two effects, only one of which is intended. The act of self-defence can have two effects: it can save a life and it can kill an aggressor. The intention to save one's own life is not unlawful; the killing of the aggressor is an unintended and accidental result of saving one's own life, and may therefore be legal or '**licit**'. However, if a person acting in self-defence uses more than necessary violence, it will be unlawful: their defence is only lawful if they repel the force against them with moderation.

Synoptic link

Link to *Chapter 3: Deontological ethics: Aquinas' Natural Law*. The principle of double effect is key to understanding Proportionalism, therefore look back at how it fitted into Aquinas' Natural Law.

Although the principle of double effect has a long history in Catholic tradition, Knauer's paper was met with opposition by many. And in 1968 Pope Paul VI's encyclical, *Humanae Vitae*, emphasised a strict deontological understanding of Natural Law and absolutely rejected some acts, such as the use of artificial contraception. This led many Catholic scholars to question the extent to which proportionate reason should play a part in Catholic thinking and behaviour.

Opposition to Proportionalism comes from those who worry that, if it were adopted, there would be nothing to stop people from performing any action at all provided that it was in proportion to the purpose or goal of the action. Others argue that there are areas of human behaviour where a priest or bishop should be free to apply proportionate reason to support people in their moral decision making in difficult or new situations.

Hoose identifies three main areas of debate about Proportionalism:

1. the distinction between a good and a right act
2. the distinction between deontological and teleological ethics
3. the distinction between direct and indirect actions.

AO1 activity 4

In Season 2, Episode 7 of *The Good Place*, Tahani and Jason's flourishing relationship threatens the integrity of the Good Place as Janet (the mainframe that keeps the Good Place intact) is feeling jealous. Eleanor and Michael decide that, to keep the Good Place going, they must break up Tahani and Jason, but Chidi warns that only the principle of double effect can justify their actions. Try to identify the following:

- the two effects of breaking up Tahani and Jason
- Michael and Eleanor's primary intention
- any unintended side-effects of Michael and Eleanor's actions
- any other options available to Michael and Eleanor to save the Good Place and secure their own safety.

Is this an appropriate use of the principle of double effect?

Proportionalist maxim

One of the most important elements of Proportionalism is the calculation of proportion between all the goods and evils involved in an action. In *Summa Theologica*, Aquinas explains that when an action contains an accidental evil (as in killing in self-defence), the good achieved by the action must outweigh the evil. The action must be in proportion.

> *Wherefore if a man, in self-defence, uses more than necessary violence, it will be unlawful: whereas if he repel force with moderation his defence will be lawful, because … 'it is lawful to repel force by force, provided one does not exceed the limits of a blameless defence'.*
>
> Thomas Aquinas, *Summa Theologica*

Proportionate reasoning is a form of practical reasoning that is specific to the principle of double effect. It is at the heart of the 'maxim', or main principle, of the proportionalists: it is never right to go against a principle unless there is a proportionate reason to justify it.

Proportionalism accepts that moral laws are good and, in general, they should not be broken. However, there are times when the principle of double effect can be applied, not as an exception to the rule, but as a reasoned way of managing a conflict between laws. For instance, in Aquinas' example of killing in self-defence, not to defend oneself would violate a primary precept, yet to kill your attacker is a violation as well. While there can never be a good enough reason to justify deliberately performing an evil action, the moral agent can weigh up the various elements of an act when faced with a conflict (such as the rules, the act itself, the consequences, the intention, the moral virtue of the individual, the method, the value and **disvalue**, and so on), to establish proportionate reason for applying double effect. The purpose of this is not to consider performing an evil action for a greater good, but to justify what is right.

Proportionalists agree that the good achieved by an action must be equal to or greater than the unintended evil it produces, but they do not agree on one way to decide whether this threshold has been met in specific circumstances.

Key term

disvalue: lack of moral importance or worth; of negative value or worth

Distinction between a good act and a right act

An area of debate within proportionalist thinking arose between the terms 'good acts' and 'right acts'. The distinction between these two terms evolved gradually in the writings of proportionalists and, at first, the terms were used interchangeably, causing some debate. Following Aquinas and the Catholic Church, a good act is the concrete action that is performed in accordance with the intention of the person acting. Natural Law gives the guidance needed to discern which actions are good. The rightness or wrongness of an action deals with whether the action should take place or not, and makes a moral judgement. While a good action should be the right thing to do, proportionalists argue that it is not always.

Hoose quotes the proportionalist scholar Bruno Schüller, who gives the example of a doctor who develops a new treatment that will benefit many people, but who is motivated by business interests and accolade. The act of developing the treatment was right, but not good. It was morally right because of the beneficial consequences for so many people, but it was morally bad because of the doctor's selfish intentions.

> *Thus, his act is morally bad because it is performed from pure selfishness. At the same time, however, it is morally right because of its beneficial consequences.* **"**
>
> Bernard Hoose, *Proportionalism: the American debate and its European roots*

Schüller gives another example of a person who, out of *agape*, wants to help someone but accidentally harms them. Their act is clearly wrong; it is not right and should never have been done. However, it was good because it was done with the best of intentions and with a virtuous disposition. So, for a proportionalist, a morally good act is not necessarily morally right and vice versa. In contrast, the traditional Catholic position is that a good act is always a right act and there is no distinction made between the two.

Distinction between an evil moral act and pre-moral/ontic evil

Part of the proportionalist debate concerning the goodness or evilness of an act is the attempt to come to a common understanding of moral terms such as '**pre-moral**', 'moral' and '**ontic**' so that the value of an action can be assessed.

The Catholic Church views ontic evil as a physical rather than a moral evil. The natural evils that occur independently of the will or action of humanity; tidal waves, droughts, or the onset of a genetic illness are examples of ontic evils, as are pain and death. In contrast, the Catholic Church considers a pre-moral evil as related to the human being who is doing the acting. It is the inclination towards evil that is part of our natural tendency as a result of the fall. Selfishness and injustice are both examples of pre-moral evils.

However, proportionalists tend to combine these two terms on the basis that ontic evils are a result of the fall and are, therefore, part of the fallenness of human nature. They are part of existence in a fallen world.

> **Key terms**
>
> *agape:* (Greek) the 'selfless love' principle which is the foundation of Fletcher's Situation Ethics
>
> **pre-moral (or ontic) evil:** for proportionalists this is an unavoidable lack of perfection that is present in all human actions. Pre-moral/ontic evil includes natural disasters, which are a result of living in a fallen world, as well as the unintended evil that is part of any decision we make.

Proportionalists argue that we should keep the elimination of pre-moral/ontic evil as our primary intention but, since this is impossible, no moral norm can expect us to completely remove all evil. Therefore, recognising that pre-moral/ontic evil exists as part of nature, we may sometimes need to perform an action that contains pre-moral/ontic evil as the lesser evil in order to achieve good. It can never be the objective of our action but can be present within the action itself.

> All our concrete actions involve ontic evils. This is unavoidable given our temporal and spatial limitations, our living together with others in the same material world, and our common sin-filled situation. **"**
>
> Bernard Hoose, *Proportionalism: the American debate and its European roots*

Pre-moral/ontic evil is not the same as moral evil or 'immorality'. For example, the act of using a blade to cut someone's body contains an element of pre-moral/ontic evil, but it does not make up the whole action. For it to become a **moral evil act**, the person's intention must be considered. If, for example, the cutting is done by a surgeon with the intention of eliminating disease, then the action is not morally evil. If it is done with the objective of killing a person out of anger, then it is morally evil (a sin). Yet there is more even than this to a moral evil action. If the action was performed unnecessarily or disproportionately by that surgeon, then it might still be considered wrong. Operating on a person who could be cured by medication and bedrest may be disproportionate and consequently immoral.

A hybrid of Natural Law: a deontological and a teleological ethic

Natural Law is usually viewed as a deontological ethical theory, and Proportionalism, being an interpretation or understanding of Natural Law, does indeed focus on the duty and rules that govern how a person 'ought' to behave. Proportionalists recognise the intrinsic value of the primary precepts and the virtues of Natural Law, as described in scripture. Proportionalism states that it is never right to go against a principle, so proportionalists accept that the most value is usually gained by obedience to Natural Law.

> There is no attempt here to justify the unjustifiable. **"**
>
> Bernard Hoose, 'Natural Law; Situation Ethics – Is There Another Way Forward?'

However, proportionalists recognise that Aquinas' Natural Law is not solely deontological, and has teleological elements to it. They claim that their understanding of Natural Law is truer than Aquinas' purely deontological understanding. Teleological ethical theories generally hold that the rightness or wrongness of an action is determined by the goal or aim of the act in producing certain types of consequences. Proportionalists recognise that morally relevant circumstances should be considered, and so they weigh up all the goods and evils involved in the situation. Therefore, in exceptional circumstances, where there is a conflict between precepts or goods and

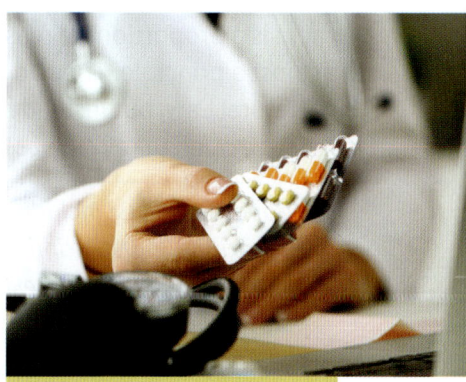

In Schüller's example, developing a new treatment for sickness is right, but it is only good if the doctor's intention is to help people.

Key term

moral evil act: an act that is defined as bad because it breaks a religious rule and is therefore immoral; includes evil intent as part of the action

AO1 activity 5

Look at each of the following acts and try to identify pre-moral/ontic evils that are part of the act. The first one has been done for you:

a) a surgeon performing an operation: damage or mutilation of a limb or organ
b) using physical force against another person:
c) punishing a criminal offender:
d) travelling to live in a foreign country:

there is a proportionate reason that could justify it, it could be right to go against a principle. They do not uphold an unchanging and absolute version of Natural Law, but instead recognise that our understanding develops and must be open to revision as our knowledge increases.

> *[Proportionalists] include such items as dignity values, institutional obligations, injustice inflicted, and the meaning of an action. Most of the time, they accept established moral norms are sufficient to guide action. In some 'cases of conflict', however, difficulties arise.* **99**
>
> Bernard Hoose, 'Natural Law; Situation Ethics – Is There Another Way Forward?'

In his 1993 encyclical, *Veritatis Splendor*, Pope John Paul II made it clear that consideration of things like consequences and intentions is insufficient for judging the moral quality of a concrete choice, and cannot alter the inherent goodness or evilness of an action.

> *Such theories however are not faithful to the Church's teaching, when they believe they can justify, as morally good, deliberate choices of kinds of behaviour contrary to the commandments of the divine and Natural Law. These theories cannot claim to be grounded in the Catholic moral tradition.* **99**
>
> Pope John Paul II, *Veritatis Splendor*

Hoose explains that proportionalists describe themselves as teleological. However, while proportionalists argue that Natural Law has always been a teleological theory, Hoose points out that there has been debate among proportionalists about what this actually means. Some proportionalist scholars have been unhappy being labelled 'consequentialists' because they argue that they consider more than just consequences to determine the rightness or wrongness of an action; they also consider values and obligations, and the intrinsic goodness of the act itself.

> *It may seem to some that 'consequence' is not a fitting label for everything that is contained in the proportionalist 'calculation'.* **99**
>
> Bernard Hoose, *Proportionalism: the American debate and its European roots*

The distinction between direct and indirect actions

Another area of debate that Hoose identifies is the distinction between **direct** and **indirect actions**. Hoose feels that this distinction is crucial to an understanding of the principle of double effect, and thus the debate about Proportionalism, but says that the distinction is not always clear.

The debate concerns how we understand direct actions and indirect actions, and whether or not they are relevant at all. An indirect action is understood, by some, to be an accidental result of a good direct action. For others, like Knauer, it is understood to be one of two immediate aspects of an action, one of which was intended and is thus 'direct', and the other of which is merely tolerated and is thus 'indirect'; the indirect action is a known by-product, not an accident. Knauer

Key terms

direct action: the immediate action that was intentionally performed

indirect action: understood differently by different thinkers, as an accidental effect of an action or as an immediate but unintended, known aspect or by-product of an act

focuses upon the intention of the moral agent rather than just their physical actions and the results of those actions. It then becomes necessary to weigh up whether the evil that is produced is in proportion to the good that is produced.

For example, the traditional understanding of Natural Law means that carrying out an abortion with the intention to abort is always evil (a sin). However, if a person's life is in danger because of an ectopic pregnancy, double effect allows a direct action to save their life (removing the compromised fallopian tube) and an indirect action (ending the life of the foetus). If the indirect action is accidental, the moral agents involved are not morally responsible for it. However, proportionalists point out that this makes no sense because the doctor knows that they will be ending the life of the foetus. The abortion is part of the action; it is not accidental but an accepted by-product of the action.

Proportionalists then go further and say that removing the foetus while keeping the fallopian tube intact is licit because even though evil is an aspect of the act, and performed directly, when one weighs up the good and the evil, there is proportionately more good achieved. However, since this involves a direct action to remove a foetus, traditional Catholic thinkers object. Proportionalists argue that the directness of the act does not matter; what matters is that more value is achieved.

Proportionality based on agape

Proportionality is based upon *agape*, but the proportionalist approach to *agape* should not be confused with Situation Ethics. Situation Ethics arose within the Protestant tradition, and it clearly rejects legalism and moral absolutes. It employs only one over-riding principle and while, like Proportionalism, it does not reject law or rules outright, it will override law if love demands it.

> *We need much more from an ethical theory than 'love will tell you what to do in the situation.'* **"**
>
> Bernard Hoose, 'Natural Law; Situation Ethics – Is There Another Way Forward?'

In contrast, Proportionalism arose from within the Catholic tradition, and is in no way a rejection of Natural Law.

Agape is an ancient Greek word that is used in scripture to mean charity or selfless action. It is central to all Christian teaching about morality, and is therefore intrinsic to Natural Law. For Aquinas, it is the most important theological virtue. It is also the basis of proportionate moral decision making. Love should motivate all morally good actions; it is not enough on its own to make an action good, but it is an essential ingredient. A loving act is not automatically right; if it brings about more disvalue than value then it is wrong. However, for the proportionalists, love for God and God's laws should be central to moral decision making.

Proportionalists recognise that deontological rules are an important part of Natural Law, but they are not all of it. There are circumstances in which it is necessary for the moral agent to consider the facts of a situation and weigh

Synoptic link

Link to *Chapter 5: Teleological ethics: Situation Ethics*. For Fletcher, the boss principle of *agape* is the only principle Christians should apply when making moral decisions.

AO1 activity 6

When wrestling with a large and difficult topic, it helps to use pictures and doodles to make the ideas memorable. Create a large A3 revision poster that defines each of the key terms for Proportionalism, and shows the relationships between them. Include a short quotation and a picture for each key term. You can doodle your own or use a picture that you have copied and pasted into place.

up the value and the disvalue that will be produced by an action. Love is an important consideration in this weighing up. It is, however, important to be aware that love alone can be mistaken. Hoose gives the example of burning heretics during the Crusades. This was an action done out of true love for God and God's law, and yet it was a horrific mistake. We might turn to the actions of Christians today and sometimes see the same thing: a burning passion for God and God's law that drives people to act in terrible ways. Love on its own is not enough to justify any action, and this is where Proportionalism differs from Situation Ethics.

Finnis' Natural Law and Proportionalism: application of the theory

The main purpose of this section of the specification is to show how Finnis' Natural Law and Proportionalism can be put into practice in real ethical situations. There is no need for an in-depth study of immigration or capital punishment and the arguments for and against each of them, but there is a need for you to understand some of the issues raised by immigration and capital punishment before looking at how Finnis' Natural Law and Proportionalism apply to them.

Immigration: what is the debate?

Immigration is a complex subject, and different countries have different immigration laws and define 'immigrants' differently. For our purposes, **immigration** involves the movement of people to live, usually permanently, in countries they were not born in. People move to another country for a wide range of reasons. Sometimes they are escaping war or persecution as an **asylum seeker** or **refugee**. Sometimes they are seeking a better quality of life as an **economic migrant**. Many people who migrate want to bring their families with them or settle near friends or other people with a similar background.

Countries usually project a positive or a negative message about immigration. After the Second World War, many countries, like the UK, welcomed immigrants, who played a central role in helping to rebuild society by working in factories and in healthcare. In contrast, many countries today are concerned about the impact of large numbers of people from overseas on demand for housing, employment, and community resources such as schools and hospitals. Some are also concerned about the social effects of immigration, as communities struggle to come to a common understanding of what it means to be a citizen and to assimilate people from different cultures. Therefore, the immigration debate is about whether or not to limit the number of people who wish to migrate, and if so, how to do it in an ethical way.

What does Finnis say about immigration?

Finnis' Natural Law holds that all people have the right to participate in any or all of the basic goods, without exception. If a person is fleeing

> ### Key terms
>
> **immigration:** the act of migrating to another country, usually for permanent residence
>
> **asylum seeker:** someone who crosses an international border to find safety from war or persecution; they are referred to as a refugee once their claim for asylum, for safety, has been accepted
>
> **refugee:** someone who crosses an international border to find safety from war or persecution; a refugee is an asylum seeker who has had their claim for asylum, for safety, accepted
>
> **economic migrant:** sometimes referred to as a migrant worker; someone who chooses to live in another country to improve their standard of living

for their life, immigrating to a country by seeking asylum is, of course, a good thing because all people must be allowed to participate in the good of life. However, this is not the only good that should be upheld. It is a requirement of practical reason that we do not arbitrarily prioritise one good over another, and so Natural Law considers the good of knowledge or the exercise of practical reasonableness to be as important as the good of life. There is, therefore, nothing inherently wrong in migration for economic reasons if moving enables a person to participate in these goods where previously they could not, and if, according to the requirements of practical reason, it does not damage the ability of others to participate in the goods.

Two other requirements of practical reason are that we should have a life plan to ensure that we can participate in the goods, and we should be detached to prevent unreasonable obsession over a project. Where immigration enables a person to pursue projects that allow them to participate in goods such as life, knowledge and friendship, then it is a positive thing. However, the requirement of detachment suggests that an individual should not obsessively pursue the project of immigration if it means risking their life on the journey and if they have no certainty about their ability to participate in the goods when they reach their destination. Yet, asylum seekers leave their homes to seek a new life because they are desperate. It may be practically reasonable to commit to the project of immigration in this situation, when there is a greater risk to life by staying put.

Finnis has, controversially, spoken out against uncontrolled immigration in the past because he feels that, over prolonged periods, it poses a great risk to the common good. **Uncontrolled immigration** is unrestricted movement of people into a country, whereas **controlled immigration** allows movement to take place but only under specific circumstances. Finnis warns that without appropriate legislation to control immigration, the long-term effect on a country would be the complete eradication of their national identity at the expense of their own freedom and community. He is concerned about the potential incompatibility of the ideals and ambitions of large groups of immigrants and those already living in the country.

> ## Key terms
>
> **uncontrolled immigration:** when there are no restrictions on the number of people who can immigrate to a country
>
> **controlled immigration:** where laws limit the number of people who can immigrate to a country, or restrict the circumstances in which immigration can take place

> *[No laws to control immigration] marks out for them a path towards, first the loss of national self-determination; and then their own replacement, as a people, by other people, more or less regardless of the incomers' compatibility of psychology, culture, relation or political ideas and ambitions, or the worth or viciousness of those ideas and ambitions*
>
> John Finnis, 'H.L.A. Hart: A Twentieth-Century Oxford Political Philosopher'

Finnis feels that modern society has become so obsessed with our individual freedom to pursue any project we please that it has taken the existence of our society for granted. When Europeans colonised countries such as the USA and Australia, wealthy white people forced their will and culture upon indigenous people at the expense of their cultural identity. Finnis seems concerned that uncontrolled immigration, over a prolonged period, will lead to a kind of 'reverse colonisation', where what is valuable within Western culture is eradicated or supressed by the culture and traditions of others. If this happened, it could be argued that the common good would be damaged if it was impossible for people to participate in all the benefits of the current society as a direct result.

Controlled immigration requires people to apply for residency or claim asylum before they settle in a country. Where the common good is unaffected, or even enhanced, by the arrival of a person from overseas, there is no reason to prevent that individual pursuing their life plan. However, many argue that immigration cannot be managed with decisions made by individuals, because there are too many people's life plans to coordinate. Therefore it is vital that there is a legitimate authority that sets and enforces rules to ensure that no one experiences a restriction of their life plan as a direct result of immigration. These rules, they argue, are essential if a society is to sustain itself.

If we support the idea that immigration is morally acceptable when it is controlled, then the next question we must ask is, 'How do we control it according to practical reason?'. Following the Golden Rule, any controls must not give preferential treatment to one person over another; they should treat everyone equally. Controls must also avoid prioritising one good over another because all of the goods are good. There are several ways in which countries have attempted to control immigration.

Some countries have a points system, which weighs the value that a potential immigrant will bring to a community. So, if someone has a skill that is needed or is well educated, and if the authorities can be sure they will not be a drain on the welfare system, then their immigration application is more likely to succeed. However, while this approach might benefit the common good, it may be viewed as Utilitarianism rather than Natural Law. We are arbitrarily prioritising the skilled or well-educated life over lives that have not had the same opportunities.

> **Synoptic link**
>
> Link to *Chapter 6: Teleological ethics: Utilitarianism*. Look at the principles of Utilitarianism. How is this approach different from Natural Law?

Some countries consider the human rights of the people involved. Refusing an immigration application may interfere with a person's right to family life or their right to practise their religion. If you cannot immigrate to live near, or with, your loved ones, you may not be able to participate in the seven basic goods to the same extent as those who live close to, or with, their loved ones. Some countries have rules that prevent people from practising their religion, pursuing education, and even playing. These rules are a threat to the goods and so allowing people living under such rules to migrate to another country enables them to participate in the goods.

However, if we only allow immigration for humanitarian reasons and restrict immigration by economic migrants, we inhibit people's freedom to choose their own coherent plan of life. We also inhibit the pursuance of the common good and disregard what people may bring to a community in terms of friendship, play, and knowledge.

The Catholic Church, based upon Natural Law, teaches that migrants should be treated as brothers and sisters, and shown love. In *Fratelli Tutti*, in 2020,

Pope Francis uses the language of what has become known as 'New Natural Law theory' to argue for the value of friendship and the common good with regard to immigration and the requirement for Christians to be neighbours to all migrants.

> *If every human being possesses an inalienable dignity, if all people are my brothers and sisters, and if the world truly belongs to everyone, then it matters little whether my neighbour was born in my country or elsewhere.*
>
> Pope Francis, *Fratelli Tutti*

Pope Francis says that political discourse no longer concerns itself with healthy debates about long-term plans to improve people's lives and advance the common good. Instead, politicians exploit people's fears for the sake of popularity, the result being a spread in extremism and suspicion, and polarisation. He calls for people to expand their circle of friends to reach others, especially those in need or those who are ignored, in a way that is not restricted by borders or nationality. There is, therefore, no room in Natural Law for discrimination against immigrants.

The Catholic Church teaches that on no account should people be treated poorly when they move to a new country. They point out that migration was a familiar phenomenon in the scriptures and specifically in the life of Christ, and refer to Christ's appeal to treat strangers with compassion in the gospel of Matthew.

What does Proportionalism say about immigration?

It is important to remember that Proportionalism is an interpretation of Natural Law, and so it is a Christian ethic. Therefore, the application of Proportionalism to the issue of immigration should recognise that the teaching of Natural Law must be followed unless there is a conflict between goods or precepts that require the application of the principle of double effect. Immigration, in general, does not cause any such conflict and so is not an issue for proportionate reason to determine.

As we have seen, Natural Law has nothing within it that explicitly forbids immigration. On the contrary, Christian teaching strongly encourages people to treat immigrants with compassion and kindness, and to remember their entitlement to the same human rights and dignity as any other human being.

> *When a foreigner resides among you in your land, do not mistreat them. The foreigner residing among you must be treated as your native-born. Love them as yourself, for you were foreigners in Egypt. I am the Lord your God.*
>
> Leviticus 19:33–34, *Holy Bible (NIV)*

The Catechism of the Catholic Church teaches that people have the right to migrate and it says that prosperous nations must welcome immigrants, but it also says that countries have the right to ensure that there are rules in place to protect the welfare of everyone concerned.

> *The more prosperous nations are obliged, to the extent they are able, to welcome the foreigner in search of the security and the means of livelihood which he cannot find in his country of origin. … Political authorities, for the sake of the common good for which they are responsible, may make the exercise of the right to immigrate subject to various juridical conditions*
>
> *Catechism of the Catholic Church, 2nd edition, paragraph 2241*

In general, then, proportionalists, like any other Catholic, are taught to accept the good of immigration and that there is no difficulty or conflict of principles involved in welcoming an immigrant into a country. In fact, the Christian virtue of love says that it is morally good to welcome and support anyone in need.

Proportionalism has developed since the 1980s, when Hoose wrote his book. Some scholars now feel it is important to balance values to arrive at the right moral action rather than simply apply the principle of double effect. For example, Garth Hallett, author of the 1995 book *Greater Good: The Case for Proportionalism*, argues that we must weigh the pre-moral/ontic good and evil inherent in an action against its moral value, and accept it as a right action only if pre-moral/ontic evil has been minimised as much as possible and it delivers more value than the alternatives. He calls this **value maximisation**. When difficulties arise, such as those that might occur if immigration is uncontrolled, proportionalists like Hallett could argue that it is in line with Catholic tradition to maximise value by applying proportionate reason in managing those difficulties.

> **Key term**
>
> **value maximisation:** an approach to Proportionalism proposed by Hallett that involves balancing the moral values in any action to maximise value as fully or nearly as fully as any alternative action

> *If Christian moral reasoning is to be both consistent and true to its past, it must be based on the balance of values; value maximisation must be its logic and its law.*
>
> *Garth Hallett, Greater Good: The Case for Proportionalism*

For example, there is some inevitable pre-moral/ontic evil when resources are shared between large numbers of people and citizens attempt to pursue their own life plans alongside many others who may have different life plans. This means that whatever action we take regarding immigration will inevitably include some pre-moral/ontic evil. However, it is the role of the moral agent to do what they can to minimise this disvalue and maximise the value. Therefore, the value gained by allowing people to move to live in other countries, pursue their life plans, contribute to new communities, obey scripture by welcoming newcomers, show love, and embrace new opportunities, among other things, must be balanced against the disvalue of having to share resources and place some limitations upon one's own life plan.

Immigration is a very emotive topic that can involve significant humanitarian concerns.

Even if it is morally good to accept all immigrants, it can be morally right to establish rules to cap the number of people who can immigrate to limit the pressure on community services and resources. It can also be morally right to pass laws that do not place unnecessary restrictions on people but do govern behaviour so that both non-immigrants and immigrants are clear about how they should treat each other.

However, it would not be acceptable to proportionalists to prevent all immigration for the sake of the common good. While the direct intention might be to preserve one's own society, this is a utilitarian approach to moral decision making that sacrifices the individual for the greater good, and places too much emphasis on consequences alone. This is inconsistent with a Christian ethic of love and compassion, and does not work to minimise pre-moral/ontic evil. It maximises value to welcome in anyone who is in dire need, including the poor and those whose lives are at risk. There is more value because more justice, love, and compassion are achieved by welcoming others and embracing friendship than are achieved by rejecting others to protect resources. This is potentially true of all immigrants, but the priority for the Christian is to protect those who are most in need because that is what scripture directs them to do. Therefore proportionalists would argue that value is maximised by welcoming the poor and the oppressed first.

> *Then the King will say to those on his right, 'Come, you who are* **"** *blessed by my Father; take your inheritance, the kingdom prepared for you since the creation of the world. For I was hungry and you gave me something to eat, I was thirsty and you gave me something to drink, I was a stranger and you invited me in, I needed clothes and you clothed me, I was sick and you looked after me, I was in prison and you came to visit me'.*
>
> Matthew 25:34–36, *Holy Bible (NIV)*

AO1 activity 7

Go through this application section of the chapter and make a list of all the occasions when a key feature of Finnis' Natural Law or Proportionalism is referred to.

Capital punishment: what is the debate?

Capital punishment is the legally authorised killing of someone as a punishment for a serious crime, such as murder or treason. There are many aims of punishment, including:

- justice, to put right a wrong and restore balance to society
- retribution, to exact revenge or repayment for a wrong committed
- deterrence, to prevent or dissuade others from committing the crime
- reformation, to rehabilitate a person so that they change their ways
- protection, to keep society safe from crime and to keep order in society.

Capital punishment cannot achieve all of these aims. For instance, while it can protect society, it cannot reform people. It also appears to violate the principle that all human life is sacred.

There are a great many issues to consider when weighing up the rights and wrongs of capital punishment, including the goods or rights of the person sentenced to death and the goods or rights of the victims and their families, the intentions and jurisdiction of the authorities, and the risk that the wrong person might be killed.

Key term

capital punishment: the legally authorised killing of someone as a punishment for a crime

What does Finnis say about capital punishment?

A requirement of practical reason is to foster the common good. The common good is the ability for everyone within a community to participate in any or all of the basic human goods. This requires a great deal of coordination by an authority, to allow people the freedom to pursue their life plans, and to manage conflict when it occurs. It makes sense that, when a member of society fails to adhere to the laws that coordinate the whole, there needs to be a system to restore the common good.

Traditionally the Catholic Church, in its observance of Natural Law, has followed Aquinas and seen capital punishment as licit. Only a lawful, God-given authority may administer the death penalty in its role as guardian of the common good and when the welfare of the community is seriously threatened by the sinfulness of one of its members. A private person may never take the life of an individual for any reason. Aquinas appeals to scripture to justify this idea.

> *And if your right hand causes you to stumble, cut it off and throw it away. It is better for you to lose one part of your body than for your whole body to go into hell.*
>
> Matthew 5:30, *Holy Bible (NIV)*

So, if an individual seriously endangers the common good, they should be killed because of the damage they can do to the whole if they continue to live.

Finnis finds this idea frightening, since there is nothing in this reasoning to prevent an innocent person from being killed to save the state, in much the same way that one might cut off a healthy hand, if it is trapped, to save oneself from drowning in a river or burning in a house fire.

> *This embarrassingly flawed argument … fails to indicate why it would not also justify the killing of innocent citizens with intent that putting them to death save the state from, say, terrorists who demand such sacrifices, as one might amputate a healthy hand to save oneself from fire or water*
>
> John Finnis, 'The Church could teach that capital punishment is inherently wrong'

E.C. Brugger, a student of Finnis and a prominent Natural Law writer, points out that the common good cannot be compared to the body as Aquinas has suggested. Members of a community are all distinct individuals in their own right, whereas hands and eyes are not. The hands and eyes serve the whole body, while the community is set up to serve the individuals within it.

When a member of society fails to adhere to the laws established to coordinate multiple life plans, there must be a response that restores the imbalance or unfairness caused by the crime. For example, a person who has stolen something must return the stolen goods, and any other advantage gained by the theft must be set right. In the case of murder, this is more challenging. A life can never be restored, and the killing of the murderer, while seemingly in proportion to the crime, will both damage the basic good of life and prevent the murderer from pursuing any life plan. Yet justice must be done, and this must be proportionate to the crime committed. It is in the best interest of the common good to remove an unrepentant criminal from society to prevent further crime, but capital punishment is not the only way to do this.

No arbitrary preference among persons is the Golden Rule: we should treat others as we would like to be treated. No one should be made to live their life purely for the benefit of others (or, in the case of capital punishment, be made to die purely for the benefit of others). This is a complete rejection of Consequentialism or Utilitarianism, and it means that it is unacceptable for an authority to kill a person through capital punishment for the benefit of society. Using another person for our own ends cannot be justified under Finnis' development of Natural Law. However, it is the role of the law and of authority to ensure that laws are clear and people are able to follow them. So, the criminal who commits a crime, in the full knowledge of the law and of the consequences of their act, cannot be allowed to carry on freely pursuing their life plan without taking responsibility for what they have done. The law must uphold and maintain the common good, therefore allowing the criminal to go unpunished is also unacceptable.

Finnis does not deny that death meets the criteria for retribution for some grave crimes. Some have argued that Aquinas' reasoning can be used to allow justice to be done and order in society to be restored through the foreseen, but directly unintended, death of the criminal. However, Finnis denies that capital punishment can ever be used to restore justice without an intention to kill, which is incompatible with God's authority and incompatible with the absolute status of the basic human values. Capital punishment is retroactive and intended as a punishment; it cannot be defended as an instinctive reaction to a threat. It seeks to restore balance and, thus, killing is its intention. Therefore, Finnis finds capital punishment unacceptable.

> *Though not disproportionate or too severe, death is not a penalty that human beings can inflict without forming an intention precisely to terminate life—to replace it with death—an intention incompatible with God's lordship over life and death.*
>
> John Finnis, 'The Church could teach that capital punishment is inherently wrong'

Some have argued that the doctrine of the Catholic Church is based on scripture and the traditions established by the early Church Fathers, and is thus inviolable. Therefore, if scripture and the Church Fathers taught that capital punishment is an acceptable way to deal with criminals, that cannot change. However, Finnis points to other Church teachings which, while correct, have required clarification over the years. In a debate with E.C. Feser, Finnis argued that the Catholic Church teaches that some people must be deprived of their freedom when they have committed a crime, but in the past, made no distinction between criminals and enslaved peoples. The doctrine was later reinterpreted to support the abolition of the enslavement of people. And if doctrine can be reinterpreted in this case, it could also be reinterpreted in the case of capital punishment.

Aquinas argued that, like animals, a serious offender lacks human dignity. The criminal has chosen to fall away from the human dignity given by God and so, like an animal, can be killed for the benefit of humanity. However, Finnis holds that while it might be true that a criminal forfeits certain rights when they commit a crime, the requirement of practical reason asks that we not reject any of the goods or reject the right of anyone to participate in them. Pope John Paul II had said that not even a murderer loses his personal dignity, and Brugger argues that it is impossible for a rational creature to lose their humanity.

> *Not even a murderer loses his personal dignity, and God himself pledges to guarantee this.* **99**
>
> Pope John Paul II, *Evangelium Vitae*

The Catechism of the Catholic Church previously said:

> *The traditional teaching of the Church does not exclude recourse to the death penalty.* **99**
>
> *Catechism of the Catholic Church*, 1st edition, paragraph 2267

However, in 2018, Pope Francis approved a new version of this paragraph, which declared the death penalty inadmissible. It now reads:

> *The death penalty is inadmissible because it is an attack on the inviolability and dignity of the person.* **99**
>
> *Catechism of the Catholic Church*, 2nd edition, paragraph 2267

This decree produced great excitement in the media because it was perceived that the Catholic Church had changed its mind. However, Finnis argues that this so-called 'development of doctrine' is simply emphasising a teaching that was already established: a person does not lose their dignity even after serious criminal acts, and more effective systems of detention have been developed to protect the common good that, unlike capital punishment, do not prevent those who have committed crimes from seeking forgiveness.

What does Proportionalism say about capital punishment?

A difficulty with the application of Proportionalism to practical ethical issues is that there is no consensus among those who call themselves proportionalists about how proportionate reason is to be applied. Proportionalism is an ethical norm rather than an ethical theory. It allows a Catholic to interpret Aquinas' Natural Law differently from the way it is traditionally taught by the Catholic Church. Aquinas taught that if the health of society demands removal of the sinner, then capital punishment is licit.

> *Therefore if a man be dangerous and infectious to the community, on account of some sin, it is praiseworthy and advantageous that he be killed in order to safeguard the common good, since 'a little leaven corrupteth the whole lump' (1 Corinthians 5:6).* **99**
>
> Thomas Aquinas, *Summa Theologica*

A more fundamental difficulty with the application of Proportionalism to capital punishment than the lack of consensus is the emphasis by many proportionalists on Aquinas' principle of double effect. This means that, in the majority of cases, the law is to be followed, and only when precepts conflict should proportionate reason step in and weigh up the values and disvalues of an action. In the case of capital punishment, there is no conflict of precepts. Capital punishment is not an indirect action, an accident, or a by-product of some other act. It is the direct action of killing a 'sinner' and, therefore, it is a moral issue about which the law should be consulted. As we have seen, the Catholic Church teaches that capital punishment is inadmissible, that to kill a criminal is a violation of the good of life and, therefore, a proportionalist would object to the use of capital punishment.

Punishment in general, according to Hoose, brings about pre-moral/ontic evil since it involves inflicting suffering for the purpose of reducing crime.

> *Clearly, punishment is a non-moral (or premoral) evil inasmuch as it consists in inflicting suffering on other human beings.*
>
> Bernard Hoose, 'The Punishment of Criminals'

Hoose goes on to argue that capital punishment is never acceptable on the basis that it cannot achieve the usual aims of punishment. In weighing up the value produced by capital punishment against its disvalue, studies show that it does not tend to deter offenders and that, in countries where capital punishment is in force, there seems to be a brutalising effect that causes higher rates of violent crime than in countries without the death penalty. As retribution it is insufficient, because there is no objective way to accurately make a punishment fit a crime and it does not consider the situation that made someone commit the crime in the first place. And it cannot enable reform because it is final and removes the opportunity for repentance in the future. However, Hoose is openly using utilitarian arguments, which concentrate on consequences, rather than proportionalist concepts to argue against capital punishment, because it does not involve a conflict of precepts.

Hallett adds that if something is clearly a sin, it has a significant disvalue, and it may not be done no matter the positive consequences. Hoose writes that the proportionalist scholar, Joseph Selling, argues that the principle of double effect has frequently been applied to cases beyond its range. Sometimes it is simply not appropriate. Selling argues that it should only be applied to cases where a direct act of good may also result in an indirect evil. It cannot be applied to justify a direct act of evil. Capital punishment is always a direct intent to kill, and thus double effect is not applicable.

> *One must consider why double effect is not applied to cases of capital punishment, imprisonment, disciplining children or civil or ecclesiastical censures, etc., and why it encounters so much difficulty when forced upon cases outside its competence, such as that of mutilation.*
>
> Joseph A. Selling, 'The Problem of Reinterpreting the Principle of Double Effect'

Some people might argue that capital punishment is a means to protect society, in some extreme cases, from those who are determined to damage or destroy it. Therefore, the intended action is to protect society, and the by-product is the killing of the criminal. Proportionalists argue that Natural Law says this is wrong. To use capital punishment for the purpose of protecting society is not an appropriate use of double effect because the killing would always be directly intended. In addition, it would be treating a person as an object rather than as a being who is intrinsically valuable. In Aquinas' example of self-defence, the killing of an aggressor is a spontaneous response to a threat; killing a criminal is planned and direct. Furthermore, protecting society is not present in the act of execution itself. It is simply a hoped-for consequence of the performance of an evil, and doing evil in the hope that good may come of it is condemned in Romans 3:8.

But would proportionalists allow the direct performance of a pre-moral/ontic evil such as killing, as long as the value it achieved outweighed that evil as a result? According to the proportionalist scholar Richard McCormick, the distinction between direct actions and indirect actions is not necessarily relevant in a discussion of capital punishment. He argues that proportionate reason requires three things according to the Catholic tradition:

Capital punishment is not the only way to ensure that society is protected from criminal activity.

1. The good that is at risk must be at least equal to the evil that would be performed in the act.
2. There is no less harmful way of protecting the good in the present moment.
3. The action must be performed to protect the good, and must not undermine that good in the future.

The pre-moral/ontic evil of human suffering brought about by the act of killing another person is such a significant disvalue that it seems hard to see how there could ever be enough value in the act to outweigh the disvalue. Especially when, in the case of capital punishment as a means of protecting society, deterring further crime and exacting justice, it can easily be concluded that there are other, less harmful ways of achieving these aims, including life imprisonment and intensive rehabilitation. It can also be argued that capital punishment undermines the good of society. The state is designed to protect the individuals living within it, and yet this protection is undermined when it is withdrawn under certain conditions.

AO1 activity 8

Make a revision chart with two columns: Finnis' Natural Law and Proportionalism. In the chart, list the main arguments that each approach gives for rejecting capital punishment as an appropriate method of dealing with criminals.

This section of the chapter will enhance your ability to **analyse** and **evaluate** the topic and help you develop your AO2 skills. For each question, think about the different positions you might take, and decide which you find most persuasive and why. It is not enough to memorise a list of 'for and against' points; you need to develop an argument.

Is Finnis' Natural Law acceptable in contemporary society?

The phrase 'contemporary society' refers to the way people live and work together in the modern age. Whether Finnis' Natural Law is acceptable to people today is dependent upon how well it helps us address modern concerns. These might include, but are not restricted to, issues like abortion, immigration, medicine, and the use of technology.

The view that Finnis' Natural Law is acceptable in contemporary society

Russell Hittinger, a critic of Finnis' Natural Law, acknowledges that Finnis and other more modern Natural Law theorists have revived interest in Natural Law and helped to make it more relevant to modern society. It is discussed in secular circles and is of relevance to modern debates about law, politics, and morality outside the realms of the Catholic Church.

Finnis' Natural Law upholds and promotes an understanding of fundamental human rights as part of the common good and the requirements of justice. This means that there are some absolute human rights, such as the right to life, that cannot be challenged for any reason, even if it would somehow have a positive consequence for the common good. This is compatible with modern society and consistent with the Universal Declaration of Human Rights that protects specific human rights.

Finnis' emphasis on the Nine Requirements of Practical Reason as the 'method' of Natural Law could be appealing to members of modern society. There is no emphasis on revelation, divine commands, or faith in the God of classical theism as the source of laws, things which are increasingly less attractive to a society that is becoming more secular. Instead, the emphasis is on reason based upon seven basic human goods that resonate with most people, and the theory provides a clear set of guidelines that have the flexibility of a teleological theory but the certainty of a deontological theory.

Finnis' seven basic human goods are self-evidently good in encouraging human flourishing for all people in all societies. This means that all people, ancient or modern, can know that these are good, not based upon some kind of non-intellectual intuition or on physical evidence or proof, but upon the self-evident intrinsic nature of the goods themselves.

The view that Finnis' Natural Law is not acceptable in contemporary society

J. Crowe points out that Finnis' Natural Law does not allow animals to have any natural rights, which is unattractive to many in contemporary society. This is because, according to Finnis, animals lack the rational capacity to pursue the basic goods. This is not surprising given that Natural Law is based upon human nature. However, there is no room for the idea that animals can pursue their own basic goods through intuition and should have their rights to do so protected. Finnis makes a sharp distinction between humans and other animals that may be unwarranted, and restricts rights to those who can rationally organise their actions to pursue the basic goods.

Crowe goes on to argue that Finnis has attempted to structure his Natural Law to deliberately exclude same-sex partnerships. Finnis has always been clear in his disapproval of same-sex relationships, but there seems to be nothing in his development of Natural Law that makes this approach necessary until he attempts to add an eighth basic good. Adding 'marital good' to his basic goods means that a basic good requires sexual intercourse to occur only between a husband and wife. However, this seems like a rather random, *ad hoc* addition. All the other goods are basic and self-evident. This 'good' is surely already covered by play, friendship, life, and religion. Without it, there is no reason why same-sex relationships cannot contribute to the basic goods.

Finnis' definition of the 'common good' lacks clarity, especially when it comes to how far community extends. This is important when it comes to modern questions about politics, immigration, and technology. Finnis argues that everyone has a duty to share in bringing about the common good for their community. But, in a contemporary society that is linked together with modern methods of communication and travel, we must question whether our responsibilities lie with our immediate physical communities alone, or whether they extend the local or national to the global community. If they do, then the laws of one country must not undermine global rules, and a country's laws about immigration, for example, cannot be in the interest of one country alone.

Valerie Kerruish argues that Finnis' account of Natural Law in *Natural Law and Natural Rights* is very abstract and sterile in its approach to ethical theory. This means that it is difficult to understand how it relates to real people who are grappling with real ethical problems in a complex world. All too often, there will be conflicts between goods, and it is very challenging for a person deep in a moral problem to remain detached enough to consider all seven of the basic goods and the Nine Requirements of Practical Reason.

AO2 activity 1

Copy the following table by selecting and summarising the points from the analysis above that you find most persuasive. Then, fill in the last row of the table, giving at least one reason why you think Finnis' Natural Law does or does not achieve the goal of being useful in contemporary society.

Goal: Finnis' Natural Law is useful for people in contemporary society	
Finnis' Natural Law achieves the goal	**Finnis' Natural Law does not achieve the goal**
Does Finnis' Natural Law achieve the goal?	

To what extent does Proportionalism promote immoral behaviour?

Consider for a moment what is meant by the word 'promote'. To promote immoral behaviour, to promote evil moral acts, Proportionalism would have to actively encourage people to do something that is immoral. The definition of immoral behaviour differs depending upon which moral theory is being discussed. Of course, proportionalists do not promote immoral behaviour according to their own understanding of acting disproportionately. So, it is necessary to consider whether Proportionalism promotes behaviour that other ethical theories would think is immoral. By asking you about 'extent', the question also implies that the answer is not necessarily straightforward and there might be some kind of middle position where Proportionalism allows, but does not promote, immoral behaviour.

The view that Proportionalism does promote immoral behaviour

Proportionalism concentrates upon weighing up the proportion of disvalue that is caused in relation to any value that is achieved. This means that proportionalists could directly will a pre-moral/ontic evil when performing a moral action. P.G. Horrigan argues that going out to deliberately rob another to feed the poor is still a directly evil act even though the person may mean well and there are positive consequences. The act is polluted by evil, and so cannot be good and has no spiritual gain. It is always wrong to choose some behaviours, but Proportionalism appears to go a step further than just tolerating unavoidable evil; it expressly seems to encourage the doing of evil so that good may come. This is condemned in scripture and by the Catholic Church (Romans 3:8).

Proportionalists try to weigh up value against disvalue in a way that, some argue, is fundamentally immoral. It leads to a situation in which it is potentially moral to sacrifice one life for the sake of another. This in an incorrect application of the principle of double effect because Christianity teaches that all lives are sacred, and no life is worth more than another. If correctly applied, double effect only *tolerates* actions that result in death or evil, it never *permits* the act of killing in the search for a good result. To weigh up consequences and intentions is insufficient for judging the moral quality of a concrete act and leads to immoral behaviour.

Proportionalism allows moral acts to be declared 'right' even if they are not 'good'. In the encyclical *Veritatis Splendor*, Pope John Paul II argued that this is because, for a proportionalist, the goodness of an action is based upon the intention of the moral agent, while the rightness of the action is based upon the probable consequences of the action and whether or not they are proportionate. We may not know the intention of the moral agent when they act and can judge their action as morally right, even if they intend something terrible that is against God's purpose for human life.

> *Consequently, concrete kinds of behaviour could be described as right' or 'wrong' without it being possible to judge as 'good or 'bad' the will of the person choosing them.* **"**
>
> Pope John Paul II, *Veritatis Splendor*

Proportionalism leads to a kind of Moral Relativism, where no act is intrinsically or absolutely forbidden, and anything can be allowed if the circumstances are right and the consequences are desirable enough. The Vatican makes it clear that any act that is an affront to human life is intrinsically wrong. Human trafficking, genocide, abortion, euthanasia, suicide, murder, mutilation, torture, and so on, are all condemned, but Proportionalism accepts the theoretical possibility that any one of these acts might be right in some situations. While the Catholic Church accepts that an evil act can be tolerated as a side-effect of a moral good, it can never be done directly. Proportionalism, on the other hand, allows an evil act to be done directly if it is a right act. This goes against the tradition of the Catholic Church and scripture.

The view that Proportionalism does not promote immoral behaviour

Proportionalists claim that the Catholic Church is inconsistent when it justifies some acts according to the circumstances but not others. For example, it allows the destruction of human life in the process of self-defence or war but declares artificial contraception and abortion to be intrinsically evil. Some proportionalists argue that they avoid such inconsistency by considering proportionate reason to be applicable in a wider range of circumstances than the Catholic Church has traditionally allowed, thereby allowing a direct abortion to save reproductive capacity, or artificial contraception to prevent starvation for a poor family with many children already.

The reason for the conflict between proportionalists and the Catholic Church was the condemnation – in the 1968 encyclical *Humanae Vitae* – of artificial contraception, sterilisation, and direct abortion (even to preserve the physical or mental well-being of someone who is pregnant or if the pregnancy would result in complications for the child) as intrinsic evils and not a matter for double effect. This is different from an action, such as taking the contraceptive pill, to alleviate a serious medical condition that has the indirect side effect of preventing a pregnancy. Such an action could be considered licit by the Catholic Church. Some proportionalists, however, allow artificial contraception to help someone who has reasons for not wanting more children. In this situation, the pre-moral/ontic good of caring for a person's welfare is unavoidably connected with the pre-moral/ontic evil of artificial contraception, and Proportionalism allows us to choose the act which produces the least evil.

Proportionalists deny that they are consequentialists as they were accused of being in *Veritatis Splendor* by Pope John Paul II. They claim to be faithful to Aquinas' interpretation of Natural Law, and to recognise that Natural Law is not purely deontological but has features of both teleological and deontological ethics. Even though the Catholic Church recognises that the purpose of moral action is to order behaviour towards God, proportionalists are condemned for doing evil so that good may come. However, proportionalists recognise that there may be intrinsic goodness in moral actions, but emphasise the unavoidable need to tolerate some evil in a fallen world. They aim to minimise the evil that one must tolerate rather than blindly follow laws that can produce terrible outcomes.

Proportionalism allows flexibility in moral decision making, which enables Natural Law to respond to new and increasingly complex moral dilemmas. For example, abortion is condemned as intrinsically evil by the Catholic Church in *Humane Vitae*. Double effect allows the removal of a fallopian tube in the case of an ectopic pregnancy, with the indirect result of the termination of the foetus. However, methods of treatment have improved as time has passed. Now it is possible to save the fallopian tube by using drugs to dissolve the foetus. Yet the Church struggles with this treatment, believing it to be a direct form of abortion. Proportionalism accepts that the termination of a foetus is an evil that adds disvalue to an act, but, when weighed against the value of preserving the fallopian tube and increasing the ability to conceive in the future, more good is achieved in a difficult and modern situation.

The view that Proportionalism allows but does not promote immoral behaviour

A good intention is not enough to make an evil act good, nor are circumstances. Lying is not good just because it was done to help someone. If someone chooses to do something intrinsically evil, nothing can make that act good. This means that while Proportionalism does not actively encourage immorality, it ultimately allows it on the basis that it fails to condemn any act as intrinsically evil.

AO2 activity 2
Summarise each argument about whether or not Proportionalism promotes immoral behaviour. Then highlight the strong arguments in green, the reasonable but not particularly strong arguments in yellow, and the weak arguments in red. Choose two weak arguments and construct a counter argument for each that demonstrates why they are weak.

Does Finnis and Proportionalism provide a basis for moral decision making for believers and/or non-believers?

Both Finnis' Natural Law and Proportionalism are ethical approaches based in Catholic theology. It is necessary to consider the extent to which they give Catholics practical support when making moral decisions. In addition, it is worth considering whether any of their ideas are transferrable to people who are not Catholic.

The view that Finnis does not provide a basis for moral decision making for believers and/or non-believers

Lloyd L. Weinreb writes that Finnis' Natural Law is based on the mistaken belief that if one reflects carefully about the human condition, the principles of moral action are a self-evident basis for the determination of concrete obligations. Finnis explicitly rejects the need to provide proof for his claims beyond the self-evident truth of the claims themselves. Finnis has very strong views against abortion and same-sex sexual acts, and he apparently claims these views are self-evident truths. However, he appears to have confused self-evidence with personal conviction. He appears to consider that any challenges to his position can be dismissed because they come from people who have simply not thought hard enough or are blinded by self-interest or bias.

There is no evidence to suggest the basic human goods are truly basic. We have a responsibility to believe only things that are supported by evidence and, while the case that Finnis makes against abortion or same-sex sexual acts, for example, appears to be supported by practical reason as evidence, it is still based on an understanding of the basic human goods being obviously good in a way that is not supported by evidence. We have no reason to agree that life, play and so on are intrinsically good or are the only basic goods on which to base our practical reasoning. Therefore, acceptance of the basic goods is an act of faith which may be unattractive to non-believers, or to anyone who feels that beliefs should be based upon reason or evidence.

The requirement of practical reason that involves respect for every basic value in every act seems unsupported. It seems to have been included to generate unnecessary moral absolutes in an otherwise flexible theory. It means that it is practically unreasonable, and therefore immoral, to will anything that does not respect all the basic human goods. Practically, it is surely necessary to prioritise some goods over others in certain situations – and Finnis agrees. For instance, if one were drowning, the good of aesthetic experience would not be the most important concern in the moment. However, to act in a way that denies this good would be immoral for Finnis, despite the fact that the good of aesthetic experience is of secondary value to the good of life, because nothing can be appreciated unless life is present.

The view that Finnis does provide a basis for moral decision making for believers and/or non-believers

Robert P. George supports Finnis against challenges from Weinreb, by pointing out that it is only the basic human goods that Finnis says are self-evident, not the practical conclusions that arise from their application. The conclusions require practical reason and are not self-evident at all. Therefore, Finnis provides a firm basis for moral decision making about issues such as capital punishment and immigration that may be appealing to religious believers and non-believers alike.

The variety of basic goods reflect the full range of ways in which a human can flourish. They are not limited to simply being alive, but demonstrate that participation in all the goods is what makes life worth living. Moral behaviour that is based on anything other than the goods is incomprehensible. George gives the example of a person who takes an extra job despite a busy life, simply for the money. He notes that such an action only makes sense if the money serves some other purpose, such as to provide for a sick relative or to save for a future project. If it is simply for the possession of the physical money alone, the action is incomprehensible because it does not further a basic good. The basic goods are a clear and rational basis for all moral behaviour.

Knowledge of the goods is based on more than vague intuition. It requires intelligent reflection on the data to understand their self-evident nature, followed by the use of practical reason to understand how best to participate in them. The goods are fundamentally necessary as a basis for moral decision making, because they provide a firm reason for moral action and can be clearly known. The goods enable us to forbid immoral choices when they prevent anything less than the full range of human flourishing.

The view that Proportionalism does not provide a basis for moral decision making for believers and/or non-believers

It is realistically impossible for a person to weigh up all of the consequences and values involved in an action. There is too much to consider and the features of an action are wildly unpredictable. While we can decide what is the most likely immediate consequence of an action, it is impossible to know anything about further far-reaching consequences or about the intricacies of an individual situation. It is, therefore, impossible to make an accurate proportional judgement.

There is a question mark over what constitutes an extreme enough situation to allow a person to break rules and perform an act that contains pre-moral/ontic evil. It is hard to see, when a conflict between moral values arises, whether the situation is extreme enough to warrant the breaking of a rule. If a starving person is without food and no one will help them, we might consider this an extreme enough situation to allow the evil of stealing to save a life. But how hungry does the person have to be?

Reason says that there are some acts that are never in accordance with God's will because they contradict the divinely created human nature and are, therefore, intrinsically evil and absolutely forbidden. It is unacceptable to then say they are allowed if the situation is grave enough. Pope John Paul II said that such theories, which try to justify deliberate behavioural choices that are contrary to the commandments of Natural Law, are not faithful to the teaching of the Catholic Church.

The view that Proportionalism does provide a basis for moral decision making for believers and/or non-believers

Proportionalists claim that we cannot judge whether an action is morally good or bad unless we consider it in its totality. This means weighing up all the factors involved in a moral action, not just considering the moral status of the action itself. Actions cannot, on their own, be judged as intrinsically good or intrinsically evil; we must refer to the context of the action. This requires the use of reason, something that is accessible to believers and non-believers alike.

Proportionalism is based in Natural Law and the Catholic tradition. This means that it should provide a firm basis for religious believers to make moral decisions because it applies principles, such as the principles of double effect and proportionate reason, which are based upon the accepted teachings of Aquinas. There should be no difficulty for religious believers in making moral decisions based on these well-established principles.

Proportionalism is realistic in its understanding of how moral dilemmas arise in a fallen world. Even a non-believer, who does not accept that imperfection arises from the fall or from sin, should be able to acknowledge that the world is imperfect and even the best decisions come with some necessary disvalue attached to them. Proportionalism aims towards actions that produce the least possible evil in the world and acknowledges that humans cannot be perfect moral beings. It has a basis in truth and experience of the world, and directs us towards achievable goals.

AO2 activity 3

There are two ways that a question could appear on an examination paper on this area:

1. A controversial statement followed by the instruction: 'Evaluate this view'.

2. A question that begins with the words: 'Evaluate the view that …'.

Write as many exam questions as you can that focus on whether Finnis and/or Proportionalism provide a basis for moral decision making for believers and/or non-believers. Then, choose the arguments that would best answer each question you have written.

What are the strengths and weaknesses of Finnis' Natural Law and Proportionalism?

This kind of question requires you to weigh up the strengths and weaknesses of Finnis' Natural Law and Proportionalism and, potentially, evaluate which arguments are the most convincing or persuasive.

The weaknesses of Finnis' Natural Law

Finnis argues that the basic human goods are self-evident and objective. This means that they are unlike anything else that we perceive in ordinary life. Ordinarily, if we wish to argue that something is objectively true, we require empirical evidence to support it, but Finnis (to avoid Hume's Guillotine) argues that the goods cannot be derived from facts about the world. J.L. Mackie argued that this amounts to a belief in something very strange, perceived by a faculty that is very odd. This is known as his 'Argument from Queerness', and Mackie points out that the claim that we just know the basic goods in spite of a lack of evidence for them is a 'very lame answer'.

> **Synoptic link**
>
> Link to *Chapter 2: Ethical thought (part two)*. Remind yourself about Hume's challenge that an 'ought' cannot be derived from an 'is', and about Mackie's challenge to Intuitionism, which is called his 'Argument from Queerness'.

S. Buckle argues that by requiring respect for every basic value in every act, Finnis not only rules out all forms of consequentialist reasoning, but he also enshrines the Catholic moral viewpoint on issues such as artificial contraception and masturbation. Finnis' Natural Law gives the appearance of allowing people freedom to choose their moral actions but, in line with traditional Catholic teaching, states that the basic good of life includes reproduction. This means that acts that do not promote reproduction, such as artificial contraception, masturbation and same-sex sexual acts, are against the basic good of life, even though denying them limits human expression and individuality.

Natural Law is based upon the understanding that human nature is rational and that reason is the path to truth. However, this understanding is not necessarily supported by evidence. Human beings are not perfectly logical computers; they make decisions based on a range of factors, some of which are emotional or based upon pressures or causes other than reason. Reasoning may be a mental faculty that is a result of evolution, rather than the purpose of human beings. Reason has helped us adapt to our environment and helped us survive, but this is not the same as it being a reliable method of finding truth or it being part of the human purpose which leads ultimately to life after death.

The strengths of Finnis' Natural Law

Finnis' Natural Law provides a firm and unalterable basis for moral decision making that Consequentialism does not. While Finnis does not ignore consequences, he argues that theories that focus on consequences alone do not explain why we should not be self-seeking or why we should be kind to others. Finnis recognises that when a moral agent is choosing a project for their lives, weighing up consequences is a practical part of making sure that an appropriate action, which will help them achieve their goals, is selected. But for Finnis, consequences are not the only relevant factor in moral decision making. The requirement to never violate the basic human goods is equally relevant and prevents unjust or immoral choices.

Finnis' approach to Natural Law avoids the rigidly deontological, biological approach of other Natural Law theorists. The 'perverted faculty argument' says that if a faculty is natural and exists for a purpose, then it is always wrong to do anything to frustrate that purpose. Edward Feser supports a version of this argument to argue that artificial contraception, masturbation, and same-sex sexual acts are wrong because they frustrate the natural purpose of the genitals. Finnis calls this approach 'ridiculous'. It leads to reasoning that means the mouth can only be used for eating and talking never kissing, and humans cannot use their hands for typing! Finnis avoids this trap by allowing that sexual activity can also be for the purpose of play or partnership between a couple. He says that only an 'inhumane fanatic' thinks that human beings are made to flourish in only one way or for only one purpose.

Finnis' Natural Law does not depend upon teachings about the beatific vision or a doctrinal understanding of Christianity. While Finnis is a Catholic, his understanding of religion in the context of the goods is broad, and allows for a range of investigations into the meaning and purpose of human existence, including atheist thinking that pursues questions about the importance of life and the existence of free will. This can be understood as a strength, in that it does not exclude non-Catholic moral agents and does not depend upon any beliefs or assumptions about life after death.

The weaknesses of Proportionalism

Proportionalists are often accused of being consequentialists or utilitarians. They are seen to be balancing the good consequences against the bad consequences of an act and making a judgement about the rightness or wrongness of it based on nothing more than this calculation. This is not what Natural Law teaches. As a deontological approach to ethics, Natural Law says that the unchanging law of God dictates that some acts are intrinsically good and some acts are intrinsically evil. To weigh the good and evil in an act is to assume that human reason is greater than the dictate of God and the Catholic Church. In this way, Proportionalism risks ignoring the intrinsic worth of some acts and all human lives.

Hoose points out that some criticise Proportionalism for undermining specific laws, such as the requirement to keep one's promises. He gives an example of a man who promises his dying friend that he will ensure that his friend's mother receives any money she is due when he dies. After his friend's death, the man finds the mother is not in need and so he gives all the money to charity. This teleological approach undermines the importance of promise-keeping because it suggests that principles can be abandoned whenever it suits someone.

Finnis argues that it is rash to assume that you can subtract disvalues from values to arrive at a net maximum or greater good, or a net minimum or lesser evil. He says that good is incommensurable. Different things bring people different kinds of pleasure or pain, they bring different types of value or disvalue to a person's life, and they are not directly comparable. He describes the attempt to weigh up value against disvalue as 'senseless' and 'arbitrary', in the same way that it is senseless to try to compare the number 6 to the mass of a book. They are different kinds of qualities and objectively impossible to measure.

The strengths of Proportionalism

Proportionalists do not simply weigh up consequences when making a moral decision. They recognise the intrinsic worth of some actions, and they acknowledge the good of God's law. However, they also recognise that there is more to moral decision making than following set laws. They claim that the Catholic Church has overstepped its jurisdiction by claiming the absolute sinfulness of some acts, like artificial contraception, that are not addressed in the Bible. They argue that there are many things that need to be considered when making a moral decision, and that considering the law and the consequences of the action are only part of the process. Considering all aspects of the moral decision is vital to ensure actions are just and people are valued.

It is unfair to argue that proportionalists disregard rules and undermine important moral principles. McCormick, in his third requirement of proportionate reason, argues that a proportionate judgement must not undermine the good of any rule in the future. Therefore, if someone were to break a promise to protect a life, it is vital that the breaking of this promise does not undermine the importance of keeping promises in general. Breaking promises is still seen as an evil; it is just tolerated so that an even greater evil can be prevented.

Proportionalism allows a moral agent to choose from a range of possible actions, rather than being restricted to obedience to the law in all circumstances. Without undermining the goodness of moral law, it gives the moral agent flexibility to serve the good in a wider range of ways. Rather than being forced to tell the truth no matter what, or not intervening to save a life for fear of acting immorally, Proportionalism allows a moral agent to act for the good in the situation they find themselves in, without compromising morality in ordinary circumstances.

How effective are Finnis' Natural Law and Proportionalism in dealing with ethical issues?

When considering the effectiveness of a moral approach, it is sensible to think about what an effective approach might look like. You could consider whether it is a practical approach, or maybe it is an approach that is efficient, reliable, or easy to understand.

The view that Finnis' Natural Law is not effective in dealing with ethical issues

Finnis does not recognise any kind of hierarchy of goods, and Russell Hittinger argues that without the goods being ordered, many moral problems become unsolvable. It is clear that some goods are more important than others. It is clearly immoral to stand beside a lake marvelling at the beauty of the sunshine on the water and not help the drowning child struggling within reach, but Finnis' Natural Law does little to suggest that one should set aside participation in aesthetic experience to save a life, and it cannot help a person to choose between goods if the Nine Requirements of Practical Reason do not help them to narrow the options.

Some scholars have tried to accuse Finnis of being a relativist because his Natural Law does not give a clear set of moral norms or rules that clarify what behaviours are morally acceptable. By leaving an individual free to formulate their own plan of life and to participate in the goods in a range of different ways according to their own preferences and culture, Finnis comes across as offering little in the way of help to those seeking understanding about how to deal with ethical dilemmas.

Finnis' Natural Law places a high priority on the place of reason in moral decision making, and plays down the role of obedience to scripture, which the Catholic Church has always considered vital. This means that there is the potential, such as in the debate about capital punishment, for reason to suggest moral behaviour that is contrary to scripture or the traditions of the Catholic Church. Feser has pointed out that by arguing against capital punishment using practical reason, Finnis has placed human reason above the wisdom of God and threatened the foundations of the Catholic Church (which had traditionally taught that capital punishment was allowed in extreme circumstances). As a result, Finnis' Natural Law is an unreliable and ineffective approach to dealing with ethical issues.

The view that Finnis' Natural Law is effective in dealing with ethical issues

Respect for every basic value in every act does not require participation in every basic value at all times. An atheist can have respect for the intrinsic value of what Finnis calls 'religious' pursuits without actually needing to participate in it themselves. This enables huge freedom and flexibility in one's moral choices, since so long as the basic goods are respected, acknowledged as goods, and no action is taken to damage them, moral agents are free to pursue those that they wish to the extent that they wish.

The Nine Requirements of Practical Reason provide objective, clear, and practical guidance for moral agents when dealing with ethical problems. They allow some freedom to choose between different moral options, but clearly rule out irrational or immoral choices. Therefore, Finnis recognises that there can be more than one morally reasonable solution to a dilemma, while guarding against an 'anything goes' approach to morality.

Finnis' Natural Law allows individuals the flexibility to manage their own life plans in many different ways; it does not instruct everyone to live in one way for one purpose. This allows humans to flourish in their own individual ways, but it also enables people to make moral choices at least in part based upon the society and the situation in which they find themselves. Practical reason provides structure, but individuals are free to develop their life plans in accordance with the problems that they face and the goals they set for themselves.

The view that Proportionalism is not effective in dealing with ethical issues

It is very difficult to answer a question about the effectiveness of Proportionalism when Proportionalism is not a theory in itself, and there is no clear agreement from scholars about how proportionate reason should best be applied to a moral situation. Proportionalism cannot be said to be effective or ineffective, therefore, since it is not clearly defined and so cannot be clearly assessed.

Proportionalism places too much emphasis on freedom to be an effective way of dealing with ethical issues. By emphasising freedom in this way, Pope John Paul II, in *Veritatis Splendor*, accuses proportionalists of failing to give enough space to duties and overemphasising the consequences of free moral choices. While free will is an important part of making good moral choices, it does not mean every free action is morally acceptable. Proportionalism misleads people by seeming to allow almost any action to be freely and deliberately chosen so long as there are enough positive consequences.

Proportionalism ceases to be effective when it allows actions that are contrary to the teaching of the Catholic Church. Pope John Paul II acknowledged that the use of proportionate reason and double effect is effective when applied to issues that scripture or the Catholic Church has no clear teaching about. However, when proportionalists allow acts that are expressly forbidden by the Catholic Church, it ceases to be authoritative and, therefore, ceases to be effective.

The view that Proportionalism is effective in dealing with ethical issues

Proportionalism is effective in dealing with ethical issues because it is flexible enough to deal with the most challenging of situations that occur in modern life. The laws that have been established through a traditional understanding of Natural Law are good as far as they go, but they were formulated when society was simpler, and much has now changed. Proportionalism allows a moral agent to manage situations in which it seems like all the available options will bring about evil.

Proportionalism engages with the process of practical reasoning in a way that the Catholic Church's interpretation of Natural Law does not. With Natural Law, it seems that reasoning is the responsibility of the moral authority (for example, the Catholic Church) on behalf of the general population. It is then the responsibility of the population to voluntarily fall into line with the rules set by the moral authority. Proportionalism is effective because it allows the individual to engage in proportionate reasoning to resolve the moral dilemmas they face; they do not have to blindly follow laws set by someone else. This seems not only more practical, but also more in keeping with Aquinas' understanding of Natural Law as a process of reasoning.

As E.V. Vacek acknowledges, Proportionalism is not some new theory that is trying to overthrow traditional ethics. It follows the principle of double effect and the application of proportionate reason, both of which are part of Aquinas' Natural Law. Natural Law has been used since the Middle Ages as a way of dealing with ethical issues; it has been adopted by the Catholic Church and it is still of interest today in its various forms. Therefore, Proportionalism, as an understanding of Natural Law, has been shown through the test of time to be an effective, reliable way of dealing with ethical issues.

AO2 activity 5

Keep a journal as you progress through the course. Record your responses or reactions when you read an argument. Sometimes you might have a strong feeling that a scholar is talking nonsense or that someone has hit the nail on the head. Writing down these reactions and the reasons why you feel that way in the moment can help you reflect and remember when you come to write an essay about the topic later.

To what extent is Finnis' Natural Law a better ethic than Proportionalism and vice versa?

When weighing up which moral approach is better, it is worth thinking about what 'better' means. An ethic might be 'better' if it is more practical, more user friendly, more efficient, more reliable, or easier to understand. The question also contains the word 'extent', which implies the answer is not necessarily as simple as one approach being better than the other; there might be a middle position.

The view that Finnis' Natural Law is better than Proportionalism

Finnis' Natural Law allows for moral absolutes, for which there can be no exceptions. This is because the definition of an action includes some account of the circumstances in which the action might be performed. For example, artificial contraception is wrong because deliberately preventing the productive nature of sexual intercourse is always wrong. In contrast, an act that prevents reproduction as an accident or as a by-product is not morally wrong. Therefore, when making a choice, people know exactly what they should and should not do with Finnis' Natural Law. In contrast, Proportionalism is not so clear because there are many variables that must be weighed in the balance.

Proportionalists distinguish between good acts and right acts, suggesting that God could require someone to perform a morally right action that they should also repent of because it is evil. This is illogical and makes a mockery of the idea of meaningful deontological rules. Finnis' Natural Law does not fall into this trap. Practical reason shows the range of ways that people can participate in the goods without the need to perform a morally evil act.

Proportionalists do not like the term 'Consequentialism' because it is used to criticise them. But, Finnis argues, Proportionalism tends to call itself a teleological ethic, rather than a consequentialist ethic, because it wants to identify with Natural Law by labelling itself in a way that makes it look like it is applying practical reason. However, Pope John Paul II rejects what he calls 'teleologism' as an error on the basis that acts are only morally good when they are rationally and voluntarily ordered towards conformity with God's will, not when they are maximising positive consequences. Finnis' Natural Law recognises that there are teleological elements to moral decision making, but focuses on the rational participation in absolute goods that cannot be violated.

Finnis' Natural Law is a clear moral theory that is consistent with Aquinas and the teaching of the Catholic Church. In contrast, Proportionalism is not a defined ethical theory as such. It involves interpreting the teaching of Aquinas from within the Catholic tradition, but there are many different proportionalists, and none of them agree on one single method of establishing the correct way to work out how a moral agent should behave, and none of them have established a method that is seen as acceptable to the Catholic Church.

The view that Proportionalism is better than Finnis' Natural Law

Despite arguments to the contrary, proportionalists do recognise that there are some intrinsically good or evil actions, provided we understand that a good or evil action is not understood purely as an abstract action, isolated from the situation in which it is performed. Instead, we should understand it as an action that includes an assessment of the morally relevant circumstances. This is better than the traditional deontological understanding of Natural Law, which assesses actions in isolation before dictating how someone should behave in a specific situation.

The Catholic Church argues that it does take circumstances into account when identifying right or wrong actions. For example, it says that lying is telling a falsehood to one who *deserves to know the truth*, and murder is killing a human *who is innocent of wrongdoing*. However, this reasoning seems to pave the way for justifications of terrible acts like vigilante justice or honour killing, which is most certainly not in line with the teaching of the Catholic Church. To attempt to make abstract rules specific does not work. Artificial contraception is defined by the Catholic Church as the use of drugs or devices 'to render one incapable of conception'. However, this is not the only reason why a person uses artificial contraception, and it suggests that reproduction is never immoral. Having a baby when one cannot afford to do so, or when one has several children already, could be argued to be fundamentally immoral in an overpopulated world facing climate change and biodiversity loss.

Proportionalists would argue that they understand that humans do not live in a perfect world. Aquinas acknowledged this when he accepted that it is moral for a person to steal food when they are starving. While Finnis' Natural Law has an element of flexibility to it, there is still an emphasis on fundamental, absolute laws that can never be violated, and it therefore risks being too idealistic to be practical. Humans do not exist in a utopia where one can perform an action that contains no evil at all. Proportionalists understand this, and incorporate it into their assessment of moral action. In contrast, Finnis cannot allow any action to violate a basic good. In theory, this means he does not allow any act at all, since all actions are contaminated by some kind of pre-moral/ontic evil.

Proportionalism is much better equipped than Finnis' Natural Law to address contemporary concerns such as artificial contraception, abortion, women's rights, and immigration, among other things. While Proportionalism is grounded in Aquinas' Natural Law, which traditionally absolutely forbids abortion and artificial contraception (as Finnis' approach also does), there is scope in Proportionalism for proportionate reason to be used to demonstrate the value in allowing direct abortion or artificial contraception in some situations. Finnis takes a much more traditional view of these moral dilemmas, a view which is less compatible with a modern understanding of a flourishing life.

The view that neither theory is better than the other

Both Finnis' Natural Law and Proportionalism are based upon the writings of Aquinas, and come from within Catholic tradition. Many of the disagreements over terminology or methodology appear to be obsessing over the technical language of small matters when the outcome is broadly the same. Both theories agree that there is a place for moral absolutes and for the principle of double effect. Neither approach believes that evil may be done for a greater good, and both agree that there are unavoidable evils that must be tolerated in some circumstances as a result of the fall. These similarities mean that neither is 'better' than the other.

AO2 activity 6

Copy and complete the following table to help you weigh up the value of Finnis' Natural Law against the value of Proportionalism. Select and summarise the points from the analysis above that you find most persuasive. Add more rows if you think there are other features that contribute to making one ethic 'better' than another. One point has been entered for you.

Goal: Finnis' Natural Law is 'better' than Proportionalism		
	Finnis' Natural Law	**Proportionalism**
Practical		
User-friendly		
Efficient		
Reliable	The ethic allows for moral absolutes based upon practical reason.	
Easy to understand		
Which ethic is 'better'?		

Practising AO1 questions

As you now know, AO1 questions may begin with one of a range of possible command words (see pages 8–9 for more detail). The following question begins with the word 'Explain' and you should now be familiar with how to answer an 'Explain' question: you must cover the broad topic area in the question in as much detail as possible, but you do not need to consider the quality of the theory or offer any views about it.

Read the past paper question below and the example paragraph written in response before completing the activity on page 171.

> *Explain John Finnis' development of Aquinas' Natural Law.*
>
> (Eduqas A Level Religious Studies, Sample Assessment Material, Component 3: Religion and Ethics, Question 1a)

Example

John Finnis developed a version of Natural Law from Aquinas[2] and sets out a method of right reasoning that helps a person work out which actions are reasonable and therefore moral[1]. He starts with what he says are basic human goods[7] or values[7] that lead to[1] human flourishing[7]. Finnis says that they are 'a general form of good that can be participated in or realised in indefinitely many ways on indefinitely many occasions'[6]. The goods are: life, knowledge, play, aesthetic experience, friendship, practical reasonableness, and religion.[1] The method of Natural Law[1] according to Finnis can be found in the Nine Requirements of Practical Reason[7]. 'Each of these requirements concerns what one must do, or think, or be, if one is to participate in the basic good of practical reasonableness.[6] These nine requirements are: a coherent plan of life, no preference among values, no preference among persons, detachment, commitment, efficiency within reason, respect for every basic value in every act, requirements of the common good, follow one's conscience.[1]

Areas for development

1. The paragraph is coherent and accurate as far as it goes, but it only states facts and does not explain them. An answer to an explain question must state the different aspects of the theory, but must also show how they function within the theory.

2. This paragraph clearly addresses the question as it talks about John Finnis' development of Natural Law. However, it borders on an 'outline' response because none of the goods or requirements are explained. There is just one sentence of explanation at the start.

3. The paragraph does not contain evidence or examples to demonstrate what the goods and requirements are or how they are to be used. The examples could appear later but, if this paragraph is representative of the whole essay, it is a weakness.

4. The response does not make use of any sources of wisdom and authority. This may not be a problem, even if no scripture appears further on in the answer, since Finnis' development is not dependent upon scripture.

5. This response makes a brief connection with Aquinas' Natural Law, but only because it is prompted by the question. Later in the response, this could be developed to show areas where Finnis developed Aquinas' work.

6. There is no requirement for scholars other than Finnis to be referenced, and including direct quotations from Finnis is a strength. However, there is nothing to show how the quotations relate to Finnis' Natural Law. They could have been used to explain the importance of the goods and the requirements or how they are to be understood.

7. There is some accurate and appropriate use of specialist vocabulary in context, but there is scope for more; for example, when explaining that the basic goods are self-evident and what this means.

Activity

a) Read the example paragraph on page 170, and identify one thing that the student has done successfully in this paragraph and one thing that could be improved.

b) Rewrite the paragraph, keeping the parts that are strong or on the right track and removing the weaknesses identified. You might find that, as you work, it becomes longer than just one paragraph, and that is absolutely fine.

AO1 practice question 1

Now it is your turn. Have a go at answering the following question. There are some points to remember underneath to help you if you are not sure how to start.

> *Explain Bernard Hoose's Proportionalism.*
>
> (WJEC A Level Religious Studies, Summer 2018, A2 Unit 4:
> Religion and Ethics, Question 2)

Since this question appeared on an examination paper, the specification has been reworded. This question would not now appear in this form. Instead, you would be asked to explain Hoose's overview of Proportionalism.

Points to remember

- Remember that Proportionalism is a development of traditional Catholic ethical thought; it is not a separate ethical theory.
- Use vocabulary that relates to the proportionalist approach to ethics, such as pre-moral/ontic evil and proportionate reasoning.
- Give examples of how the principle of double effect and proportionate reasoning have been developed by proportionalists, and how this differs from a more firmly deontological approach to Natural Law.

AO1 practice question 2

Now try this question by yourself.

> *Apply Finnis' Natural Law to the issue of immigration.*
>
> (Eduqas A Level Religious Studies, Summer 2019, Component 3:
> Religion and Ethics, Question 3a)

Practising AO2 questions

When writing a response to an AO2 question, you must remember that you are being examined on your ability to analyse and evaluate effectively. Analysis involves a detailed examination of something and you should pick apart the concept to look for its strengths and weaknesses. Evaluation involves judging the quality or importance of the concept. You are expected to analyse and evaluate throughout the whole of your response; you are not expected to include long passages explaining knowledge and understanding.

Read the past paper question below and the example paragraphs written in response before completing the activity on page 174.

> *'Proportionalism deals effectively with all ethical issues.'*
> *Evaluate this view.*
>
> (WJEC A Level Religious Studies, Sample Assessment Material, A2 Unit 4: Religion and Ethics, Question 5)

Example 1

Proportionalism deals effectively with all ethical issues[2] because it is a flexible ethical theory[1]. Rather than sticking with deontological[6] rules come what may, it is prepared to allow an act that contains pre-moral[6] evil because it is right to do so in the circumstances. This does mean that evil will sometimes be produced, but the action is right[6] if the evil is proportionately less than the good[6] that is produced by the same action. The practical reasoning of Proportionalism is not new but it has been discouraged in favour of obedience to the teachings of the Catholic Church. It is much more adaptable to modern society[1] than other versions of Natural Law and it can deal more[1] effectively[2] with the complexity of modern dilemmas[1]. For example, immigration is much more complex now than it was in the past because the global population has increased, and an understanding of human rights has been established, which makes it much harder to ignore the needs of people who wish to move away from difficult lives and access more opportunities [3].

Areas for development

1. There is some valid analysis of some of the issues raised by the question, but the paragraph is one-sided and offers no analysis of the debate surrounding these issues or alternative arguments. There is also no evaluation to justify the judgement that has been made.

2. The paragraph clearly addresses the question.

3. The paragraph contains an example to illustrate the point being made, but it could be made more specific by identifying why an increase in the global population and/or human rights make society more complex, and, more importantly, how Proportionalism deals with these challenges more effectively than other developments of Natural Law.

4. There is no mention of scholarly views.

5. There is no attempt to make connections with other areas of the course. While connections should not be forced, if it is relevant to the question, an answer could refer to other theories that are more or less successful.

6. There is some accurate use of specialist language in context.

Example 2: an improved response

Proportionalism deals effectively with ethical issues[2] because it is flexible[1]. Rather than sticking with deontological[6] rules come what may, it is prepared to allow an act that contains pre-moral[6] evil because it is right[6] to do so in the circumstances. This means that evil will sometimes be produced, but only if it is proportionately less than the good[6] produced by the same action. However, the Catholic Church objects to this approach, arguing it allows too much freedom[1] at the expense of moral duty and obligation[1]. Pope John Paul II criticised Proportionalism as[4] 'consequentialist'[6]. The weighing up of consequences is unreliable[1] and scripture states[1], in Romans[3], that no one may do evil so good may come. While Proportionalism is attractive[1], it is ineffective[2] at dealing with all[2] ethical issues in this way. It is only effective[2] at managing moral problems when there is a conflict of[1] values[6] or a choice between two evils[1]. For example, if someone convicted of a crime wants to move to a new country to escape capital punishment, Proportionalism would have to weigh up the [3] value[6] of respecting the criminal's life plan, against the[3] disvalue[6] of a member of society avoiding justice [3]. However, these are very unusual moral issues[1], not all moral issues[2], and Proportionalism therefore has limited reach.

What went well

1 This paragraph includes a consideration of counter-arguments and weighs what is good and bad about Proportionalism, coming to a reasoned judgement.

2 This paragraph contains regular reference to the wording of the question throughout.

3 The paragraph contains an example and explains how it demonstrates the conflict being referred to. It also contains a relevant reference to scripture.

4 Mention of the Pope is an appropriate reference to scholarly views.

5 This response does not make use of connections with other areas of study, but it could go on to do so in the rest of the response.

6 There is accurate use of specialist language in context.

Activity

a) Read Example 1 on page 172 and identify three things that could be developed to improve the analysis or the evaluation.

b) Read Example 2 on page 173. This time the evaluation and analysis are much more effective. Make a list of at least three things that you think the student has done that makes the paragraph better than Example 1.

AO2 practice question 1

Now it is your turn. Have a go at answering the following question. There are some points to remember underneath to help you if you are not sure how to start.

> *'Finnis' Natural Law is a practical ethical approach for contemporary society.' Evaluate this view.*
>
> (WJEC A Level Religious Studies, Summer 2019, A2 Unit 4: Religion and Ethics, Question 4)

Points to remember

- This question focuses on how useful or useable Finnis' Natural Law is in the modern world. Remember to give arguments on both sides of the debate and support them with evidence and reasoning. For example, you can point out that Finnis' Natural Law allows people to freely choose their own plan of life in accordance with the seven basic goods that, together, allow full human flourishing.
- Give plenty of examples, throughout your essay, to illustrate how useable or unusable Finnis' Natural Law is for contemporary society. For example, you could use the example of abortion to show that there are some acts that Finnis' Natural Law still forbids, even when a person is in desperate need.
- Use the ideas of the scholars that you have seen mentioned in this chapter or in other chapters. You can refer to Fletcher, Bentham, or Mill to challenge Finnis' deontological approach to ethics, or you could refer to Divine Command theorists, like Adams, to suggest a return to scripture and God's commands rather than flawed human reason.

AO2 practice question 2

Now try this question by yourself.

> *'The strengths of Proportionalism, as an ethical theory, clearly outweigh its weaknesses.' Evaluate this view.*
>
> (WJEC A Level Religious Studies, Summer 2019, A2 Unit 4: Religion and Ethics, Question 5)

Mark schemes for all exam questions can be found at www.eduqas.co.uk and www.wjec.co.uk.

The #BeKind movement has many strands, and one form of it was given a new lease of life in February 2020 after the death of former *Love Island* host Caroline Flack. #BeKind takes a stand against the trolling and bullying that has become prevalent in online culture. On 16 February 2020, Kirstie Allsopp tweeted, 'If we want people to #BeKind it has to be universal … So start being kind about everyone, even those you disagree with'.

Traditional interpretations of moral laws make pronouncements that absolutely condemn certain behaviours and actively promote others. As people navigate life, with all its complexities, they can find themselves coming into conflict with these kinds of moral absolutes. For example, within Christianity there has been a history of criticising sexual and romantic relationships outside the confines of heterosexual, monogamous marriage, including same-sex relationships and polyamory. Many people who have found themselves in conflict with these moral laws have felt excluded, shamed, and judged.

So, to what extent is morality about following strict laws and rules, and to what extent is it about being kind to people even when we do not agree with them?

In this chapter you will consider Joseph Fletcher's approach to ethics: Situation Ethics. You will learn about the features of the theory, and how it might be applied to contemporary ethical issues such as same-sex relationships and polyamory. You will discover that it developed, within sections of Protestant Christianity, as an alternative to Natural Law, and it allows a moral agent to consider moral problems on a case-by-case basis with the single principle of love in mind, rather than applying a general principle.

Situation Ethics takes a very different approach to sexual ethics than the legalistic ethical system of Natural Law.

AO1

This section of the chapter will enhance your **knowledge** and **understanding** of the topic and help you develop your AO1 skills.

Joseph Fletcher's Situation Ethics – his rejection of other forms of ethics and his acceptance of agape as the basis of morality

Joseph Fletcher's Situation Ethics arose in the United States of America in the 1960s, as a reflection of the social and cultural context of the time. Fletcher was a Protestant minister who became interested in what is known as American Pragmatism, that is, working out what is practical rather than focusing on ideology or doctrine. Fletcher's Situation Ethics was an attempt to reject **dogma** from within the confines of Christianity.

Fletchers' rejection of other approaches within ethics

In his foreword to *Situation Ethics: The New Morality*, written in 1966, Fletcher describes Situation Ethics as a 'non system' of morality:

> *The reader will find a method here, but no system. It is a method of 'situational' or 'contextual' decision making, but system-building has no part in it.*
>
> Joseph Fletcher, *Situation Ethics: The New Morality*

Fletcher argued that Jesus did not use a system of ethics, and that ethics requires no system. Fletcher felt that his ethical perspective was not new at all, that its roots lie in Christianity, but that he had given it a new, contemporary outlook.

Legalism

Religious ethics had traditionally considered the Bible to be the basis of moral excellence. The Catholic Church followed Natural Law, with its absolutist, deontological approach to moral behaviour, while Protestant traditions had a **puritanical** approach to ethics, placing faith firmly in the commands of scripture, which should be obeyed regardless of how much sense they made. These strict, absolutist approaches to ethics are known as **legalism**. They tell everyone what to do, setting rules and laws and seeing that infringements are punished. There is no room for individual circumstances to be considered because the rules are absolutely good, set by God or reasoned through **casuistry**, and cannot be broken. Fletcher found such a complex web of laws and rules very restrictive.

Key terms

dogma: a fixed set of rigid principles or beliefs that must be accepted without question

puritanical: rigid adherence to strict rules of moral behaviour that forbid pleasure

legalism: conformity to law or to a strict religious or moral code

casuistry: the application of general ethical principles to particular cases of conduct (as in Natural Law)

> *Any web thus woven sooner or later chokes its weavers.* **"**
>
> Joseph Fletcher, *Situation Ethics: The New Morality*

Fletcher regarded legalism as suffocating, binding, and rigid. If you enter into a moral decision with prefabricated rules and regulations that must be followed, the rules will take priority over the people in the situation.

Antinomianism

Fletcher equally disparaged **antinomianism**. Existentialists like Jean-Paul Sartre and Simone de Beauvoir had taught people that we can make ourselves and have sole responsibility for our own behaviour. This approach meant that people could make their own ethical decisions, free from the direction of any other eternal being or from all set ethical standards. Fletcher was concerned that such an approach to moral behaviour was directionless, leading to an *ad hoc*, lawless, and unprincipled approach to ethics. De Beauvoir saw no connection between one moment and the next, and thus rejected any basis for generalising moral principles or laws. This produced an 'anything goes' ethics, with no way of judging behaviour as good or bad, or right or wrong, and allowed people to justify any action at all. Antinomianism literally means 'against law' and enables people to enter into a situation without principles. This approach was warned against in scripture.

Peter and Paul saw some gentiles taking the offer of freedom from the law too literally, and living as though their actions did not matter.

> *Live as free people, but do not use your freedom as a cover-up for evil; live as God's slaves.* **"**
>
> 1 Peter 2:1, *Holy Bible (NIV)*

Fletcher saw the same problem in Christians who claimed to be 'spirit led' in their moral decision making; it led to random, unpredictable, erratic decision making.

> *They follow no forecastable course from one situation to another. They are, exactly, anarchic – i.e. without a rule. They are not only unbound by the chains of law, but actually sheer extemporisers, impromptu and intellectually irresponsible.* **"**
>
> Joseph Fletcher, *Situation Ethics: The New Morality*

Fletcher's rationale for using the religious concept of '*agape*'

Fletcher favoured a middle way to making moral decisions; one that took the flexibility of antinomianism and the structure of legalism, but left behind both the chaos and suffocation of those approaches. In Situation Ethics, the moral agent takes the principles of their community into every moral situation and treats them respectfully as illuminators. However, if the situation requires it, they are prepared to set those illuminators aside.

Key term

antinomianism: 'against law'; the idea that people are under no obligation to obey the laws of ethics or morality as presented by religious authorities

Synoptic link

Link to *Chapter 8: Determinism and free will: free will.* In the section on 'Concepts of Libertarianism', you will meet the work of Jean-Paul Sartre who taught that we are free and solely responsible for our own ethical decision making. Sartre's ethic implies that we are not bound to any system of morality at all.

The principle upon which the decision to set them aside rests is the religious concept of '**agape**', which comes from the New Testament. This is the one and only law or rule of Christian ethics for Fletcher.

Agape is a Greek word that is roughly translated as 'selfless love' or sometimes as 'charity'. It is distinct from other Greek words for love, such as *philia* (the love of deep friendship) and *eros* (romantic love). It is the kind of love that is an unconditional care or concern for the wellbeing of others. It is selfless compassion for other people, which does not require anything in return. As a way of making moral judgements, Fletcher preferred using love to look at the situation a person is faced with, rather than rigid rules or doing whatever the moral agent feels like in the moment.

Fletcher saw *agape* as being the kind of compassion advocated by Jesus and Paul. He gives the example of a person who has escaped from an asylum and is searching for a person they want to kill. For Fletcher, legalism says that, when asked, you should tell the would-be murderer where their intended victim is hiding so that if he finds and kills his victim, only one sin is committed (murder) instead of two (murder and lying). However, situationism would allow the lie because it is more loving to save a life. The only obligation a moral agent has is to love; there is no obligation to follow any other law or rule. It is vital that the moral agent uses rules as illuminators, but never as directors. *Agape* is the only absolute rule, and the responsible moral agent decides if the law or the wisdom of the Church serves love in the situation in front of them before making a decision about the best course of action. For Fletcher, legalists idolise the law and antinomians throw the baby out with the bath water.

> The situational factors are so primary that we may even say 'circumstances alter rules and principles'.
>
> "
>
> Joseph Fletcher, *Situation Ethics: The New Morality*

The role of conscience

Fletcher took issue with the traditional concept of conscience. He acknowledged the following four theories of conscience, each of which he went on to reject:

1. moral intuition
2. guidance from the Holy Spirit
3. an internalised value system inherited from culture
4. reason making moral judgements.

Fletcher was sympathetic to Aquinas' belief that conscience is reason making moral judgements. However, he rejected the idea that the conscience is something that we have. Instead, it is something we do; it is a verb rather than a noun. It is antecedent, looking forwards into the future at decisions that will be made, rather than consequent, looking backwards at decisions that have been made in the past. It weighs up, constructively, the most loving decision. Conscience is vital in moral decision making because it is the process of directing decision making, weighing up the best action in the circumstances.

> *Paul spoke of conscience in two of his letters, to Rome and Corinth, and tended to give a new twist to the Greco-Roman idea by treating it as a director of human decisions rather than a reviewer.*
>
> Joseph Fletcher, *Situation Ethics: The New Morality*

What all this means is that Fletcher advocated taking a Christian approach to ethics that is more flexible than the traditional Christian approaches of following the law as it is presented in commands from scripture or Natural Law. Instead, he argued that Situation Ethics follows the example of Jesus, focusing on love being the main motivation for moral actions. For Fletcher, it was vital that human beings did not approach ethics without any guidance at all but, instead, that they considered love the driving purpose behind any law. If love was not served by the law, then the law should be abandoned in the name of doing the loving thing.

For example, the law in Exodus instructs us never to lie, kill, or steal. In general, love is best achieved by sticking to these laws, and if these things are avoided, life will be better than if they were not avoided. However, there are some circumstances in which lying, killing, or stealing could bring about a loving outcome, and it would be selfless and compassionate to do them. For example, if a murderer asks for the whereabouts of someone they would like to kill, we might reject the command against lying to save the life of another person. If a terminally ill person asks to be helped to end their life, it might be more loving to help them, rather than obey the law that forbids killing. Fletcher does not advocate abandoning the law altogether. Rather, he suggests that the law should be observed so long as it produces a loving outcome; the moment it ceases to serve love, it should be ignored.

> *[Situation Ethics] focuses on cases and tries experimentally, not propositionally, to adduce, not deduce, some 'general' ideas to be held only tentatively and lightly. It deals with cases in all their contextual particularity, deferring in fear and trembling only to the rule of Love.*
>
> Joseph Fletcher, *Situation Ethics: The New Morality*

Synoptic link

Link to *A Level Religious Studies for Eduqas: Philosophy of Religion*, Chapter 4: Challenges to religious belief: religious belief as a product of the human mind. Remind yourself of Freud's understanding of conscience as the working of the super-ego, an internalised value system that has been imposed on us by our upbringing and culture.

AO1 activity 2

Fletcher gives four specific cases to test his ethical theory. He gives no solutions. Here is one of the cases.

A terminally-ill man has the chance to take costly medication to prolong his life for a while or he will die within six months. He has three choices:

- Take the medication: he will have to borrow money to pay for the medication, and if he lives more than six months, his life insurance will be cancelled when it comes up for renewal. His wife and family will be in debt for the cost of the medication and will be left with no insurance money to provide for them.

- Do nothing: the life insurance will be left intact, and his family will be left with some financial security.
- Kill himself: the pay out from the life insurance will be much higher and his family will be well provided for.

What is the role of conscience in this situation? What would be the most loving thing to do in your opinion?

The biblical evidence used to support Situation Ethics

Fletcher was an American episcopalian minister. This means that he was a Protestant, not a Catholic, and that he had, at the time, strongly held Christian beliefs. It also means that he looked to scripture for authority about how people should behave, rather than the Catholic Church's teaching.

Fletcher believed the teachings of Jesus and Paul in the New Testament clearly directed that, while the law is an important illuminator that shows us the best way to behave in general, it should not be the focus of worship and should not be set in stone to the extent that it is put before the people who are designed to serve.

> *Then he said to them, 'The Sabbath was made for man, not man for the Sabbath.'* 99
>
> Mark 2:27, *Holy Bible (NIV)*

Fletcher believed that a relativistic approach was evident in the work of Jesus, who healed the sick on the Sabbath instead of worrying about the law that forbade work, and forgave the adulterous woman instead of stoning her according to the law. Fletcher felt that the best way to be loving depends upon the situation, and so if it is more loving to break a law then, following Jesus' example, that is the good thing to do.

> *Jesus straightened up and asked her, 'Woman, where are they? Has no one condemned you?'* 99
> *'No one, sir,' she said.*
> *'Then neither do I condemn you,' Jesus declared. 'Go now and leave your life of sin.'*
>
> John 8:10, *Holy Bible (NIV)*

> *Looking for a reason to bring charges against Jesus, they asked him, 'Is it lawful to heal on the Sabbath?'* 99
> *He said to them, 'If any of you has a sheep and it falls into a pit on the Sabbath, will you not take hold of it and lift it out? How much more valuable is a person than a sheep! Therefore, it is lawful to do good on the Sabbath.'*
> *Then he said to the man, 'Stretch out your hand.' So he stretched it out and it was completely restored, just as sound as the other.*
>
> Matthew 12:10–13, *Holy Bible (NIV)*

Synoptic link

Link to Component 1: A study of Christianity, Religious concepts and religious life, Religious life, Key moral principles. The key moral principles of Christianity include love thy neighbour.

Link to *Chapter 3: Deontological ethics: Aquinas' Natural Law* and *Chapter 4: Deontological ethics: Finnis' Natural Law and Proportionalism. Agape* or love is a theological virtue that is fundamental to all Christian approaches to ethics.

The teachings of Jesus

The parable of the Good Samaritan is a good example of Fletcher's understanding of the kind of behaviour that is required by *agape*.

The lawyer is asking Jesus to whom he is obligated to show love, and indicates that he intends to go no further than he is obliged to by law. Fletcher found this kind of legalism to be self-serving. While the law can be constructive and illuminating, when people hide behind the letter of the law they are putting themselves before others. He called this 'cheap legalism' and considered it an attempt to escape the higher demands of the spirit.

Jesus commands the lawyer to go and behave in the same way as the Samaritan. Like Jesus, Fletcher believed that the situationist must be prepared to get dirty and take risks to care for others. *Agape* is not limited by geography or religion; it extends to all those who need help. The situationist, like the Samaritan, risks making the wrong moral judgement when they act, and if they do, they will have to accept the consequences. But when they deliberate in love, they are working to protect others, rather than themselves.

> *On one occasion an expert in the law stood up to test Jesus. 'Teacher,' he asked, 'what must I do to inherit eternal life?'*
>
> *'What is written in the Law?' he replied. 'How do you read it?'*
>
> *He answered, '"Love the Lord your God with all your heart and with all your soul and with all your strength and with all your mind"; and "Love your neighbour as yourself."'*
>
> *'You have answered correctly,' Jesus replied. 'Do this and you will live.'*
>
> *But he wanted to justify himself, so he asked Jesus, 'And who is my neighbour?'*
>
> *In reply Jesus said: 'A man was going down from Jerusalem to Jericho, when he was attacked by robbers. They stripped him of his clothes, beat him and went away, leaving him half-dead. A priest happened to be going down the same road, and when he saw the man, he passed by on the other side. So too, a Levite, when he came to the place and saw him, passed by on the other side. But a Samaritan, as he travelled, came where the man was; and when he saw him, he took pity on him. He went to him and bandaged his wounds, pouring on oil and wine. Then he put the man on his own donkey, brought him to an inn and took care of him. The next day he took out two denarii and gave them to the innkeeper. "Look after him," he said, "and when I return, I will reimburse you for any extra expense you may have."*
>
> *'Which of these three do you think was a neighbour to the man who fell into the hands of robbers?'*
>
> *The expert in the law replied, 'The one who had mercy on him.'*
>
> *Jesus told him, 'Go and do likewise.'*

Luke 10:25–37, *Holy Bible (NIV)*

Contact with a dead body was considered unclean and the Priest particularly, but also the Levite, would have been instructed to avoid uncleanliness. If they assumed the man was dead or would shortly die, when they passed by on the other side of the road they were avoiding any risk to themselves by following the letter of the law. Taking this approach protected them from condemnation.

The teachings of Paul

1 Corinthians 13 is a famous chapter from the Bible, which is often read at weddings because of its focus on the character of love. However, this passage is not about the romantic love between a husband and a wife.

This passage is about *agape*. This is translated as charity by some, but it is the unconditional care or concern for other people that was seen in the actions of the Samaritan in Luke 10:25–37.

> *If I speak in the tongues of men or of angels, but do not have love, I am only a resounding gong or a clanging cymbal. If I have the gift of prophecy and can fathom all mysteries and all knowledge, and if I have a faith that can move mountains, but do not have love, I am nothing. If I give all I possess to the poor and give over my body to hardship that I may boast, but do not have love, I gain nothing.*
>
> *Love is patient, love is kind. It does not envy, it does not boast, it is not proud. It does not dishonour others, it is not self-seeking, it is not easily angered, it keeps no record of wrongs. Love does not delight in evil but rejoices with the truth. It always protects, always trusts, always hopes, always perseveres.*
>
> *Love never fails. But where there are prophecies, they will cease; where there are tongues, they will be stilled; where there is knowledge, it will pass away. For we know in part and we prophesy in part, but when completeness comes, what is in part disappears. When I was a child, I talked like a child, I thought like a child, I reasoned like a child. When I became a man, I put the ways of childhood behind me. For now, we see only a reflection as in a mirror; then we shall see face to face. Now I know in part; then I shall know fully, even as I am fully known.*
>
> *And now these three remain: faith, hope and love. But the greatest of these is love.*
>
> 1 Corinthians 13:1–13, *Holy Bible (NIV)*

Agape is not based upon whether or not the other person is likable or deserving. It is, purely and simply, altruistic compassion for another person.

Agape is about seeking the neighbour's interest with a careful eye on all the factors in a situation. For Jesus, and for Fletcher, *agape* is what the law is all about. The spirit of the law is to be found in loving God and your neighbour so, if following the law takes a person away from love, then the law should be abandoned.

Fletcher says that faith, hope, and love are the commitments that identify the Christian. He felt that both Jesus and Paul replaced the precepts of the Torah with the living principle of *agape*, with 'good will in partnership with reason'.

AO1 activity 3

Chapter 1 mentioned the story of Jamel Dunn, a 32-year-old man whose body was found in a lake in Florida, three days after he had drowned. Later, a video of his drowning appeared on social media. It had been filmed by five teenagers, who had mocked as they watched Jamel drown, and who had failed to help or to call for assistance. They faced no charges as they did not break any laws.

- What risks would the teenagers have faced if they had tried to help the drowning man?
- Could a law reasonably insist that people step in to help those in trouble? Why? Why not?

Fletcher claimed that agape is risky, but you practise agape to protect others, not yourself.

Situation Ethics as a form of Moral Relativism, a consequentialist and teleological theory

Situation Ethics is, by design, a **relativist** theory. This means that Fletcher did not think there are absolute standards of right or wrong. However, he did not agree that there are no moral principles that should be obeyed at all. He called Situation Ethics 'principled Relativism', with love as the principle that should be followed in all situations. He saw law as subservient to love, so that when a decision has to be made, the law can be set aside if it is more loving to do so. Fletcher felt that moral decisions should be made in relation to love; any action is acceptable if, and only if, it aims at a loving outcome, and what is loving depends upon the people involved and the situation.

> *Christian Situation Ethics is not a system or program of loving according to a code, but an effort to relate love to a world of relativities through a casuistry obedient to love.* **"**
>
> Joseph Fletcher, *Situation Ethics: The New Morality*

Fletcher takes a consequentialist approach to ethics. This means that Situation Ethics focuses upon the results or outcome of an action, rather than the action itself. We should be careful here, however; Fletcher did point out that the conscience – the process of moral decision making – is not about looking back retrospectively and wondering if one did the right thing. It is about looking forward to the possible outcomes and judging which result will be the most loving. Situation Ethics is, therefore, concerned with the consequences in as much as they are the result of our actions that will most affect the people in the situation. The outcome is what affects people, and that should be the focus of moral action. Fletcher quotes Bishop Kenneth Kirk by saying:

> *'Every man must decide for himself according to his own estimate of conditions and consequences; and no one can decide for him or impugn the decision to which he comes. Perhaps this is the end of the matter after all.'* This is precisely what this book is intended to show.
>
> Joseph Fletcher, *Situation Ethics: The New Morality*

Key term

relativist: the view that 'right' or 'wrong' are not absolute, fixed, objective, or unchanging, but are to be judged in relation to something else, such as how much love they produce or the culture that someone is based in; it means morality can be understood differently by different people

Fletcher's approach is also considered teleological. A theory is teleological when it involves an explanation of good as an end goal to be achieved, and for Fletcher the end goal of morality should be helping people. Rules are only good when they serve people. When people serve the law at all costs, they miss the purpose of morality. The aim of all morality, for Fletcher, is love. Therefore, any moral action is only good if it serves love; there is no absolute good or bad action, and there are no duties beyond being loving.

Joseph Fletcher's Situation Ethics – the principles as a means of assessing morality

The boss principle of Situation Ethics

Situation Ethics has just one general rule, and this is the commandment to love God through your neighbour. This is often described as the 'boss principle'.

> *What a difference it makes when love, understood agapeically, is boss. When love is the only norm. How free and therefore responsible we are!*
>
> Joseph Fletcher, *Situation Ethics: The New Morality*

Agape is concern for the wellbeing of a neighbour and even an enemy. It is an attitude rather than a feeling. The commandments that have been treated as absolute laws in the past are seen, by Fletcher, as guides rather than rules. The commandment that states we should tell the truth is an illuminator but must be disregarded if obedience to it means that love is not served. Fletcher gives medical examples where rigid observance of the law might prevent a doctor revealing to a woman that she is about to marry a man with a sexually transmitted infection, or might prevent a doctor from sterilising a woman with a heart condition who would risk death if she became pregnant again.

Fletcher states that the Greek word *agape* is easier to understand when describing this boss principle. It is a living principle that embodies the spirit of all other 'laws' that are found within the Torah, and means that they can be disregarded if they are not loving in practice. In Greek, there are four different words for 'love'. *Eros* is passion or sexual desire. *Philia* is friendship and *storge* is love for family. These kinds of love are selective, exclusive, and emotional. *Agape*, on the other hand, is an attitude of benevolence, literally goodwill. It is unsentimental, loving of the unloving and undeserving.

The four working principles

The **four working principles** of Situation Ethics – Pragmatism, Relativism, Positivism, and Personalism – are described by Fletcher as 'presuppositions'. This means that they are believed to be true but there is no way to prove they are true. Fletcher thought it important that moral agents are aware of these underlying assumptions before making moral decisions so that they can guard against unfairness or prejudice.

Synoptic link

Link to *Chapter 4: Deontological ethics: Finnis' Natural Law and Proportionalism*. Look at Proportionalism based upon *agape* and notice the difference between Situation Ethics and Proportionalism. They are both Christian approaches to ethics and so they both value *agape*. However, Situation Ethics has only one value, *agape*, whereas Proportionalism weighs up a range of values, including the law, when making a decision. With Proportionalism, the law is always good and is never simply abandoned.

AO1 activity 4

a) Select four short Bible quotations, of no more than 20 words each, that you feel sum up Fletcher's Situation Ethics. Give a reason why you chose each quotation.

b) Learn each quotation and the reason you chose it off by heart. You could write the quotations and reasons on sticky notes and place them somewhere you visit regularly, such as the fridge door or your bedroom mirror.

Pragmatism

The first working principle is Pragmatism. Pragmatism means being practical. Sometimes to make progress, we must do what works best in the situation. Fletcher talks about this as taking a success posture, where, to be good or right, an action must work effectively to achieve a loving result. This approach is mentioned by Paul:

> *'I have the right to do anything,' you say   but not everything is beneficial. 'I have the right to do anything' – but I will not be mastered by anything.*
>
> 1 Corinthians 6:12, *Holy Bible (NIV)*

Pragmatism is choosing what is most constructive or what works best in a situation, rather than what is lawful. Paul was pointing out that while new Christians could consider themselves free from the law, that did not mean that any behaviour at all was good.

> *To be [morally] correct or right a thing – a thought or an action – must work.*
>
> Joseph Fletcher, *Situation Ethics: The New Morality*

The end to which an action should work is a meta-ethical question that relies on faith or commitment to an idea. Only after it has been decided what we are to have faith in, can ethics go to work. Here, the idea or aim that must be worked toward is love. The ethical action must practically work towards the goal of love.

Relativism

The second of the four working principles is Relativism.

> *The situationist avoids words like 'never' and 'perfect' and 'always' and 'complete' as he avoids the plague, as he avoids 'absolutely'.*
>
> Joseph Fletcher, *Situation Ethics: The New Morality*

There is only one absolute that applies when it comes to ethical decision making, and that is love. This is the 'why' of Situation Ethics, the reason for action, and it never changes. Relativism relates to the tactics that are practically employed when actually making ethical decisions. These are the things that are always subject to change; the 'how' or the 'what' of Situation Ethics.

However, Situation Ethics is not anarchy. To be relative means to relate to something, and there needs to be an absolute principle – a boss principle – to which everything relates. In Situation Ethics, this is agapeic love.

> *It relativises the absolute, it does not absolutise the relative.*
>
> Joseph Fletcher, *Situation Ethics: The New Morality*

Fletcher argued that love must be applied and related to each moral decision-making situation. Only love is constant; everything else is variable.

Key term

four working principles: one of two sets of guiding principles of Situation Ethics to help people assess the most loving action in any given situation; they are Pragmatism, Relativism, Positivism, and Personalism

Rigid observance of the law takes individual situations and forces them to fit to unbending rules. Fletcher argued that, instead, moral behaviour was about working out how to respond differently to each unique moral situation with the only absolute principle of love.

Positivism

The third working principle is Positivism. This is shorthand for '**Theological Positivism**', which Fletcher contrasts with **Theological Naturalism**.

Theological Naturalism uses reason, based on human experience or natural phenomena, to dictate what it is acceptable to believe or have faith in. An example of this kind of approach to moral decision making is Natural Law. In contrast, Theological Positivism '**posits**' or puts forward propositions of faith without reference to reason. Faith comes first: thinking is supported by faith, rather than faith being supported by thinking. Propositions of faith are not necessarily against reason but they are outside the realms of reason. In Situation Ethics, the moral agent has faith that love is the only absolute and, with that faith, uses reason to help them to decide what the most loving thing is to do in a situation.

> *Christian ethics 'posits' faith in God and reasons out what obedience to his commandment to love requires in any situation.* **"**
>
> Joseph Fletcher, *Situation Ethics: The New Morality*

Just as a utilitarian cannot prove their presumption that happiness is the highest good, the Christian cannot prove that God is love. Fletcher agrees here with Hume that we cannot climb across the gap from descriptive 'is' statements to prescriptive 'ought' statements through steps of logic, but Fletcher goes on to say that to arrive at an 'ought' requires a leap of faith across the gap. It is a voluntary decision of faith to say yes to the statement that God is love and that love is good.

Personalism

The fourth and final working principle is Personalism. This puts people at the centre of decision making, not things or laws.

> *The legalist is a what asker, (What does the law say?); the situationist is a who asker (Who is to be helped?).* **"**
>
> Joseph Fletcher, *Situation Ethics: The New Morality*

Fletcher argued that Jesus' disciples were commanded to love *people* not principles, laws, or objects. Things are only good if they are good for, or good to, somebody. Kant argued that we should treat people as ends, never merely as means, and Fletcher agreed that ethical decisions should be made for the sake of a person and never a thing. There is nothing individualistic about this ethic: good derives from the needs of people, who are members of a society and have neighbours, and true existence consequently involves personal relationships with others.

Key terms

Theological Positivism: starting with faith, rather than reason, to arrive at religious beliefs

Theological Naturalism: using reason, based on human experience or natural phenomenon, to arrive at religious beliefs

posits: suggests something is true

Joseph Fletcher
(1905–1991)

Fletcher argued that God is a personal being, that people were created *imago dei*, and so people are of primary concern in Christian ethics. He argued that it is not the unbelieving who invite damnation but the unloving; because God is love, atheists are saved by the very God whose existence they deny.

The four working principles together show that Situation Ethics focuses on action and decision making. It asks how to do the most loving thing in any situation, and is unconcerned with dogma. Rules are no more than helpful guides, and a mature ethical decision maker will not be bound by rules but will make a practical decision based on love for the person in the unique situation.

AO1 activity 5

Match the following quotations from *Situation Ethics: The New Morality* by Joseph Fletcher to one or more of the working principles, and give a reason why you think the quotation illustrates your chosen working principle(s) well.

a) 'Love is of people, by people, and for people. Things are to be used; people are to be loved.'

b) 'The divine command is always the same in its *why* but always different in its *what*, or changeless as to the *what* but contingent as to the *how*.'

c) 'The good is what works, what is expedient, what gives satisfaction.'

d) 'Aesthetic and ethical propositions are like faith propositions, they are based upon choice and decision. The "leap of affirmation" is essential to all three.'

The six fundamental principles

Fletcher describes the following **six fundamental principles** as the heart of Situation Ethics. While Situation Ethics has similarities with more secular approaches like Utilitarianism, the six fundamental principles describe the method through which Christians should make their moral decisions, with the central goal of achieving the most loving outcome.

Love is the only good

> Only one 'thing' is intrinsically good; namely, love: nothing else at all.
>
> Joseph Fletcher, *Situation Ethics: The New Morality*

This principle tells us that only love is intrinsically good in and of itself, independent of any other factors. Legalists claim that commands from God or natural laws, such as the command to preserve life, are intrinsically good and actions like murder are intrinsically evil. However, Fletcher argues that what makes an act good or evil is whether or not it helps people in the situation they find themselves in, and to say anything else brings us to a contradiction. To say that some acts are intrinsically evil forces a person to do evil in some situations.

For instance, for the legalist, lying is evil but lying to protect someone's life may be a 'lesser evil'. This suggests that some acts are still evil and require forgiveness but are, in some way, the right thing to do. This makes a false distinction between what is 'good' and what is 'right'. It also puts the legalist

Key term

six fundamental principles: one of two sets of guiding principles of Situation Ethics to help people assess the most loving action in any given situation; they are: love is the only good, love is the ruling norm of Christianity, love equals justice, love for all, loving ends justify the means, and love decides situationally in the position of having to say that it is sometimes right to go against the command of God. Fletcher calls this confused, muddled, and contradictory. He says that to lie in such a situation is good. It does not require repentance because it is done in love. Telling the truth is only valuable in as much as it loves people, because only love is good.

Love is the ruling norm of Christianity

> *The ruling norm of Christian decision making is love, nothing else.* 〞
> Joseph Fletcher, *Situation Ethics: The New Morality*

Maria Skobtsova was made a saint in the Russian Orthodox Church. She is said to have taken the place of a young Jewish girl in the gas chambers in Ravensbrück concentration camp.

This principle states that when a Christian makes a moral decision, the only thing they must never set aside is the rule to love. While Christians get some illumination from laws in scripture, there are situations where law offers no support at all. For example, Fletcher speaks of the command against killing. If this law is absolute, acts like suicide are also absolutely forbidden. However, Mother Maria (Maria Skobtsova), who is said to have taken the place of a young Jewish girl in the Nazi gas chambers, essentially died by suicide. She sacrificed her life to save another. The legalist is forced either to condemn such an action or make exceptions to the rules.

The German anti-Nazi pastor and theologian Dietrich Bonhoeffer allowed exceptions to the command against killing if the victim was not innocent, for instance in the case of war or capital punishment. He was involved in a plot to assassinate Hitler, yet he would have been forced by his own ethic to leave a man to die painfully if he were trapped in a burning plane wreck pleading to be shot. Fletcher sees love as a distillation of the law, where love has been extracted or filtered out, with the legalistic husks thrown away as rubbish. A Christian can employ law when it is loving to do so, but any commandment can and should be violated if it serves love to do so.

Love equals justice

> *Love and justice are the same, for justice is love distributed, nothing else.* 〞
> Joseph Fletcher, *Situation Ethics: The New Morality*

For Fletcher, love, justice, and prudence are not separate virtues. Justice is love fairly shared out. It is love using reason to work out problems and calculate duties, resources, obligations, and opportunities. Fletcher followed Augustine (see page 255) in saying that love is careful and diligent in serving the neighbour as well as it can. He argued that love must be carefully balanced and thorough in its calculations. This is an intellectual process that allows a Christian to work out how best to distribute love to neighbours. Fletcher recognised that we never have just one neighbour at a time, so fairness requires that love must do all it can to take everything into account and make sure love is fairly shared out. This is a social enterprise, not an individual one.

Fletcher mentioned segregation as an example of where people have differentiated wrongly between love and justice. He does not understand how a Christian gospel could preach love while simultaneously withholding justice from Black people under segregation laws. Fletcher says that *agape* must form a coalition (an alliance) with Utilitarianism, replacing their pleasure principle with the agapeic calculus: 'the greatest amount of love for the greatest number of neighbours'.

Love for all

> *Love wills the neighbour's good whether we like him or not.*
>
> Joseph Fletcher, *Situation Ethics: The New Morality*

The biblical commands not to murder, lie, or steal are all about the relationship we have with other people. To love your neighbour is to show them kindness and fair treatment. In 1 Corinthians 13, Paul describes love as being non-preferential. This means that your neighbours are not just the people that you like; they are everyone who needs love. The gospels tell us that they include enemies and strangers.

Agape is not emotional, preferential love like *philia* or *eros*, which we cannot be commanded to feel. *Agape* is practical. It is a voluntary decision to act in a benevolent way. It is not simply pleasing people; you would not give heroin to an addict just because they wanted it. Instead, *agape* is action for the neighbour's sake, even if they do not deserve it and even if they are unlovable. It is altruistic but may sometimes involve self-love if, and only if, that would benefit the neighbour. Fletcher gives the example of a ship's captain who should keep themselves alive, even at the expense of some passengers, if it means that the rest of the ship will be brought to safety. Love also requires us, sometimes, to put ourselves in harm's way, sacrificing ourselves if it is more loving to other people. This good will for others is non-reciprocal; it requires nothing in return and describes the relationship between God and humanity as well as relationships between humans beings.

Loving ends justify the means

> *Only the end justifies the means; nothing else.*
>
> Joseph Fletcher, *Situation Ethics: The New Morality*

For Fletcher, the ends are the results of an action. If the consequence is loving, then whatever steps a person has taken to get there are justified. Fletcher said that unless there is a purpose to an action, it is simply a meaningless, random accident. An action only becomes meaningful because of the purpose it serves. Ends and means are inseparable, and their goodness is relative to each other.

However, this does not mean that the situationist can do whatever they like. Means are ingredients that should be selected carefully, just as you would select ingredients for a recipe, because they contribute to the final

Synoptic link

Link to *Chapter 6: Teleological ethics: Utilitarianism*. Read about the main principle of Utilitarianism to achieve the greatest happiness for the greatest number.

189

product. The means should be fitting and proportionate to the ends. An action may sometimes be good and sometimes be evil; it depends on the situation. Fletcher claims that surgeons must sometimes mutilate bodies to save them, and that nurses must sometimes lie to some mentally ill patients to calm them for treatment, but only because in some situations the ends justify the means. There is no guilt derived from these actions, only sorrow that there is not a less tragic circumstance. According to Fletcher, there are four factors involved in moral decision making: the end, the means, the motive, and the foreseeable consequence. All of these should be balanced on love's scales. There are lots of possible ends for ethical actions, but the only end that is good in itself is love.

Love decides situationally

> Love's decisions are made situationally, not prescriptively.
>
> Joseph Fletcher, *Situation Ethics: The New Morality*

Many people want a prefabricated morality, a morality that has been built in advance, because they can lean on its strong, unyielding rules. It gives comfort and security, whereas conscience is a burden. Moving from law to love is a risk, full of the anguish of decision making. But the law cannot dictate moral decisions with generalisations or abstractions. This would not produce a loving result because moral decisions concern a living reality and situations change. Fletcher described the case of a pregnant woman in Arizona who was told her child *might* be affected by a drug called thalidomide that had been prescribed to help with extreme morning sickness. The doctors advised abortion, but the law generalised that abortion was wrong. In court, the judge denied her appeal. Eventually, her husband took her to Sweden where the abortion was carried out and the baby was found to be very badly deformed. Fletcher declared that deciding to have the abortion would have been a loving decision even if the baby had turned out to be unaffected. It was a risky decision, not knowing what the outcome would be, but it was responsible in the moment of decision.

Actions are only right *because*, *when*, or *while* they are loving. Situation Ethics takes as full account as possible of the context or environment of every moral decision. The rights and wrongs of a situation are relative to love, but once the course of action is chosen, the obligation to pursue it is absolute.

Fletcher's Situation Ethics: application of the theory

The main purpose of this section of the specification is to show how Situation Ethics can be put into practice in real ethical situations. There is no need for an in-depth study of the history of same-sex relationships and polyamory, but you do need to understand the issues raised by traditional religious responses to both before looking at how the theory of Situation Ethics applies to them.

AO1 activity 6

The 2003 film *Touching the Void* is about a real-life event that took place in 1985, when mountaineers Joe Simpson and Simon Yates made the first successful ascent of Siula Grande in the Peruvian Andes. During their descent, Simpson was accidentally lowered over the edge of a cliff and he found himself hanging in mid-air unable to climb back up. Yates was unable to pull Simpson to safety by himself and could not see or hear him to understand the problem. After holding on for over an hour and a half in extreme weather, Yates began to lose traction in the snow; he was at risk of falling to his death. Yates had two choices available to him:

- cut the rope to save himself
- try to hold on and hope someone came to the rescue.

Use the six fundamental principles of Situation Ethics to reason what the most loving course of action is in this situation. What are the 'risks' in this decision?

Homosexual relationships: what is the debate?

A same-sex relationship is a romantic and intimate, sometimes sexual, relationship between two people of the same gender. Some traditional Christian interpretations of the Bible may suggest that God commands Christians to avoid same-sex relationships.

This is because some Christian denominations teach that God created marriage as a permanent and sacred covenant for one man and one woman, and sexual intercourse as the physical union of the couple for the purpose of producing children and raising them in a family unit.

> *That is why a man leaves his father and mother and is united to his wife, and they become one flesh.* **"**
>
> Genesis 2:24, *Holy Bible (NIV)*

Some Christians have used these verses to suggest that being gay or bi is a choice that can and should be resisted because it is against God's creative purpose. However, not all Christians agree that the Bible is specific or consistent on this matter. In addition, many argue that being gay or bi is biologically determined. If this is the case, when religious laws are interpreted in this way, they command people to resist their very nature. Christianity has spent a lot of time considering and debating the teaching about same-sex sexual relationships and weighing up what it means for Christians.

In recent years, the debate has been less about whether same-sex relationships are acceptable and more about the way in which religious law should treat people who are gay or bi; this is what Fletcher was interested in. Christian churches have begun to turn their attention to the way in which they treat gay and bi members of their congregations. The Catholic Church distinguishes between performing same-sex sexual acts and being gay or bi.

Same-sex sexual acts are described as 'intrinsically disordered', on the basis that they are not reproductive and are, therefore, absolutely forbidden. Gay and bi people are called to live a chaste life, to always be respected, and never to be treated with violence or malice. As such, Pope Francis has not changed any doctrinal teaching and has reaffirmed the Catholic Church's teaching about same-sex sexual acts. However, he has worked hard to examine the issue of pastoral care for people in same-sex unions, calling for less judgement, more understanding, and an equal welcome for gay and bi people in church.

The Protestant approach to same-sex relationships is more varied. Some Protestant churches, such as the United Reformed Church in 2016 and Methodists in 2021, have embraced same-sex unions. However, the official positions of the Church in Wales and the Church of England are more complex. Both Churches teach that marriage is a lifelong and faithful union between a man and a woman, and that sex is only acceptable within a heterosexual marriage. However, more recently, there have been moves to consider whether Church teaching or practice should be adjusted to fit the needs of society.

What does Fletcher say about homosexual relationships?

When Fletcher was writing in the US in the 1960s, there were strict legal constraints against same-sex relationships. Gay and bi people could be imprisoned or chemically castrated in an attempt to punish or prevent same-sex sexual activity. Christians often cite Leviticus 18:22 as an example of God's command against same-sex relationships.

> 'Do not have sexual relations with a man as one does with a woman; that is detestable.'
>
> Leviticus 18:22, *Holy Bible (NIV)*

An interpretation of Natural Law is that it forbids same-sex sexual acts on the basis that they do not promote reproduction and cause disorder in society. However, Fletcher rejected this legalistic approach. He did not distinguish between different types of relationships and wrote that sex is only wrong in Situation Ethics if it hurts someone. Fletcher said that if a couple are of sufficient maturity, cause no harm to society, and do not themselves believe they are doing something wrong, there is no reason why sexual intercourse should not be a private matter. This is the approach taken by the Wolfenden Report, published in the UK in 1957, which declared that it should not be the duty of the law to concern itself with sexual immorality, only with challenges to public order, decency, or injury.

> The triple terrors of infection, conception, and detection which once scared people into 'Christian' sex relations (marital monopoly), have pretty well become obsolete through medicine and urbanism.
>
> Joseph Fletcher, *Situation Ethics: The New Morality*

Widespread conversations about safe sex and medical advancements mean that the fear of sexually transmitted infections no longer govern people's behaviour in the way that they might have done in the past, and what was once an activity that was considered dangerous outside of marriage is now an activity for pleasure and partnership. This is true for all sexual relationships.

While Fletcher rejected the legalistic approach, and society during his time appeared to be more accepting of sexual freedom, he was at pains to point out that the law can act as an illuminator. In some cases, he argued that it would be wise to advise people to restrict their sexual behaviour for practical reasons; for example, laws against underage sex are there to protect the welfare of children. However, this is a situational approach, not a legalistic one. He also pointed out that *agape* does not simply give people what they want: it is not enough that one person wants a sexual relationship with another person, what is important is the love created by the relationship. Two people who are in a relationship that causes one or both of them physical, psychological, or emotional harm are in a relationship that damages *agape*. A relationship based on preference is bound to be self-serving to some degree because if you are with someone because you like them, then you are with them because they make you happy. However, if the relationship is more about your own gratification than about the well-being of the other person, Fletcher questioned whether or not love is being served.

But this is not really a matter for public legislation. It is a private matter between a couple, regardless of their sexuality. It is also not about the morality of sex itself, but more to do with the motives behind sexual acts. In Fletcher's view there are greater moral problems in the world than questions of sex and sexuality and, in the interests of justice, there is no reason why a mature adult cannot decide such matters for themselves.

> *The ethical 'pharisees' (of whom there are too many) fail to see that the most evil and descriptive traits are not those of the sexual appetite, which is biologically given and morally neutral in itself, but the irrational emotional passions such as hate, fear, greed, ulcerous struggles for discrete status – all of our self-regarding (sinful) and antisocial impulses.*
>
> Joseph Fletcher, *Moral Responsibility: Situation Ethics at Work*

What does Situation Ethics say about homosexual relationships?

One of the first things to remember about Situation Ethics is that the boss principle of *agape* is to be applied to the individual person in each situation, not to abstract concepts or ideas. Therefore, Situation Ethics cannot make a general pronouncement about the goodness or badness of same-sex relationships in theory. Situation Ethics does not apply any absolutes to the issue of same-sex relationships because it is all relative to love. Therefore, the question is not: Are same-sex relationships morally acceptable? The question is: Is this particular same-sex relationship going to promote *agape*?

Fletcher argued that same-sex relationships are not a matter for legislation. They are a private matter.

Agape is, of course, non-preferential. Romantic and sexual relationships are not, in and of themselves, *agape*; they are better described as *philia* or *eros*. However, Situation Ethics does not rule out the possibility of partners in a relationship showing *agape* towards each other, and it does not prohibit *agape* from being shown to them or by them. The unique circumstances of each relationship must, therefore, be assessed to see whether or not *agape* is served or obscured by the relationship. This is the case for all romantic and sexual relationships, not just same-sex relationships. Any relationship that is abusive or manipulative is unacceptable according to the principle of *agape*.

Since we cannot use Situation Ethics to make general pronouncements, we must consider the people involved in a specific situation. Let us, therefore, consider a hypothetical couple, two men who wish to embark on a new relationship. Personalism means that we put the well-being of each of them before religious or human laws. We must look at their situation and see how much love can be achieved from their relationship. If the relationship creates *agape* – if they are both consenting, make each other happy, show each other respect, and look out for each other in a compassionate and kind way – then it is not anyone else's business to decide whether the relationship should be permitted.

Agape is only threatened when the outsider with their rule book becomes involved. If we were to forbid this couple from being together, *agape* could suffer. It could cause emotional pain. Telling two people that their urges are sinful and evil, that they must feel something different and that they are rejected by God because of their desires, would certainly cause them significant distress, both in the short term and long term. The agapeic calculus – 'the greatest amount of love for the greatest number of neighbours' – tells us that such legalistic attitudes have caused significant trauma to gay and bi people over the years, especially when people have felt compelled to undergo conversion therapy or hide their sexuality from those they love.

However, if a second hypothetical straight, gay or bi couple were to embark upon a new relationship, we might not come to the same conclusions. If, for instance, one member of the partnership felt pressured into the relationship or if one member of the partnership was emotionally or physically abusive, then we would consider the relationship to be entirely self-serving for one person. Situation Ethics would consider it more loving to attempt to liberate someone from such a toxic situation in the name of *agape*, by whatever loving means are necessary.

There are no absolutes about specific issues in Situation Ethics. It is not the goal of Situation Ethics to pronounce same-sex relationships right or wrong. The only thing that is good is love, and any means that bring about love are good. This is true of all relationships. Fletcher felt very strongly that the time for condemning gay or bi people was over. He believed it was time for a loving approach to those who have been marginalised and discriminated against. Fletcher was quoting the work of his contemporary humanist thinker L. Kirkendall when he said that moral conduct enables relationships with others to be more trusting and appreciative, which increases the capacity of people to work together. Antinomian behaviour that is self-centred and recognises no obligation to others is dangerous. Sex is not wrong unless it is malicious, callous, or if it hurts or exploits others. Sex laws should protect the vulnerable, such as children, prevent public nuisance and prevent assault, violence, duress, or fraud. Otherwise, same-sex relationships – like all romantic relationships – are a private matter.

> ### AO1 activity 7
> Read the section above about the application of Situation Ethics to same-sex relationships, and note down every time one of the four working principles or the six fundamental principles of Situation Ethics are mentioned.

> *Moral conduct is that kind of behaviour which enables people in their relationships with each other to experience a greater sense of trust, and appreciation for others; which increases the capacity of people to work together; which reduces social distance and continually furthers one's outreach to other persons and groups; which increases one's sense of self-respect and produces a greater measure of personal harmony.*
>
> Lester A. Kirkendall, 'Searching for the Roots of Moral Decisions'

Polyamorous relationships: what is the debate?

A **polyamorous relationship** is a romantic and/or sexual relationship between more than two people, a relationship that all the participating parties are aware of and fully consent to. It is not the same as cheating and it is not the same as **polygamy**, which is being legally married to more than one person at the same time. Polyamorous relationships tend to emphasise the importance of consent, openness, honesty, and trust so that all the members of the relationship flourish and are not hurt. Some countries are beginning to recognise polyamorous relationships. For example, Somerville in Massachusetts has become the first US city to give members of polyamorous relationships the same rights as married couples.

As previously stated, Christianity has traditionally taught that sex should be between one man and one woman within the confines of the sanctity of marriage for the primary purpose of reproduction. Therefore, it should not come as a surprise that any sexual relationship that falls outside this definition is considered morally wrong. The Bible does not speak of polyamory as such (although the practice of polygamy appears in the Old Testament and is not expressly condemned), but it is clear that sex outside marriage is morally unacceptable and that monogamy is God's intention.

> *But since sexual immorality is occurring, each man should have sexual relations with his own wife, and each woman with her own husband.*
>
> 1 Corinthians 7:2, *Holy Bible (NIV)*

> *Marriage should be honoured by all, and the marriage bed kept pure, for God will judge the adulterer and all the sexually immoral.*
>
> Hebrews 13:4, *Holy Bible (NIV)*

For Christians, a marriage is a covenant, not only between the man and the woman, but God as well. Therefore, extending a relationship beyond two people is not simply a matter of personal choice. It is important that it is in accordance with God's will. The Catholic Church's teachings are clear that sex must only happen between a married couple.

> *The sexual act must take place exclusively within marriage. Outside of marriage it always constitutes a grave sin and excludes one from sacramental communion.*
>
> *Catechism of the Catholic Church,* 2nd edition, paragraph 2390

The Church of England has attempted to appear less absolutist in its approach to modern relationships, but currently maintains the teaching that sexual intercourse is for married couples only.

What does Fletcher say about polyamorous relationships?

Fletcher does not use the term 'polyamorous' in any of his writings. However, he does write at length about sex, and talks about the morality of unmarried sex, same-sex sexual acts, and monogamy. He rejected legalistic approaches to sex, and this included the traditional Christian view about the purpose and value of sex.

Key terms

polyamorous relationship: a romantic and intimate, sometimes sexual, relationship between more than two people, which all the participating parties are aware of and fully consent to

polygamy: being legally married to more than one person at the same time

> *The idea in the past has been that the ideal fulfilment of our sex potential lies in a monogamous marriage. But there is no reason to regard this idea as a legal absolute. For example, if the sex ratio were to be overthrown by disaster, polygamy could well become the ideal or standard.*
>
> Joseph Fletcher, *Moral Responsibility: Situation Ethics at Work*

Fletcher argued that there was no reason why premarital sex should be prohibited by law. He valued the freedom of the individual to choose their own moral behaviour relative to what is most loving. He looked to the writings of Paul for support in this regard.

> *I am convinced, being fully persuaded in the Lord Jesus, that nothing is unclean in itself. But if anyone regards something as unclean, then for that person it is unclean.*
>
> Romans 14:14, *Holy Bible (NIV)*

Sex outside of the confines of marriage, and therefore polyamory, is only wrong if an individual thinks it is wrong. However, a sexual act that is harmful to another person is wrong. So, the emphasis upon honesty and openness within polyamorous relationships is vital if such relationships are to be considered morally acceptable. For Fletcher, a moral decision must be personal – it must consider the wellbeing of the people involved, rather than valuing rules or laws – and the most important thing in any moral decision is treating others with love.

> *Sarcasm and graft are immoral but not sexual intercourse unless it is malicious, callous, or cruel.*
>
> Joseph Fletcher, *Moral Responsibility: Situation Ethics at Work*

This means that no sexual act is ethical if it exploits (what Fletcher meant by 'graft') or hurts another person. Therefore, there must be care and commitment in premarital sex acts for them to be moral, and there is no reason why this cannot be the case in a polyamorous relationship.

Fletcher said that Situation Ethics is not interested in reluctant virgins and technical chastity. People can have sex without love and love without sex, and if people do not believe it is wrong to have sex outside marriage, then it is not wrong unless they hurt themselves, their partners, or other people. The morality of sex is relative to how much *agape* is shown to the people involved. The six fundamental principles of Situation Ethics show us that love is the most important thing, and that people and the situations they find themselves in should always be considered first when Christians make moral decisions.

What does Situation Ethics say about polyamorous relationships?

Situation Ethics does not make a general pronouncement about the goodness or badness of polyamorous relationships in theory. The boss principle of *agape* is applied on an individual basis to each person in each situation. Whether polyamory is acceptable is relative to love. So, as we saw with same-sex relationships, the question is not: Are polyamorous relationships morally acceptable? Instead the question is: Is this polyamorous relationship going to promote *agape*?

Legalistic approaches to relationships beyond those of a husband and wife are clear. The Divine Command Theory generally views sexual relationships as created by God for the purpose of reproduction. They are commanded by God as permanent, binding, and unbreakable. They are for one man and one woman, and extra-marital relationships are prohibited. This means that any sexual encounter outside of the relationship between a married couple, after marriage, is considered adulterous. In addition, premarital sex is taught to be against God's command.

However, Situation Ethics could question the value of commands like these. Widespread access to artificial contraception means there is no longer any practical reason to reject sexual relationships outside of monogamous, heterosexual marriage, since unwanted pregnancy can be prevented and the availability of condoms means sexually transmitted infections do not hold the same fear as they did in the past.

The legalist approach of Natural Law also forbids polyamorous relationships. The primary precepts show that the purpose of sex is reproduction. God created marriage to enable sex for the purpose of reproduction, and what God joins together, no one must separate.

However, for Situation Ethics, the issue of polyamory falls outside the concern of the law. As far as sex is concerned, the law should protect the vulnerable, meaning the underage and those who might be victims of abuse. It should also ensure that society is not harmed or disturbed by public acts that might not be loving to others. However, beyond these circumstances, sexual acts are private matters. Therefore, if a group of people who know what they consent to and treat each other with dignity choose to enter into an honest relationship together, provided it allows for, or promotes, *agape*, Fletcher did not think it was the business of the law to judge whether it is right or wrong.

Fletcher was clear that we must not fall into the trap of absolutising the relative. This means that we cannot make a general judgement about polyamorous relationships being good or bad, or right or wrong. We can only look at an individual situation and judge it relative to how much love is produced. It is important to remember that the boss principle of *agape* is not the same as the love that we show to a family member, a friend, or a lover. These feelings of love are better described as *philia* or *eros,* and they are quite different from the rational, compassionate treatment of other people represented by *agape*. *Agape*

Fletcher saw no reason for monogamy to be the only way of having a fulfilling relationship.

may be demonstrated through a polyamorous relationship, but it may not be. If three people put the other members of the relationship before their own happiness, showing them kindness, respect and looking out for their needs, then *agape* may be there. Such a relationship will be self-serving to some degree, as each person chooses to be with the other people because they make them happy. However, *agape* requires that if one person wishes to leave the relationship, then they must be allowed to leave because their well-being is paramount.

A polyamorous relationship can contain three or more people who are communicative and discuss their relationship together, have an equal status in the relationship, and are committed to each other, just as a relationship of two people can. If each person in the relationship is aware of the needs of their partners, and they each do all they can to support each other, Fletcher would argue that it is not the business of the law to interfere in this relationship. If the partners do not think the relationship is wrong, all the partners are adults, they are not compromising public decency, and no one is getting hurt, then they are doing nothing wrong. Fletcher refers to an incident in California, in the 1960s, where police uncovered a wife-swapping club and there was outrage when it turned out there were no laws to stop it. According to Fletcher:

> *It is doubtful that love's cause is helped by any of the sex laws that try to dictate sexual practices for consenting adults.* **"**
>
> Joseph Fletcher, *Situation Ethics: The New Morality*

On the other hand, if one or more partners is unhappy, jealous, or made to feel less important than another partner, it may be a different story. In this instance, while happiness alone is not the primary goal of Situation Ethics, the unhappiness experienced by one or more partners is a sign that *agape* is not being served. In an agapeic relationship, everyone listens to each other's concerns and discusses them openly. If one partner is dominating or manipulative, treating the others as objects rather than individuals, then it does not enable *agape*. Everyone in the relationship should be fully consenting, and there should be complete honesty between them. Here, Situation Ethics would have concern for the people in the relationship rather than any laws or rules that forbade the act of polyamory itself.

> *Monogamy may be an ideal, but it is not an idol.*
>
> Joseph Fletcher, *Situation Ethics: The New Morality*

A marital relationship is not to be pursued to the detriment of the individual people involved. Situation Ethics would reject a polyamorous relationship if it causes unhappiness or harm, not because it idolises monogamy, but because in that particular instance, agape is not present.

AO1 activity 8

In April 2021, singer Willow Smith revealed that she is polyamorous on a talk show hosted by her mother, Jada Pinkett Smith. Her grandmother, who was also present, struggled with the revelation. Make a list of reasons why Fletcher would argue that Smith should be able to participate in polyamorous relationships, and a list of reasons why others may think she should not.

This section of the chapter will enhance your ability to **analyse** and **evaluate** the topic and help you develop your AO2 skills. For each question, think about the different positions you might take, and decide which you find most persuasive and why. It is not enough to memorise a list of 'for and against' points; you need to develop an argument.

To what degree is *agape* the only intrinsic good?

Remember, to say that *agape* is intrinsically good means that part of the essential nature of *agape* is that it is good. When considering whether *agape* is the only intrinsic good, it is sensible to think about the range of possible answers to this question. You could consider whether or not *agape* itself is intrinsically good, or you could consider whether there are other things that might be considered intrinsically good too.

The view that *agape* is the only intrinsic good

Jesus seems to have insisted on the primary status of *agape*, as did Paul in his address to the Corinthians. Jesus claimed that love of God and neighbour is the base on which all the law and commands rest. Paul said that love was the greatest moral virtue of all. These words appear to confirm that *agape* is indeed the only intrinsic good, and that any act which serves love is only good because of the love that it aims towards.

Paul Tillich argued that the idea of acts being intrinsically and eternally decreed has been used by failing political and religious systems as a way to hold on to power. The idea that certain behaviours are eternal and absolute means that humans are required to obey laws that suit the law makers, rather than doing what the situation requires. Tillich argued that only love is intrinsically good; only love has the power to be relevant to each situation without losing its eternal validity in a changing world. Tillich said that love can transform so that it is relevant in any time or situation; it is the ideal for history as a whole, no matter what the situation.

For Fletcher, love is not a 'thing' for a person to have or be. It is an action, something that a person does. It does not present an ideal form of generalised, perfect behaviour. Instead, it must be applied in different circumstances and, in each situation, if the loving thing is done, that will be the good thing. Laws can be followed or laws can be broken, but what matters is that the loving thing is done. Fletcher felt that, to some extent, he had Martin Luther and even Karl Barth on his side. Both presented arguments that agreed there are times when disobedience to the law is the loving thing to do.

The view that *agape* is not intrinsically good

Fletcher is a theological positivist. He requires that human beings have faith that *agape* is good because it cannot be proven through reason. This is non-rational rather than irrational, but the requirement for faith is a far cry from any kind of evidence to support the belief in the intrinsic goodness of *agape*. Humans are expected to trust that no action is intrinsically good but that any action is acceptable if it serves love. We are given no reason why love is better than religious or human laws.

Situation Ethics fails to distinguish between actions that are good and actions that are right. Proportionalists argue that while something like *agape* might be intrinsically good, that does not mean that it is always the correct thing to do. It might be good to love, but that does not mean that it is right to do something just because it is loving. For instance, it might be loving to want to end someone's suffering, but that does not justify killing.

Bernard Hoose, in his account of the Catholic approach of Proportionalism, argues that love is not enough to make an action morally good. He points out that terrible acts have been performed in the name of love. He gives the historical example of burning heretics by well-intentioned Christians. He points out that these acts were performed from a fervent love of God and God's message, but they were terribly wrong.

The view that *agape* is one among several intrinsic goods

Situation Ethics states that *agape* is the only intrinsically good thing and that there are no actions that are intrinsically bad. William Barclay argued instead that *agape* does not change the intrinsic nature of any action. He gave the example of a dangerous drug used by doctors to treat a disease. Such a drug would be kept under lock and key, rationed, and managed carefully. It would never be treated as though it was anything other than dangerous, even if it was sometimes used for a good purpose. There are some actions that should always be controlled because they are always bad, and other actions that are always good. It is not straightforward to just abandon such a concept.

Pope Pius XII, in a radio message in 1952, stated that treating *agape* as the only law is an act that attempts to justify decisions that are in direct opposition to the law of God, which was upheld by both Jesus and Paul. By challenging the morality of the Catholic Church, Pope Pious XII saw the 'new morality' of Situation Ethics as attacking the person of Christ himself. He made it clear that God has forbidden a range of acts, including sexual acts, and they are intrinsically bad and therefore sinful. Obedience to God's law is intrinsically good. The teaching of Situation Ethics is, he argued, expressly forbidden.

Jesus and Paul did not suggest that love was the only thing that was intrinsically good. In 1 Corinthians 13, Paul says that faith, hope, and love are all important. In addition, in Galatians 5:22, Paul lists a range of other things that appear to be 'good'. He includes love along with joy, peace, patience, kindness, and faithfulness.

AO2 activity 1
Look through the nine arguments about the degree to which *agape* is the only intrinsic good, and rank them according to how convincing or persuasive you find them. Award a 1 for the least convincing argument and a 9 for the most convincing argument. Explain your choices for the most convincing and least convincing arguments.

Does Fletcher's Situation Ethics promote immoral behaviour?

It is useful to consider what is meant by the word 'promote'. To promote immoral behaviour, Fletcher would have to be actively encouraging people to do something immoral. For Fletcher, immoral behaviour involves acting contrary to love and, of course, he does not promote immoral behaviour according to his own understanding of the term. However, we can consider whether he promotes behaviour that other theories would consider immoral, and we can also consider whether Situation Ethics allows, rather than actively encourages, immoral acts.

The view that Situation Ethics promotes immoral behaviour

The Catholic Church cites Romans 3:8 when it says that it is never acceptable to do evil to produce a good outcome.

> *Why not say – as some slanderously claim that we say – 'Let us do evil that good may result'? Their condemnation is just!*
>
> Romans 3:8, *Holy Bible (NIV)*

Fletcher's fifth fundamental principle states that loving ends justify the means. This means that absolutely any action can be considered acceptable if there is a 'good' outcome. Killing, torture, rape, abuse, lying, and slander are all fair game in moral decision making, as long as one can foresee desirable consequences. The Catholic Church would argue this actively promotes immoral, sinful behaviour.

Barclay, writing in 1971, argued that removing laws to give individuals the freedom to decide their own morality is a mistake.

> *Once a thing is not forbidden, it may be felt not only to be permitted, but to be encouraged. It could be argued that what the law permits, it approves.*
>
> William Barclay, *Ethics in a Permissive Society*

Barclay gave the example of university students being allowed to have students of the opposite sex stay overnight in their rooms. A university that permits this, according to Barclay, promotes it. Barclay felt that it was important to maintain rules and laws so as to uphold a clear moral standard. For him, the university should enforce rules about students' sexual activities to encourage moral behaviour.

Barclay went on to point out that Fletcher makes a big assumption that an unmarried person somehow requires sex to feel fulfilled. He argued that Fletchers' examples involving sex often allow a 'wrong' to make a 'right'. To seduce a woman 'for her own good' or to have sex with a man to 'cure' him of his tendency to prefer children is morally unacceptable. Barclay points out that there are right and wrong ways to solve a problem, and using sex as a cure, thereby abandoning moral law, forgets that there may be more effective ways of managing problems.

The view that Situation Ethics does not promote immoral behaviour

It is not possible for Situation Ethics to promote immoral behaviour. Fletcher said that moral acts require consideration of love alone in each specific situation. The only actions that are immoral are those that are unloving. Situation Ethics does not promote actions that are unloving, and so cannot promote immoral behaviour.

Tillich argued that the promotion of legalism as an eternal law has historically been used to maintain the authority of those in power, especially at times when their power is seen to be failing. Martin Luther and Paul struggled against law and argued that only love can adapt to the needs of each individual situation in a changing world without losing its eternal dignity and validity. Therefore, love cannot promote immoral behaviour, while law certainly can.

Fletcher observed that it is nonsense for scholars like Barth to condemn certain acts as intrinsically morally evil, and yet acknowledge that sometimes God may command a person to do them. For example, killing is condemned as intrinsically evil, yet in some situations, God commands that an evil act is performed – such as when he commanded Abraham to kill his son, Isaac. This means that it becomes good to do evil, which is nonsense. Fletcher's approach is to say that no act is intrinsically evil, and therefore, to do a loving thing is always to do something good. There is no contradiction here, and so Situation Ethics does not promote immoral behaviour.

The view that Situation Ethics allows, but does not promote, immoral behaviour

Barclay pointed out that the vast majority of Fletcher's numerous examples are drawn from abnormal, unusual, or extraordinary situations. Most people are highly unlikely to find themselves in such extreme situations, and it is much easier to see the value in Situation Ethics in these examples than it is to think that laws can be abandoned at will in everyday life.

At no point in his writing does Fletcher suggest that any particular action is commanded by God. In his selection of four final examples in the appendix to *Situation Ethics: The New Morality*, he does not give solutions to the problems. He argues that the most loving thing must be done, but it is up to the reader to determine what that loving action is. In other examples throughout the book, Fletcher implies that certain actions are allowed by love rather than commanded. Therefore, while Situation Ethics does allow immoral actions such as killing, lying, or stealing, it never commands that they must be done.

Situation Ethics promotes only that people should behave in love towards each other. However, Fletcher emphasised personal freedom to choose the most loving action for oneself. This puts no protection in place to guard against the abuse of Situation Ethics for personal gain. Barclay pointed out that humanity is not perfect. Love can make mistakes, it can be distorted; and freedom from law, when love is not perfectly present, is dangerous. It leaves too much room for selfishness, cruelty, or damage.

To what extent does Situation Ethics promote justice?

This question includes the word 'extent', which implies the answer is not necessarily a question of whether Situation Ethics promotes justice or not does promote justice. There might be some kind of middle position, whereby Situation Ethics supports justice or enables justice, yet does not actively promote it.

The view that Situation Ethics promotes justice

The third of Fletcher's six fundamental principles is that love equals justice. Justice, for Fletcher, is the same thing as love; therefore, it is at the heart of ethical decision making and cannot be separated from Situation Ethics. Throughout his writing, Fletcher repeatedly explains that the purpose of Situation Ethics is to ensure that people are treated fairly, and that the rigid observance of the law that leads to people being treated unjustly is avoided.

Barclay protested that laws should not be abandoned in favour of *agape*, on the basis that there are certain acts that we surely can never approve of. The examples he gives are the legalising of consenting same-sex relationships, the easing of divorce regulations, and the eligibility of unmarried parents to have the same rights as those who are married. He considers that such behaviours are not private matters but, in fact, affect the lives of others. However, in contemporary society, all of these things are acceptable and, one might argue, society is fairer for it.

Fletcher pointed out that it is not possible to make general judgements about what is right or wrong that will apply universally. He said that it all depends upon the situation. Love, and therefore justice, would not judge a person who has sex for money because they are starving, in the same way as it would judge a person who has sex because they want an expensive item of clothing. Situation Ethics promotes justice because it considers all the factors involved in a situation which make that situation unique, and it comes to a judgement that is fair for the person at the centre of it.

The view that Situation Ethics does not promote justice

Barclay questioned whether love and justice can really be the same thing. He points out that other great thinkers, such as Reinhold Niebuhr, have described *agape* as transcendent, beyond this world, whereas justice is

AO2 activity 2

Look at the following example that Fletcher gives:

In 1945, in the final year of the Second World War, the *Enola Gay* dropped an atomic bomb known as 'Little Boy' on Hiroshima. Three days later, they dropped another on Nagasaki. There was division within the US government about whether or not the weapon should be used, whether Japan should be warned, and whether the targets should be civilian as well as military.

a) Would Situation Ethics promote the use of the atomic bomb? Why or why not?

b) Would Situation Ethics allow the use of the atomic bomb? Why or why not?

c) Would legalistic approaches to ethics allow or promote the use of the atomic bomb?

d) Do you think the use of such a weapon was moral or immoral? Why?

something that applies firmly in the real world. Emile Brunner saw justice as something that is applied between groups, while love concerns the relationships between individuals. Fletcher's claim that love and justice are the same is in direct conflict with these definitions.

Legalism promotes the good of society at the expense of individual freedom, and individualism promotes the good of the individual at the expense of society. Yet, society and the individual are inseparable from one another. Human beings do not act in a vacuum, and any so called 'private' moral action necessarily has some effect upon other people. Situation Ethics takes little account of this, and in placing certain actions in the realm of private morality, does not promote fairness for everyone. In Fletcher's many examples, he allows the freedom of the individual at the expense of society.

Situation Ethics appears to pick and choose to whom love should be shown. While Fletcher referred to Jesus' command that we should love our neighbours and our enemies, he also suggested that Situation Ethics must apply an adapted version of Utilitarianism: we must show the greatest love for the greatest number. However, this is not love fairly shared out. For example, sacrificing the lives of civilians for the sake of a shorter war is not showing justice to those civilians, and tipping people out of an overcrowded lifeboat is not showing justice to those who drown as a result.

The view that Situation Ethics supports, but does not promote, justice

Tillich argued that love implies equality, in the sense that the one who loves and the one who is loved are equal to each other. But in practice, equality – justice – is not guaranteed by love. Tillich gave the example of ancient Greece, where there was political equality among all those who were free, but inequality between free people and enslaved people. Love can be restricted and distorted, and this may lead to discrimination and injustice.

The idea of love is well-meaning and positive, but it is highly interpretive. What seems loving to one person may not seem loving to another. Love underpins all Christian ethical approaches, but how to be loving has been interpreted very differently through the ages. It seems loving in the twenty-first century to ensure people have equal rights regardless of their sexual preference. However, in the past, it may have appeared loving to restrict same-sex relationships because they were considered harmful to the individuals involved and to society. It seems, then, that love makes justice possible, but does not clearly describe what actions are fair in practice.

'Justice' has a number of different definitions. For instance, it can be fair treatment, upholding of the law, or administering punishment or reward. However, regardless of the definition, justice needs adjudication to ensure it is impartial, reasonable, and fair. Unfettered freedom for people to make their own decisions in what they feel is love could easily give rise to chaotic and unfair actions, even if those actions are performed from a loving motive.

AO2 activity 3

Read the following quotation:

> *We ought not to hesitate to break a law that is in all conscience unjust, that is to say, unloving.* "
>
> Joseph Fletcher, *Situation Ethics: The New Morality*

Do you agree? What problems can you see occurring if ordinary civilians choose to break laws that they believe are unjust?

How effective is Situation Ethics in dealing with ethical issues?

When considering the effectiveness of a moral approach, it is sensible to think about what an effective approach looks like. Is it an approach that is clearly described? Or maybe it is an approach that is flexible, or reliable, or an approach that offers sufficient guidance to deal with life's challenges?

The view that Situation Ethics is highly effective in dealing with ethical issues

Fletcher demonstrated the effectiveness of Situation Ethics in dealing with difficult ethical issues. He gave the example of two groups travelling on the Boone Trail, in the eighteenth century, to establish new settlements in Kentucky. Both groups were threatened by indigenous Americans and both groups included nursing mothers, whose babies were crying loudly and putting the groups at greater risk. The first group was caught and killed but the second group made it to safety because the mother killed her baby to ensure her group was not discovered. The law would not have offered guidance in such a difficult situation. Situation Ethics allowed the mother to decide what to do, when the law would have paralysed her.

Tillich argued, in *Morality and Beyond* (1963), that both Catholicism and Protestantism have made the 'yoke' of morality heavier with the emphasis on obedience to laws and rules despite Jesus' desire to make moral decision making easier. This suggests that the flexibility of Situation Ethics in dealing with complex moral situations is more effective than the weighty burden of the law.

Tillich argued that Situation Ethics is part of the solution to the problem of ethics in a changing world. There needs to be an immovable principle that is the basis from which change can happen, as society changes and needs to evolve, but which keeps ethical behaviour grounded in an eternal standard of good. This can be found in the boss principle of *agape*. It is above law but follows the clear directive of Jesus in a changing world.

The view that Situation Ethics is not effective in dealing with ethical issues

According to Hoose, Situation Ethics is 'too vague'. While the debate about the importance of circumstance and consequence is an important one, Hoose feels that Situation Ethics is underdeveloped and, consequently, unsatisfactory. More is needed when dealing with ethical issues than just being told 'love will tell you what to do'.

Barclay argued that, just as a child needs guidance when learning to do the right thing, or a flautist needs lessons before they are able to play the flute by themselves, a moral agent needs guidance and support before being given the freedom to go off and make loving decisions according to the situation. Humanity cannot be trusted to make ethical decisions in a reliable way without the guidance of law.

Prefabricated rules, rules that have been set down in advance, simplify ethics. Barclay pointed out that they save people from making difficult, and often dangerous, moral judgements for themselves. No one has to decide from scratch or worry about whether they have made the wrong choice. Morality should be easy, and people should be able to trust the law to lead them in a direction that has been decided in advance by minds that may be more capable than theirs of making reliable ethical judgements.

The view that Situation Ethics is partially effective in dealing with ethical issues

Hoose pointed out that problems arising from the moral agent themselves can never be cured by a system of ethics. If 'love is lacking', then a person will do what they want, no matter what rules are in place to encourage them to make different choices. Love is not enough.

> *Love's presence or absence does not tell us whether or not an action is morally right. Love merely encourages, or rather, demands, a sincere search.*
>
> Bernard Hoose, *Proportionalism: The American Debate and its European Roots*

This means that while Situation Ethics has identified a vital part of Christian ethics, which is fundamental to good moral decision making, it has not gone far enough to discover what really makes an action moral.

Situation Ethics is brave and risky according to Fletcher. It means that people must take responsibility for their actions rather than blindly obeying rules and ignoring the consequences of their actions. However, the whole purpose of normative ethics is to identify a system that can be trusted to work out what is good or evil. Situation Ethics firmly rejects the use of any system whatsoever, and so there is no objective way to judge how effective it is.

Situation Ethics awards humanity freedom and commands us only to love. There can be nothing bad about either of these things. Both are required in scripture and are fundamental to a Christian understanding of ethics. However, Fletcher offered no training before sending moral agents out on their own to face the challenges of the world. He assumed, as John Robinson did, that Situation Ethics is 'the only ethic for man come of age' (Robinson, *Honest to God*). But Barclay pointed out that human beings are not 'of age'. They are not perfect, and a person who is set free to make important moral decisions needs to be trained and trustworthy if they are going to function without the guidance of the law.

AO2 activity 4

Create a short survey to find out if friends and family think that Situation Ethics is an effective method in dealing with ethical issues. You could ask questions such as:

- Do you think we should always obey the law, no matter what?
- Under what circumstances do you think breaking a law is the right thing to do?
- What does it mean to tell someone that they should always be loving?

Review the data you have collected. Did any of your friends and family raise any interesting arguments? Do they think that Situation Ethics is an effective ethical theory? Do you agree? Why or why not?

Should *agape* replace religious rules?

This kind of question asks you to consider whether *agape* is a suitable substitute for the laws put in place by Christianity. It might be useful to consider the nature of *agape* as a guiding principle, rather than a law. This is because it performs a different function. Instead of instructing people about specific actions they may or may not perform, it is an attitude that guides moral decision making in each individual situation.

The view that *agape* should replace religious rules

Dietrich Bonhoeffer understood rules and principles as tools that can be thrown away when they are no longer of use. This means that there are rules and principles that a situationist can rely on while they are useful, but once they cease to be useful, they can be set aside. They can be abandoned completely if they are broken, or they can be saved until they are needed in the future. *Agape* is the principle that helps a person decide on the usefulness of a religious rule or principle and, therefore, it should replace them as the governing principle of ethical behaviour.

Barclay described *agape* as a highly intelligent thing. It requires reason and involves working out what is most loving rather than mindlessly obeying prefabricated rules that do not necessarily help people in the specific circumstances they find themselves in. Fletcher described *agape* as thinking supported by faith, and saw it as the only way for people to take moral responsibility for their actions. In contrast, religious rules can be blind, out of touch with the 'headaches and heartbreaks' of real life.

Moral behaviour requires moral agents to look at the difficulties faced by others with compassion and sympathy rather than judgement or self-righteousness. Legalism encourages people to judge others experiencing their own unique difficulties. It leads people to force others into even more damaging situations. For example, many worry that the current tightening of US abortion laws, done in the name of saving the lives of the unborn, could lead to greater harm, as some people are pushed towards illegal and unsafe abortions out of desperation and others proceed with pregnancies that might cause them damage.

The view that *agape* should not replace religious rules

Fletcher himself pointed out that Situation Ethics does not offer a system of ethics to replace traditional religious rules. He even went so far as to say that there is no such thing as a Christian ethical system. He argued that Jesus had no system of ethics (although many Christians would respond that Jesus followed Jewish law). Jesus' actions and words challenged the rigid observance of religious rules at all costs. For instance, he did not encourage his followers to work on the Sabbath whenever it suited them, but he did say that if someone was suffering, helping them to alleviate their pain on a Sabbath was reasonable and compassionate. Therefore, *agape* should not replace religious rules, it should underpin and guide them.

Laws are necessary to manage behaviour. Barclay gave the example of a game. Without rules, games make no sense. Without a referee, a game of football cannot take place. While Situation Ethics would be wonderful in a world where human beings are perfect, human beings are flawed, unreliable, and careless. They need the guidance provided by religious rules and laws.

Situation Ethics does not give much space for the grace of God. To encourage the use of personal, subjective reasoning above the role of God in a difficult moral situation is to put human reason above God's grace and power. Christianity teaches that God is omnipotent, omnibenevolent, and personal. This means that believers are required to trust in God's will and plan for them, and not override his commands with their own reasoning.

To what extent does Situation Ethics provide a practical basis for making moral decisions for religious believers and non-believers?

Again, by asking you about 'extent', this question implies the answer is not necessarily that Situation Ethics provides a practical basis for moral decision making or not. There may be other conclusions, whereby Situation

---

AO2 activity 5

Summarise the arguments from this section onto flash cards. Choose the argument that you feel is most powerful and write the following:

- one reason why you find this argument powerful
- a quotation from a scholar that supports the argument
- a direct challenge to the argument you found powerful
- one reason why the challenge you have written could be successful
- an example to demonstrate the success of the challenge
- a decision regarding whether the initial argument or the challenge is more persuasive
- one reason why you made that decision.

Now choose the argument that you find least powerful and do the same.

Ethics provides some degree of support but is not always or completely practical. An examination question may also ask you to consider the extent to which this is practical for people who hold religious beliefs, or those who do not. You should consider whether your answer would be different if it refers to people who are not religious.

The view that Situation Ethics provides a practical basis for making moral decisions for religious believers/non-believers

Situation Ethics does not promote antinomianism. It does not suggest that the law should be abandoned and ignored in the pursuit of love. Fletcher valued the role of law in society and understood that religious rules, for the most part, guide people along a good moral path. He believed that laws are usually 'pretty safe' and are a way of translating value judgements (judgements made, by society, about what is good) into formal social disciplines that everyone can abide by. However, sometimes the law cannot address situations that are unusual or difficult and, in these cases, Situation Ethics offers people guidance about the right thing so that they do not end up paralysed by inaction.

Religious believers may agree that religious rules usually guide people along a good moral path. However, non-believers have no reason to prefer religious rules. But non-believers may agree that since even secular law does not address every unusual or difficult case, Situation Ethics can help individuals to make decisions when the law fails.

Non-believers may agree that Situation Ethics is practical since love is something that anyone, regardless of religious belief, can support. The '#BeKind' movement demonstrates the need for compassion for people when we make moral choices, and one does not need to have a religious belief to agree that we should be kind to each other.

The view that Situation Ethics does not provide a practical basis for making moral decisions for religious believers/non-believers

The risk provided by complete moral freedom is too great. While it is wonderful, in theory, to have complete freedom to choose the most loving action in any situation, this is too idealistic. People can easily use this freedom to perform selfish, corrupt, even cruel actions, and there is nothing in Situation Ethics to prevent it. The damage that can be done by allowing this level of freedom is huge if a person is not truly acting with *agape*. Situation Ethics is impractical because it does not safeguard against the likelihood of abuse.

Barclay argued that the law is the distillation of experience. The long history of human experience has contributed to the production of moral laws, and this should not be dismissed. It should be taken seriously as a guide to the actions that are proved to be harmful or injurious and the actions that are proved to be beneficial. This is far more practical than a moral free-for-all.

Non-believers may argue that since Situation Ethics places its faith in God and the teachings of Jesus on love, it is not practical as a basis for making moral decisions. Religious values often lead people to do terrible things. Just because an act is motivated by love does not mean that the act will not be morally abhorrent. For instance, forcing a faith on another person might be done out of love and concern for their afterlife, but it doesn't make it practical or morally right.

The view that Situation Ethics provides some practical support for making moral decisions for religious believers/non-believers

The view that Robinson, in *Honest to God*, wrote that there is no suggestion in the gospels that ethical approaches based on Christianity are only for religious people. He claimed that they are for all people because they are based upon human nature and date back to God's created purpose for humanity. Jesus' teaching on love is practical for all because it is in line with God's purpose for humans, but still allows people to work out the best action in the situation they are faced with.

Fletcher gave many examples to illustrate how *agape* might be applied in different ethical situations. His principles give guidance about how people should understand love, and he drew from both religious and non-religious ethicists to support his arguments. However, since each moral situation must be assessed according to its own specific circumstances, and Fletcher gives no rules or methods for how to do this, the moral agent is left to work it out for themselves.

Fletcher did not dismiss the role of law or of religious rules in ethical decision making. They can still operate and be a practical guide for people who are making moral decisions. Equally, moral agents are able to dismiss laws that appear to be impractical in a specific context. For example, laws forbidding stealing will usually be upheld, but if stealing is the only way to survive, it is loving and good to steal. However, Fletcher did not indicate exactly what level of need is required for a law to be abandoned. It is unclear whether one needs to be on the brink of starvation to be allowed to steal, or if a lesser feeling of hunger would make it acceptable.

AO2 activity 6

Look at the following example that Fletcher gives:

In Italy, during the Second World War, a priest was involved in the bombing of a Nazi train by the underground resistance. To persuade the culprit to surrender, the authorities began killing 20 hostages a day. The priest refused to give himself up because he was the only person available to help his parishioners gain forgiveness for their sins. After three days, a fellow resistance fighter betrayed the priest to stop the killing.

a) Which was the loving action in this situation and why?

b) If you had difficulty in deciding which was the most loving action, why did you find it difficult?

c) Do you agree with Fletcher that the priest's method of decision making was practical? Give three reasons for your answer.

Practising AO1 questions

As you now know, AO1 questions begin with a range of possible command words (see pages 8–9 for more detail). The following question begins with the word 'Examine'. 'Examine' questions require you look at a particular aspect of a complex issue in significant depth. It asks for more detail than an 'Explain' question and, as a result, the subject of the question may be fairly narrow.

Read the past paper question below and the example paragraph written in response before completing the activity on page 212.

> *Examine why Fletcher used 'agape' as the basis for Situation Ethics.*
>
> (Eduqas A Level Religious Studies, Summer 2019, Component 3: Religion and Ethics, Question 4a)

Example

Fletcher[6] used the concept of *agape* as the basis for his 'new morality'[6] of Situation Ethics because[2] he felt that *agape* is unconditional love for others regardless of whether you like them or can get anything back from them[1]. Fletcher[6] used the teaching of Jesus as the basis for[2] Situation Ethics. Jesus taught that we should love our neighbour as we love ourselves.[1] This means that we should show love to anyone who is nearby. Jesus also said that we should love our enemies.[1] This means that we should show love to people regardless of whether we like them or not. Fletcher said[6] that we should use this way of making moral decisions because[2] it is structured without denying us our personal freedom to choose our moral actions for ourselves. Fletcher felt that it is a better approach than[1] legalism[7] because[2], while legalism is a[1] binding, choking 'web' of laws[6], Situation Ethics gives you the freedom to make moral decisions according to the particular person[1] who is in need in front of you and allows you to make difficult decisions when the law would condemn you no matter what you do.

Areas for development and what went well

1 This paragraph contains relevant knowledge and understanding. There is a brief definition of *agape*, which is helpful, but the student does not linger too long on this and gets right on with answering the question.

2 This paragraph clearly addresses the question.

3 The paragraph does not contain any examples or evidence. There is a mention of Jesus teachings, but specific examples would be beneficial. Alternatively, one of Fletcher's examples could be included.

4 The response makes no use of sources of wisdom and authority. However, they would be useful because Fletcher's reasons for using *agape* are based upon his understanding of the Bible.

5 This response takes no opportunity to make connections. An example of how a legalistic approach like Natural Law might respond to an ethical issue could be used, to show why Fletcher might reject it.

6 Fletcher is the only scholar that needs to be quoted or paraphrased in an answer to this question. While other scholars can be used in support, they are unnecessary.

7 The language used is appropriate but there is scope for more sophisticated and technical language to be used.

Activity

a) Read the example paragraph on page 211, and identify one thing that the student has done successfully and one thing they could improve.

b) Improve the example paragraph by correcting the weakness you identified.

AO1 practice question 1

Now it is your turn. Have a go at answering the following question. There are some points to remember underneath to help you if you are not sure how to start.

> *Apply Fletcher's Situation Ethics to ethical issues relating to homosexual relationships.*
>
> (WJEC AS Level Religious Studies, Summer 2018, AS Unit 2:
> An Introduction to Religion and Ethics and the Philosophy of Religion, Question 1a)

Points to remember

- This is an 'apply' question, so you need to use the features of Fletcher's Situation Ethics to show how it can be used to make an ethical decision about same-sex relationships.
- Make sure that you use the most appropriate principles of Situation Ethics to highlight the ethical issues that best relate to same-sex relationships. For example, you could show how a decision must be practical and just in its treatment of same-sex couples. You can also show why alternative ethical decision-making approaches would be rejected by Fletcher.
- Give examples of the kinds of relationships that Fletcher might have accepted or rejected. For example, you could mention that Fletcher would have rejected relationships that are self-centred or abusive, regardless of the type of relationship it is.

AO1 practice question 2

Now try this question by yourself.

> *Explain why Fletcher rejects the ethical approaches of legalism, antinomianism and the role of the conscience.*
>
> (Eduqas AS Level Religious Studies, Summer 2018, Component 3:
> An Introduction to Religion and Ethics, Question 3a)

Practising AO2 questions

When writing a response to an AO2 question, you must remember that you are being examined on your ability to analyse and evaluate effectively. Analysis involves a detailed examination of something and you should pick apart the concept to look for the strengths and the weaknesses. Evaluation involves judging the quality or importance of the concept. You are expected to analyse and evaluate throughout the whole of your response; you are not be expected to include long passages explaining knowledge and understanding.

Read the past paper question below and the example paragraphs written in response before completing the activity on page 215.

> 'Situation Ethics is a practical way for religious believers to make moral decisions.' Evaluate this view.
>
> (Eduqas A Level Religious Studies, Summer 2019, Component 3: Religion and Ethics, Question 4b)

Example 1

Situation Ethics is not a practical way for religious believers to make moral decisions.[2] There is no clear guidance for them[1] when making decisions, so they don't know what to do. A religious believer requires God's guidance[1]. They need laws and rules. Barclay[4] noted that 'People do not want freedom. They want security'[4]. Security is more practical[2]. Fletcher[4] himself said that making loving decisions is 'risky'[4]. So, Situation Ethics is impractical[2]. Hoose acknowledged[5] that love is not enough[1] to make an action moral or immoral and there are terrible decisions that are made by people who really love God[4]. Situation Ethics allows people to do terrible things[1] and claim they are loving when they are not. That is an impractical method[2] of morality. Situation Ethics has no system[1] that prevents awful actions and so it is impractical[2].

Areas for development

1. There is some valid analysis. However, this single paragraph is one-sided and offers no counter argument, deeper analysis, or evaluation. It would be better to spread these arguments over the whole essay, and instead use this paragraph to analyse and evaluate one or two points more deeply. There is a good use of scholarly ideas that could be improved by weighing up how effective they are. A judgement is made at the end of the paragraph and supported with a reason.

2. This paragraph focuses on the two aspects of the question throughout: religious believers and practicality.

3. The paragraph does not contain examples or evidence to support the arguments.

4. There are plenty of references to scholarly points of view and their relevance to the arguments are briefly explained. However, there is no sense of weighing up the arguments or considering counter arguments.

5. There is a brief attempt to make a relevant connection to Proportionalism. This could be developed further by considering how it might be more practical to take into account other things as well, such as goods and values.

6. The language used by the candidate is appropriate, but the paragraph lacks specialist language specific to Situation Ethics.

Example 2: an improved response

At first glance Situation Ethics seems highly impractical[2] for religious believers facing difficult moral dilemmas. This is because there is no clear guidance[1] and no way that believers can know if they are making good moral decisions. William Barclay[4] notes that 'people do not want freedom. They want security'[4]. The responsibility of decision-making is too great.[1] There is too much room for error[1] in Situation Ethics and no protection[1] that prevents people from making bad decisions that are not in accordance with God's will. However, legalistic[6] religious guidance has been restrictive[1]. Prefabricated laws[6] do not allow decisions that are pragmatic[6] or personal[6]. For example, a committed, loving, same-sex couple going about their own private business would be condemned as[3] sinful[6] and the harm done by shaming people in this way is significant.[3] The desire for security is laziness[1] on the part of the moral agent. Fletcher[4] requires religious believers to step up because loving decisions are 'risky'[4]. This may be challenging but is a far more practical[2] way of making ethical decisions in the real world where sometimes there is no clear and easy solution[1].

What went well

1 There is now a sense of weighing up the good and the bad aspects of the arguments.

2 This answer contains regular reference to the wording of the question throughout.

3 There is now a more detailed use of a worked example to illustrate a point.

4 There is still appropriate evidence of scholarly points of view and quotations from them. These are now weighed up and a counter argument offered.

5 To make room for analysis and evaluation in this paragraph, the student has decided to remove the connection to Proportionalism. Elsewhere the answer could consider how Proportionalism is more (or less) practical because it considers the values and disvalues beyond love alone when deciding on a moral action.

6 There is some accurate use of specialist language in context.

Activity

a) Read Example 1 on page 213 and identify three things that could be developed to improve the analysis or the evaluation.

b) Read Example 2 on page 214. This time the evaluation and analysis are much more effective. List at least three things you think the student has done to make their answer better.

AO2 practice question 1

Now it is your turn. Have a go at answering the following question. There are some points to remember underneath to help you if you are not sure how to start.

'Agape (selfless love) should replace all religious rules.'
Evaluate this view.

(WJEC AS Level Religious Studies, Summer 2018, AS Unit 2:
An Introduction to Religion and Ethics and the Philosophy of Religion, Question 1b)

Points to remember

- The question asks you to focus on whether love should replace religious rules. You could weigh up whether this was what Fletcher, or Jesus for that matter, was advocating. You could consider whether both rules and love are needed, or whether the rules are ultimately the most loving approach.
- Give plenty of examples throughout the essay, to back up your arguments and illustrate your ideas. For example, you could give examples showing how helpful or unhelpful rules relating to same-sex relationships have been in the past. Alternatively, you could discuss Hoose's idea that terrible things can be done in the name of love and give specific examples.
- Use the ideas of the scholars that have been mentioned in this chapter or in other chapters. Think about the other ethical approaches you have studied so far, and whether the rules that they present are any more effective at guiding morality than a command to 'be loving'.

AO2 practice question 2

Now try this question by yourself.

'Religious believers must reject Situation Ethics as a basis for making moral decisions.' Evaluate this view.

(Eduqas AS Level Religious Studies, Summer 2017, Component 3:
An Introduction to Religion and Ethics, Question 3b)

Mark schemes for all exam questions can be found at www.eduqas.co.uk and www.wjec.co.uk.

Teleological ethics: Utilitarianism

On 30 August 1941, the Prime Minister, Winston Churchill, authorised the development of a UK nuclear weapons programme. The US dropped an atomic bomb on Japan in 1945, at the end of the Second World War, and since then countries, around the world have been investing in nuclear weapons programmes.

The UK Government's website tells us that the UK possesses nuclear weapons to preserve peace, prevent coercion, and deter aggression. In other words, other countries are put off using their nuclear weapons against the UK because they know that if they do, the costs to them would outweigh any benefits. The UK government argues that abandoning the nuclear deterrent would put the country at greater risk, and therefore continued investment in our nuclear weapons programme is for the greater good.

Those who support the continued use of nuclear weapons as a deterrent say that this is the reason we have not had a third world war. They argue that nuclear weapons have saved millions of lives and have kept peace between countries. This is a greater benefit than any harm caused by possessing them. Yet others point out that the existence of these weapons is the cause of continued conflict across the globe, and the main victims are always civilians. For these people, there is no justification for continuing to develop weapons of mass destruction.

Can we justify an action that will benefit the majority, even if a minority may be harmed?

In this chapter, you will study Utilitarianism as presented by Jeremy Bentham and John Stuart Mill. You will learn the different approaches of Act and Rule Utilitarianism, and how they might be applied to the contemporary ethical issues of animal experimentation for medical research and the use of nuclear weapons as a deterrent. You will understand Utilitarianism as a secular approach to ethics that is characterised by the memorable phrase, 'the greatest good for the greatest number'.

Can we justify the possession of weapons of mass destruction if the threat of their use benefits the majority?

This section of the chapter will enhance your knowledge and understanding of the topic and help you develop your AO1 skills.

Classical Utilitarianism: Jeremy Bentham's Act Utilitarianism

While the classical formulation of Utilitarianism was most fully developed in the work of Jeremy Bentham, it has its roots in the works of thinkers such as Plato, Aristotle, and Epicurus.

> *For we recognise pleasure as the first good innate in us, and from pleasure we begin every act of choice and avoidance, and to pleasure we return again, using the feeling as the standard by which we judge every good.*
>
> Epicurus, *Letter to Menoeceus*

Utilitarianism is essentially **hedonistic** because it is concerned with maximising happiness or pleasure. It values 'happiness' or 'pleasure' as the greatest good, and the basis for all ethical action. Bentham and Mill use both these terms interchangeably. Act Utilitarianism says that one must weigh up the amount of happiness produced by any action and perform only acts that maximise happiness.

Utilitarianism is a broadly **secular** theory. Some utilitarian scholars, like John Gay, had expressed utilitarian principles in religious terms, because they saw happiness as something approved of by God. However, Bentham discarded religious tradition and social convention, and was more concerned with legal and social reform.

Bentham's theory of 'utility' or 'usefulness'

The word '**utility**' means usefulness. Following David Hume, Bentham – writing in the late eighteenth and early nineteenth century – understood right actions as actions that produce pleasure and reduce pain. The law should work towards the goal of maximising pleasure and minimising pain. If a law or action does not do this, then it is wrong. This is known as the **principle of utility** and the logical implication of it, for some utilitarians, was to identify the course of action that produced the greatest happiness for the greatest number. This is known as the '**greatest happiness principle**'. However, Bentham was concerned that the greatest happiness principle could lead to the sacrifice of the minority, and believed it was better to approximate the happiness of all members of the community.

The ultimate aim

For Bentham, the ultimate aim of all moral action is to pursue pleasure and avoid pain. He begins this discussion in Chapter 1 of *Introduction the Principles of Morals and Legislation*.

Key terms

hedonistic: concerned with maximising happiness or pleasure

secular: having no connection with religion

utility: how useful an act or object is in bringing about pleasure or happiness

principle of utility: Bentham developed the principle of utility which states that an action is right if it promotes pleasure and reduces pain

greatest happiness principle: according to Utilitarianism, an action is right if it produces the greatest happiness for the greatest number

> *Nature has placed mankind under the governance of two sovereign masters, pain and pleasure. It is for them alone to point out what we ought to do, as well as to determine what we shall do. On the one hand the standard of right and wrong, on the other the chain of causes and effects, are fastened to their throne.*
>
> Jeremy Bentham, *An Introduction to the Principles of Morals and Legislation*

Bentham observed that all creatures, including human beings, are motivated by pleasure and pain. They desire pleasure and should, therefore, behave in a way that promotes or maximises pleasure. This applies on a personal level, through private morality, as well as on a public level, through government and law. Pleasure is the sole element of good, and is the one thing by which all actions can be judged.

Utilitarianism argues that the pleasure of others is as important as one's own pleasure. Therefore, Utilitarianism differs from Ethical Egoism because, when assessing the goodness or badness of an action, one must consider the pleasure of the whole community and not just the pleasure of the individual. Any system of law that is set up should consequently have happiness as its main goal and, therefore, Bentham thought it was important that government is democratic so that the happiness of the people is safe in the hands of the people themselves.

Bentham took a **quantitative** approach to happiness. This means that he was more interested in the amount of happiness that is achieved in an action, rather than in differentiating between different types of happiness and establishing the best-quality happiness.

> **Synoptic link**
>
> Link to *Chapter 1: Ethical thought (part one)*. Refresh your memory about Ethical Egoism and Stirner, and make sure you understand how Ethical Egoism differs from Utilitarianism.

> **Key term**
>
> **quantitative:** a term applied to Bentham's assessment of happiness – concerning amount (of happiness, as opposed to quality)

> *The utility of all these arts and science, – I speak both of those of amusement and curiosity, – the value which they possess, is exactly in proportion to the pleasure they yield. Every other species of pre-eminence which may be attempted to be established among them is altogether fanciful. Prejudice apart, the game of pushpin is of equal value with the art and science of music and poetry. If the game of pushpin furnishes more pleasure, it is more valuable than either.*
>
> Jeremey Bentham, *The Rationale of Reward*

Pushpin was a children's game. Bentham described it as innocent and available to everyone. In contrast, he saw the arts and sciences as enjoyed by only a few people, and recognised that enjoyment of them was very subjective. The arts and the sciences do bring happiness, but the only way in which they are better than a game is when they bring a greater quantity of happiness by, for instance, distracting people from the business of war. In themselves, they are no better than any other kind of pleasure.

Bentham spends a whole chapter talking about different types of pleasure and pain. All types of pleasure and pain can come under the rule of law, and if someone performs an act that produces pain, they can be punished as a result. However, whether or not they are punished is something that needs to be weighed up according to the circumstances. The sensation of pleasure or pain is subjective to the individual. In addition, pleasure and pain can sometimes be mixed together in the same action. Bentham was not interested in establishing which types of pleasure and which types of pain were most significant. He was more concerned with the quantity of both.

The principle of utility

The principle of utility is, therefore, the general governing principle that one ought to act to produce maximum happiness and reduce pain. For some, the logical implication is that Utilitarianism must identify the greatest happiness for the greatest number (the greatest happiness principle).

> By the principle of utility is meant the principle which approves or disapproves of every action whatsoever, according to the tendency it appears to have to augment or diminish the happiness of the party whose interest is in question: or what is the same thing in other words, to promote or to oppose that happiness. I say of every action whatsoever, and therefore not only of every action of a private individual, but of every measure of government.
>
> Jeremy Bentham, *An Introduction to the Principles of Morals and Legislation*

This means that the law should be governed by the principle of utility. Right actions promote happiness, and wrong actions decrease it or bring about pain. An act should only be required by law if it promotes a greater balance of happiness over pain when weighed against the alternatives. Punishments and rewards can be set into the legal system to act as motivators, but laws, once established, can be broken if greater happiness is achieved by doing so.

> … extraordinary occasions may now and then occur, in which the happiness of the people may be better promoted by acting, for the moment, in opposition to the law, than in subservience to it.
>
> Jeremy Bentham, *A Fragment on Government*

Bentham believed that moral debates come about not because people disagree with the principle of utility (although they might try to argue that they do), but because they disagree about how it should be applied. Bentham felt it was impossible to disapprove of the principle of utility in a coherent way, and rejected religious principles that interfere with the principle of utility. He mentioned the principle of asceticism as the opposite of utility. Ascetics live a life of extreme self-denial, turning away from sensual pleasures. Religious ascetics may even seek pain. Bentham felt that making oneself miserable is, however, a private matter. The difficultly comes if such principles extend to making others miserable, as is the case with holy war and religious persecution.

AO1 activity 1

Choose five actions you have performed today. For each action, work out what pleasure motivated you to act. For example:

Action	Motive
ate breakfast	to feel satisfied and no longer hungry, to experience a pleasant taste
went to the gym	to feel energised, to work towards the goal of becoming stronger and fitter

The hedonic calculus

The principle of utility says that a moral agent should, in each unique moral situation, look at the options and perform the action that produces the greatest happiness for the greatest number. This requires a method to weigh up the happiness or pain experienced by everyone associated with an action. Bentham suggested that there are seven criteria that should be used to measure the quantity of happiness or pain that is created by an action and that, together, these criteria form the **hedonic calculus**.

> **Key term**
>
> **hedonic calculus:** the seven criteria by which Bentham attempts to measure happiness and determine whether or not an act is right

Criterion	Definition	Application
Intensity	The power or strength of the sensation of happiness or pain that is felt by the people involved. This can only be weighed up after all the other criteria have been considered.	These six criteria should be used when an individual is working out the moral course of action in private matters.
Duration	How long the happiness or pain will last. The longer it will last, the greater its value in the calculation.	
Certainty	How sure we can be that the happiness or pain will follow the action. Greater value is given to sensations that we can be sure will follow.	
Remoteness (propinquity)	How soon it will be before the happiness or pain will be experienced. The sooner the better!	
Richness (fecundity)	The likelihood that the act will lead to more sensations of the same kind. The more likely it is that the act will lead directly to more happiness being felt in the future, the greater its value in the calculation.	
Purity	How free the act is from being contaminated by sensations of the opposite kind. A pleasurable act that is polluted by pain will be of a lower value in the calculation.	
Extent	How many people will be affected by the happiness or pain that is caused by the act. It is worth more, the more people that are involved.	This criterion should be added if the action applies to more than one individual.

> *Sum up all the values of all the pleasures on the one side, and those of all the pains on the other. The balance, if it be on the side of pleasure, will give the good tendency of the act upon the whole, with respect to the interests of that individual person; if on the side of pain, the bad tendency of it on the whole.*
>
> Jeremy Bentham, *An Introduction to the Principles of Morals and Legislation*

Bentham provided a clear methodology for calculating the happiness and pain in each action: the values of both happiness and pain are added up to see, on balance, whether an act is good or not. A good act will have a greater quantity of happiness than pain. Bentham also requires that the calculation be repeated for each person who is affected by the action, and then the balance of pain and happiness is calculated for the total number of people concerned.

The purpose of the law is to increase the total amount of happiness in a community and reduce or exclude everything that diminishes happiness by rewarding good behaviour and punishing bad behaviour. But Bentham made the point that punishment in itself causes pain, and so is to be avoided wherever possible. The principle of utility only justifies punishment if the pain caused is out-balanced by a greater reduction in pain overall or an increase in happiness. Where punishment cannot deter or prevent crime, is too expensive, or there are better ways to achieve the same aim, it is pointless. Every situation is different and so the work of the courts is to work out the most appropriate punishment in the situation. The hedonic calculus is to be used to weigh up whether a specific punishment should take place. For example, it must be *certain* that the punishment will act to deter reoffending or similar offences by others in the *future*. The positive effect must be *immediate*. And so on.

But there are limits to the remit of the law. There are situations in which the law should not attempt to direct the conduct of members of the community, because they concern matters of personal choice and do not concern others. For instance, punishing same-sex sexual acts is inappropriate because, so long as the relationship is consensual, it concerns only those involved.

Jeremy Bentham (1748–1832) left his body to medical science and, following his instructions, his mummified remains are dressed and displayed for public viewing at University College London.

> *There are few cases where it would be expedient to punish a man for hurting himself: but there are few cases, if any, in which it would not be expedient to punish a man for injuring his neighbour.* 99
>
> Jeremy Bentham, *An Introduction to the Principles of Morals and Legislation*

AO1 activity 2

Consider the following fictitious scenarios:

a) A drug is being developed for use in humans to combat the effects of a virus that is responsible for a pandemic, killing millions and making many millions more sick. Rats could be injected with the drug to indicate how safe it is to use in humans.

b) The nuclear weapons of a small country are very out of date. The government of the country believes the weapons should be updated so that they can be used in defence if the country is ever attacked. This will cost billions of pounds and require underwater test detonations.

For each scenario, look at the seven criteria of the hedonic calculus for all the people involved, and consider how much happiness or pain will result. What action do you think should be performed in each situation?

Act Utilitarianism

'**Act Utilitarianism**' is a term that has been applied to Bentham's Utilitarianism retrospectively; it was introduced by Richard Brandt in the 1950s. Act Utilitarianism generally means that each individual moral act is weighed in the balance separately, with no requirement to follow the same set of rules in every situation. In other words, act utilitarians believe that the principle of utility should be applied on a case-by-case basis.

Bentham lived in a society that had rules and laws, but he recognised that they were not always useful in producing happiness. He therefore proposed legal reforms that aimed to enable greater happiness, but he did not advocate that the law should be abandoned altogether. He recognised that it was not necessarily practical to apply every element of the hedonic calculus on every single occasion.

> *It is not to be expected that this process should be strictly pursued previously to every moral judgement or every legislative or judicial operation. It may, however, be always kept in view.*
>
> Jeremy Bentham, *An Introduction to the Principles of Morals and Legislation*

This means that Bentham can be called an act utilitarian because he rejected the idea that set traditions and laws must be applied blindly, regardless of the situation. Instead, he advocated that people should be mindful of the criteria of the hedonic calculus when making moral and legal decisions so that maximum happiness for individuals and the community can be produced.

Act Utilitarianism as a form of Moral Relativism, a consequentialist theory, and a teleological theory

Bentham's brand of Act Utilitarianism is a form of Moral Relativism. This is because it does not hold that an action is inherently good or evil. It is only good or evil in relation to how much happiness or pain is produced as a result. Consequently, it is inappropriate for a law to apply to all instances of an action in the same way; each situation is different and must be considered in the light of all the influencing factors.

> *These circumstances, all or many of them, will need to be attended to as often as upon any occasion any account is taken of any quantity of pain or pleasure, as resulting from any cause.*
>
> Jeremy Bentham, *An Introduction to the Principles of Morals and Legislation*

Bentham is characterised as an act utilitarian who required that each moral act is weighed on a case-by-case basis.

Bentham's brand of Act Utilitarianism is also a consequentialist theory because the process of weighing up happiness or pain involves a consideration of the consequences or potential consequences of an action. The seven criteria of the hedonic calculus concern the likelihood of an action resulting in more happiness than pain.

Act Utilitarianism is considered a teleological theory on the basis that the purpose or goal of an action is to produce the greatest happiness for the greatest number. This applies equally to individuals who are contemplating their own behaviour and legislators who are writing laws.

> *Now private ethics has happiness for its end: and legislation can have no other.* ”
>
> Jeremy Bentham, *An Introduction to the Principles of Morals and Legislation*

John Stuart Mill's development of Utilitarianism

John Stuart Mill admired Bentham, and agreed that social and legal reform could be achieved through the greatest happiness principle.

Mill was an empiricist. He claimed that the fact that happiness is what people desire is evidence that happiness is the first principle on which ethical action should be based. He took a naturalist view that since people desire happiness, happiness must be what is good.

However, Mill rejected Bentham's idea that all happiness is the same.

Not all pleasure is the same

Utilitarianism had come under criticism from scholars like Thomas Carlyle, who called it 'pig philosophy' on the basis that it was too simple-minded and appeared to value the pleasure of animals as highly as the pleasure of humans. This caused difficulty because it suggested someone could be just as happy choosing to live in a state of passive, unproductive ignorance, rather than striving to become an educated, productive, and useful member of society.

Mill recognised that people come to a deeper understanding of happiness through education and experience. Those who have experienced a full range of pleasure – both the simple kind that animals experience, and the more advanced, human pleasures – understand that humans require more than just sensory pleasure to live a happy life. Mill took a **qualitative** approach. He claimed that while the quantity of happiness should be measured, this was not enough to fully appraise the happiness created by an act. The quality of the happiness that is creates must also be considered.

John Stuart Mill (1806–1873)

Key term

qualitative: a measure of the standard or value of an item, experience, or situation

> *It is quite compatible with the principle of utility to recognise the fact that some kinds of pleasure are more desirable and more valuable than others. It would be absurd that while, in estimating all other things, quality is considered as well as quantity, the estimation of pleasure should be supposed to depend on quantity alone.*
>
> John Stuart Mill, *Utilitarianism: On Liberty and Other Essays*

Mill distinguished between higher and lower pleasures.

Lower pleasures

Lower pleasures are important and are considered, by Mill, to be good. They are sensual or physical pleasures that a person may have in common with animals, such as the pleasure gained by eating a meal or being warm. Mill pointed out that such pleasures are easily obtained.

> *It is indisputable that the being whose capacities of enjoyment are low, has the greatest chance of having them fully satisfied.*
>
> John Stuart Mill, *Utilitarianism: On Liberty and Other Essays*

Higher pleasures

Human beings have the capacity for intellectual pleasures that animals do not. These **higher pleasures** are of a higher quality, and include things such as education, rational thinking, and appreciation of art. Mill felt that it was these pleasures that distinguish us from animals, and it is a lack of these pleasures that can make life unsatisfactory for a human. It is more challenging to gain satisfaction from these pleasures; it is often hard work to achieve them. But those who have experienced them will always choose them over lower pleasures because they recognise their higher value and gain much more happiness in life as a result.

> *It is better to be a human being dissatisfied than a pig satisfied; better to be Socrates dissatisfied than a fool satisfied. And if the fool or the pig, is of a different opinion, it is because they only know their own side of the question. The other part to the comparison knows both sides.*
>
> John Stuart Mill, *Utilitarianism: On Liberty and Other Essays*

These higher pleasures are sometimes contaminated by dissatisfaction or suffering: think of the struggling artist or musician who survives on very little to continue with their work. However, Mill noted that in these cases, someone who has experienced the higher pleasures would not give them up for a lower pleasure, even though there is suffering involved.

> *Few human creatures would consent to be changed into any of the lower animals, for a promise of the fullest allowance of a beast's pleasures; no intelligent human being would consent to be a fool, no instructed person would be an ignoramus, no person of feeling and conscience would be selfish and base, even though they should be persuaded that the fool, the dunce, or the rascal is better satisfied with this lot than they are with theirs.*
>
> John Stuart Mill, *Utilitarianism: On Liberty and Other Essays*

Key terms

lower pleasures: a term used by John Stuart Mill to identify inferior pleasures of the body

higher pleasures: a term used by John Stuart Mill to identify superior pleasures of the mind

Mill believed that the best people to choose between pleasures and judge their worth are those who have experience of both higher and lower pleasures. These people will be well-educated and intelligent and, where they disagree over the worth of one pleasure or another, the majority have the final decision.

Conformity to historical rules (Rule Utilitarianism)

Mill wrote that happiness is most likely to be achieved when society leaves people alone to pursue their own private pleasures as they wish. However, for society to run effectively, this freedom must be subject to rules that are established for the happiness of society in general. Utilitarianism has been criticised for being too time consuming, since in an emergency situation, no one has time to work out every element of the hedonic calculus to ensure that the greatest happiness for the greatest number is being produced. However, Mill responded by saying that people should go into moral situations with the knowledge and experience that has been accumulated through all the years of human experience. We can enter moral situations with ready-made rules or laws that have been calculated according to the primary principle of utility. There is no requirement to work out every problem on the spot. Just as a sailor would not go to sea without being prepared, the moral agent can be prepared for any moral situation they encounter.

> *Being rational creatures, they go to sea with it ready calculated; and all rational creatures go out upon the sea of life with their mind made up on the common questions of right and wrong, as well as on many of the far more difficult questions of wise and foolish.* **"**
>
> John Stuart Mill, *Utilitarianism: On Liberty and Other Essays*

While Mill did not use the term **Rule Utilitarianism**, he has since been associated with it. This means that he understood that a morally right action is one that conforms to a pre-prepared moral rule that has already been justified by the principle of utility. Most of the time, people can follow these pre-prepared moral rules without having to perform any calculations. However, Mill did not believe that people should stick rigidly to such rules no matter what the situation. He recognised that almost all moral theories grapple with the problem of conflicting moral rules, and acknowledged that there are times when rules must be abandoned in pursuit of the principle of utility.

> *Thus, to save a life, it may not only be allowable, but a duty, to steal, or take by force, the necessary food or medicine, or to kidnap, and compel to officiate the only qualified medical practitioner.* **"**
>
> John Stuart Mill, *Utilitarianism: On Liberty and Other Essays*

> *If the principle of utility is good for anything, it must be good for weighing these conflicting utilities against one another, and marking out the region within which one or the other preponderates.* **"**
>
> John Stuart Mill, *Utilitarianism: On Liberty and Other Essays*

AO1 activity 4

Consider the following examples of pleasure, and divide them into higher pleasures and lower pleasures. Make a list of the problems you come across when you attempt to do this.

a) eating a meal that you made from scratch

b) meeting a friend for a coffee

c) going to see your favourite band

d) training to run a marathon

e) reading a trashy novel.

Key term

Rule Utilitarianism: a view associated with John Stuart Mill; rule utilitarians believe that by using the principle of utility, one can draw up general rules, based on past experiences, which would help to keep this principle and so should be obeyed

225

Mill is, as a result, characterised as being a 'weak rule' utilitarian. This is because he admits that there are times when the rules must be set aside. At these times, a moral agent should return to the principle of utility: to maximise pleasure and minimise pain. 'Strong rule' utilitarians argue that there can be no exceptions to rules that are based on the principle of utility.

Mill argued that the principle of utility gives society a duty to protect people. Therefore, he advocated rules that would provide education and political expression to women. Mill claimed that any men who opposed such rules did so from base or lower motives, and denying women access to such things would prevent an opportunity for the development of happiness.

The harm principle

A good example of a rule that Mill put forward is the **harm principle**. This principle states that an individual must be allowed the freedom to pursue pleasure as they wish, unless they will cause harm to others by doing so. There is no other reason for interfering. Mill also said that even if a person wishes to perform an action that could cause harm to themselves, it is not acceptable to interfere if they are capable of making such a decision for themselves.

> The sole end for which mankind are warranted, individually or collectively, in interfering with the liberty of action of any member of a civilised community, against his will, is to prevent harm to others.
>
> John Stuart Mill, *Utilitarianism: On Liberty and Other Essays*

This freedom enables people to pursue pleasure and, therefore, happiness in their own individual ways, and to develop culture and character as a result. That everyone has the right not to be forced into behaving in a particular way is a rule that contributes to human happiness. But the desires of one member of the community must not be allowed to diminish happiness for others. For example, this means that a person is free to engage in consensual sex of any variety, whether outside of marriage or with a partner of the same sex, because it causes no harm to other people. Mill said that it is not good enough to compromise someone's freedom by arguing it is for their own good or they would be happier in the long run. While such arguments might allow a person to challenge someone's behaviour, they are not reason enough to force them to moderate their actions or punish them. In addition, the harm principle protects minority groups from restrictions placed on them by the majority, something that could result from the greatest happiness principle. For instance, enslavement of a minority could be justified using the greatest happiness principle, because it brings happiness to the majority. However, the harm principle protects the interests of the minority so that this cannot happen.

Mill gave exceptions to the harm principle. He pointed out that children or those who are in the care of others do need to be protected and so cannot have complete freedom. Controversially for today, he also advocated that

Key term

harm principle: a principle created by Mill that argues the only reason power can be rightfully exercised over another person, against their will, is to prevent harm to others

'backwards states of society' – societies that do not conform to a Western understanding of culture – should have less freedom and more restrictive leadership.

Mill recognised that rules potentially cause some harm, but overall, any harm is balanced by the benefits. For example, while people should be free to do what they want, they should be compelled to prevent bad things happening to other people. So long as they are not putting themselves in danger, a person should be forced by law to help a drowning child; the negative action of forcing a person to act is outweighed by the benefit of saving the child's life. This is another exception to the harm principle because it compels a person to act against their own free will to help the drowning child.

> *There are also many positive acts for the benefit of others, which he may rightfully be compelled to perform; … such as saving a fellow creature's life, or interposing to protect the defenceless against ill-usage.* **"**
>
> John Stuart Mill, *Utilitarianism: On Liberty and Other Essays*

Mill's Utilitarianism as a hybrid teleological and deontological theory

Like Bentham's Act Utilitarianism, Mill's Rule Utilitarianism can be viewed as a teleological theory. This is because the purpose, or *telos*, of a law is creating the greatest happiness for the greatest number.

However, Mill's Rule Utilitarianism can also be viewed as a deontological theory. This is because once the principle of utility has been used to establish a law, a moral agent has an obligation to obey it. Mill claimed that all moral agents have a sense of duty that arises from recognising happiness as the ethical standard and a desire to be part of the wider society.

> *Every person, except an absolute monarch, has equals, everyone is obliged to live on these terms with somebody … in this way people grow up unable to conceive as possible to them a state of total disregard of other people's interests.* **"**
>
> John Stuart Mill, *Utilitarianism: On Liberty and Other Essays*

Utilitarianism: application of the theory

The main purpose of this section of the specification is to show how Utilitarianism can be put into practice in real ethical situations. There is no need for an in-depth study of animal experimentation for medical research and the use of nuclear weapons as a deterrent, but you do need to understand some of the issues these topics raise before looking at how the theory of Utilitarianism applies to them.

AO1 activity 5

Create a table with two columns to distinguish between the features of Act Utilitarianism and the features of Rule Utilitarianism. (Remember that higher and lower pleasures are *not* a feature of Rule Utilitarianism. They are just part of Mill's approach in particular.)

AO1 activity 6

Imagine you are opening a brand-new school or college and you have to decide on rules for your staff and students. The rules must help the school community to be happy. What rules would you devise? Can you think of any exceptions to the rules you have made?

Animal experimentation for medical research: what is the debate?

Animals are extensively used for the benefit of humans in all sorts of ways, as food, for sport, as a source of clothing, for transport, and to further our scientific knowledge. This section is solely concerned with the use of animals for medical research.

The use of animals for medical research is currently considered necessary by the majority of scientists. It has enabled humans to discover huge amounts about how living bodies work, and there is still a great deal we need to know and understand to treat illnesses in humans and animals effectively. While people take part in medical trials to find out if drugs that have been developed are safe to use, animal testing plays a critical role in developing the drugs in the first place. This is because it is considered unethical to experiment on humans in this way, and variables such as temperature and food can be controlled more effectively in a laboratory environment. Using animals for medical research has allowed us to develop vaccines and other vital medical treatments in humans and animals. Without the use of animals, progress against diseases like cancer and HIV would be severely hampered.

There are strict laws in the UK that regulate the use of animals for experimentation. However, many people have grave concerns about the use of animals for medical research. As well as concerns about the conditions in which the animals are kept, they believe that deliberately inflicting suffering upon a creature that will gain no benefit from it is cruel. They also argue that experimenting on animals is often ineffective because the human diseases being researched do not necessarily appear naturally in animals, and must be artificially created in the laboratory. Many treatments that look promising in the laboratory later fail in human medical trials.

Those who challenge the use of animals for medical research argue that animals should have rights, just as humans do.

What does Bentham say about animal experimentation for medical research?

As far as Bentham is concerned, an act is moral if it promotes happiness and immoral if it promotes suffering. Humans have the capacity to experience both happiness and suffering, but what about animals? Animals are not moral agents and so are not the subject of much of Bentham's writing. Yet it is reasonable to assume that they too can feel happiness and can suffer. If they could not, there would be no moral problem when humans treat animals in any way they like. There is no reason to assume a pebble is concerned when a child kicks it along a path, but a kicked dog yelps in what we can assume is pain. This is the most important consideration for Bentham.

> *The day may come when the rest of the animal creation may acquire those rights which never could have been withholden from them but by the hand of tyranny. The French have already discovered that the blackness of the skin is no reason why a human being should be abandoned without redress to the caprice of a tormentor. It may one day come to be recognised that the number of the legs ... are reasons equally insufficient for abandoning a sensitive being to the same fate. What else is it that should trace the insuperable line? Is it the faculty of reason, or perhaps the faculty of discourse? But a full-grown horse or dog is beyond comparison a more rational, as well as a more conversable animal, than an infant of a day or a week or even a month old. But suppose they were otherwise, what would it avail? The question is not, can they reason nor can they talk? But, can they suffer?*

Jeremy Bentham, *An Introduction to the Principles of Morals and Legislation*

The insuperable line Bentham refers to is the line that marks the point at which one must start treating another being with care because it can suffer.

Many argue that animals are subordinate to humans because they are not as intelligent or because they cannot use language. Bentham argues that the capacity to feel happiness or pain is the only factor that should influence how you treat another being. It is the most basic requirement that enables any creature to care about anything. Therefore, while some people argue that animals are less important because they are less intelligent or cannot use language, Bentham argues that the interests of animals and humans are worth the same (pushpin is as good as poetry), because they are based upon a shared capacity for happiness or pain. If an animal suffers when it is experimented on, their suffering must be weighed in the balance when deciding if experimenting on animals for medical research is acceptable.

However, Bentham elsewhere made the declaration that killing animals is acceptable provided there is a clear purpose to it and the animal is not made to suffer unnecessarily. Killing for food, defence, or medical experimentation were good reasons for Bentham. Killing or harming for enjoyment was not.

> *Sir, —I never have seen, nor ever can see, any objection to the putting of dogs and other inferior animals to pain, in the way of medical experiment, when that experiment has a determinate object, beneficial to mankind, accompanied with a fair prospect of the accomplishment of it. But I have a decided and insuperable objection to the putting of them to pain without any such view.*

Jeremy Bentham in a letter to the editor, *The Morning Chronicle*, 4 March 1825

What does Mill say about animal experimentation for medical research?

Mill was not primarily concerned with writing about animal experimentation. However, his development of Utilitarianism can be applied to this issue, and he did have something to say about the treatment of animals. Mill was prepared to apply his harm principle to all creatures that have the capacity for suffering. For Mill, we should be free to do what we please provided it does not harm anyone else. While he did not mention animals, he did make exceptions for those beings, such as children, who are not yet capable of choosing intelligently for themselves; they may have their freedom curtailed.

In other works, Mill went on to point out that adults do not have the freedom to mistreat a child in their care because a child does not have the capacity to understand what is in its own best interests. The law should protect children, even from their own parents, to ensure they are not subjected to mistreatment. This suggests adult humans have the same duty of care towards animals. Mill expressly said that when decisions must be made on behalf of those who cannot do so for themselves, they should be taken only for the benefit of those concerned. Thus, animals cannot be treated as possessions or harmed simply for the benefit of others.

> *The reasons for legal intervention in favour of children apply not less strongly to the case of those unfortunate slaves and victims of the most brutal part of mankind, the lower animals.*
>
> John Stuart Mill, *Principles of the Political Economy with Some of Their Applications to Social Philosophy*

Mill advocated that the law should protect the interests of animals, even against their owners, to ensure that they do not experience unnecessary suffering. He argued that no one should dismiss the very real suffering of animals because of some other abstract rule or value that they hold. This does not mean that we should never experiment upon animals. However, it does mean that unnecessary cruelty and suffering should be avoided. Mill's primary aim was the greatest happiness for the greatest number, which included maximising happiness and removing or minimising suffering. Therefore, laws that govern the treatment of animals, including how they are used in medical research, should always look to remove or minimise suffering.

What does Utilitarianism say about animal experimentation for medical research?

The application of Utilitarianism to this issue has sparked the interest of modern utilitarians. The Australian philosopher Peter Singer is well known for saying that current arguments supporting the use of animals in medical research are guilty of **speciesism**.

> **Key term**
>
> **speciesism:** a prejudice or attitude of bias in favour of the interests of members of one's own species and against those of members of other species

> *Speciesism – the word is not an attractive one, but I can think of no better term – is a prejudice or attitude of bias in favour of the interests of members of one's own species and against those of members of other species.*
>
> Peter Singer, *Animal Liberation*

In his 2005 work, *Animal Liberation*, Singer argues that if we say animals should be experimented on for the benefit of humans because we are somehow more important, that our interests count for more, we are using the same kind of argument as those that support white supremacy or the subjugation of women. In Singer's view, suffering is equivalent to suffering, no matter who or what is experiencing it.

> *The basic element – the taking into account of the interests of the beings, whatever those interest may be – must, according to the principle of equality, be extended to all beings, black or white, masculine or feminine, human or non-human.* **"**
>
> Peter Singer, *Animal Liberation*

However, Mill's idea that not all happiness is the same could be used to support an argument that animal happiness or suffering is of less value than human happiness or suffering. And, if animals are less capable of higher pleasures or mental suffering because they have a lesser intellect or less capability for language, it follows that when medical research must be carried out, it is acceptable to inflict suffering upon those less capable of higher pleasures or mental suffering than upon those who are more capable of experiencing them.

Singer objects to the idea that lesser intellect is a justification for animal experimentation. He gives the example of a crazed attacker who lurks in a park and kidnaps passers-by to experiment upon them. Once humans hear about the danger, they are likely to experience dread. In contrast, an animal is unlikely to experience a similar dread of being experimented on. However, Singer argues that if the experience of dread is justification for carrying out animal experimentation, consistency requires us to permit experiments on human children, people who are unconscious, and people with cognitive disabilities, since they cannot experience dread either. To object in these cases and not when we consider animals is speciesist.

Singer argues that animals may even suffer more than humans, as it is impossible to explain to them what we are doing and reassure them that they will come to no harm. A wild animal cannot distinguish between an attacker and someone who has come to save them, and so may experience extreme fear even when a human is being kind. In contrast, we can talk to a human and explain the risks, to which they can consent.

> *If possessing a higher degree of intelligence does not entitle one human to use another for his or her own ends, how can it entitle humans to exploit nonhumans for the same purpose?* **"**
>
> Peter Singer, *Animal Liberation*

Bentham's approach requires simply that we weigh the suffering and happiness of humans and animals using the hedonic calculus. The pain experienced by the animal must be balanced against the pain experienced by the person who is suffering from an illness that the experiment is designed to cure. For example, the extent and intensity of the pain must be considered. If thousands of mice must be tortured and killed to prevent the mild suffering of one person with a non-terminal skin condition, all other criteria in the calculation being equal, the experiment should be abandoned. However, if the patient's suffering is severe and the disease is highly contagious, the experimentation is justified, all other criteria in the calculation being equal.

AO1 activity 7

Research UK laws that govern animal experimentation for medical research. Do any of these laws reflect utilitarian principles? Do any of the laws reflect Singer's accusation of speciesism?

All the factors from Bentham's calculus must be weighed in the balance for all the parties involved, and this includes both humans and animals. Not all animal experiments require extreme suffering for the animals: some creatures may simply be observed in certain environments. But others may be killed without being used for experimentation at all because they are surplus to requirements. The killing of those animals for no greater good may lack fecundity or richness, since it leads to nothing positive for anyone involved. However, since Bentham rejected the idea that any being had rights that could not be challenged, if experimentation on a small number of animals would enable a larger number of animals or humans to gain more happiness and less suffering overall, then this is acceptable.

Mill wanted the law to be based upon the principle of utility ('to maximise pleasure and minimise pain') and believed that the principle should apply equally to people and animals. He believed laws could be formulated which set down that if animals must be used for medical research to reduce human suffering, animal suffering should be avoided or minimised.

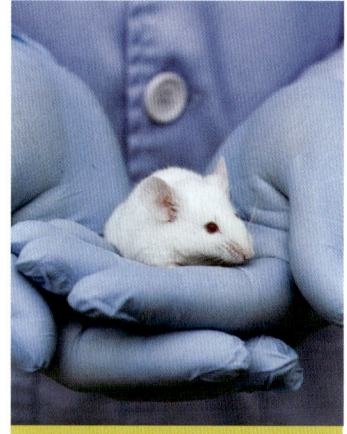

Singer accuses those who use animals for their own benefit of speciesism.

The use of nuclear weapons as a deterrent: what is the debate?

The debate surrounding the possession of nuclear weapons as a deterrent is complex, even more so than a general discussion about the ethics of war. The UK began its nuclear weapons programme in the 1940s, towards the end of the Second World War, at a time when the majority of the world had lived through two lengthy world wars and seen an enormous amount of death and destruction. The use of atomic bombs on the cities of Hiroshima and Nagasaki hastened the end of the war, but came at an enormous cost to life, killing not just military personnel but also many civilians. The issue here is whether or not it is ethical for a nation to possess nuclear weapons as a way to discourage other countries from launching a nuclear attack. However, even though a nation may possess nuclear weapons with the intent to prevent war, there is little point in possessing them unless at least one of the following propositions is also true:

- they intend to use the weapons if necessary
- they want to convince other nations that they intend to use them if necessary.

If nuclear weapons are being kept for the purpose of deterrence, a nation should only use them in self-defence. Another country would have to attack first and the country targeted would have to be willing to retaliate. If it is clear that a nation would never use their nuclear weapons, under any circumstances, they would not have a deterrent effect.

This means that there needs to be some consideration of the following questions.

- Is it morally acceptable to use nuclear weapons in self-defence?
- Can the use of nuclear weapons ever be considered capable of producing maximum pleasure and minimum pain in any situation?
- Who might be morally legitimate targets for nuclear weapons?

What does Bentham say about the use of nuclear weapons as a deterrent?

It should go without saying that Bentham, who lived between 1748 and 1832, had nothing to say about the use of nuclear weapons, which were developed as a result of scientific breakthroughs in the 1930s. However, war and the prevention of war were certainly issues of concern for those living in the eighteenth and nineteenth centuries. Bentham wrote 'A Plan for Universal and Perpetual Peace' in 1789, after the Seven Years War between Britain, France, and later, Spain.

> *It is not the interest of Great Britain to keep up any naval force beyond what may be sufficient to defend its commerce against pirates. … It is not the interest of Great Britain to keep on foot any regulations whatsoever of distant preparation for the augmentation or maintenance of its naval force.*
>
> Jeremy Bentham, *A Plan for Universal and Perpetual Peace*

Bentham saw all war as essentially ruinous. He believed that there was nothing in the nature of war that could possibly be considered of benefit to anyone involved. In his view, the best way to deter nations from war was through the use of defensive confederations. He suggested that nations agree peace treaties and work together towards disarmament – towards the reduction of military forces and weapons – to ensure that peace is maintained. Rather than building up more weaponry, Bentham argued, within his own historical situation, that the best deterrent is collaboration over trade rather than creating a military defence.

What does Mill say about the use of nuclear weapons as a deterrent?

Mill, who lived between 1806 and 1873, also lived before the development of nuclear weapons. Therefore, he too had nothing to say on the topic of nuclear weapons as a deterrent. However, his views on war in general are relevant.

> *But war, in a good cause, is not the greatest evil which a nation can suffer. War is an ugly thing, but not the ugliest of things.*
>
> John Stuart Mill, *The Contest in America*

Mill was writing, in England, about the American Civil War. He felt that war was sometimes necessary, and in this case he saw it as an opportunity to end enslavement. Even though Mill recognised that many people would die and that the war could go on for a long time, war was justified by the greater happiness that could result. Mill's view of the American Civil War could be used to suggest that if it is possible for the possession of nuclear weapons to bring about a greater good in the long term, their possession and even their use might be justifiable.

What does Utilitarianism say about the use of nuclear weapons as a deterrent?

Utilitarianism is a consequentialist theory that considers everyone's welfare when making a moral decision. This means that any deliberation over the possession of nuclear weapons must weigh up the happiness and suffering of the people in the country that owns them and everyone else who may be affected. Act Utilitarianism requires us to measure happiness on a case-by-case basis, but Rule Utilitarianism accepts that there is a place for rules or principles concerning the possession of nuclear arms.

Possessing nuclear weapons as a deterrent involves threatening to use them to deliberately destroy civilian populations in order to convince would-be aggressors to remain cooperative. An example of a rule or principle that could be relevant to rule utilitarians on this matter is the **principle of discrimination**. This principle states that harming civilians is unacceptable and rule utilitarians may, consequently, argue that it is acceptable to have nuclear weapons as a deterrent so long as there is no realistic threat to civilian life.

> **Key term**
>
> **principle of discrimination:** the principle that determines who are appropriate targets in war and who should be immune from attack

However, Act Utilitarianism does not necessarily forbid having nuclear weapons as a deterrent if there is more happiness in the world as a result. Because Utilitarianism is a consequentialist theory, there is no suggestion that anyone has absolute rights, and while attacking the innocent is usually not the way to increase happiness, the consequences of not being prepared to use nuclear weapons could be worse.

However, if nuclear weapons are used against civilians, it is certain that there would be a great deal of pain in both the short and long term, and not just to those living in the country targeted. The duration of suffering would be significant, as countries around the world manage the consequences of such a catastrophic event, which might include an escalation in violence. Furthermore, the threat of using nuclear weapons must be believable if they are to be effective as a deterrent; there must be plans for how they will be deployed. People will experience anxiety if they believe they may be at risk from a nuclear attack and the intensity of the fear will increase with increasing hostility between nations. And the fear does not just affect the nations in dispute; it affects everyone who is aware of the growing risk. The extent of the suffering caused by the threat to use or the actual use of nuclear weapons is significant, and no happiness that is produced as a result can ever be pure in nature; it will always be contaminated by pain.

For utilitarians, all acts are possible if they create more happiness or diminish pain. A strong rule utilitarian may not accept the targeting of civilians under any circumstances, because it is a slippery slope leading to more and more exceptions to the principle of discrimination in the future and, consequently, more killing and less well-being. Yet, Mill suggested that failing to engage in war can sometimes be immoral. Possessing nuclear weapons and not being prepared to use them could be worse than using them, if failing to engage means that there is a greater loss to life and freedom overall. Mill's harm principle says that people should be free to do what they want unless their actions cause harm to others. The use of nuclear weapons to deter nations from harming each other may be a way to ensure countries are free to operate however they wish, provided they do not interfere with the freedom of other nations.

A country's nuclear strategy could state that it would only deploy weapons against military targets and not against civilian targets. However, this might not be enough to deter some would-be aggressors, in which case the deterrent would be ineffective and ultimately lead to more suffering. Alternatively, a nation could posture and bluff, with the intention of deceiving another country into believing they would use nuclear weapons when in reality they would not. Leaders could make announcements, publicise weapons testing, and display their nuclear capabilities to add weight to their empty threat. Yet, this relies upon the lie being convincing enough to cause another nation to back down, and risks escalating hostilities.

In March 2021, the UK Prime Minister, Boris Johnson, announced plans to increase the country's nuclear weapons stockpile as a deterrent.

Bentham believed that disarming and working towards trust and collaboration is the best way to avoid war. If the possession of nuclear weapons escalates mistrust and fear between countries, then possessing them could make a volatile situation worse. However, if the expected consequences of disarming are worse than going through with using those weapons as a last resort, then it may be legitimate to continue to keep them as a deterrent. If other countries continue to own nuclear weapons, the decision to keep them for defence can be viewed as an appropriate response. While possessing nuclear arms comes at a cost, both a financial cost and a cost to people's well-being, failing to deter an aggressor could come at an even greater cost. For example, over 55 million people were killed during the Second World War. Yet, that cost is considered worthwhile by the majority given that failure to resist the Nazi regime may have cost many more lives and freedoms.

Some argue that a country must possess a strong nuclear capability in order to be an effective deterrent. They argue that any attempt to attack a nuclear nation would be futile – certain to fail – and so would be pointless. However, others argue that a nation who fears the threat from a nuclear power could be encouraged to strike first to disable or weaken that power. If this is the case, then any threat on the part of the country with nuclear arms could be counterproductive and potentially make things worse. Bentham's idea was that the adversary needs to be reassured that no one intends to be aggressive. Disarming would be a reassuring tactic.

AO1 activity 8

Research the UK's current position on the possession of nuclear weapons. Can you identify how the UK's nuclear weapons programme aims to deter other nations from engaging the UK in nuclear warfare? Do you think the UK nuclear weapons programme reflects utilitarian principles?

This section of the chapter will enhance your ability to analyse and evaluate the topic and help you develop your AO2 skills. For each question, think about the different positions you might take, and decide which you find most persuasive and why. It is not enough to memorise a list of 'for and against' points; you need to develop an argument.

To what degree is pleasure the sole intrinsic good?

In Utilitarianism, a theory of usefulness, it is necessary to consider which consequences are good or useful and should therefore be promoted. Bentham and Mill propose that happiness or pleasure is good or useful. To say this is to claim that part of the essential nature of pleasure is that it is good, and that it is not possible to say the same thing about any other quality. When answering a question like this, you could consider whether or not pleasure is intrinsically good, or whether there are other things that might be considered intrinsically good as well as, or instead of, pleasure.

The view that pleasure is the only intrinsic good

It makes sense to argue that pleasure is the only intrinsic good. Utilitarianism, as a theory of usefulness, promotes behaviour that is good *for* people rather than behaviour that is good in and of itself. Behaviour that promotes happiness clearly benefits people. R.E. Goodin argues that if we were forced to choose between actions that are good *for* someone and actions that help no one, we would surely choose the first option. Bentham himself challenges asceticism as pointless action that is little more than empty gesture. Actions that promote pleasure always cause positive results for people that can be seen in the world, and so pleasure is clearly the only intrinsically good goal.

Pleasure is a vital part of a positive life experience. It is the one thing that human beings seek universally, and the one thing that we can all agree will improve our quality of life. A life without pleasure is a grim prospect, and there are a wide range of activities that people can participate in that will give them pleasure. It is, therefore, a reasonable assumption that pleasure is not only intrinsically good but also the only intrinsic good, because it is the one thing that seems be common to the behaviours that we pursue in our lives.

According to the ancient Greek scholar Epicurus, pleasure ensures that people live a good life. He claimed that it was impossible to live a pleasant life without being wise, honest, and just. The drive to be good comes from a desire for pleasure because if we are mean, unkind, or unfair, it leads us towards a life of conflict, misery, and displeasure. The drive for pleasure even leads us to moderate our behaviour, because too much of something pleasurable can cause us pain and suffering (for example, too much food can make you ill).

The view that pleasure is not intrinsically good

Utilitarians themselves cannot agree on what the goal of a useful action should be. Bentham and Mill spoke of happiness or pleasure, but there are now 'preference' utilitarians who argue that the goal of a useful action is not happiness or pleasure, but what the majority prefer. Others, like Moore, can be characterised as utilitarian, but seem to be more concerned with ideals, and some seem to prefer welfare as the sole good. If utilitarians are so divided on what the one goal of a useful action should be, then it is unconvincing to claim that pleasure is the one thing we can rely upon to be good in and of itself.

Pleasure is so subjective that there is no way it can be considered a suitable standard by which to judge moral behaviour. Everyone has a different understanding of what brings them happiness, and there is no way we can standardise such experiences. If a group of people were surveyed about the things that cause them pleasure or pain, or asked to rate their pain experience, there would be a wide range of answers and no consensus. Pleasure is, therefore, an inadequate sensation to be described as the sole intrinsic good and used as a basis for moral behaviour.

Pleasure is not the only intrinsic good because pleasure makes a person docile and inactive, and does not encourage them to strive to become better. It is dissatisfaction, anger, and desire that drive people to achieve, to do things, and improve themselves. J.J.C. Smart gave the example of two brothers, one docile and content and the other dissatisfied and striving for more. The second brother achieves more in his life, learns more, and changes the world, whereas the first brother, who is easily satisfied, does very little.

The view that pleasure is one among several intrinsic goods

The idea that pleasure is the sole intrinsic good does not account for behaviour that we value but that does not bring about pleasure. Goodin points out that the marathon runner endures agony to turn in a personal best time, and a soldier may undergo torture rather than betray their troop, but these actions are not done for the purpose of gaining pleasure. There are other reasons why we value acts – maybe the welfare of others, or ideals like truth, friendship, or beauty – which are intrinsically good and would justify these behaviours more effectively than pleasure alone.

It seems more likely that the welfare of oneself and others is the sole intrinsic good, not pleasure. 'Welfare' utilitarians would argue that welfare is critical even when an action does not immediately bring about happiness

> ### Synoptic link
>
> *Link to Chapter 2: Ethical thought (part two).* Take a look back at Chapter 2 to see Moore's understanding of Intuitionism and his objections to Ethical Naturalism.

or involves sacrificing happiness for some apparently greater purpose. For example, a drug addict may gain pleasure from drug use, but it is considered more moral to refuse to supply them with drugs and instead support them to become drug-free. This might bring more pain in the short term but is in the interest of their welfare. Welfare as an intrinsic good explains why people value actions like hard work or altruism, even when they do not bring happiness directly to oneself or even to others.

Pleasure is too narrow a gauge for goodness. We can experience great amounts of pleasure by artificially stimulating our brains for hours at a time, isolated from other people who are doing the same thing. Yet, this is not generally considered to be a life well lived. Many would argue instead that real life is more important, even if it would mean a lesser quantity or quality of happiness. While a happy life or a life with a minimum of pain may well be desirable, it is not necessarily the only thing that makes living worthwhile.

To what extent do Act Utilitarianism and Rule Utilitarianism work in contemporary society?

This question is asking you to compare Act Utilitarianism and Rule Utilitarianism to see which is more usable. The key phrase is, however, 'contemporary society'. The question is asking you to assess whether Utilitarianism is able to answer the ethical challenges raised in today's world. For instance, nuclear weapons were not a feature of Bentham and Mill's world, but can we use Utilitarianism to tackle the moral dilemmas that their existence creates.

The view that Act Utilitarianism works in contemporary society

Act Utilitarianism allows people to decide what to do in new situations that are not adequately addressed by existing, perhaps outdated laws. A focus on rules or laws leads people to obey or even idolise them long after they cease to be suitable for contemporary society. For example, a rule that forbids artificial contraception may have made sense in a society that required healthy levels of reproduction to maintain economic growth. However, in a society where overpopulation is a real problem, where environmental issues are a pressing concern, and where people want to avoid unwanted pregnancies and sexually transmitted infections, to insist on a rule that forbids artificial contraception may seem irrational. Act Utilitarianism enables people to free themselves from such rules.

AO2 activity 1

Robert Nozick proposed a thought experiment known as the Experience Machine.

Suppose that scientists built an experience machine that can stimulate your brain to perfectly reproduce any pleasurable experience. The machine guarantees you a life of bliss and, once you are plugged in, you forget that you are in a virtual reality and think you are living in the real world. All the time, however, you are floating in a tank with electrodes attached to your brain. You know that the machine will never break down and it is safe from sabotage. (For ideas about the Experience Machine, watch Red Dwarf Series 2, Episode 2 where the crew play the Virtual Reality game 'Better Than Life'.)

a) Is it enough to feel pleasure or is there something that is more important to you?
b) Would you plug yourself in? Why or why not?

Act Utilitarianism considers the interests of everyone affected by a moral action. Both those positively and those negatively affected, and those near and far are taken into account in the hedonic calculus. It is, therefore, better than an egoistic approach to ethics, which requires us to look after only our own interests.

When considering animal testing for medical research or the use of nuclear weapons as a deterrent, Act Utilitarianism encourages moral agents to consider the consequences of a wide range of possible actions in the circumstances. This approach is realistic rather than idealistic. Act Utilitarianism helps real people make real choices and consider the very real consequences of those choices; it does not describe a perfect society where actions are permitted or forbidden. For example, there are some terrible illnesses for which solutions cannot be found without animal experimentation. However, Act Utilitarianism would recognise the pain felt by an animal too, and would attempt to balance the act with the real results to bring about the best possible result in the circumstance.

The view that Act Utilitarianism does not work in contemporary society

Act Utilitarianism is accused of being excessively complex and therefore difficult to use in contemporary society. Bentham himself pointed out that excessive complexity could add to the harm that is caused in some situations. For instance, when considering punishment for criminal offences, excessive complexity could cause disproportionate suffering to the person who is being punished. When applying the hedonic calculus, Bentham felt moral agents should avoid moral decisions that are unnecessarily complicated. While this sounds reasonable, it does not help people make moral decisions in our increasingly complex modern world.

Act Utilitarianism allows intrinsically immoral actions to take place if they bring the greatest happiness for the greatest number. Therefore, a judge and jury can knowingly convict and punish an innocent person to prevent a riot, a doctor can kill a person and use their organs to save five other lives, and a nuclear bomb can be used to kill thousands of innocent people so that a larger or more densely populated country can display its superior power. There are some actions that are intrinsically wrong, and therefore if Act Utilitarianism can justify immorality, it does not work in contemporary society.

Act Utilitarianism is impractical in contemporary society because it would undermine the trust that is necessary for society to operate and for countries to have positive relationships with each other. If 'anything goes' then that means that lying, breaking promises, and sabotage are all acts that are on the table. No one would be able to go into a hospital and feel confident that the doctors will do all they can to ensure that they leave healthy! A country could not trust a neighbouring nation not to use their nuclear weapons to attack rather than simply deter. We could not believe anything that others say or count on people to fulfil their promises. Society would become very unstable and it could not function effectively.

The view that Rule Utilitarianism works in contemporary society

Following historic rules designed to bring the greatest happiness to the greatest number means that people are less likely to jeopardise other people's happiness. For instance, a rule that states 'do not kill' protects individuals and society from harm. While act utilitarians argue that the individual must make each decision for themselves, rule utilitarians justifiably argue that there are too many opportunities for mistakes if individuals are left to make all decisions for themselves.

Unlike Act Utilitarianism, Rule Utilitarianism does not undermine the trust that enables society to function effectively. Historic rules mean that you can, on the whole, trust judges and juries to come to the right decisions, and you can trust doctors to act in the best interests of each individual patient.

Like Act Utilitarianism, Mill's Rule Utilitarianism still allows individuals the freedom to choose actions that do not harm other people. For example, it is possible for adults to make choices about their own sex lives if they are consenting and do not cause any kind of harm. Yet, it also allows general rules that protect the happiness of everyone in society. Furthermore, rules that undermine people's freedom can be challenged and rules can change if the needs of society change, since the rules are based only upon what will produce the greatest happiness for the greatest number.

The view that Rule Utilitarianism does not work in contemporary society

Mill's Rule Utilitarianism contains too many exceptions to make any real sense. His harm principle allows exceptions for children and for those who cannot make choices for themselves, which feels perfectly reasonable. It means that an adult should act on a young person's behalf until such times as they can make their own moral decisions. Children are also protected by law to ensure they are not ill-treated by their parents. However, Mill went on making exceptions until it seems that only the elite are free to make their own moral decisions. For example, he argued that 'backwards states of society', societies that do not conform to a Western understanding of culture, should have less freedom and more restrictive leadership. This colonialist attitude may have been in keeping with his time but it is out of date and unacceptable today.

Rule Utilitarianism ends up collapsing into Act Utilitarianism if it wishes to avoid being overly restrictive. Blanket rules like 'do not kill' do not allow for difficult or unique situations. Exceptions could be built into the rule so it becomes, for example, 'do not kill, except in special situations that justify killing such as self-defence or war'. However, the more exceptions there are, the harder it is to see the difference between Act Utilitarianism and Rule Utilitarianism. Another alternative is to generate more specific rules, such as 'only kill when your life is threatened and there is no other way save your own life.' Yet, again, the more detailed and specific the rules get to accommodate special circumstances, the more like Act Utilitarianism it looks.

Rule Utilitarianism risks becoming a complex web of laws and rules that are impossible to navigate as contemporary life throws up new and increasingly difficult moral problems. General rules do not usually account for all the different moral problems people may encounter, and complex rules are required to cover such a wide range of things, including online behaviour, complex medical procedures, and cyber warfare. Navigating all the rules could easily become impossible for the ordinary person, leading them to ignore the rules and make decisions for themselves anyway.

To what extent does Rule Utilitarianism provide a better basis for making moral decisions than Act Utilitarianism?

A question that begins with a statement declaring one form of Utilitarianism 'better' than another will require you to give some thought to what it is that makes a moral theory 'better' or 'best'. It may be that you consider one to be more practical, or more compassionate. Maybe the best theory will be more flexible or produce fairer results. It is sometimes helpful to begin by offering an analysis of what 'better' means before weighing up which theory meets your criteria.

The view that Act Utilitarianism is better than Rule Utilitarianism

It is better for an ethical theory to be rational. Rule Utilitarianism is essentially rule worship. It involves commitment to rules even if it will not maximise happiness to follow them in a specific situation. The rules themselves become sacred, rather than the happiness produced by the moral action. This seems irrational if the goal is to create the greatest happiness for the greatest number. Therefore, Act Utilitarianism is 'better' because it focuses on the goal of greatest happiness in each situation.

Act Utilitarianism fits in better with a secular approach to ethics because it does not rely on an outside agent to establish moral laws and ensure their goodness, an outside agent that has historically been God. This is more attractive in contemporary society, which tends to be more secular than religious.

If we act to produce the maximum amount of usefulness in every individual action, then we will ensure the greatest happiness for the greatest number. This seems like a more effective way to ensure that everyone lives a happy life than insisting people follow rules that might maximise happiness in a general way, but often require people to perform individual actions that do not bring about the most happiness for everyone involved.

AO2 activity 2

In 2017, anthropologists at Oxford University published the results of a survey of 60 cultures from around the globe. They believe they have discovered seven universal moral values:

- Love your family.
- Help your group.
- Return favours.
- Be brave.
- Defer to authority.
- Be fair.
- Respect others' property.

Does this mean that fixed rules are required for moral behaviour, or can we pursue these values without setting any rules in place?

The view that Rule Utilitarianism is better than Act Utilitarianism

It is better for an ethical theory to be practical, so that it can be used in real life. Rule Utilitarianism seems to fall in line with more conventional methods of moral decision making, like Aquinas' Natural Law. It prevents an 'anything goes' approach, ensuring the minority are protected against behaviours that would maximise the happiness of the majority at the expense of the minority.

Act Utilitarianism involves the weighing up each individual action, which is an impractical way to run a society, and can enable people to justify terrible actions in the name of the 'greater good' (framing an innocent person to prevent a riot, for example). However, Mill's harm principle means that Rule Utilitarianism protects people from this aspect of Act Utilitarianism, by limiting the freedom of people to pursue pleasure and minimise pain for themselves when it might cause harm to others.

It is better for an ethical theory to ask only what is reasonable, and Act Utilitarianism is too demanding. It is not reasonable for a moral theory to expect an individual to favour the well-being of a stranger over their own child, yet Act Utilitarianism requires us to evaluate everyone as equals. Act Utilitarianism also expects people to do this every time that they have a moral decision to make, and this is wildly impractical for individuals in their day-to-day lives. The rules of Rule Utilitarianism are a short-cut that allow people to quickly assess what they should do because they have been formulated in advance.

The view that both forms of Utilitarianism are equally good/bad

Even act utilitarians find it beneficial to obey rules the majority of the time. They are prepared to make exceptions in unusual situations, but Bentham advocated following laws, and did not expect people to assess every action against every criteria of the hedonic calculus every time they act. The hedonic calculus only needs to be applied when the rules are inadequate or inappropriate.

It is not possible to predict consequences with any degree of accuracy. Both forms of Utilitarianism leave us only able to judge the moral worth of an act after it has taken place. Act Utilitarianism forces a moral agent to decide on the best course of action based on what they think might happen all things considered, and Rule Utilitarianism forces a moral agent to follow a rule that is based on what has happened in the past. Neither approaches are guaranteed to predict the outcome that will produce the greatest happiness for the greatest number in each specific situation.

No form of Act or Rule Utilitarianism provides a concrete way of measuring happiness or whatever useful quality must be measured. Happiness, wellbeing, or ideals are not quantifiable in a mathematical way; they cannot

AO2 activity 3

Make a list of all the weaknesses of Act Utilitarianism that you can think of. How might an act utilitarian defend themselves against each accusation?

For example: *Act Utilitarianism allows immoral actions if they create the greatest happiness for the greatest number.* **But** *an act utilitarian would counter this by arguing that the hedonic calculus includes an obligation to minimise suffering for other people, so an act is very unlikely to be considered moral if it is contaminated by pain.*

Now do the same for Rule Utilitarianism.

be measured in units, and weighing them up is very abstract and subjective. Therefore, neither form of Utilitarianism provides an objective way to measure the morality of an action, whether they set rules in place or not.

Does Utilitarianism promote immoral behaviour?

To promote immoral behaviour, Utilitarianism would have to actively encourage people to do something that is immoral. Immoral behaviour, according to Bentham and Mill, involves acting in a way that maximises pain or minimises happiness. Of course, they would never have promoted immoral behaviour according to their own definition. However, we can consider whether Utilitarianism promotes behaviour that other theories believe to be immoral, and we can consider whether Utilitarianism allows, rather than actively encourages, immoral acts.

The view that Utilitarianism does promote immoral behaviour

Utilitarianism allows two wrongs to apparently make a right. This is something Christian teaching and Natural Law has long objected to. In Romans 3:8, the Bible declares that we may not do evil so that good may come. However, Utilitarianism allows any act if it brings about a pleasurable result. Utilitarians would, for example, allow stealing, lying, and violence if it created the greatest happiness for the greatest number.

Utilitarianism is strangely impersonal. It treats everyone as equals and so does not prefer one person's pleasure or pain over another's. This means we cannot put the needs of a loved one who is suffering above our own needs or the needs of anyone else, and this impersonalism is highly impractical since we are most likely to know how to bring pleasure to, or ease the pain of, those who are closest to us. It is more efficient and more in line with human nature to help those closest to us, to those in our families or friendship groups.

Goodin says that Utilitarianism tends to be criticised by those who are politically right wing because it can be used to justify the redistribution of property in the interests of producing the greatest happiness for the greatest number, even if that redistribution involves body parts! Goodin refers to Gilbert Harman's example of a surgeon presented with a healthy patient who is an organ donor. Utilitarianism would allow the doctor to harvest their organs for the benefit of five sick people in need of transplants. Yet, Utilitarianism is equally challenged by those who are politically left wing, because it can be used to justify an unfair distribution of wealth, where a minority has all the benefits and the majority has nothing, provided the benefits bring more happiness to the minority overall.

The view that Utilitarianism does not promote immoral behaviour

Mill's differentiation between higher and lower pleasures is helpful. While lower pleasures are rather simple and inadequate for assessing moral behaviour, higher pleasures are richer and lead to a better society, more enjoyment, and a more fulfilling life. There is nothing immoral about these things.

R.B. Brandt said that Utilitarianism leaves a place for rules like 'keep your promises' and 'tell the truth', so it is unlikely to promote immoral behaviour. These rules can be regarded as directives that usually point out a person's duty. They are reasonably taught to children and they guide everyday decisions, saving people time. They also tend to correct any biases we might have when faced with complex situations that require individual calculation, when we may be tempted to favour our own interests.

There is utility in following some existing rules that are not formulated by the hedonic calculus! The greatest happiness for the greatest number will be promoted if we follow some of the existing rules, because of human fallibility and a tendency to promote our own interests. Part of the calculation prior to performing a moral action can include whether or not it is more useful to calculate the decision oneself or to follow a current moral rule.

The view that Utilitarianism allows but does not promote immoral behaviour

It is difficult to see how any act that promotes an outcome in which happiness is maximised and pain is reduced or removed could possibly be immoral. The act of lying, for example, can only be immoral when it results in pain or suffering. Lying is surely justified if is saves a life or protects someone from unnecessary pain. Mill's harm principle even offers a safeguard to protect people from harm when others are weighing up the acts that bring them the most happiness. Yet, acts that bring happiness are not always pure. Contamination is inevitable, and therefore immoral behaviour (in the form of pain) may be allowed as people seek to bring about the best possible result, even if they are not actively promoting pain. For instance, I may cause pain to my child by lying to them that their pet rabbit ran away rather than cause them the greater pain of knowing it was killed by a fox.

Pleasure alone can lack dignity and be selfish, and seeking pleasure can lead to immoral behaviour. Bentham's assessment that all pleasures are equal shows that anyone can do anything provided it brings the greatest happiness for the greatest number, and this can be used to justify terrible actions. A popular example is that of the sadistic guards. Ten guards who gain pleasure from the torture of one prisoner could justify their actions on the basis that their pleasure outweighs the prisoner's pain. While Mill's idea that not all pleasures are the same could lead us to challenge the guards' justification, because the pleasure they experience is a lower pleasure and not worth much as a result, happiness or pleasure is still an inadequate basis for behaviour because there is such diversity in what people find pleasurable. While the vast majority of people would reject the actions of the guards as immoral, that may be because we do not share their enjoyment of torture.

Utilitarianism requires that a moral agent has a reason for the decisions they make. That reason is that an action produces the greatest happiness and the least pain. In this way, Utilitarianism does not promote blindly following rules or acting on a whim. Moral actions must be justified as producing happiness. However, although Utilitarianism does not promote immorality, the fact that humans are fallible creatures means it does leave room for people to justify immorality on the basis that an action was judged to facilitate happiness.

To what extent does Utilitarianism promote justice?

Justice is generally considered to mean 'fairness', so this kind of question expects you to weigh up how fair Utilitarianism is, and whether fairness is something that Utilitarianism actively advocates or if it is a natural but unintended consequence.

The view that Utilitarianism promotes justice

Utilitarianism recognises that the value of a resource differs from person to person, and does not measure utility in terms of the amount of a resource someone has access to. For example, the utility you will gain from a pound coin will be different depending on whether you are wealthy or you are poor. The first pound you earn is worth more than the millionth. A pound will bring little joy to a millionaire, but it could make a world of difference to someone who earns less than a pound a day. The same can be said of food: the first slice of cake may bring great happiness but the tenth will probably make you feel sick. In this way, Utilitarianism naturally promotes justice because it weighs the happiness gained from a fair distribution of resources according to a person's need.

Mill understood Utilitarianism to be the perfect example of loving your neighbour as you love yourself; it is the Golden Rule in practice. It promotes justice because it treats the happiness of everyone as equally important and valuable. Mill's harm principle also ensures that the vulnerable are protected. Mill argued that Utilitarianism mirrors Jesus when Jesus promoted justice by putting the welfare of others before himself to reduce their suffering.

Utilitarianism is concerned with the welfare or happiness of people. The calculations performed by act utilitarians and the rules formulated by rule utilitarians have people's well-being at their heart because they are concerned with minimising injustice, pain, and suffering. Utilitarianism treats all people as equals, and values everyone's happiness and pain the same, regardless of who they are. People are treated fairly, and so Utilitarianism is concerned with promoting justice.

AO2 activity 4

Sometimes, Utilitarianism is accused of justifying any action that produces more happiness. In this way, acts like lying become morally acceptable if they produce a greater amount or better quality of happiness. Is this a reasonable criticism?

a) Are there any actions that you consider absolutely immoral, regardless of the circumstances?

b) Can you imagine a circumstance in which Utilitarianism would be able to justify such an action based on it producing the greatest happiness for the greatest number?

The view that Utilitarianism does not promote justice

Utilitarianism does not give us a way to differentiate between one person who experiences a lot of pleasure and ten people who experience a little pleasure. This could lead to injustice if one person experiences quantitatively more happiness than ten others when the happiness is shared out. It also means there is no reason why we should not promote terrible things, such as the enslavement of other people, provided quantitatively more happiness is experienced as a result. This is clearly not something that either Bentham or Mill would have wanted, but it is an inevitable consequence of a utilitarian approach to moral decision making.

According to Pope Francis, Utilitarianism treats people as objects. There is no sense of sanctity of life or of absolute moral values or principles that value people as important regardless of the situation. This means that an individual is expendable if it is perceived that they lack 'usefulness' in bringing about happiness. For example, if someone is sick, with no hope of recovery, killing them becomes the most useful action to reduce suffering. This sounds like a positive outcome, but Pope Francis sees it as unjust to reduce a person to a thing and treat them as undeserving of care.

Brandt points out that it does not matter to the act utilitarian how happiness is distributed, provided the greatest happiness for the greatest number is achieved and happiness is not diminished by an action. This could result in a situation in which half the population is left unhappy while the other half has their happiness doubled. The overall happiness is the same, and so there is no moral difficulty. This is clearly in conflict with our general understanding of justice.

The view that Utilitarianism allows but does not promote justice

As a relativist theory, Utilitarianism does not forbid particular behaviours no matter what. This means that it is open to injustice because there are no actions that are off the table and those who are in the minority count for less. However, it must be noted that Utilitarianism does not set out to make the minority suffer or encourage actions that are deliberately cruel to a small number. Therefore, while Utilitarianism may allow the minority to experience injustice when it is the least terrible option, it sets out to maximise happiness and minimise suffering in every action.

Utilitarianism generally does not place particular value on the ideas of duty or personal character. Other ethical systems suggest that these things are important to ensure that justice is promoted: doing one's duty is vital if promises are to be kept or if the vulnerable are to be protected, and good personal character is vital if someone is to show loyalty or to treat others fairly. Yet, Utilitarianism only values the sum total of happiness created and, if this is at the expense of a small minority, then that is hard luck.

While Bentham and Mill were clearly concerned with the administration of justice in terms of ending enslavement, and treating women, prisoners, and the poor fairly, Utilitarianism does not require every individual to value these things as well. Utilitarianism is simply concerned with maximising happiness. This may allow justice to be done, but justice is not a central principle of Utilitarianism, and Utilitarianism does not promote justice as part of its decision-making process.

To what extent does Utilitarianism provide a practical basis for making moral decisions for religious believers and non-believers?

There are two parts to this question: first, you are asked to consider if Utilitarianism is a practical ethical theory, and secondly, you are asked if it is practical for religious people and/or non-religious people. It is important to distinguish between believers and non-believers in your answer because each group has different views on what behaviours are ethical.

The view that Utilitarianism provides a practical basis for making moral decisions

Utilitarianism is practical for non-believers because it uses empirical evidence, not divine revelation, to guide moral decision making. It considers the interests of all people, and uses evidence from human experience to deduce the correct action. This is a very scientific approach of using sensory evidence and observation to come to a conclusion.

Utilitarianism is attractive to believers even though it is not based on divine revelation. Mill believed that Utilitarianism was consistent with Christian morality:

> *If it be meant that Utilitarianism does not recognise the revealed will of God as the supreme law of morals, I answer that a Utilitarian who believes in the perfect goodness and wisdom of God necessarily believes that whatever God has thought fit to reveal on the subject of morals, must fulfil the requirements of utility in a supreme degree.*
>
> John Stuart Mill, *Utilitarianism: On Liberty and Other Essays*

Happiness is a relatively simple concept to use to resolve moral dilemmas. It does not require dependence upon divine revelation or the will of God. Nor does it require complex analysis of a range of goods, virtues, or principles. Happiness is something that everyone can experience, making Utilitarianism highly practical.

The view that Utilitarianism does not provide a practical basis for making moral decisions

We do not have utility meters implanted into our foreheads that can be read like electricity meters by anyone who wants to see what we are experiencing.

Every mind is a mystery to every other mind and, consequently, no one can fully understand the experience of happiness or suffering experienced by others so that they can measure it and decide on the moral action. The moral agent is forced to guess what someone else would think or feel, and this is not a practical basis for making moral decisions.

Utilitarianism commits the Naturalistic Fallacy. It tries to draw ethical conclusions from empirical evidence, even though ethical facts are not the same as natural facts. This error in logic makes utilitarian judgements rationally invalid and, as a result, Utilitarianism cannot provide a practical basis for making moral decisions.

Consequences are exceedingly unpredictable. It is surely impractical, therefore, to make moral decisions based upon the predicted consequences of an action when it is not possible to know, in advance, what the outcome of a particular action will be. In addition, it takes an unreasonably long time to calculate what the moral thing to do is if the hedonic calculus is used properly. It is impractical to expect time to stop while a moral agent guesses all the possible consequences of each possible action and chooses the one that will produce the greatest happiness for the greatest number. It is more practical to follow rules or laws that give a general guide to moral action.

The view that Utilitarianism provides some practical support for making moral decisions

Bentham's Act Utilitarianism provides practical support for moral decision making in the form of the hedonic calculus. This guides the moral agent, showing them what to weigh in the balance, but leaves it up to the moral agent to do the calculating for themselves. It requires a moral agent to take responsibility for their actions, but gives them some help so that they are not making a random guess as to the best course of action.

Mill's Rule Utilitarianism is more practical because it allows people to use historic rules to help them make quick decisions based on the wisdom of others. However, Mill does not require people to rigidly follow these rules no matter what. He recognised that there will be times when someone must use the hedonic calculus and take responsibility for their own moral decision making. Therefore, some guidance is given, but individuals are still free to make decisions themselves, including deciding when it is appropriate to break historic rules.

Religious believers could turn to Utilitarianism to resolve moral dilemmas when scripture does not provide clear guidance about what to do. There is nothing in Utilitarianism that is fundamentally at odds with the moral decision making discussed in the New Testament. Jesus taught people to be compassionate, and clearly showed an interest in maximising wellbeing. Utilitarianism enables these things too. While Utilitarianism does not require a belief in God or an absolute moral standard, it gives some guidance that Christians could find useful in some situations.

Synoptic link

Link to *Chapter 2: Ethical thought (part two)*. Look back to chapter 2 to read about the objections to Ethical Naturalism and what is meant by the Naturalistic Fallacy.

AO2 activity 6

Consider the following scenarios. Can the following actions be justified using utilitarian principles? Do you think that they are 'good' ethical actions?

a) A politician lies to the public so they can win enough votes to get into power and improve society by expanding the welfare system and funding education.

b) A business uses all the water resources in a developing nation to create and sell their product. They donate billions of pounds of their profit to charities promoting child welfare.

c) A pharmaceutical company tests their products on large numbers of caged primates, causing them significant suffering, so that it can get results quickly. The resulting drugs are used to treat millions of cancer patients effectively and affordably.

Practising AO1 questions

As you now know, AO1 questions begin with a range of possible command words (see pages 8–9 for more detail). The question below begins with the word 'Compare'. 'Compare' questions require you to show the similarities and differences between two approaches. You do not need to consider the quality of the approaches or offer any views about them. It is better to discuss the approaches together, comparing each aspect of them in turn, rather than describing one approach and then describing the second approach.

Read the past paper question below and the example paragraph written in response before completing the activity on page 250.

> *Compare Act and Rule Utilitarianism.*
>
> (Eduqas AS Level Religious Studies, Summer 2017,
> Component 3: An Introduction to Religion and Ethics, Question 2a)

Example

Act Utilitarianism[2] says that *a good moral action is one that produces the greatest happiness for the greatest number of people in each individual action. That means that you have to weigh up the happiness achieved every time you act*[1]. For example, if you are deciding whether or not to steal, you would ignore the rules and just weigh up whether or not it is ok to steal in the situation you find yourself in. You would consider why you want to steal and, if you were starving and wanted to steal food, you would decide that there would be more happiness if you stole food than if you starved to death.[3] A problem comes up when we use this example, though, because if a person wants to steal for the fun of it, then they can because it would make them happy to steal.

Areas for development

1 The response shows some knowledge and understanding of what Act Utilitarianism is, and has some understanding of how this compares with a more rule-based approach. However, there is no clear attempt to address Rule Utilitarianism.

2 This answer does not fully address the question because there is no sense of comparison, and Rule Utilitarianism is not covered in the paragraph shown.

3 There is an attempt to develop an example, although there is no attempt to use the hedonic calculus or demonstrate a method of how one might weigh up whether it is morally acceptable to steal.

4 It is not appropriate for students to use sources of religious authority in this response about a non-religious ethical theory.

5 The student has not made any connections with other approaches that have been studied, but this is unnecessary here.

6 There is no reference to any scholars in this paragraph. Bentham and Mill are examples of scholars who have been characterised as act or rule utilitarians, and it would be useful to use them to help with the comparison between the approaches.

7 No specialist vocabulary is used.

Activity

a) Read the example paragraph on page 249 and identify two strengths and two weaknesses.

b) Improve the example paragraph by rewriting it to correct the weaknesses you identified.

AO1 practice question 1

Now it is your turn. Have a go at answering the following question. There are some points to remember underneath to help you if you are not sure how to start.

Apply Bentham's hedonic calculus to the use of nuclear weapons as a deterrent.

(WJEC AS Level Religious Studies, Summer 2018, AS Unit 2: An Introduction to Religion and Ethics and the Philosophy of Religion, Question 2a)

Points to remember

- This is an 'apply' question, so you need to use the hedonic calculus criteria (intensity, duration, certainty, remoteness, richness, purity, and extent) to show how one might make the decision to possess or develop nuclear weapons as a way of deterring others from attacking.
- The hedonic calculus considers happiness and suffering, and so it can be used to forbid actions as well as permit actions.
- Give examples and use short quotations from Bentham where relevant. Do not forget to explain any quotations that you use or paraphrase.

AO1 practice question 2

Now try this question by yourself.

Explain the main features of Act Utilitarianism.

(Eduqas AS Level Religious Studies, Summer 2019, Component 3: An Introduction to Religion and Ethics, Question 5a)

Practising AO2 questions

When writing a response to an AO2 question, you must remember that you are being examined on your ability to analyse and evaluate effectively. Analysis involves a detailed examination of something and you should pick apart the concept to look for the strengths and the weaknesses. Evaluation involves judging the quality or importance of the concept. You are expected to analyse and evaluate throughout the whole of your response; you are not expected to include long passages explaining knowledge and understanding.

Read the past paper question below and the example paragraphs written in response before completing the activity on page 253.

> 'Act Utilitarianism is not relevant in modern society.'
> Evaluate this view.
>
> (Eduqas AS Level Religious Studies, Summer 2017, Component 3: An Introduction to Religion and Ethics, Question 1b)

Example 1

Act Utilitarianism is irrelevant to modern society[2] because it is very time-consuming[1] to calculate the consequences[6] of every single action[1]. As a hedonist[6], Bentham said we should 'sum up all the value of pleasure on one side and all the value of pain on the other side'[4]. But, in an emergency situation, we do not have time for that[1]. For example, if there are two people in a burning building and we have time to rescue one, we cannot expect the victims to wait while we calculate the[3] relative[6] happiness achieved by saving one and allowing the other to die.[3] However[1], Act Utilitarianism is relevant to modern society[2] because it is compassionate. Instead of following[1] deontological[6] rules and laws that ignore the specific situation, Act Utilitarianism considers the pain of the individuals in question.[1] Bentham said that it was acceptable to act in opposition to law rather than in subservience to it[4], because that might be the best way to achieve happiness. However, it is possible to develop laws and rules that show compassion. The more pressing issue is that[1] Act Utilitarianism[2] should be practical and useable[1] in modern society[2], which it is not if it is too time consuming to apply.[1]

Areas for development

1 There is a clear sense of evaluation and analysis in this paragraph. The student shows two sides of the argument and concludes.

2 The paragraph is appropriate for an AO2 question and clearly relates to Act Utilitarianism, however there is little mention of the specifics of what makes this difficult or suitable for modern society in particular.

3 The student develops an example to illustrate their point clearly. They could have considered using an example that relates more to modern society if they were struggling to address that part of the question. For instance, Bentham would have been unlikely to have been concerned with road traffic accidents, but the strengths and weaknesses of Act Utilitarianism in such an example may still be valid.

4 There is plenty of evidence of scholarly points of view, and these are quoted or paraphrased in an appropriate way. It is possible that an opposing scholar could be used to support a challenge to Bentham.

5 The student mentions deontological approaches, and could develop this to consider whether approaches like Natural Law would be more or less relevant to modern society than Act Utilitarianism.

6 The language used by the student is appropriate and specific to Utilitarianism.

Example 2: an improved response

Act Utilitarianism is irrelevant to modern society[2] because it is very time consuming to calculate the[1] consequences[6] of every single action in a fast-paced, global society[1]. As a hedonist[6], Bentham said we should 'sum up all the value of pleasure on one side and all the value of pain on the other side'[4]. But in an emergency situation, when faced with multiple pressures, or when managing large numbers of people, we do not have time for that[1]. For example, if there are multiple casualties in a motorway crash and we have time to rescue one person, we cannot expect all the victims to wait while we calculate the[3] relative[6] happiness achieved by saving each individual.[3] However[1], Act Utilitarianism is relevant to modern society[2] because it is compassionate. Instead of following[1] deontological[6] rules and laws that ignore the complexities of modern life, it considers the pain of the individuals in question. However, it is possible to develop laws and rules that show compassion, and[1] Mill's weak rule approach allows for exceptions to rules[4] to be made if this produces greater happiness. The more pressing issue is that[1] Act Utilitarianism[2] should be practical and useable[1] in modern society[2], which it is not if it is too time consuming to apply.[1]

What went well

1 The sense of evaluation and analysis has been retained, but now the student relates their reasoning specifically to issues in the modern world. They mention the pace of life and the amount of people who may now be affected by a moral decision.

2 This paragraph is still appropriate to AO2, and now it references Act Utilitarianism and modern society in a more convincing way.

3 The new example is more appropriate to the developed point that is being made, and seems more in keeping with a modern dilemma.

4 There is still appropriate evidence of scholarly points of view. The student has chosen to refer to Mill as a contrasting argument now.

5 The student mentions deontological approaches, and could develop this to consider whether approaches like Natural Law would be more or less relevant to modern society than Act Utilitarianism.

6 The language used by the student remains appropriate and specific.

Activity

a) Read Example 1 on page 251 and identify one thing that could be developed to improve the analysis or the evaluation.

b) Example 2 on page 252 is an improved version of Example 1. Read it and identify how the student has improved their response.

AO2 practice question 1

Now it is your turn. Have a go at answering the following question. There are some points to remember underneath to help you if you are not sure how to start.

'Act Utilitarianism provides a better basis for making moral decisions than Rule Utilitarianism.' Evaluate this view.

(Eduqas A Level Religious Studies, Summer 2018, Component 3: Religion and Ethics, Question 5b)

Points to remember

- The question asks you to weigh up whether Act Utilitarianism or Rule Utilitarianism is better for making decisions. You can use the ideas of Bentham and Mill to exemplify these approaches, and you should consider what criteria you want to use to determine what 'better' is.
- Give plenty of examples to illustrate your ideas throughout the essay. For example, you could include an example that shows how rules can help people make moral decisions, and contrast it with an example that shows how using the hedonic calculus enables people to make a decision that takes all of a situation into account.
- Use the ideas of the scholars from other areas of ethical study. For example, you could use the Natural Law theorists and proportionalists to challenge Utilitarianism where relevant to the question.

AO2 practice question 2

Now try this question by yourself.

'Pleasure is the only true basis for morality.' Evaluate this view.

(WJEC AS Level Religious Studies, Summer 2018, AS Unit 2: An Introduction to Religion and Ethics and the Philosophy of Religion, Question 2b)

Mark schemes for all exam questions can be found at www.eduqas.co.uk and www.wjec.co.uk.

Lionel Shriver's novel *We Need to Talk About Kevin* is the story of a mother (Eva) whose son (Kevin) kills several students from his high school. In the book, Eva tells us that she had been ambivalent about having a child, in denial during her pregnancy and that she struggled to be a mother to a challenging child. At times during Kevin's childhood, Eva thinks there is something 'wrong' with Kevin's behaviour and they have a cold relationship, but his father (Franklin) loves and defends him, believing him to be misunderstood.

As he grows up, Kevin 'resists' toilet training, appears to encourage others to self-harm, manipulates his peers, is involved in 'accidents' that injure others, and accuses a teacher of sexual abuse. Eva is often unclear whether or not she believes Kevin's versions of events, and feels that he pretends to cooperate when his father is around. Eva and Franklin experience marital difficulties and discuss divorce as Franklin refuses to listen to Eva's concerns.

The parents of the children who die blame Eva for poor parenting. Her lack of love for Kevin, his genetic makeup, his parents' divorce, or his mother's behaviour during pregnancy could all have contributed to creating a personality that led to the killings. Or is Kevin fully and solely responsible for the choices he made?

In this chapter, you will study the religious concept of predestination as presented by Augustine and Calvin. You will also consider the concept of Determinism as presented by scholars such as Locke, Pavlov, Hobbes, and Ayer; and you will think about the implications of these concepts on moral responsibility and religious belief. For example, if our actions are all determined, is there any point in formulating normative systems of ethics? If our destination is decided before we are born, does it make any sense for God to blame us for our sins? Does it make any sense to punish people when they commit crimes or reward them for acts of heroism?

Are we free to make our own choices, or are we controlled by our genetic makeup and the things that have happened to us?

AO1

This section of the chapter will enhance your knowledge and understanding of the topic and help you develop your AO1 skills.

Religious concepts of predestination

The religious concept of **predestination** – the belief that God has already decided what will happen and, specifically, has already elected certain souls for salvation – is extremely complex, and is dependent upon a number of other theological claims. Christian scripture teaches that human beings have **free will** to choose their actions and are held accountable for their sins. However, this belief must be balanced with other beliefs, such as the omniscience of God, who is all-knowing, and the omnipotence of God, who is all-powerful. God must know what we will do before we do it, and must decide what happens to us when we die. To suggest otherwise limits God by suggesting we have power that God does not. Therefore, religious concepts of predestination are rooted in beliefs about the nature of God and God's relationship with humanity.

Augustine

Augustine of Hippo lived in North Africa from 354 to 430 CE and had a great influence on the development of Christian doctrines. Augustine's thinking on predestination is woven into his writings on other issues and is sometimes unclear. His ideas evolved as he responded to different theological problems, so he appears to change his mind over time.

For nearly twenty years, a controversy with another theologian, Pelagius, occupied a great portion of Augustine's writings, and wrestling with the controversy shaped Augustine's understanding of predestination. Pelagius and his supporters had challenged the Christians in Rome, who thought it did not matter how they behaved because they were saved by God's **grace** (by the gift of mercy shown to humanity that rescues some from sin through Jesus' death on the cross). However, Augustine objected to Pelagius' claim that behaving morally could bring salvation because it suggested that people have the power to save themselves, without God's help, and appeared to make Christ's sacrifice on the cross redundant.

Augustine was keen to ensure that God was seen as omnibenevolent, omnipotent, and omniscient (supremely good, powerful, and knowing). Sin must be the work of humanity, not of God, and salvation can only be achieved in accordance with God's will and in accordance with Paul's teaching.

> *In him we were also chosen, having been predestined according to the plan of him who works out everything in conformity with the purpose of his will.*
>
> Ephesians 1:11, *Holy Bible (NIV)*

Key terms

predestination: the belief that God has already decided what will happen and, specifically, has already elected certain souls for salvation

free will: the belief that God allows humanity the ability to choose between different courses of action

grace: for Augustine, the gift of mercy shown to humanity that rescues some from sin through Jesus' death on the cross

Synoptic link

Link to *Chapter 8: Determinism and free will: free will*. Take a look at the teachings of Pelagius, to whom Augustine was objecting.

Doctrine of Original Sin

In the book of Genesis, Adam and Eve commit the first sin in the garden of Eden. By eating the forbidden fruit, they turn away from God's will and fall from the perfect state in which they were originally created. This event brings sin and death into the world. Drawing on the book of Romans, Augustine understood this event as **original sin**:

> *Therefore, just as sin entered the world through one man, and death through sin, and in this way death came to all people, because all sinned.* "
>
> Romans 5:12, *Holy Bible (NIV)*

According to Augustine's doctrine of original sin, when God created people, they were perfectly good and were given the gift of free will with which they could choose to obey God. When Adam sinned, that perfect state was corrupted and Adam's free will was damaged. Because all of Adam's descendants were seminally present (present in his semen), he condemned not only himself but all of humanity to a state of guilt from original sin.

> *For God, the author of natures, not of vices, created man upright; but man, being of his own will corrupted, and justly condemned, begot corrupted and condemned children. For we all were in that one man, since we all were that one man who fell into sin by the woman who was made from him before the sin.* "
>
> Augustine, *The City of God*

Before the fall, Adam and Eve were immortal and innocent. Had they stayed obedient, they would have remained in this state for eternity and would not have died. However, Augustine argued that they had already decided to turn away from God by the time the devil, in the form of a serpent, tempted them to eat the forbidden fruit, and so they cannot pass the blame on to the devil. Their fall was the result of their own free choices.

An essentially free human nature

When Adam was created by God, *imago dei*, he was created with free will – with **liberum arbitrium** – to choose not to sin. Although damaged by original sin, Adam's descendants still have free will. For Augustine, without human free will, God would be the author of sin and could not be considered omnibenevolent. Without human free will, God is not justified in punishing those who do evil. Therefore, a human must be morally responsible for sin by acting freely according to their own desires.

Key terms

original sin: the condition of sinfulness and guilt that all humans are born into, caused by the first sin of Adam and Eve, and passed down through the generations

liberum arbitrium: (Latin) free will to choose

Synoptic link

Link to *A Level Religious Studies for Eduqas: Philosophy of Religion*, Chapter 3: Challenges to religious belief: the problem of evil and suffering. Refresh your memory about Augustinian-type theodicies, and ensure you understand the nature of evil as *privatio boni* and the role of human freedom in evil and suffering.

The loss of human liberty to our sinful nature

Augustine recognised that there was a difference between original sin and individual sin. Human beings are born with original sin, which has damaged their free, human nature and contaminated it, meaning that all humans share in Adam's guilt. And having inherited Adam's original sin, humanity is now predisposed to commit individual sin. Human liberty (*libertas*) has been lost, and while people still have free will to make choices, their free will has been distorted by sin and so they only desire evil.

Like scales that already have weights on one side, human beings are inclined towards sin.

Augustine gave the example of a set of weighing scales where one side is already stacked heavily with weights. While the scales still work, from this position it is impossible for any weight placed on the other side to have any real effect. This means that human beings are free, but only to sin. The guilt from their original sin has made it impossible for them to freely choose good by themselves.

The role of concupiscence

Original sin came from an intense desire that led Adam away from God. Augustine called this **concupiscence**. It is the desire for earthly pleasures and refers to all forms of human desire, but especially sexual pleasure. Since the fall, humans are slaves to their desires; they are weak willed and cannot remain faithful to God's commands.

According to Augustine, all infants exist because of sexual intercourse. It is through this act that original sin is passed on to offspring and how concupiscence continues in individuals. Baptism can cleanse the stain of original sin but does not remove the tendency towards concupiscence. Only one child has ever been born free of concupiscence: Jesus Christ, who was born to a virgin and conceived without semen, was free from original sin and, consequently, from concupiscence.

Humanity as a 'lump of sin'

In the New Testament, Paul describes the analogy of a potter with a lump of clay. The clay is useless until the potter has acted upon it and fashioned it for a purpose.

> Does not the potter have the right to make out of the same lump of clay some pottery for special purposes and some for common use? 🙾
>
> Romans 9:21, *Holy Bible (NIV)*

Augustine saw humanity like this lump of clay, but contaminated. He described humanity as ***massa peccati***, a lump of sin.

> ## Key terms
>
> ***libertas***: (Latin) liberty
>
> **concupiscence**: the desire for earthly pleasures
>
> ***massa peccati***: (Latin) a lump of sin

While individual humans may consider it unfair that we are lumped together in this way, Augustine believes this feeling arises because we do not really understand the enormity of our sinfulness. Humanity is universally affected by original sin, and it is impossible for an individual to perceive this truth. Sin contaminates the whole of human life, from the moment of our conception, and dominates all human decisions.

God's grace and atonement for the Elect

Since the whole of humankind is born in a state of sinfulness, God would be perfectly justified in punishing the whole of humanity by sending everyone to hell. However, God is loving as well as just. While all should be held accountable for their sinfulness, God has chosen to save some of the condemned through **atonement**, when the life and death of Jesus reconciled God and humanity. It is through God's grace alone that the illness of sin can be cured.

> **Key term**
>
> **atonement:** the reconciliation of God and humanity through the redemptive life and death of Jesus

Pelagius argued that humans can freely decide to be good for themselves and can earn their salvation through merit. However, Augustine regarded this as a heresy, as against the teaching of the Christian Church, because it would make Jesus' death redundant. For Augustine, humanity is incapable of making good choices as a result of the fall because all are tainted by original sin.

> *But there is an opinion that calls for sharp and vehement resistance – I mean the belief that the power of the human will can of itself, without the help of God, either achieve perfect righteousness or advance steadily toward it.*
>
> Augustine, *The Spirit and the Letter*

Augustine argued that humans do not deserve to be saved, and cannot be rewarded for good deeds. Salvation is not a reward based upon merit or virtue; it is a free gift from God to the undeserving. It is not given to everyone; it is particular, not universal. While everyone is contaminated by sin and unable to free themselves from it, God's grace can free them and God elects some to receive that gift.

Augustine refers to the parable of the workers in the vineyard. In this parable, a landowner promises to pay workers one denarius for a day's work. He hires a group of workers early in the morning and pays them one denarius. He then hires extra workers towards the end of the day and pays them the same wage. Those who worked all day complained.

> *But he answered one of them, 'I am not being unfair to you, friend. Didn't you agree to work for a denarius? Take your pay and go. I want to give the one who was hired last the same as I gave you. Don't I have the right to do what I want with my own money? Or are you envious because I am generous?'*
>
> Matthew 20:13–15, *Holy Bible (NIV)*

Augustine clearly argued that Christians should believe in both predestination and free will.

The payment to those who started work at the end of the day was not a reward for hard work; it was the fulfilment of a promise made by the landowner. In the same way, salvation is not a reward for good behaviour; it is a gift from God and a fulfilment of God's promise to humanity of eternal salvation. To those who complained that this does not seem fair, Augustine replied that God is not required by justice to save anyone, because all humans are tainted by original sin and it is just for sinners to be punished. However, because God is loving, God has the desire to save humanity. God has freely chosen to show mercy to some people and, by the gift of grace, saves them from damnation. With infinite knowledge, God has decided in advance – has predestined – who will be saved. Human beings fail to understand God's choice because, in their fallen state, they are incapable of understanding this divine mystery.

It is unclear from Augustine's writings if he was suggesting **double predestination** or **single predestination**. Double predestination is the belief that God has selected, in advance, who will be saved and who will be damned. It means that God creates some souls with the express intention of punishing them, and some of Augustine's writings do seem to imply this. However, scholars like John Hick and Alister McGrath suggest that Augustine favoured single predestination. This means that God has selected some people for salvation (the **Elect**) and actively chosen to give them the gift of grace. The remainder of the undeserving (the **Reprobates**) are simply left to their just punishment.

Obedience to the laws in scripture is not the way to salvation; no one can be saved simply by doing good deeds. Scripture simply highlights the acts that are only possible for humans to choose if they have been given God's grace. This grace is irresistible, and those whom God has chosen will remain faithful to God until death.

According to Augustine, humans are free and responsible in the sense that their acts are their own; they are an expression of the desires that stem from their own fallen nature which inclines them towards sin. Therefore, humans are also predestined in the sense that they are free only to sin. God foreknew how they would act and chose some for salvation through God's grace.

> ## Key terms
>
> **double predestination:** God has selected, in advance, some souls for damnation and others for salvation
>
> **single predestination:** God has selected, in advance, some souls for salvation
>
> **Elect:** also sometimes called Saints; those chosen by God, before the creation of the world, to receive salvation
>
> **Reprobates:** those not chosen by God as one of the Elect are predestined to receive just punishment for their sinful nature

AO1 activity 1

Complete a revision 'work out'. Download an interval timer to your phone or find one online, and set it so that you have 4 minutes' work with 1 minutes' rest for 20 minutes (four rounds). In each of your four work sessions, answer one of the following questions:

a) What did Augustine mean by 'original sin'?
b) Why did Augustine believe that evil was the fault of humanity rather than God?
c) How did Augustine think we can be free and yet predestined?
d) How did Augustine think the elect are saved?

John Calvin

John Calvin was a French Protestant reformer who approached the issue of free will and predestination with Augustine's teaching very much in mind. However, Calvin's theology challenged Augustine's thinking and Catholic tradition. It is particularly important to be aware that Calvin's **Doctrine of Election** was not central to his theology and teaching. It was more an inevitable consequence of some of his other teachings about the nature of God and the role of scripture. Calvin wrote about predestination in the first edition of *Institutes of the Christian Religion*, which was published in 1536, and in each subsequent edition, the doctrine became more detailed and developed as he defended it from attack. The influence of Calvin's teaching was central to the Second Synod of Dort in 1618–1619, which was called by the Dutch Reformed Church to settle the conflict between Calvinism and the Arminians (the followers of Jacobus Arminius) who placed greater emphasis on human free will.

Doctrine of Election

Calvin saw predestination as a decree of God that was decided before creation, independent of any human action.

God has **pre-determined** some people (the Elect) for eternal life and others (the Reprobates) for damnation. God chooses the Elect according to God's will, not according to the behaviour of humanity or – in contrast with the teaching of another Protestant reformer, Martin Luther – on a free decision of faith. Calvin admitted that this was a frightening idea, but the importance of this doctrine is that everything about our eternal condition is within God's power and control.

> *The decree, I admit, is, dreadful; and yet it is impossible to deny that God foreknew what the end of man was to be before he made him, and foreknew, because he had so ordained by his decree.*
>
> John Calvin, *Institutes of the Christian Religion*

Calvin based his teaching firmly upon scripture, which he saw as the fundamental authority on God and faith. He referred to Paul's letters to the Romans and the Ephesians as clear and incontrovertible evidence of predestination as he saw it.

> *For he chose us in him before the creation of the world to be holy and blameless in his sight. In love, he predestined us for adoption to sonship through Jesus Christ, in accordance with his pleasure and will.*
>
> Ephesians 1:4–5, *Holy Bible (NIV)*

The absolute power of God

This understanding of God's will as the sole reason for the election or damnation of human beings is based upon the nature of God as creator and sustainer of the world. God does not abandon God's creation to the workings of nature or to chance. Through God's providence – care and guidance through the Holy Spirit – God controls everything in the universe. Nothing happens unless God wills it, therefore every single person is predestined for salvation or damnation according to the deliberate will of God that is unaffected and uncaused by human actions or decisions.

Key terms

Doctrine of Election: the Calvinist teaching of predestination: God's unchangeable command that from before the creation of the world, God would save some (the Elect) for eternal life, while others (the Reprobates) would be sentenced to 'eternal damnation'

pre-determined: something decided in advance

Synoptic link

Link to *Chapter 8: Determinism and free will: free will*. Read about the teachings of Arminius, with whom Calvin disagreed.

The corrupted nature of humans

Calvin refers to Augustine throughout *Institutes of the Christian Religion*. He follows Augustine in saying that while Adam was initially created by God as perfectly good and with free will, in the fall, humanity's free will was corrupted through original sin. God predestined that Adam would fall and drag humanity down with him. Following Augustine, Calvin could not accept that any human action, coming from such corrupted and wretched beings, could possibly affect the outcome of God's judgement in any way; people are powerless to influence their eternal fate, so nothing that they do can change God's plan for them.

However, Calvin did not believe that people should sit back and do nothing because God's decision about their eternal future is unalterable. While one's final state is predestined by God, an individual can still make decisions over the course of a lifetime. Calvin advocated that all should seek God's grace by living a life that is pleasing to God. The ability to do this will make no difference to God's decision about whether or not an individual is saved, but it is a sign that they may be numbered among the Elect. Protestants suffered persecution in France in the sixteenth century and, for Calvin, persecution was also a sign that God had elected someone for salvation.

The Elect and the Reprobates

One significant difference between Calvin and Augustine is Calvin's clear preference for double predestination. Calvin taught that God has made a positive decree from the outset that some should be saved and some should be damned.

> *All are not created on equal terms, but some are preordained to eternal life, others to eternal damnation; and, accordingly, as each has been created for one or other of these ends, we say that he has been predestinated to life or to death.*
>
> John Calvin, *Institutes of the Christian Religion*

God not only foresaw the fall of Adam and the ruin of Adam's descendants, God's will actually brought it about. Calvin said we cannot know the reason for God's judgements. However, God's power is exercised over the Elect when they are chosen, and over the Reprobates when they fulfil God's purpose, yet God remains pure. God is just in punishing the Reprobates because they have turned away from God, but God did not simply know in advance that this would happen, God decreed it. In Calvin's view, God predestined humans for their election or reprobation before the fall. This means that the fall was the method by which God carried out predestination.

> *Those, therefore, whom God passes by he reprobates, and that for no other cause but because he is pleased to exclude them from the inheritance which he predestines to his children.*
>
> John Calvin, *Institutes of the Christian Religion*

John Calvin was a French, Protestant Reformer whose teaching was at the heart of the Calvinist/Arminian controversy.

Calvin saw the death and resurrection of Christ as a historical event for the forgiveness of human sin. But he could not accept that Christ would be unable to attract all of humanity to himself. Yet, it is an observable fact that not everyone has faith in the gospel. Therefore, for Calvin, the rejection by some of God's grace is evidence that God has ordained some for damnation. Calvin also could not accept that natural laws would destroy God's creation through death. Therefore, it is the work of Adam that brought death into the world, and this too is in accordance with the decree of God.

Unconditional election

While '**unconditional election**' is not Calvin's phrase, it is used by Calvinists to explain that the sins of the Elect are forgiven only through the grace of God and this does not depend upon human good behaviour. There is no need for a Christian to be anxious about whether they are good enough before God because God's grace is a free gift and is unconditional. There is nothing they can do that will have any effect on God's choice, so they cannot lose their election by making a mistake. No one can enter heaven unless they have received God's grace and have been elected on the basis of God's will alone. Any holiness displayed by a person is not the reason for election, it is the result of election.

> *We learn from the Apostle's words, that the salvation of believers is founded entirely on the decree of divine election, that the privilege is procured not by works but free calling.* **"**
>
> John Calvin, *Institutes of the Christian Religion*

Limited atonement

Limited atonement does not refer to some kind of limitation on Christ's ability to save humanity from sin. Instead, it refers to the limited number of people who will receive Christ's gift. The majority of Christian Churches have taught that salvation through Christ's death on the cross was for everyone, although not everyone will accept the gift. However, while Calvin himself did not use the phrase 'limited atonement', Calvinism rejects the idea that God can desire to do something and human beings can influence, reject, or render it ineffective. Calvinists believe that God's will cannot be circumvented or foiled because God is omnipotent. Only some are saved because God must have desired to save only some from the outset. Therefore, Christ's death was only for the Elect.

Irresistible grace and the perseverance of the Elect

God's **irresistible grace**, through Christ's death, ensures the elect are **justified**. This means that they have been saved, regardless of their actions in this lifetime. However, the elect will also always obey God's will because they are **sanctified** and there is nothing they can do to resist God's commands. The omnipotent God forms each person's will and so, through the power of God's Holy Spirit, each person will choose what God expects

---

Key terms

unconditional election: the Elect are chosen purely through God's will

limited atonement: Christ's death and atonement for humanity's sins was for the Elect only

irresistible grace: the Elect cannot resist the calling of God

justified: saved by the death of Jesus Christ on the cross

sanctified: given the ability to obey God's will

of them. This is, according to Calvinism, the **perseverance of the Elect**: once someone is a member of the Elect, they cannot commit **apostasy**; they cannot give up their faith. Anyone who appears to turn away from their faith was not a member of the Elect to begin with. God cannot fail and Christ would not allow his faithful to be taken from him. God has the will and the power to redeem whomever God chooses, so it cannot be possible for God to lose to human weakness and sin.

While no one can know who has been elected and who has been damned, a tendency towards faith and obedience to God's law is a clue that someone has been chosen. However, it is not possible to be certain. Those who appear to be among the Elect or the Reprobates cannot know for sure that they have been saved or condemned. All should strive, therefore, to follow God's commands in the hope that they are among the Elect.

> ## Key terms
>
> **perseverance of the Elect:** the Elect cannot commit apostasy (give up their faith); the Holy Spirit ensures this
>
> **apostasy:** give up, or fall away from, one's faith

> *If the end of election is holiness of life, it ought to arouse and stimulate us strenuously to aspire to it, instead of serving as a pretext for sloth.* "
>
> John Calvin, *Institutes of the Christian Religion*

The Five Points of Calvinism

The five central principles of Calvin's teaching are summarised in the Five Points of Calvinism, which were set down at the Synod of Dort. They can be contrasted with the Five Articles of Remonstrance presented by the Arminians (see page 307), and are usually remembered by English speakers using the acronym TULIP:

T   Total depravity: Humans have an inherently sinful nature and are incapable of good works by themselves.

U   Unconditional election: Election is not dependent upon anything that humans do. It makes no difference if you do good works or have faith. A person is elected on the basis of God's will alone.

L   Limited atonement: Not everyone will be elected. God elects some and actively condemns others. This is known as double predestination.

I   Irresistible grace: There is nothing that humanity can do to resist God's call. The Elect will be redeemed because God's power is absolute, and humans do not have the power to overturn it.

P   Perseverance of the Elect: It is impossible to turn away from God, and the Elect will remain faithful to God regardless. This is a sign that God has chosen them.

> ## AO1 activity 2
>
> Choose three quotations from Calvin and place them in the centre of a piece of A4 paper. Around the outside, in your own words, write as many statements as you can that help to explain what Calvin meant in each quotation. See if you can include reference to all Five Points of Calvinism.

Concepts of Determinism

The concept of **Determinism** is an ancient one, and what it means has changed over time. However, since about the seventeenth century, it has been understood to mean that every event has a cause. If every event has a cause, all human actions, mental states, decisions, and choices, whether in the past or in the future, are all the effects of **antecedent causes**; that is, they are all the effects of causes that happened before they occurred. They are, therefore, fixed and unalterable. This means that the human understanding of free will – the idea that we have significant control over our own actions – is an illusion. The future is set as part of a mechanistic (machine-like) chain of cause and effect, and there are no meaningful alternatives to our actions. This is known as **universal causation**: the laws of cause and effect occur to everything that exists in the universe, without exception.

Determinism does not require any belief in a god or metaphysical entity who controls human actions. It is a materialist concept, which means that all events can be explained in their entirety by the laws of nature as described by Newtonian physics, and that nothing exists beyond physical matter. It differs from predestination because predestination claims that human destiny is laid out by a divine being and cannot be changed. Determinism, on the other hand, does not require an omniscient being. It argues that current events are dependent upon preceding causes, and future events can be predicted by looking at current events. If current events were different, the future would be different. This means, in theory, that it is possible to predict the future if we have enough knowledge of current events.

The implications of Determinism will be explored in depth later but it is worth noting now that if Determinism is true, human action is outside of human control and, consequently, it seems that we cannot be held morally responsible for our actions. This implies that to judge, punish, or reward a person for their behaviour is pointless, since they could not have acted differently.

There are two broad approaches to Determinism which were described by William James, writing in the late-nineteenth century: Hard Determinism and Soft Determinism. Hard Determinism can be further subdivided into philosophical, scientific, and psychological Determinism.

Hard Determinism

Hard Determinism is the belief that all actions are caused and, therefore, determined, meaning that there is no such thing as 'free' choice. It is an **incompatibilist** approach: there are no exceptions to causation and, as such, causation and free will are incompatible. Both cannot be believed at the same time; either we are free or we are not.

> ### Key terms
>
> **Determinism:** the philosophical idea that all events are necessarily the effect of antecedent causes
>
> **antecedent causes:** causes that happened before an event that occurs later
>
> **universal causation:** the laws of cause and effect occur to everything that exists in the universe, without exception
>
> **Hard Determinism:** the proposition that all actions are caused and therefore determined, meaning that there is no such thing as a 'free' choice
>
> **incompatibilist:** the view that free will and Determinism cannot co-exist

William James, while not a determinist philosopher himself, described the universe – as viewed by hard determinists – as an iron block. There are no possibilities for events other than the ones that occur. Such apparent possibilities are illusory and were never possibilities at all.

> *It professes that those parts of the universe already laid down absolutely appoint and decree what other parts shall be. The future has no ambiguous possibilities hidden in its womb.*
>
> William James, *The Will to Believe and Other Essays in Popular Philosophy*

Philosophical Determinism

The philosopher John Locke wrote about freedom and Determinism in *An Essay Concerning Human Understanding*. Locke lived before James was born, and so would not have made use of the terms 'Hard Determinism' and 'Soft Determinism', and some of his writings lean towards Soft Determinism. However, his ideas are useful to a discussion of **Philosophical Determinism**.

Locke, writing in 1689, pointed out that 'will' and 'freedom' are both powers. So, to ask whether our will is free is a nonsensical question, like asking whether one power has the power of another power.

> *And it is as insignificant to ask whether a man's will be free, as to ask, whether his sleep be swift or his virtue square.*
>
> John Locke, *An Essay Concerning Human Understanding*

Locke argued that 'freedom' and 'will' are two different powers. Freedom is the power to be able to do, or not to do, something. Will is the power to wish or desire that something is the case. We can ask if a person is free, but we cannot ask if our will is free.

Locke made the point that if we are going to apply the term 'free' to a person, then we need to be clear about what it is we mean. Locke gave the example of a tennis ball that is hit around by a racket or lying still at rest. We do not consider the ball a free agent because it does not have the power of thought and so cannot have any preference for whether it moves or not. However, it is not simply the power of thought that makes an entity free. Locke gave a second example of a man who falls from a broken bridge. This man cannot be considered free either because, while he does have the power of thought and can prefer not to be falling, he does not have the power to act on his thoughts and change his situation. Locke went further still and gave a third example of a man who hits himself or his friend in an uncontrollable movement of his arm, such as a tic or convulsion. In this case, the man has the power of thought and he can prefer not to move his arm and, usually, he can even act on this preference. But, in this particular instance, the specific movement is against his preference and not within his power to control, so we would not consider his action free.

Key term

Philosophical Determinism: the 'hard determinist' philosophical position which argues that all events are necessarily the effect of prior events and conditions subject to the laws of nature

Locke's fourth analogy is more complex:

> *Again, suppose a man be carried, while fast asleep, into a room, where there is a person he longs to see and speak with; and be there locked fast in, beyond his power to get out; he awakes, and is glad to find himself in so desirable company, which he stays willingly in, i.e., prefers his stay to going away.*
>
> John Locke, *An Essay Concerning Human Understanding*

The man has the power of thought, has a preference, and decides based on that preference. Yet we still struggle to call him free. This is because the man can only be considered free if he has the power to do what he chooses. The man seems to be free because he prefers to stay. However, his freedom is an illusion that would quickly disappear if he got up and tried the door. Freedom, then, requires the ability to think, prefer, and then do the very thing that you prefer.

> *Liberty is not an idea belonging to volition, or preferring, but to the person having the power of doing, or forbearing to do, according as the mind shall choose or direct. Our idea of liberty reaches as far as that power, and no farther. For wherever restraint come to check that power, or compulsion takes away that indifference of ability on either side, to act, or to forbear acting, there liberty and our notion of it presently ceases.*
>
> John Locke, *An Essay Concerning Human Understanding*

The hard determinist can, however, look at Locke's example and point out that the locked door is not the only thing that checks the man's power to act. The man cannot will himself to leave because the presence of his close friend is a factor that determines his preference. While the man believes that he has made the choice to stay, in fact he could not have chosen differently even if the door had remained unlocked, because he wants to spend time with his friend. This leads us to another question raised by Locke: Am I free to will what I will?

John Locke's example of the sleeping man can be used by hard determinists to show that free will is an illusion.

According to Locke, when a person acts, their action comes from their will which, in turn, comes from their preference. No one has the power not to will; it is necessary that we will something. For example, if a man is walking and is told to stop, he must either will that he stops or will that he keeps going. He must prefer one of the two options, and the option he prefers will be the one that causes him the greatest pleasure and the least pain.

So, if a person must necessarily will something, are they free to choose what they will? Locke thought this a very strange question. To ask if a person wills what they will creates an infinite chain of wills, each one determining the next. In Locke's view, such a question was too ridiculous to answer. However, he indicated later that the will to act is caused by a desire for pleasure or, more powerfully, a desire to remove misery. When a person decides to act, they are caused to do so by their strongest desire to remove any feeling of unease; for example, a feeling of hunger causes the desire to eat and so a person eats.

Locke is considered to present a position more consistent with Soft Determinism when he says later that humans can weigh up or examine their desires. So, while people are determined by their judgement of what causes the greatest relief from unease, they have the power, or freedom, to suspend their judgement until they have weighed up the most desirable action.

AO1 activity 3

Read the following scenario.

Stella is the designated driver on a night out with her friends and her mother says she must have the family car back by midnight. Stella picks up her three friends. They go to a busy pub and get separated. At 11:30pm, Stella starts trying to find her friends so that she can drive them home. One friend is very drunk and is in the bathroom. Another is chatting to a close friend and it is difficult to persuade her to leave. Stella texts her mother to tell her she will be late because she cannot leave her friends. Stella's mum is angry and forbids her from taking the car for a night out in the future. Was Stella free to obey her mother's rule? List all the possible causes you can find that prevented Stella from acting freely.

Scientific Determinism

Scientific Determinism is based upon the observation of cause and effect in the universe. Newton's first law of motion states that everything in motion or at rest remains in motion or at rest unless an external force acts upon it. Therefore, if an object is stationary, it will remain stationary unless a force (such as someone kicking it or throwing it) causes it to move. If an object is in motion, it will remain in motion unless a force (such as friction or air resistance) acts upon it. Therefore, when a physical event occurs, it is the result of an external cause or force. If this is true of all physical events, then it must also be true of human actions because they too are physical events. The implication is that causes and effects stretch back through time, in a chain, from this moment to the first moment of the Big Bang. Equally, it means that, given the physical state of things in the present moment, there is only one possible future that could exist as a direct result of current causes.

The scientific method is an empirical approach, in which knowledge is gained by following a series of methodical steps to propose and test a hypothesis. Science must always be prepared to analyse new data and re-evaluate previous hypotheses. Scientific investigations into the make-up of the organisms that exist on Earth have led some to suggest that human behaviour is determined by factors that are inherited from parents, and our actions may, therefore, be outside our control.

Biological Determinism – also known as Biologism, Biodeterminism, and Genetic Determinism – is the claim that a person's characteristics are inherited from their biological parents and are, therefore, fixed at the moment of conception; they are governed by our **genetic inheritance**. This means that not only are our physical characteristics – such as height, sex, and skin tone – dictated by our **genes**, but so too are our behavioural characteristics, such as sexuality and criminality. This implies that there are no other factors that significantly govern a person's behaviour, and there is nothing to be done to change their behaviour if they inherit a gene that predisposes them to, for example, addiction or violence.

Key terms

Scientific Determinism: a form of Hard Determinism based on the theory of causation; for every physical event there is a physical cause, and this causal chain can be traced back to the Big Bang

genetic inheritance: characteristics are passed from parents to their offspring through DNA

genes: units of DNA that control the development or function of characteristics in an organism

A range of scientific discoveries support the position of biological determinists.

- In the nineteenth century, the theory of evolution by means of natural selection was developed by Charles Darwin and Alfred Russel Wallace. They proposed that species have gradually developed over a long period of time, with characteristics passed from generation to generation to enable the survival of the fittest.
- Gregor Mendel, a nineteenth-century Austrian botanist and monk, is considered the father of modern genetics. By experimenting on pea plants, he developed the principles of heredity, identifying dominant and recessive genes and explaining how parents pass characteristics on to their offspring.
- In the twentieth century, Oswald Avery and his team proved that DNA (Deoxyribonucleic Acid) is the chemical responsible for inheritance because it contains all the information required to make genes.
- The Human Genome Project, which ran between 1990 and 2003, was an international research project that sequenced and mapped all the genes in the human body.

The implications of these developments have been significant. For some, it has led to the belief that genetic traits are unchangeable. There is a rigid causation in operation, and it does not matter what we do, an individual cannot change their genes. This means that if a set of parents have genes with dominant traits that make them criminals, then their child will be a criminal too, no matter what social and environmental measures are put in place.

In the early 1900s, Francis Galton coined the term 'eugenics' to describe the use of selective breeding to improve the inherent qualities of a race. He advocated the strict regulation of marriage and family size to remove 'undesirable' physical characteristics and behavioural traits from the human population.

> *It has, indeed, strong claims to become an orthodox religious tenet of the future, for eugenics cooperate with the workings of nature by securing that humanity shall be represented by the fittest races. What nature does blindly, slowly, and ruthlessly, man may do providently, quickly, and kindly.*
>
> Francis Galton, 'Eugenics: Its Definition, Scope and Aims'

This led to the introduction of compulsory sterilisation laws in the US and Germany in the early-twentieth century. People with mental and physical disabilities, as well as prisoners, were forcibly sterilised in an attempt to remove their 'defective genes' from the gene pool. During the Second World War, the Nazi regime took this a step further and killed people with mental health difficulties and disabilities. Eugenics was also used in the past to classify women, non-white people, people with disabilities, and LGBTQ+ people as inferior or defective. Today, greater knowledge of the human genome has led some to suggest we could look for 'kill' switches, to enable us to turn off problem genes in a bid to prevent obesity, cancer, addiction, or other 'undesirable' behaviours.

It is difficult, in the twenty-first century, to hold on to a strong form of Biological Determinism and argue that genes are the only factor that dictate a person's destiny, and that inheriting a specific collection of genes makes certain physical characteristics and behavioural traits inevitable. This is because research has demonstrated that both genetic and environmental factors have a role to play in a person's decisions and behaviour. Upbringing, wealth, diet, and so on all influence how a person's genes present and how the individual responds to the circumstances they find themselves in.

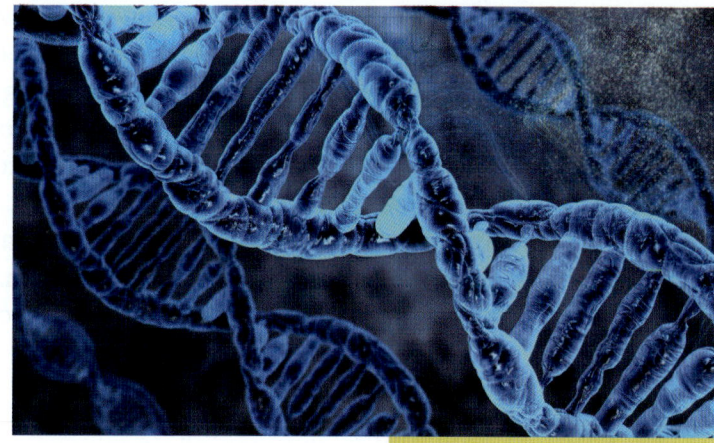

If Biological Determinism is correct, our genes determine our moral behaviour, and so we are not free.

For example, Cystic Fibrosis is a genetic disease, but whether a person with the gene has mild or severe symptoms is, in part, influenced by environmental factors, such as wealth, nutrition, and stress.

Studies have shown the complex relationship between genetics and environment that impacts upon human behaviour. In Finland in 2014, a study of 900 offenders revealed two genes associated with violent crime. Those with the genes MAOA or CDH13 were found to be thirteen times more likely to have a history of violent crimes. Yet the lead author of the study, Jari Tiihonen, warned against the idea of screening the population for these genes. He argued that criminal behaviour is complex and shaped not only by genes, but also by environmental factors. This is supported by the Dunedin Study, which took place in 2002 in New Zealand. It found that people with the MAOA gene who had been abused as children were more likely to be antisocial and aggressive adults than people with the gene whose childhood had been more stable.

There is, therefore, a complex relationship between genetics (our human nature) and the environment (our nurture or upbringing). Nevertheless, human actions are still determined. The cause that operates on a person may be genes alone, or it may be a mixture of genes and the environment; either way, a person does not have free will because their will is dictated by a combination of external factors that includes their genetic make-up.

Psychological Determinism

Whereas Biological Determinism looks to internal physiological factors – genes – as the cause of human behaviour, **Psychological Determinism** looks to external factors – how we are nurtured. Parents, teachers, the media, and cultural norms all play a part in conditioning, or nurturing, a person to behave in a certain way. Psychological Determinism states that moral actions are motivated by drives for things like happiness or self-interest, which are outside the control of the individual agent and conditioned into them through repeated experience. Therefore, psychological determinists argue that a person cannot be considered to have free will.

AO1 activity 4

Identify the three most important points about Biological Determinism that you think will be useful to you when writing a response to an exam question. Write these three points as headings on a flashcard. Then read the section again and add additional details, examples, and key vocabulary under each heading.

Key term

Psychological Determinism: a form of Hard Determinism based on the study of human behaviour; all actions, thoughts, and feelings are the inevitable outcome of complex psychological processes

Ivan Pavlov was a Russian, Nobel prize winning physiologist who is best known for his research on classical conditioning. Pavlov and his team worked with dogs in experiments regarding digestion. During these experiments, the dogs were often fed so that their saliva production could be measured. Salivation is an involuntary reflex that occurs to aid the digestion of food. Pavlov noticed the dogs salivating not just at the sight or smell of food, but in anticipation of it, often in response to environmental cues like the movements of the person who usually fed them. This led him to move his study to focus on this aspect of the dogs' behaviour.

The trigger that causes an automatic response like salivation (in this case the food presented to the dogs) is known as an unconditioned stimulus, and the dogs' automatic response (in this case salivation) is an unconditioned response. Pavlov introduced a neutral stimulus (in this case the sound of a metronome) to the dogs. Initially, the dogs did not respond because they did not connect the metronome with food. However, introducing the sound of the metronome to the dogs as a conditioning stimulus moments before the food was given meant that after a few times, the metronome (now the conditioned stimulus) could be played on its own and it would cause salivation (now a conditioned response). The behaviour became learned or conditioned.

The ability of all creatures, including human beings, to learn what is dangerous or advantageous through conditioning is a vital part of survival, and Pavlov's research demonstrated that hard, set laws can explain and predict animal behaviour. These results imply that actions are the result of a long chain of conditioned reflexes, and therefore cannot be described as free. Once associations have been acquired and established, responses are automatically produced.

Pavlov's approach was developed by others who are known as behaviourists. For example, B.F. Skinner used an approach called operant conditioning on rats and pigeons to show that free will is an illusion. Animals placed in his 'Skinner Box' received reinforcers or punishment for engaging in behaviours such as pressing levers or pecking a key. They would receive a positive reinforcer or reward, such as a food pellet, for desirable behaviour. Negative reinforcers removed an unpleasant stimulus, such as an electric current running through the box, in response to desirable actions. These reinforcers strengthened desirable behaviour by making it more likely that it would be repeated. Punishers weakened undesirable behaviour by providing an unpleasant experience such as a shock. According to Skinner, all behaviour can be explained as a result of operant conditioning, and therefore a person who commits a crime has no real choice. They are propelled in this direction by environmental circumstance and personal history that has conditioned them to act in the way that they do.

Synoptic link

Link to *Chapter 1: Ethical thought (part one)*. Take a look back at the section on Psychological Egoism. This determinist theory suggests that human moral action is always driven by a person's self-interest.

Pavlov is best remembered for his work with dogs to demonstrate his classical conditioning method.

AO1 activity 5

Watch an episode of *Supernanny*, *It's Me or the Dog*, or *Dog's Behaving Badly*. In all of these programmes a process of conditioning (often similar to operant conditioning) takes place to alter the behaviour of the children or pets in the family. See if you can identify the conditioned stimuli and the conditioned responses in the episode you have chosen.

Soft Determinism

Soft Determinism is the belief that actions are caused but they also have an element of free will. It is a **compatibilist** approach because causation and free will are compatible; both can be accepted at the same time without contradiction.

Soft determinists argue that all events are caused by antecedent causes, but that human beings can still be considered free, and therefore morally responsible, if we define free will in the correct way. Incompatibilists argue that there is a contrast between caused actions and free action. If an action is caused, then it cannot be considered free. Classical compatibilism argues for the liberty of spontaneity: that freedom is simply the ability to act according to one's own desires, unhindered by external obstacles, and there is no contrast between caused and free acts.

The incompatibilist approach of hard determinists says that all actions are the effects of antecedent causes. They say that for a moral agent to be considered free, they would have to be able to act independently of all causes, but, since this is impossible, no moral agent is free. However, Thomas Hobbes, writing in the seventeenth century, thought that this was nonsense.

Thomas Hobbes

The seventeenth-century philosopher Hobbes agreed that every action performed by a moral agent is necessarily caused and, therefore, determined. An uncaused action does not exist and there is no need to invoke additional explanations for an action beyond the causes that preceded it; the cause of an action is both necessary and sufficient to explain it. Hobbes gives the example of a dice being thrown: the way that the dice lands is determined by the position of the hand, the surface of the table, the force of the throw, and so on.

For Hobbes, 'freedom' does not mean uncaused, it means that human action is not coerced, and it is this that makes Hobbes a soft determinist. The word 'free' is applied to the person rather than the will, the desire, or the inclination. A person who is locked in a cell has limited freedom; they are prevented from leaving, even if they wish to, by an external cause. Freedom is, then, the absence of something that prevents a person from acting in accordance with their own desires. A free person is someone who is not hindered or prevented by any external obstacle from doing what they wish to do.

Hobbes described two kinds of freedom. Firstly, there is unhindered movement of any physical body. This is the absence of an external cause or constraint that prevents a being from performing an action. For example, water runs freely down a hill, within the necessary limits of a channel, provided there is no dam to prevent it, and I can breathe freely provided there is nothing smothering my face. These kinds of freedom do not require any kind of mental process or what Hobbes calls 'imagination'.

Key terms

Soft Determinism: the proposition that all actions have elements of free will within causally-determined boundaries

compatibilist: the view that free will and Determinism are not contradictory but, rather, are entirely compatible

Secondly, there is voluntary motion that is dependent upon mental processes. This is the performance of actions that come from within the moral agent that can therefore be called voluntary. These causes are dependent upon mental processes, and are in accordance with a person's will or desire. Voluntary actions are not necessarily rational actions, as sometimes people do act in irrational ways, but they are the result of deliberation, and reflect a person's preferences or aversions. We might refer to these as internal causes, as they come from within the moral agent. For example, I am free to walk to the fridge, even though that action is caused by my strong desire to eat, if I am not prevented from doing so by any external constraint.

By distinguishing between these two types of causes, it is possible to agree with hard determinists that a moral agent is caused, but to challenge them by arguing that causation is compatible with freedom.

Hobbes gives the following example of a free action:

> When a man throws his goods into the sea for fear the ship should sink, he does it nevertheless very willingly, and may refuse to do it if he will: It is therefore the action of one that was free.
>
> Thomas Hobbes, *Leviathan*

When the man throws his belongings into the sea he acts freely because the act is consistent with his **internal cause**, with his immediate desire to save the ship from sinking. However, a man who throws his belongings into the sea when the lurch of the ship causes him to drop what he is carrying does not act freely. The **external cause** or coercion means that he acts independently of his own will or desire.

However, a person's will is still brought about by antecedent causes such as preferences, aversions, and their capabilities. These causes are necessary – they are required for the will to exist – and they are sufficient, therefore nothing else is needed. Therefore, what a person wills is also necessary. Ultimately, Hobbes believed that God is the uncaused causer of all things, so he argued that the chain of causation that accounted for the will leads back to God.

> Liberty, and Necessity are Consistent; as in the water, that hath not only liberty, but a necessity of descending by the Channel; so likewise in the Actions which men voluntarily doe: which because they proceed from their will, proceed from liberty; and yet, because every act of mans will, and every desire, and inclination proceedeth from some cause, and that from another cause, in a continuall chaine, (whose first link is in the hand of God the first of all causes,) proceed from necessity.
>
> Thomas Hobbes, *Leviathan*

A.J. Ayer

Writing in 1954, A.J. Ayer agreed with other determinists that human beings are subject to cause and effect. He argued that, in fact, Determinism is the only way in which human beings can be held morally responsible for their actions.

Key terms

internal cause: a cause that exists within or originates from the mind of the moral agent, e.g. a desire for food

external cause: a cause that exists outside the control of a moral agent, e.g. being locked in a room

Synoptic link

Link to *A Level Religious Studies for Eduqas: Philosophy of Religion*, Chapter 1: Arguments for the existence of God: inductive. Look back at the cosmological argument to remind yourself of Aquinas' Second Way: the Uncaused Causer.

> *Either it is an accident that I choose to act as I do, or it is not. If it is an accident, then it is merely a matter of chance that I did not choose otherwise; and if it is merely a matter of chance that I did not choose otherwise, it is surely irrational to hold me morally responsible for choosing as I did. But if it is not an accident that I choose to do one thing rather than another, then presumably there is some causal explanation of my choice: and in that case we are led back to Determinism.*
>
> A.J. Ayer, *Philosophical Essays*

To hold someone morally responsible for their actions requires us to reconcile freedom and Determinism. Moral agents cannot be responsible if their actions are simply uncaused accidents of chance. For us to be held to account for them, they must be caused by our own, free actions.

Ayer said that some compatibilists try to reconcile freedom and Determinism by defining freedom as the 'consciousness of necessity'. In other words, they define freedom as an awareness of the causes that operate upon them. But Ayer rejected this; he said that it is not what we normally mean by freedom, and it does not get to the root of the problem. Knowing the causes of an action does not give a person control over it.

Instead, Ayer argues that an action is free if it is not constrained. A free action is necessarily caused, or determined, because it is possible to explain a free action with reference to the prior events that brought it about. However, this is different from a constrained action that is not free but is forced or compelled. A constrained action is one in which the moral agent had no other option available to them because of the circumstances in which they found themselves. This contrasts with Hard Determinism, which argues that a caused action is the opposite of a free action, so if our actions are caused, they cannot be free.

> *And if the circumstances are such that no reasonable person would be expected to choose the other alternative, then the action that I am made to do is not one for which I am held to be morally responsible.*
>
> A.J. Ayer, *Philosophical Essays*

Ayer gave an example of a kleptomaniac (someone who suffers from a mental illness that causes an uncontrollable desire to steal) and a thief. A thief can go through a decision-making process before they steal. As a result of this process, they can resolve to steal or not, and should be capable of acting in accordance with their decision. However, the kleptomaniac can resolve whatever they like, but will steal anyway. The kleptomaniac is constrained by their illness, and we may be reluctant to hold them morally responsible because they could not control their actions.

> *A kleptomaniac is not a free agent, in respect of his stealing, because he does not go through any process of deciding whether or not to steal. Or rather, if he does go through such a process, it is irrelevant to his behaviour. Whatever he resolved to do, he would steal all the same. And it is this that distinguishes him from the ordinary thief.*
>
> A.J. Ayer, *Philosophical Essays*

Ayer acknowledged that the feelings and processes that led to the thief's decision to steal were as equally caused as the kleptomaniac's actions.

Why, then, do we say that the thief is free, when their actions are just as much mapped out by causes as the kleptomaniac's actions? Ayer required three conditions to be present for a caused act to be considered free:

1. A different choice must be possible.
2. The action must be voluntarily chosen.
3. No other being forced or compelled the agent to choose that action.

If these conditions are met, then the moral agent has acted freely, not because their action was the result of chance, but because the moral agent was not constrained or forced to behave in the way that they behaved.

Ayer still considered that there were questions to be addressed, however. While an individual who voluntarily gets up and walks across a room may not feel constrained in the same way that they might if someone pointed a gun to their head, this does not mean that causation does not operate just as powerfully when it is invisible. And if the thief was caused to act, then why consider them free? Ayer's answer was that causal laws explain human actions but do not compel them, except in a metaphorical sense. Determinism is described in such a way that it tends to imply that one event is in the power of another. Ayer argued that this is not literally the case and, in fact, they are just correlated; there is a relationship between them. When one event occurs, another also occurs in relation to the first, but this metaphor leads to the mistaken idea that freedom and cause must be in conflict.

> *We tend to form an imaginative picture of an unhappy effect trying vainly to escape from the clutches of an overmastering cause.* **"**
>
> A.J. Ayer, *Philosophical Essays*

All that is required for something to be a cause is that, in the specific circumstances, the effect could have only occurred if the event we are calling 'the cause' was present. If Determinism is correct, then the future is predictable by looking back at past causes. However, no one else, no god or higher mind, has decided this for us. All that is meant is that it is theoretically possible to deduce what will happen by looking at a set of facts about the past. It does not mean that a person's actions are pointless or that we are constrained by the past.

The implications of Determinism and predestination

The implications of Hard and Soft Determinism on moral responsibility

The term 'moral responsibility' implies that a person's behaviour is within their control and that, at the time they acted, they possessed that control. However, Hard Determinism states that a person's actions are caused by external events that they do not have control over. The work of Pavlov and behaviourists such as Skinner suggest that events experienced by a moral

AO1 activity 6
Try using a memory palace – Sherlock Holmes' method of memorising information – to memorise the soft determinist approaches. This is a system that helps you memorise information by placing the ideas you want to remember in familiar locations. Select a place that you are so familiar with that you can navigate around it with your eyes shut, like your home. Walk around your chosen place in a logical manner, identifying interesting or significant items, then match the ideas you want to memorise to the items you have identified. For example, if one of your items is a candle and Ayer's thief example is the thing you wish to remember, you could imagine a thief sneaking into your home and stealing your candle. To remember the facts in the future, imagine yourself back in your home and go through the special objects you selected.

agent in their past dictate the choices they make in the present. People are conditioned to act in a certain way in response to specific stimuli and cannot, therefore, be said to be in control of their actions. Similarly, science demonstrates that a moral agent's DNA, inherited from their parents, dictates their physical characteristics and character traits. A person's genetic inheritance, therefore, dictates how they will behave in any given situation.

Yet, control does not tell the whole story. It is generally accepted that there are some individuals who cannot be held morally responsible for their actions even though they appear to choose them. For instance, animals, very young children, and people with dementia are not considered morally responsible for their actions, even though they appear to be in control and choose how to act, because they do not understand what they are doing. In contrast, a healthy adult is able to deliberate rationally before they do something, and it is this ability that suggests they should be morally responsible. Yet, if Hard Determinism is correct, then the process of weighing up what to do before making a decision is subject to cause as well. A person may feel as though they are deliberating, and that they could choose from a range of possible options, but this sense of freedom is illusory and the choice they make has already been determined by antecedent events. Consequently, the ability to reason does not make a person morally responsible either.

Moral responsibility requires that a moral agent could have done otherwise. If Hard Determinism is true, then the occurrence of an event is made inevitable by causes that occur in the past. Therefore, if a moral agent's action are not within their own control, because they are unavoidable, it makes no sense to hold them responsible. Since a person cannot choose whether or not they exist and cannot dictate the content of the laws of nature, the consequences of antecedent causes are not a moral agent's responsibility. The man in Locke's room was not responsible for remaining there because he could do nothing else; his remaining in the room was beyond his control. Locke considered that thoughts could also be determined. He gives an example of a man being tortured on the rack, who cannot think of anything other than pain. The power to will is directed by our desire to seek pleasure and avoid pain. If this is the case, some would argue that we can never choose other than we do, and therefore we cannot be held responsible.

However, soft determinists argue that free will and Determinism are compatible and, consequently, people can be held morally responsible for their actions. If we are free to act as we choose, then we are responsible for our actions. As Ayer pointed out, freedom is the opposite of compulsion, not Determinism. If a person's action is uncaused or random, then it is ridiculous to hold that person responsible for an action. Moral responsibility only makes sense if actions are caused. Therefore, provided a moral agent's actions are not forced, the actions are within their control, and it makes sense to hold them morally responsible for their actions. Similarly, Hobbes regarded an agent morally responsible provided the cause of their action is internal and in accordance with their will.

The worth of human ideas of rightness, wrongness, and moral value

Moral responsibility implies that a person has a duty or an obligation to act in one way rather than another way; for example, a teacher has a moral responsibility, a duty, to educate their students. This duty then implies that there are certain behaviours, attitudes, or actions that are good, valuable, or right, and others that are bad or wrong; for example, a teacher who fails to educate their students is not doing their duty, and is failing to do what is right or is actively doing something wrong. Immanuel Kant argued that our sense of duty, the idea that we ought to act one way rather than another, implies that we can do so. Therefore, Determinism suggests that ideas of right and wrong are inherently meaningless because it makes no sense to say that a person acts wrongly or should act differently if they had no other choice.

However, Determinism could find human ideas of right and wrong extremely useful. For psychological determinists, human moral values are important training tools that are used to condition and then predict human behaviour. These are used all the time by educators and parents who wish to encourage desirable behaviour in children. Religious institutions add power to their concepts of right and wrong by encouraging members to consider moral laws to be equivalent to God's objective will. Giving human behaviour moral status is valuable because society can use that status to mould individual behaviour to produce the most beneficial actions.

Ayer argued that moral terms such as 'good' or 'bad' have no objective value, but are used as a persuasive tool to encourage others to conform to subjective standards of behaviour. This does not necessarily make human ideas of morality worthless; it simply means that these human ideas of right and wrong cannot be scientifically measured and proved to be correct. Carl Rogers pointed out that science cannot comment upon the worth of human ideas of morality. It can investigate and describe many aspects of human moral beliefs, but it cannot comment upon their worth without being given subjective, unscientific, standards by which to measure them.

Locke thought that moral ideas of right and wrong are valuable because he believed that they are God's laws. Pleasure and pain help to motivate people to perform moral actions that are in accordance with those laws of God, and although people do sometimes make poor judgements, a person can temporarily put off the moment of feeling a desire to act while they weigh up which action would be in accordance with God's laws. However, other philosophers take a more clearly hard determinist position and argue that in the example of the sleeping man, it makes no difference if we tell the man that he should get up and leave. If the door is locked, it does not matter what laws are in place, or what pleasure or pain he feels, and it does not matter what act of weighing up takes place, he will still be forced to remain in the room.

Hobbes, as a compatibilist, argued that a person who acts voluntarily does so freely, even though they cannot choose their own will. Liberty is the absence of anything that constrains a person's ability to act in accordance with their own desires. Some might argue that the existence of moral laws can act as a constraining factor and remove our free will. However, others might say that while voluntary actions are always caused, there is nothing that prevents someone from choosing to disobey a law. The sense that we should obey a law can act upon a person in such a way that they voluntarily obey it, but it does not constrain them from acting against the law.

The value in blaming moral agents for immoral acts

A person can respond with blame or praise when someone does something. Yet responding with blame or praise only make sense if someone is morally responsible for their behaviour. Blame implies that a person deserves some kind of punishment as a result of something they have chosen to do. A hard determinist might argue that it is practical to punish someone for breaking a criminal law because such punishment can act to deter future law-breaking or in some way can protect society from crime, but this would not mean that the individual has any personal responsibility. However, if someone acts to break a moral law, without any ability to behave differently, it is difficult to see how blame in any way prevents immorality or makes the world a better place.

Psychological Determinism suggests that praise and blame are valuable tools that can be used to train, nurture, or condition a person to behave in a certain way. Praise operates as a positive reinforcer to encourage desirable behaviour. Blame operates as a punisher to discourage undesirable behaviour. This is useful to deter behaviour that we deem 'wrong' or 'bad' rather than to provide justice in response to immoral actions. However, if Biological Determinism is correct and DNA is the main determiner of moral behaviour, it is difficult to see any value in blaming someone for their immoral actions. There is nothing that an individual can do to change their DNA, and so their actions are not their fault, and blame will not change this fact.

Is there any value in blaming someone for their immoral behaviour?

Although Ayer did not comment on the value of blaming moral agents for their actions, his approach to Soft Determinism can be applied to the issue. According to Ayer, moral actions can be called free when the moral agent has not been compelled to perform them. We can observe that a fear of blame is potentially, but not necessarily, a compelling factor that forces a person to act against their own will. If that fear is strong enough to compel, then the resulting act cannot be called free. However, just because fear of blame could compel some people to act against their own will, this is not a reason for us to avoid blaming people for their actions. Ayer's explanation of Soft Determinism was descriptive rather than normative. He was explaining compatibilism, not pronouncing what we should or should not do. Therefore, it is up to us whether we conclude that blaming people for their actions is valuable, but it is only logically possible to blame a person who is not compelled to act through a fear of that blame.

However, for Hobbes, all actions are caused, and fear is just one among many internal causes. A person acts freely when they are afraid of blame because they willingly act according to their desires. Blame can be used by society as a tool to discourage immorality and protect the population from harmful behaviour.

Synoptic link

Link to Chapter 2: Ethical thought (part two). Remind yourself of A.J. Ayer's Emotivism and his understanding of the meaning of ethical language.

Locke appears to believe that there is a right way to behave. He argues that, while a person will necessarily do what they will and that the will is formed from a desire for pleasure or pain, everyone has the power to put off acting on their desire until they have weighed up what the good moral action is. True happiness is found in actions that are intrinsically good, but we are often caused to act by a desire for immediate happiness. Therefore, blame can be applied to those who are impatient and act impulsively, making bad choices, rather than taking the time to reason correctly.

The usefulness of normative ethics

Normative ethics is useful in setting out the details of a person's obligations and how they should be achieved. Science can help to describe some aspects of moral action or can investigate the causes of a moral action, but it is not equipped to make the kinds of value judgements that normative ethics makes. Normative ethics can also be useful as a tool for conditioning human behaviour. Therefore, for the behaviourist, normative ethics can help to train people to behave in the way that any particular ethical system considers desirable. There is no reason from a psychological standpoint to argue that one ethical system is better than another.

Ayer argued that normative claims or judgements do not describe facts about the world. They cannot be verified, and they cannot be said to be true or false. They are emotive utterances that attempt to influence others by calling their attention to certain features of a situation. Ayer acknowledges that when a person makes a moral judgement of this kind, they often have reasons for doing so. The reason might be that their action will bring the greatest happiness for the greatest number (Utilitarianism) or that the rule they have established can be derived from observation of the natural world (Naturalism). Reasons are given to try to cause others to agree and change their own behaviour accordingly, but they have no basis in fact. Ayer has often been accused of encouraging loose moral behaviour by saying that we should not use normative ethics or that we should live without any kind of ethical policy. However, these are normative statements, and he carefully avoided making any statements of this kind.

Locke argued that it is difficult to accurately judge what is good. He said that a healthy mind and a healthy body are required for good ethical judgement, and that education from an early age is vital if people are to learn how to discern what is good. This suggests that normative ethics could be useful to guide a person's moral reasoning processes and could potentially assist those who did not benefit from the necessary early education. It is important for Locke that in our human weakness we are persuaded to understand that even though virtue and religion do not bring happiness straight away, the happiness they do bring will ultimately be greater than any immediate thing. Normative ethics can help a person to understand, and eventually desire, a real good.

Hobbes' writing about morality is mixed with his political writings. Hobbes argued that since human nature tends towards selfishness and is governed by a fear of death, people are often rather ineffective in choosing the right way to behave. Hobbes therefore argued that society is best governed by an absolute ruler whose power supersedes religious rules, and that obedience to the absolute ruler is essential even if people believe that a command from that ruler is morally wrong. Unquestioning obedience to a normative system of ethics would not only establish a peaceful and cooperative society, but it would also ensure life after death, because any wrong actions are the fault of the absolute ruler, not the individual who performed them.

The implications of predestination on religious belief

The teachings of Augustine and Calvin on predestination are intrinsically linked with, and arise from, their beliefs about the nature of God and God's relationship with humanity. Predestination was not a central teaching for either of these scholars, but was the necessary result of other Christian doctrines. This means that it is not possible to deny predestination without making fundamental changes to essential Christian doctrine, which Christians would find unacceptable.

The link between God and evil: Is God responsible for evil?

If God predestines humanity for salvation or reprobation, there are implications for the relationship between God and evil. Opponents of Augustine and Calvin argued that if God predestines all human actions, then God allows, creates, or even performs evil. If this is the case, as Pelagius argued, then sin is not sin at all; sin is completing tasks that are ordained by God. Sin is only sin when someone deliberately turns against God of their own free will, not when they perform an action that they are coerced into doing. Therefore, for Pelagius, the only sinner is God, because God has predestined human actions and humans are, as a result, not free to turn against God of their own free will.

However, this is an unacceptable position for Christians, who believe God is all-loving. Both Augustine and Calvin must, therefore, be able to explain how God has power over all creation and predestines everyone's futures without being responsible for their evil acts. Some of Augustine's texts appear to show that God only chooses the Elect and leaves behind the Reprobates. If this is correct, God does not cause evil and sin, but leaves some people to their own evil and sin. However, critics may argue that God therefore performs evil by omission. God fails to save some from suffering when it is within God's power to do so.

The Christian doctrine of the fall teaches that human beings are responsible for the introduction of evil into the world. Both Augustine and Calvin's teaching is in line with this doctrine. Sin cannot be attributed to God in any way because God created humanity with a perfect and free nature. It was Adam's choice to disobey God that corrupted human nature and brought with it the requirement for punishment. This doctrine requires a belief in the free will of Adam. While Augustine and Calvin teach predestination, Adam must have been given free will initially so that God cannot be blamed for human sin.

AO1 activity 7

Each day, take one header from the list below concerning the implications of Determinism on moral responsibility. Set a timer for 5 minutes and write a list of as many things as you can that relate to this heading. Once the 5 minutes are up, check your list against your notes or this book. How many things did you get right? How many ideas did you miss? Make a separate list of the missing points. These are the ones you should focus on in your revision.

- The worth of human ideas of rightness, wrongness and moral value.
- The value of blaming moral agents for immoral acts.
- The usefulness of normative ethics.

Synoptic link

Link to *A Level Religious Studies for Eduqas: Philosophy of Religion*, Chapter 3: Challenges to religious belief: the problem of evil and suffering. Look at what the problem of evil means for the character of God.

For Calvin, however, Adam's choice to disobey God was in accordance with God's will. While Augustine believed all human beings were created perfectly good before the fall, Calvin taught that some of humanity was created for damnation from the outset. The implication that concerned Calvin's opponents was that this appears to make God the author of evil. God appears to have created humanity with the express purpose of ensuring some, including Adam, would sin.

Arminius' concept of predestination attempted to resolve the problems described above by placing more emphasis upon free will. God permitted Adam to choose sinful acts, while at the same time disapproving of the choice. Sin is a terrible thing but, according to Arminius, God knows the full range of acts that could occur as a result of any given set of circumstances and knows, therefore, whether a person will do a good deed or commit a sin. God will approve of the former and disapprove of the latter, without causing either action. In this way, Arminius argued, God cannot be the author or cause of evil in the world. However, this view of predestination was condemned by the Synod of Dort because it suggests that God's grace can be resisted, and therefore suggests that humans may have power over their own destiny in a way that God does not. This is the very idea that Augustine and Calvin were trying to avoid with their doctrine of predestination, since they were concerned with emphasising God's sovereignty and power over all of human action.

It is also important to Augustine, in particular, that God is not viewed in combat with an equal and opposing power of evil. The doctrine of predestination supposes that there is one God, and God is the sole authority over all things. This means that for Augustine and Calvin, God has complete authority over evil, but evil is allowed to remain in accordance with God's divine plan. For both scholars, God has no moral obligation to remove evil, because God did not cause evil and it is a just punishment for the sins of humanity.

The implications for God's omnipotence and omnibenevolence

Both Augustine and Calvin were keen to affirm God's nature as all-powerful, all-loving, and all-knowing. Predestination fully supports the idea of God as all-powerful with supreme authority over all things. If human beings can decide their own destiny, they are placed on a par with God, and some events must, necessarily, be outside God's control. This is an unacceptable situation for both Augustine and Calvin. Sin must be the responsibility of people because God is not the author of evil; yet people must also be incapable of saving themselves because they are utterly dependent upon God. In addition, there is nothing that humanity can do to resist God's power and will. God's grace is irresistible and, having been elected, a person cannot commit apostasy because God cannot fail by allowing human sin and weakness to succeed against divine election.

The criticism of predestination is that by apparently choosing who is saved and who is damned independent of the actions of individual people, God appears to be acting arbitrarily. However, for Calvin, God does not do anything by accident. Everything that occurs is part of God's divine plan, even if humanity is too weak or sinful to understand it. This view of predestination removes the need for people to be concerned about whether they are saved or damned; what happens to them is in God's hands, so they cannot mess it up or mistakenly damage God's plan for them. God saves because God wishes to, not because God can be influenced or controlled by human beings.

Yet many argue that if God is truly omnipotent, God can do anything, and so everyone should be saved. Or they argue that if God is truly all-powerful, God could have created a world in which everyone freely chooses the good, so that there would be no need for reprobation. The implication is that either God lacks the power to do these things and is not all-powerful, or God lacks the will to do these things and is, therefore, not all-loving. However, neither Calvin nor Augustine saw any need for God to be responsible for saving everyone. No one person deserves, has earned, or is owed salvation by God; anyone that God saves is saved purely by God's mercy and love. In addition, the doctrine of predestination does not require God to do anything illogical. There is a paradox in expecting that God could act in a way that is logically unreasonable: it is as unreasonable to request that God create a square circle as it is to expect God to create a world in which people freely choose the good. For free will to exist, evil choices with real consequences – such as reprobation or punishment for disobedience – must also exist.

An omnibenevolent God is not responsible for sin, but is the sole author of salvation from sin through Christ. Augustine objected to Pelagius on the basis that Pelagius argued people can save themselves through good works, therefore appearing to render Christ's death on the cross unnecessary. For Augustine, good works do not bring about salvation. For Calvin, even faith does not bring about salvation. It is not the act of choosing faith that causes a person to be saved. Faith is no more than a sign that someone has been saved by God. While God is omnibenevolent, God has no moral responsibility to save everyone from eternal damnation.

Augustine argued that God was just in allowing a person to be left to the sin that was fair punishment for their own choices. Calvin taught that God's justice requires a person to be actively damned for their sinfulness; but, because God is all-loving, he has elected to save some through the death and resurrection of Christ. This is evidence of God's divine love for humanity; it is a free gift for the undeserving that cannot be earned. Therefore, predestination is evidence of both God's supreme power over everything and his complete goodness in saving a portion of humanity.

Pelagius argued that damning the innocent, such as unbaptised infants, is not consistent with God's omnibenevolence. He found it abhorrent that God would hold babies responsible for the sins of the first man, and saw nothing of God's nature reflected in this view of predestination. Yet, for Augustine, there cannot be a human who is innocent of sin. Since all are contaminated with the same original sin, God makes the choice to save the elect for no other reason than because it is God's will. Arminius protested that an all-loving God would never decree evil by creating people just so they could be condemned to sin. Yet, to suggest that God's decision as to who is saved and who is damned can be influenced by the desires or actions of individuals is to challenge God's authority, which is absolute.

The use of prayer

God's decision to predestine some for salvation and others for damnation is irresistible according to Augustine and Calvin. Arminius counter-argued that this makes it difficult to imagine that there is any real use for prayer or sermons if this is the case. In Christian tradition, **prayer** is for thanksgiving, petition, confession, and praise. But why petition God or confess your sins if your destiny has been predestined and nothing you can do can make any difference?

Augustine teaches that one certainly should pray to God. He argues that since God already knows the content of a prayer, and has already predestined that certain benefits will be granted to some individuals, prayer is humanity's way of demonstrating cooperation with God's plan.

> *Prayers, also, are of avail to procure those things which He foreknew that He would grant to those who offered them; and with justice have rewards been appointed for good deeds, and punishments for sins.*
>
> Augustine, *The City of God*

According to Augustine, there is no need for a person to pray for what they desire because God already knows what they want before they ask for it. Instead, people ought to pray to increase their desire for God so that they might be ready to receive what God is preparing to give them. The purpose of prayer is not so much to influence God as to increase focus and attention on the will of God and openness to God's will.

Calvin taught that humankind is destitute of all goodness and people are incapable of doing anything to gain salvation for themselves. Therefore, they must look beyond themselves for salvation in the person of Christ. Prayer is a sign that someone is a member of the Elect. It is necessary as a means of seeking God, and Calvin argued that faith without prayer can never be genuine. Prayer is a form of communication with God; it helps a person to sustain their faith in God and understand God's will. Calvin addressed the criticism that prayer seems pointless if God is all-knowing, explaining that prayer is for the sake of the person praying and not for God.

> *It is very absurd, therefore, to dissuade men from prayer, by pretending that Divine Providence, which is always watching over the government of the universes is in vain importuned by our supplications, when, on the contrary, the Lord himself declares, that he is 'nigh unto all that call upon him, to all that call upon him in truth' (Psalm 145:18).*
>
> John Calvin, *Institutes of the Christian Religion*

Key term

prayer: a devout petition to God or to an object of worship

Synoptic link

Link to *A Level Religious Studies for Eduqas: Philosophy of Religion, Chapter 5: Religious experience (part one)*. Look at the experience of prayer according to religious believers. Can prayer have any effect on God? Can it have any effect upon the believer?

The existence of miracles

Miracles are usually understood to be God's intervention in the world. If predestination is correct, then God performs miracles to achieve God's purpose for creation. The act of creation itself is a miracle, and the resurrection of Christ for the salvation of humanity from sin is also miraculous; they are both examples of divine action in the world. According to Augustine, miracles are evidence of a person's faith in the work that God accomplishes in the world. Since God has predestined humanity for election or reprobation, any miracle that is performed by God will be in accordance with God's plan, and does not affect who God has decided to elect. However, some might question why an omnipotent God needs to perform miracles if everything has been predestined according to God's plan from the moment of creation. God should not need to intervene in the workings of the world because God's plan is perfect, and God is unchanging.

It can be argued that if God performs a miracle in the world, then this interferes with human free will: God's action in the world compromises faith, as humans are no longer free to decide whether they believe in God if God is working before their eyes. However, miracles do not interfere with human free will because humans are already constrained by sin because of the fall. This is because, as Augustine taught, the fall tainted Adam with original sin which was then passed down to the rest of humanity, therefore removing their freedom and leaving them free only to sin. If God works a miracle in the world, then it cannot damage human free will any further than humanity has already damaged it. Therefore, a miracle is God's work in a fallen world, which allows humanity to have the faith that they cannot choose on their own. That faith allows them to be freed, by God, from the bondage of sin and death. According to Augustine, miracles are evidence of a person's faith in the work that God accomplishes in the world. Miracles allow the elect to receive salvation in accordance with the will of God.

Perseverance in prayer may be a sign that a person is one of God's Elect, according to Calvin.

Synoptic link

Link to *A Level Religious Studies for Eduqas: Philosophy of Religion*, Chapter 6: Religious experience (part two). Look at the way that different scholars define a miracle, and consider the reasons why religious believers might accept that miracles occur.

AO1 activity 8

Create sensory cues for yourself that will help you to remember the vital ideas in this section. Music, pictures, food, or smells that you associate with clear ideas are really helpful, and those reminders should be added to your notes as visual cues. For example, to remember terms like *massa peccati*, I might picture a big plate of spaghetti because to me, the Latin term looks like 'mass of spaghetti'. For irresistible grace, I might use a picture of a magnet drawing an object towards it. Make sure you include teaching from the key scholars Augustine and Calvin, and include ideas that relate to:

a) the link between God and evil
b) the implications for God's omnipotence and omnibenevolence
c) the use of prayer and the existence of miracles.

This section of the chapter will enhance your ability to analyse and evaluate the topic and help you develop your AO2 skills. For each question, think about the different positions you might take, and decide which you find most persuasive and why. It is not enough to memorise a list of 'for and against' points; you need to develop an argument.

Should religious believers accept predestination?

This question focuses upon the beliefs of those who are religious. Therefore, you are expected to consider whether the theory of predestination is consistent with other religious beliefs, whether it is morally acceptable for religious believers, or whether there are any logical difficulties with predestination that provide challenges for religious believers, rather than non-religious people. The scholars we have studied – Augustine and Calvin – come from a Christian tradition. However, you could relate this question to another religion you have studied.

The view that religious believers should accept predestination

Predestination is the only possible explanation for human action if someone believes in an omnipotent creator of all things. To suggest that humans have any control over their actions, or what happens to them in the afterlife, damages a religious understanding of God's sovereignty. Humans cannot influence God's will because humans do not have power over God, and God is not subject to change in the same way that humans are. Religious believers should accept that their destiny is in the hands of God.

Religious believers should accept predestination because it removes pressure and anxiety from their lives. The alternative would otherwise be to accept rigid observance of religious laws or perfect, unwavering faith. Augustine acknowledged that if a religious believer allows their fate to rest in the hands of God, they no longer need to worry that they have failed to uphold some small area of God's will that is easily forgotten in a complex world with so many concerns. It is up to God to decide a person's destiny, and believers can relax and feel reassured that their fate is already taken care of.

Predestination is the only logical conclusion if one believes that God is transcendent and, therefore, exists outside of time. It makes no sense to suggest that people have any responsibility for their behaviour in a universe that is planned, created, and controlled by a timeless, omniscient being. To suggest people have free will is to give them more power and significance than is logically possible.

The view that religious believers should not accept predestination

It is completely contrary to God's omnibenevolent character to accept the theory of predestination. It turns God into a torturer who takes delight in human suffering. Arminius argued that Calvin's understanding of God makes God the author of evil and is in no way the omnibenevolent being presented by the New Testament. Morally, there can be nothing good about a God who deliberately predestines some people to eternal damnation (as Calvin taught), regardless of their actions or wishes. And there can be nothing good about a God who abandons people to such torture regardless of their behaviour (as Augustine taught). A God that pre-determines a person's eternal fate in either of these ways is an arbitrary or partisan kind of God, not the God of Christianity.

Predestination allows people to adopt a lazy attitude to morality. If a religious believer accepts predestination, they can ignore all moral laws and standards of acceptable behaviour because their actions cannot affect the pre-determined future that God has decided for them. This was exactly what Pelagius saw happening among Roman Christians, which led to his rejection of predestination. Christian moral behaviour is important because it demonstrates that God is being treated with respect, it affects other members of society, and it must affect the way in which a just God ultimately rewards or punishes someone in the afterlife.

It is illogical to claim that humanity is responsible for evil if they are not free to make choices for themselves about their behaviour. Immanuel Kant argued that 'ought' implies 'can'. This means that if a moral code requires someone to perform a certain moral action, they must be free to carry out that action. The only logical belief that is possible for religious believers is that humanity has free will. This is because God has set a standard for moral behaviour in the Bible. If a religious believer accepts the doctrine of predestination, then they accept that God has set an impossible standard they can never hope to achieve because they are only capable of sin. However, if humans have free will, then they can choose to act in accordance with God's standard if they wish.

The view that religious believers could accept predestination

Religious believers base their faith upon their own personal relationship with God, formed through prayer and personal experience. It is nonsense to attempt to dictate what a religious believer 'ought' to believe because that would circumvent true faith in God. It is possible for a believer to accept predestination if they believe that God is the creator and sustainer of the world, and that God is actively involved and interested in the world. However, it is equally possible that they could reject it on the basis that God has given them the gift of free will.

There is nothing illogical about accepting God as the omniscient and omnibenevolent creator of everything and that God decides the outcome of all human endeavour. Yet, if a religious believer chooses to reject predestination, this is also a reasonable belief because human experience tells us that our decisions are meaningful and change the course of our lives. Ultimately, religious believers can reasonably accept both positions.

If Calvin or Augustine are correct, it is important that religious believers are left alone to decide whether they accept predestination for themselves. This is because their faith must either come from themselves or be fixed by God. If it were possible for a believer's faith to be fixed by the Christian Church, then their faith would not be genuine; it would be nothing more than a mindless obedience to a human authority. To make belief in predestination mandatory is to allow the Church to control human will.

To what extent does God predestine humanity?

This kind of question focuses upon a religious understanding of predestination, and here we are being asked about the relationship between God and humans. Setting aside arguments about whether or not God exists, it is important to consider religious beliefs about God's nature and the nature of humanity. As before, the scholars we have studied – Augustine and Calvin – come from a Christian tradition. However, you could respond to this from the perspective of another religion that you have studied.

The view that God predestines humanity

If God exists, God must predestine humanity because the Bible says that God's power and authority over the whole of creation is absolute. It is impossible for God's will or purpose to be altered by any decisions of humanity because God has power over all creation, and nothing that humans can do could go against God's will.

> *His divine power has given us everything we need for a godly life through our knowledge of him who called us by his own glory and goodness.*
>
> **2 Peter 1:3**, *Holy Bible (NIV)*

As John Feinberg argues in his 1986 book *Predestination and Free Will*, God has absolute power over all creation. This means that everything that occurs is because God has directly planned, willed, and acted to direct it, not simply because God knew in advance that it would happen.

> *God's will covers all things … God's good pleasure and good purposes determine what he decrees.*
>
> John Feinberg, *Predestination and Free Will: Four Views of Divine Sovereignty and Human Freedom*

AO2 activity 1

Look up the following Bible quotations. Which support the concept of free will and which support the concept of predestination, and why?

- Jeremiah 1:5
- John 6:44
- Romans 13:2
- 1 Corinthians 10:13
- Galatians 5:13
- 2 Timothy 1:9
- 1 Peter 1:2
- Revelation 3:20

God's omniscience means that God must predestine humanity because if God knows what will occur (not just what might occur) in the future, then the future must be set. Feinberg points out that God's omniscience cannot be explained without the doctrine of predestination. Arminius argued, against Calvin, that God knows the full range of possible events for any given situation (he called this middle knowledge). However, Feinberg argues that this is not enough. God must know not only what can possibly happen, but what will actually happen. If this is the case, then the future is set by God and humanity must be predestined.

Scripture teaches that our behaviour has nothing to do with our salvation: Jesus offered redemption to the sinner who was crucified next to him, yet he constantly challenged the Pharisees who obeyed God's laws meticulously. It is, therefore, clear that humanity cannot be saved by good works but must trust in God's will.

> Then he said, 'Jesus, remember me when you come into your kingdom.' Jesus answered him, 'Truly I tell you, today you will be with me in paradise.'
>
> Luke 23:42–43 *Holy Bible (NIV)*

The view that God does not predestine humanity

God cannot predestine humanity because this would make God the author of evil. If God predestined human actions as Augustine or Calvin describe, then God would have designed things so that Adam would take the fruit from the tree in direct conflict with God's own command. Even if God's act of predestination only involved electing or reprobating humanity rather than controlling their individual actions, predestination renders life on Earth entirely meaningless, and begs the question of what the purpose is in having religious belief at all if nothing we do makes any difference about where we end up in the afterlife.

If God predestined humanity, scripture would be inaccurate. Scripture shows that Adam and Eve made choices that were not in accordance with God's will. It shows God being angry with individuals who try to defy God's will. It also shows that God is pleased with those who listen and have faith. Jesus clearly tells people how they should behave, and so God must allow human beings the ability to choose whether or not they obey these commands, or they have no purpose, and God's anger and joy are a pretence.

According to Pelagius, God does not predestine humanity. Human beings save or damn themselves with their moral choices on Earth. God created humanity *imago dei* and has, therefore, given people the ability to reason so that they can distinguish between good and evil. God has given them the gift of scripture to help them to understand how they should behave, but it is their free choices that determine what happens to them in the next life. This view is consistent with the human experience of decision-making, and appears more coherent with the idea that God's justice requires human actions to be rewarded or punished.

Synoptic link

Link to *Chapter 8: Determinism and free will: free will*. Many of the arguments against Augustine and Calvin come from their contemporaries: Pelagius and Arminius. Look up some of the key terms from these scholars to help you understand how they fit together.

According to Arminius, for God to predestine humanity in the way that Calvin describes, God would have to act in a way that is paradoxical to God's nature. God would be damning Reprobates because of their sinfulness, but they would not actually have been sinful because they would not have been rebelling against God. They would have been acting in accordance with what God had decreed!

To what extent does Hard Determinism illustrate that humanity has no free will?

This question asks you to consider whether the existence of cause and effect within the universe leads to an acceptance of the Hard Determinism position that there can be no freedom at all for moral agents, or whether a compatibilist view of the coexistence of Determinism and free will is more convincing.

The view that Hard Determinism makes free will impossible

According to Scientific Determinism, if free will is true then the laws of nature, which were fixed before the human race existed, can be violated by humans and therefore are shown to be false. This is nonsense. Humans are physical beings in a physical world, and are subject to the same laws as all other physical matter. There is no way that there can be an explanation of human actions which shows that humans are exempt from the laws of nature that have existed from the moment of the Big Bang.

In the nineteenth century, Pierre Laplace argued that since the universe consists of cause and effect, then theoretically, if a being existed that is intelligent enough to know all the forces operating in nature and the position and movements of everything in the universe, this being would know every action that a human would ever perform. This theoretical being is known as 'Laplace's Daemon'. It does not matter if such a being exists, or even if such a being could know everything. This form of Scientific Determinism argues that the fact that all the laws of nature are potentially knowable is enough to show that every thought and action is an inevitable result of the blind forces of nature's laws, and not free will.

Denial of free will comes from a misunderstanding of the nature of causation. Human action is not caused by someone whispering instructions or controlling us through hypnotism. Actions are caused by our own bodies and internal physical states (for example our DNA, the chemical composition of our brains, or sensations of hunger and thirst) and by our psychological make-up. In addition, human actions are not the result of one single cause; they occur when a range of specific circumstances come together in one moment in such a way that makes it impossible for someone to act differently. The decision to drink a glass of water comes not only from feeling thirst, but also the circumstances that

AO2 activity 2

The 2014 film *Interstellar*, directed by Christopher Nolan, follows a group of astronauts searching for a new home for humanity. While on a space mission, Cooper is able to travel in such a way that he can see all events from outside time, as if they are all happening at the same moment, and can act to influence the past. If someone can witness all events from outside time, what does this mean for the concepts of free will and predestination?

led to a failure to drink for several hours, the availability of water, a lack of more enjoyable drinks, the need for distraction from other tasks, and so on. Philosophical Determinism shows that if all these circumstances collide, a person will inevitably drink a glass of water and can do nothing else.

The view that Hard Determinism makes free will unlikely

In the seventeenth century, Baruch Spinoza said that humans believe themselves to be free because they are conscious of their actions but unconscious of the causes of their actions. In fact, Spinoza's Philosophical, Hard Determinism shows that the belief that we do anything freely is an illusion or a 'waking dream'. This is, according to Spinoza, because the beliefs of the mind are dictated by the state of the body. He saw mental decisions and bodily appetites as being part of the same process. Beliefs are conditioned into us, and are part of the causal process through which our bodies move and cause further effects in the world.

Those who argue for free will say that a moral agent is free to choose a different action if they so desire. This is a very weak understanding of free will. A person chooses to eat an apple because they are hungry and it is in front of them. They could have freely chosen the orange but they did not, because they do not like oranges, or because they had already eaten an orange that day, or because the apple looked fresher. There is no difference between accepting that there are a different set of psychological or physical causes in operation when a different decision is made, and saying that the agent could choose differently if they wished to. It just means that we do otherwise if we are caused to do otherwise. It does not mean that we could do otherwise under the conditions.

The view that Hard Determinism fails to illustrate that humanity has no free will

Soft Determinism shows that while cause and effect do exist and operate on all physical matter, they are compatible with our ability to act freely. Humans can choose how to act because we are part of the causal chain; we do not need to transcend the causal chain. Effect follows cause, but the causal chain stretching backwards only looks rigidly fixed, as philosophical determinists claim, because we are looking at it retrospectively. If, when presented with two equally possible options, I made a different choice on one occasion, the chain of events would look different when I looked back at it. Provided an option is possible and it is chosen in accordance with a person's desires, the person acts freely.

Anthony Flew argued that there are no universal psychological laws that completely explain the human ability to make choices. Although Skinner believed that he could potentially account for all human behaviour, he never managed to establish an equation that could control or predict all human actions. Whenever a person does something, there are all kinds of mental, emotional, social, chemical, and physiological aspects involved in the action. Scientific explanations for decision making are limited because humans are more than just physical objects. They are conscious, self-aware moral agents.

Philosophical determinists may argue that people are compelled to act by their strongest desire in the situation, which is outside their control. However, this argument is false. However much a moral agent wants to do something, they can refrain from doing it. Human beings are not helpless creatures that are ruled by their desires. It is possible for a person's desires to change; they can fall in and out of love, they develop and break habits, and they can act in ways that go against both their long-term and short-term desires.

AO2 activity 3

The 1932 dystopian novel *Brave New World* by Aldous Huxley depicts a world in which humans are mass produced to create a strict social hierarchy. Embryos are manufactured for their genetic qualities, such as intellectual capacity, so that the resulting people are both suitable for, and content with, specific roles in society. Then their behaviour is conditioned so that their destiny is inescapable.

Give three reasons why an individual in this kind of society would be deprived of free will, and three reasons why you think it could be possible for them to act against their conditioning.

What are the strengths and weaknesses of Hard and Soft Determinism?

It is important that a response to a question like this is still an evaluation of strengths and weaknesses, and not just a list of strengths and weaknesses. Here are some examples of the strengths and weaknesses of each position, and you will find many more throughout the rest of this AO2 section. However, in an essay, you must go on to weigh up these arguments, and consider whether or not they are persuasive and why.

The strengths of Hard Determinism

Hard Determinism is supported by a wide range of academic disciplines. Physics, biology, philosophy, psychology, and history all demonstrate cause and effect. It is the height of arrogance for humans to believe themselves special enough to be excused from causal influence and capable of transcending what no other being or object in the known universe can transcend. Humans are physical beings that are part of the universe, and the disciplines that explain the universe tell us that cause and effect operate everywhere.

Society is based upon the assumption of cause and effect; society does not work without cause and effect. Programmes and books about child raising make use of conditioning techniques for parents who wish to raise well-balanced children. Teachers, law makers and judges also rely upon the assumption that people can be trained to behave well and, if they misbehave, the consequences of their actions will cause a person to behave differently in the future.

The weaknesses of Hard Determinism

Hard Determinism contrasts 'cause' with 'freedom', and claims that all actions are caused. To falsify the idea of Hard Determinism, it is only necessary to find one example of something that is not caused and then the theory collapses. Quantum physics has provided evidence that not every event in the universe is caused, and has demonstrated that some particles act in unpredictable ways, not because we do not know their causes, but because causal laws are no longer clearly defined at this subatomic level. Therefore quantum physics is enough to demonstrate that the premise of Hard Determinism is flawed.

Hard Determinism removes human dignity and devalues human behaviour. If Hard Determinism is true, then moral actions are pointless because nothing we do is within our control. Deterministic psychology, such as behaviourism, underestimates the uniqueness of human beings and their ability to design their own futures and change the course of their lives if they wish. Flew points out that humans are not helpless cogs in a machine or victims of circumstance. Even if we can predict what someone will do in a specific situation, it does not mean that they were unable to act any differently.

The strengths of Soft Determinism

Soft Determinism is a compromise that allows the cause and effect identified by scientists to coexist with human freedom and, therefore, moral responsibility. Soft Determinism allows human actions to be meaningful, because they are caused by the moral agent themselves and not by random chance or an external event. However, it also recognises the inescapable nature of causality in the universe.

Soft Determinism admits that there is a difference between causes that are internal and those that are external to a moral agent. Internal causes are those that originate from within; they are consistent with the personality, desires, and intentions of a moral agent. Internal causes, therefore, allow for moral responsibility because they show that the actions a moral agent performs reflect the person that performs them. It is incorrect to say that the moral agent is not responsible for them, because they come from who they are as a person.

The weaknesses of Soft Determinism

Soft Determinism's understanding of human freedom is exceedingly narrow. To argue that a 'free' action is simply consistent with our desires or is an action that has not been forced, is not the same thing as saying that it belongs to the moral agent. William James was unimpressed with such definitions of freedom, calling them a 'quagmire of evasion', and he felt that they avoided the real issue of whether there can ever be any kind of event that is not determined by a prior cause. Soft determinists are forced to admit that our will is caused by something external to us so, in reality, the 'freedom' offered by Soft Determinism is not at all what we mean when we describe someone as 'free'.

In 1924, American lawyer Clarence Darrow defended two teenage boys, Leopold and Loeb, who had kidnapped and murdered a younger boy, Bobby Franks. Darrow successfully argued that the two teenagers should be excused the death penalty on the basis that the boys did not choose their own upbringing, experiences, or psychological state.

> *What has this boy to do with it? He was not his own father; he was not his own mother; he was not his own grandparents. All this was handed to him. He did not surround himself with governesses and wealth. He did not make himself and yet he is compelled to pay.*
>
> Clarence Darrow, 'The Trial of Leopold and Loeb'

Darrow argued that to hold the boys responsible for their actions involved blaming them for their personalities, which were caused by events beyond their control. It is surely unreasonable to consider an internal cause to be the fault of the moral agent, because internal causes come from events further back in the chain of causality; which leads us back to Hard Determinism.

AO2 activity 4

Consider the strengths and weaknesses of Hard and Soft Determinism described in this section.

a) Place the arguments in rank order, with number one being the argument that you find most convincing and number eight being the argument that you find least convincing.

b) For each argument, try to give a reason why you think it is successful or convincing. Are there any arguments that you cannot justify at all?

c) For each argument, try to think of a counter-argument or a reason why you can challenge it. Are there any that you think are so successful that there is no way to challenge them?

d) In an evaluation question, you will be expected to establish whether one perspective is more persuasive than another. As a result of your work in a) to c), what is your opinion? Is Hard Determinism a strong theory or a weak theory? Is Soft Determinism a strong theory or a weak theory? Give a reason for your judgement in each case.

Is moral responsibility an illusion?

A person must have moral responsibility if they are to be reasonably praised or blamed for their actions. This question asks you to consider whether the sense that a person can be held accountable for their behaviour is real or imaginary. If it is real, then a person could be rewarded or punished for what they do because they deserve it, rather than because it is a practical way of training people to behave in a desirable way.

The view that moral responsibility is an illusion

If it is impossible for a moral agent to act differently than they do, then it is not possible for a person to take moral responsibility for their actions. Humans think they are acting freely because the causes acting upon them are unconscious. However, all the events that led up to each decision a person makes stem from a chain of antecedent causes that led back before their birth and are outside their control. There is, therefore, no moral responsibility and no sense in any praising or blaming a person for their actions.

Some thinkers point towards intentions or desires as an indication that humans can have freedom and, therefore, moral responsibility. However, intention and desire are no more than consequences in the chain of cause and effect. A person has a desire because of the state of their physical body or the shape of their personality. These things are determined by biological and psychological causes and are, therefore, outside a person's control. While conscious thought does make a human different from a cog in a machine, it is still ultimately not up to us how we behave.

Just because we experience the sensation of making moral choices, this does not mean that our moral choice-making is real. In Locke's example of the man in the locked room, the man believed that he stayed in the room freely but the appearance of freedom was completely illusory. Humans believe they are free to choose, but this is because they are unaware of the causal factors that operate upon them. They cannot, therefore, be held responsible for choices that are ultimately outside their control.

Scholars like Saul Smilansky and Galen Strawson argue that moral responsibility is an illusion, but that it is a necessary illusion. Strawson argues that free will is impossible because when we act, we do so because of the way that we are. To be morally responsible for the way we are requires us to deliberately cause ourselves to be the way we are, but this is impossible. Smilansky argues that it is, however, useful to society for us to believe that we are responsible. He argues that belief in the free will offered by compatibilism, while false, is enough to motivate us to continue to attempt to behave morally.

The view that moral responsibility is not an illusion

Soft Determinism demonstrates that people act intentionally, in accordance with their desires or their own will. Provided that a person has not been compelled to act or restrained from acting, their behaviour is not simply mechanical. Our desires and our will indicate the kind of people we are. Our ability to desire one action rather than another, and then perform the action we desire, is the very definition of moral responsibility. It is not Determinism that robs us of the power to do things, it is constraint.

Researchers have performed experiments on the brains of conscious patients, and have identified the area of the brain where decision making occurs: the parietal cortex. While the experiments themselves say nothing about moral responsibility, they do indicate that the experience of decision making that directly precedes action is not an illusion. This could be interpreted to mean that a moral agent is responsible for their actions, since an action is dependent upon a very real prior decision that occurs in a specific part of a person's brain.

Jean-Paul Sartre argued that we are ultimately responsible for everything that we do. This is because from the moment we are born, we begin to create our own personalities through the decisions we make in our lives. And, because we make ourselves, we are fully responsible for every decision we make, and we can do anything. To pretend that decisions are not our responsibility is to act in bad faith and to lie to ourselves about the reality of life. There is no one else to blame when we make mistakes, and there is no one who can save us from the consequences of our own decisions.

Determinism argues that we act because of causes that stretch back in time, and that our actions are an inevitable consequence of those causes. However, this a simplistic description of what occurs. While there are certainly causes that operate upon a moral agent, each individual does not exist in a separate bubble attached to their own causal chain. Instead, we interact with others and our environment. There are an infinite number of causes that affect each other and, in a unique moral moment, a person with their own unique history will act personally, not mechanically. Only they can have responsibility for their action, because no single cause can account for the person who responded in that moment to that individual dilemma.

> ### Synoptic link
>
> Link to *Chapter 8: Determinism and free will: free will*. Be aware of the scientific knowledge that can be put forward in support of the existence of free will.

AO2 activity 5

The 1998 film *Sliding Doors* showed two lives that the main character, Helen, could have lived depending upon whether or not she caught a train. In the life where she catches the train, she discovers her boyfriend cheating on her and leaves him. In the life where she misses the train, she remains unaware of his infidelity. In each storyline, Helen's life takes a very different track.

a) Can Helen be described as free if her decision to leave or stay with her boyfriend is the result of a chain of causes? Give two reasons for your view.

b) Was it possible for Helen to leave her boyfriend in the version of her life where she remains unaware of his infidelity? Does this mean that she was free to do so? Give two reasons for your view.

To what extent does predestination influence our understanding of God?

Once again, this question concerns the religious understanding of free will and predestination. Many of the previous arguments about predestination that we have considered can be recycled here, provided that they are redirected to respond to the specific question asked. It is also relevant to consider whether teachings about predestination would influence someone's decision to have faith at all. The scholars we have studied – Augustine, Calvin and their contemporary challengers – come from a Christian tradition. However, there is no reason why you cannot respond from the perspective of another religion you have studied.

The view that predestination affects our understanding of God and is, therefore, important

If a religious believer considers humanity to be predestined, then this tells them that God is omnipotent and omniscient, the creator and sustainer of all things. This enables them to turn to God with faith, trusting that God will provide for them and look after them in the afterlife. It enables believers to understand that the purpose of their own lives is ordained by God, and to understand that if there are things in life that they do not understand, then they can trust in God who is in control.

As Augustine showed, predestination is vital if one is to avoid pride in one's own abilities. If people can save themselves through good works, there is no reason to seek God, and this could lead to humans placing themselves on the same level as God in terms of power and moral authority. Augustine was less concerned with preserving a sense of human self-worth and more concerned with acknowledging the authority and power of God. Salvation is a free gift from God that is entirely undeserved and has nothing to do with any human worthiness or skill.

Arminius objected to Calvin's form of predestination on the basis that it fails to make Christ the basis of election. It no longer matters whether one has faith in Christ as a means of salvation. Instead, people are victims of God's will. This view of predestination makes God both arbitrary and partisan, unworthy of worship or human obedience. This negative portrait of God is further highlighted by Arminius' point that God would have had to create some humans specifically for the pleasure of condemning them; it would mean that God could decree evil.

All of Arminius' objections to Calvin's form of predestination boil down to what it means for our understanding of the nature of God. What does Calvin's predestination say about God's nature if God creates humans with the ability to make choices but ultimately determines what happens to them without reference to those choices? What does it mean for God's nature if God preordains some as Reprobates before they are even created? What does it mean for God's nature if, as some scholars understand Calvin,

God changes humanity's ability to use their freedom after the fall? All Christian teachings about free will and predestination have an impact on human understanding of the nature of God and God's relationship with human beings.

The view that predestination is not important for our understanding of God

All of the scholars that we have studied, including Augustine, Pelagius, Calvin, and Arminius, agreed that God is omnipotent and omnibenevolent. None of them disagreed about God's nature, yet they disagreed over the extent to which we are free or predestined. This suggests that predestination is not important for our understanding of God, because it is not an inevitable conclusion of religious faith in the God of Christianity.

No one actually knows if we are predestined or not. It is a theological debate, and people take positions in the debate for political purposes. It benefitted the Catholic Church to accept Augustine's view of predestination over Pelagius' view because while Pelagius advocated pure behaviour, his theology damaged the authority of the Catholic Church by suggesting that a person's fate was in their own hands; it suggested that there was no reason why anyone should continue to obey Church edicts. Similarly, the Calvinist theology of predestination won out against the Arminians because the Dutch Reformed Church was concerned that the Arminian view challenged their traditions. It was a foregone conclusion that the Arminians would lose, even before the Synod of Dort was called. Therefore, predestination is only important for a religious understanding of the position of Church institutions and not vital to our understanding of God.

Predestination was not central to the theology of Augustine or Calvin. It was a result of other ideas about the nature of God and human salvation. Therefore, predestination does not influence a believer's understanding of God; it is brought about as a result of their understanding of God. If a believer focuses on the sovereignty of God, as Augustine and Calvin did, then predestination is a reasonable conclusion. However, if a believer focuses on God's love, then they may not understand predestination as inevitable.

It is more important that the concept of predestination gives people an understanding of the human condition and moral responsibility, than it gives people an understanding of the nature of God. If humans are predestined, the practical implications for behaviour, punishment, and sin are huge. If humans are free, the same is also true. The role of prayer, the work of Churches, and the importance of moral law and the scriptures are all affected by a belief in predestination. This is more important than a human understanding of God, because God is transcendent and largely unknowable anyway. Whereas the importance of other considerations such as moral behaviour, prayer, or the work of the Church affect everyday life.

AO2 activity 6

a) Look at the arguments above that say predestination is important for our understanding of God, and pair each one with a counter-argument that says predestination is not important for an understanding of God. You may want to add arguments and counter-arguments of your own.

b) Decide which argument in each pair is the strongest. Give one reason for your decision, and an example or evidence to back up your judgement.

Exam support

Practising AO1 questions

As you now know, AO1 questions may begin with one of a range of possible command words (see pages 8–9 for more detail). You should now know how to deal with any of these words when they appear. You have also seen the importance of making sure that you answer all aspects of the question in front of you throughout your answer.

Read the past paper question below and the example paragraph written in response before completing the activity on page 298.

> *Explain Hard Determinism with reference to philosophical, scientific and psychological concepts.*
>
> (Eduqas A Level Religious Studies, Summer 2018, Component 3: Religion and Ethics, Question 1a)

Example

Pavlov[6] developed[1] classical conditioning[7], which gives a psychological explanation of the principles of Hard Determinism[2]. He showed that there are set laws that explain and predict animal behaviour, showing that the present is simply the effect of[1] antecedent causes[7] that act upon the mind.[1] Pavlov[6] and his team noted that the dogs in his lab would salivate in anticipation of receiving food, even when no food was present[3]. Pavlov[6] demonstrated that this[1] involuntary, unconditioned response[7] could become conditioned by[1] training the dogs to associate a conditioning stimulus of a metronome being played as food was produced. Eventually, the playing of a metronome alone would produce salivation[3]. Salivation became a[1] conditioned response[7] and therefore was completely[1] mechanistic, predictable[7], and not free.[1] He said that behaviours 'proceed according to as rigid laws as do any other physiological processes'.[6] This means that behaviour in dogs or, as other[1] psychologists[2] showed, in humans can be seen as the result of[1] universal causation[7], a result of Hard Determinism[2] and therefore, utterly[1] incompatible[7] with free will.[1]

What went well

1. The paragraph is thorough, accurate, and relevant, explaining the facts of Psychological Determinism from Pavlov in detail.

2. This paragraph clearly addresses the question at the start, and refers to it again at the end of the paragraph where words such as 'psychologists' and 'Hard Determinism' are used.

3. The paragraph contains evidence from Pavlov's studies where it talks about his experiments on dogs to demonstrate an understanding of classical conditioning.

4. The response does not make use of any sources of wisdom and authority. This is not a problem, as in a question such as this, it is unnecessary.

5. This response has not made any connections with other approaches. However, these connections should not be forced, and this paragraph is packed with plenty of relevant and useful information.

6. In this paragraph, the only scholar who is necessary is Pavlov, and he is used throughout the response. A quotation from Pavlov has been embedded into the answer with an explanation.

7. There is a significant amount of specialist vocabulary that has been used in this response. It is used appropriately and accurately throughout.

Activity

a) Read the example paragraph on page 297 and identify three things that the student has done successfully in this paragraph.

b) Make a list of things that must be added to complete the entire essay and ensure that it fully answers the question.

AO1 practice question 1

Now it is your turn. Have a go at answering the following question. There are some points to remember underneath to help you if you are not sure how to start.

Explain the arguments of the philosopher John Locke and the psychologist Ivan Pavlov in support of Hard Determinism.

(WJEC A Level Religious Studies, Summer 2019, A2 Unit 4: Religion and Ethics, Question 1)

Points to remember

- Make sure that you include every aspect of the question in your answer: John Locke, Pavlov, and Hard Determinism.
- Try to show how the examples of the locked room from Locke and the dogs from Pavlov can be used to support Hard Determinism, rather than just retelling the stories.
- Use vocabulary that relates to the Hard Determinism, such as 'incompatibilism', 'universal causation', and 'antecedent causes'.

AO1 practice question 2

Now try this question by yourself.

Explain religious concepts of predestination with reference to St Augustine and John Calvin.

(Eduqas A Level Religious Studies, Autumn 2020, Component 3: Religion and Ethics, Question 3a)

Practising AO2 questions

As you now know, AO2 questions always require analysis and evaluation. You should now know how to pick apart the details of any issues that you raise and to weigh up the quality of any arguments that you present. You have also seen the importance of making sure that you answer the question carefully.

Read the past paper question below and the example paragraphs written in response before completing the activity on page 301.

> *'All human life is predestined by God.' Evaluate this view.*
>
> (Eduqas A Level Religious Studies, Autumn 2020, Component 3: Religion and Ethics, Question 3b)

Example 1

Human life is not[2] predestined[6] by God[2]. We are free to act however we like because otherwise there would be no such thing as moral action. You have to be free to be able to do something right or wrong[1]. Locke said that we are like people who have been[4] locked in a room[3] and think that we are free, but it is actually an illusion[4]. But[1] he is wrong[4] because[1] the man in the room can at least try to get out at any time[4]. That part of his freedom is still in place so we cannot be predestined[2]. However[1], science shows that humanity is predestined[2]. It says that we have been predestined[2] by our genes which have been passed down to us from our parents. We might also be predestined[1] by our upbringing and experiences because[1] they can have a big effect upon us. If this is true, which it is because it is science, it shows that God is the power and is in control of all human action. If human life is not predestined[2], God can be controlled by what humans want and God is little more than just one of us[1].

Areas for development

1 There is some valid analysis, but the student has muddled predestination and Hard Determinism, which makes it more difficult to sustain confident analysis and evaluation.

2 The paragraph makes an attempt to address the question, but struggles to remember the difference between predestination and Hard Determinism.

3 The examples that are given do not demonstrate successful arguments for or against predestination because they are focused on a more general consideration of Determinism.

4 There is a mention of a scholarly view, but it does not clearly demonstrate a view that is relevant to the question.

5 There is no attempt to make connections with other areas of the course. There is no need to force a connection, however it is possible that there could be links to the problem of evil, to religious experience, or to any other normative ethical theory.

6 There is some accurate use of specialist language in context, but not much outside the word that is used by the question.

Example 2: an improved response

It can be argued that human life is not predestined by God.[2] As[1] Arminius[4] argued, if[1] predestination[2] were true[1], it would make prayer and moral action meaningless[3] because there is nothing that anyone could do to influence God or affect their ultimate end.[1] He argued; 'From this doctrine it appears to them as though it were impossible for all their diligence to be useful'.[4] Predestination[2] would make the whole point of the religious experience of prayer – to freely develop a relationship with God – into a futile exercise[5] because it would make no difference at all. However, scripture clearly states that[1] God has, in fact, predestined[2] humanity[1]. Ephesians 1:11 tells us that humans were chosen by God according to a divine plan.[3] In fact[1], free will[6] would make all God's plans meaningless because they could be foiled by human choices. This would be a challenge to God's power and[1] sovereignty[6]. Augustine pointed out that it is only through God's[4] grace[6] that the[4] elect[6] can make any good choices through the[4] salvation[6] of Christ on the cross.[4] Therefore, it seems unlikely that human life is completely free from[1] predestination[2] because God's power and grace is the reason that God is worthy of worship in the first place. If[1] human life is not predestined[2], God is subject to human whims or superseded by human actions and God is little more than just one of us.[1]

What went well

1 This paragraph contains plenty of critical analysis and evaluation on both sides of the argument.

2 This paragraph contains regular reference to the wording of the question throughout.

3 The paragraph contains a couple of examples where there is evidence for or against predestination.

4 The student has included reference to Arminius and to Augustine in their answer, so there is scholarly support for both sides of the argument.

5 There is a brief reference to the purpose of prayer, which is a link to religious experience from the Philosophy paper. The student has not laboured this connection as it would distract from the question.

6 There is accurate use of specialist language in context.

Activity

a) Read Example 1 on page 299 and identify three things that could be developed to improve the analysis or the evaluation.

b) Read Example 2 on page 300. This time, the evaluation and analysis are much more effective. Make a list of six things that you could add to the answer if you were going to finish off the AO2 essay response.

AO2 practice question 1

Now it is your turn. Have a go at answering the following question. There are some points to remember underneath to help you if you are not sure how to start.

> *'The philosophical concept of Hard Determinism clearly illustrates humanity has no free will.' Evaluate this view.*
>
> (Eduqas A Level Religious Studies, Summer 2018, Component 3: Religion and Ethics, Question 1b)

Points to remember

- Remember that this question is asking you to evaluate the philosophical concept of Hard Determinism rather than predestination, and there is no need to reference God as the being that sets a person's destiny.
- As well as making use of scholars such as Locke, you could also use Sartre (discussed in Chapter 8) to support the idea that philosophy can illustrate we do have free will. You can also use other scholars not found on the specification if you wish, provided they focus on whether Hard Determinism clearly illustrates a lack of free will.
- Remember, you can argue that other approaches, such as science or psychology, might illustrate a lack of free will more clearly than philosophy. This is also a valid line of argument.

AO2 practice question 2

Now try this question by yourself.

> *'Hard Determinism is far more convincing than Soft Determinism.' Evaluate this view.*
>
> (WJEC A Level Religious Studies, Summer 2018, A2 Unit 4: Religion and Ethics, Question 5)

Mark schemes for all exam questions can be found at www.eduqas.co.uk and www.wjec.co.uk.

Determinism and free will: free will

We began Chapter 7 thinking about Lionel Shriver's novel *We Need to Talk About Kevin*. We considered whether Kevin's character and behaviour were determined by poor parenting, genetic makeup, or other environmental factors.

Eva, Kevin's mother, feels that Kevin is intelligent and that, even from a young age, he chose his actions carefully. She believes he presented himself as cooperative and enthusiastic to his father, but cold, calculating, deliberately cruel and deceptive to her. While Kevin's childhood is not idyllic, he had a loving father and a fairly standard home life, and others in a similar position do not act as Kevin did. Is it possible that a person can make free choices about their actions, choices that override their genetic makeup or the influence of environmental factors?

In this chapter, you will study the religious concept of free will as presented by Pelagius and Arminius. You will also consider the philosophical concept of Libertarianism as presented by Sartre and inferred from the work of Sirigu and Rogers. You will consider the implications of these concepts on moral responsibility and religious belief. For example, is there any value in blaming or praising moral agents for their actions? (Is there any purpose in blaming Kevin for the killings or praising him when he appears sorry?) What does it mean about God's nature if he rewards people purely for their moral effort?

Does it make sense to praise or blame people for their behaviour?

This section of the chapter will enhance your knowledge and understanding of the topic and help you develop your AO1 skills.

Religious concepts of free will

The religious concept of free will is extremely complex and is dependent upon a number of other theological claims. It is interwoven with Christian understanding of God's nature, human nature, and the existence of evil and sin. Christian teaching and tradition contain the idea that humans have been given the gift of free will by God, but this must be balanced with the belief in God's sovereignty as an all-powerful being who created everything *ex nihilo*. Any religious notion of free will must be understood within the context of Christian teachings about the fall, sin, and atonement. It is not the same as philosophical concepts of **Libertarianism**, which may be secular and do not rely on beliefs about the nature of God and revelation from scripture.

Pelagius

Pelagius was a contemporary of Augustine. In the early-fifth century, he was living in Rome and was concerned about the poor moral standards of Roman Christians, who seemed to try to justify their actions by arguing that they ultimately had no control over anything they did. He felt that Augustine's teaching on predestination left no place for people to make choices and take moral responsibility for their actions. Most of Pelagius' writings have survived only as fragments of letters or as quotations in the work of his opponents such as Augustine, as Augustine responded to Pelagius' challenges to his thinking on predestination. Therefore, when piecing together Pelagius' teachings, we must recognise that what we have is inherently biased because Pelagius' words have been presented by a fierce opponent. Other contemporaries, such as Julian of Eclanum and Celestius, also developed the approach that has become known as Pelagianism. Thus, there are some ideas attributed to Pelagius that we cannot be sure are his, as they are not seen in the selected writings of Pelagius that are still available to us.

One big area of debate between Augustine and Pelagius concerned human nature. Pelagius rejected the idea that sin comes from human weakness and that humans are powerless on their own to do anything good at all. For Pelagius, God's gift of free will is genuine and complete, so humans are responsible for their sin. However, religious concepts of free will are interwoven with an understanding of God as supreme authority. Pelagius did not completely deny predestination, but he understood it very differently to Augustine. Predestination, for Pelagius, is interwoven with God's foreknowledge of future human decisions: God is omniscient and has foreknowledge of who will be saved through their own free choices. Those

Key terms

ex nihilo: (Latin) out of nothing

Libertarianism: a philosophy that holds that human beings are free, have free will, and concepts of Determinism are false

Synoptic link

Link to *Chapter 7: Determinism and free will: Determinism.* Look back at the teaching of Augustine on predestination to remind yourself why Pelagius would make this accusation.

who are saved are not chosen independently of their own will; they choose for themselves, but God already knows what they will choose.

The role of original sin

Christian teaching states that humans are sinful and require salvation; on this, Augustine and Pelagius agreed. However, they disagreed about the origins and nature of sin. Neither scholar wanted to accept that an omnipotent God could be responsible for the creation of evil or the existence of sin. Augustine taught that evil originated from Adam's original sin and that humans are incapable of good without God. In contrast, Pelagius argued that human beings are born in a sinless state and, when they sin, they do so from free choice and are, therefore, responsible for their actions. He argued that God does not expect humans to obey laws that it is impossible for them to obey, so it is possible for humans to make good choices. There is, in other words, no excuse for failing to choose good because it is perfectly possible to be good.

> *In fact, man is truly good for the very reason that these people say he is not: that he has freedom to choose good or evil. Within the heart of man there is no overwhelming compulsion to act in one way or the other.*
>
> Pelagius, 'Letter of Pelagius to Demetrias, AD 385'

Pelagius argued that it was possible, in theory, for a person to live a sinless life, even before Jesus was born. He named biblical figures, including Abraham, Isaac, and Mary (the mother of Jesus) as examples of people who lived lives without sin.

> *'I once more repeat my position: I say that it is possible for a man to be without sin.'*
>
> Pelagius as quoted in Augustine, *On Nature and Grace*

Sin is a voluntary action, not something that is inherited. Adam's sin is not passed down the generations to the rest of humanity, and it cannot compromise our ability to do what is good. Adam's sin is an example of sinful behaviour that humans often choose to follow, but humans can obey God's commands and choose not to sin.

Original sin does not involve the transmission of personal guilt that leads people to damnation. It would be unjust of God to condemn all of humanity for the sin of one man. Human nature is not crippled or transformed by sin because sin is not a substance. It is not something that can change or weaken our essential human nature. It is an action.

Pelagius, therefore, promoted **asceticism** (self-disciplined avoidance of sensual pleasure) as the ideal lifestyle for Christians. In contrast to Augustine's approach, which allowed sinful behaviour in Christians to be accepted as an unfortunate tendency that was outside a person's control, Pelagius taught that only the morally upright should be allowed to become part of the Catholic Church. Each individual is responsible for their own moral destiny, and is expected to work towards moral perfection.

Key term

asceticism: self-disciplined avoidance of sensual pleasure

Pelagius reasoned that if sin is impossible to resist then it could not be called sin at all! Sin is only sin when someone deliberately turns against God of their own free will, not when they perform an action that they are compelled to perform. This means, Pelagius argued, that infants who die without being baptised are not damned because they have not yet sinned. To suggest that God holds infants responsible for the sins of someone else is completely inconsistent with the all-loving, merciful nature of God.

Humanity maturing in God's image

Before Adam and Eve ate fruit from the tree of knowledge, they did not know the difference between good and evil, something that is required for freedom of choice. Prior to this sin, they were innocent, like children. Their obedience was like that of a little child who knows no better. To become mature, they needed to learn for themselves. God gave them the opportunity to learn by placing the tree in the Garden of Eden. If God had instructed Adam and Eve to eat, they would have obeyed like children. By forbidding them to eat, God gave them a free choice. Just as a teenager defies their parents as part of their journey into adulthood, Adam and Eve defied God and started the human journey of maturing into God's image.

> *Thus, the story of their banishment from Eden is in truth the story of how the human race gained its freedom: by eating fruit from the tree of knowledge, Adam and Eve became mature human beings, responsible to God for their actions.*
>
> Pelagius, 'Letter of Pelagius to Demetrias, AD 385'

No one is totally good or totally evil, but people can build up good habits or bad habits. Humanity has built up a habitual tendency to sin, and continued participation in the world encourages even more sin. However, if we become habitually inclined to good, it is easier to do good in the future. Pelagius held that Christians should steadily advance towards perfection by adopting the ascetic life and ridding themselves of excess. Augustine found this teaching offensive, since it implies that humans can become perfect, just as God is perfect.

Free will is used to follow God's laws

Augustine believed that people have free will, but it is limited by sin. In contrast, Pelagius believed that people possess complete freedom of will and are totally responsible for their own sinful actions. Human nature is not compromised or incapacitated by weakness; such imperfection would reflect negatively on God.

According to Pelagius, there is no need for divine grace to ensure good behaviour. Everyone, including non-Christians, are capable of choosing to follow God's laws by themselves. Augustine objected to this teaching on the basis that it implies human beings are responsible for their own salvation and threatens God's omnipotence.

Synoptic link

Link to *A Level Religious Studies for Eduqas: Philosophy of Religion*, Chapter 3: Challenges to religious belief: the problem of evil and suffering. Refresh your memory about Augustinian-type theodicies, and ensure you understand the nature of evil as *privatio boni* and the role of human freedom in the existence of evil and suffering.

Pelagius was condemned as a heretic by two different popes. He then disappeared from historical records.

> *If only Christians were good, then God would not be good, because he would have denied the rest of humanity the freedom to choose goodness. The goodness we see in pagans is proof of the goodness of God. He has granted every person, regardless of race or religion, the freedom to choose good or evil.*
>
> Pelagius, 'Letter of Pelagius to Demetrias, AD 385'

In his letter to Demetrias, an aristocratic woman who had renounced her wealth to live as a nun, Pelagius emphasised that commands from God are meant to be obeyed. He did not accept human frailty as an excuse for failing to do God's will. He claimed, in contrast to Augustine, that it is possible to freely choose to obey God. God created humanity in full awareness of their capabilities, and did not place any obligation on them to do what is impossible. Perfection is possible, and a moral duty for all people. This means that it is possible to gain salvation through good behaviour and freely chosen obedience to God's commands. This teaching prompted Augustine to accuse Pelagius of rendering Christ's death on the cross as pointless if salvation can be gained by good works alone.

The role of grace in salvation

While Augustine believed God's grace was irresistible, in that our free will must be liberated by grace if we are to develop the desire to do good, Pelagius believed that humans have freedom and responsibility. This was controversial, with Augustine claiming that Pelagius appeared to be arguing that there was no purpose in divine grace. However, Pelagius did not deny grace. He understood grace differently from Augustine, as the way that God supports humans to make good decisions.

Pelagius has been described as understanding grace in three different ways.

- Firstly, Pelagius suggests that humanity has been created with **natural grace** (also known as original grace). This is the grace given to people by God as a gift at birth. Natural grace concerns the abilities that humans are born with that make them human, such as reason and free will to choose to avoid sin. This is the capability that distinguishes humans from the rest of the animal kingdom.

> **Key terms**
>
> **natural grace:** the gifts of reason and free will that are an essential part of the human nature created by God
>
> **revelation:** the gift of God's law and the example of Jesus' life on Earth, given to humanity through scripture

> *God made man in his own image; and so he intends each of us to be like him. God has made many animals stronger and faster than human beings. He has given many animals teeth and jaws that are more powerful and sharper than the finest sword. But he has given man intelligence and freedom. We alone are able to recognise God as our maker, and thence to understand the goodness of his creation.*
>
> Pelagius, 'Letter of Pelagius to Demetrias, AD 385'

- Secondly, Pelagius appears to understand grace as including God's gift of **revelation**. This is both the revelation of God's commands and the example of Jesus' life on Earth as revealed by scripture. Jesus is the example of a sinless, perfect human that we should try to imitate, and his actions and teachings show us what is required of us. God has, therefore, provided us with all the guidance we need to understand our moral obligations, and it is up to the individual to decide what to do.

Those who are saved are those who choose to follow God's commands and Jesus' example.

> *In the person of Jesus Christ, the inner spiritual law is made fully manifest for us. His words explain the spiritual law, and his life and death exemplify it. Through him we are reborn as new men and women, because we can see clearly how we should live.*
>
> Pelagius, 'Letter of Pelagius to Demetrias, AD 385'

- Thirdly, Pelagius understands that humanity is not yet perfect. Therefore, God gives us **pardon**. This is the gift of forgiveness, given to those who work to act correctly and repair any evil that they have done. The grace of pardon is forgiveness for sin that is offered through the death of Christ. While Augustine accused Pelagius of making Christ's death on the cross pointless, Pelagius retained the idea that human beings require God's forgiveness for sin and that the death of Jesus was essential to that forgiveness. Salvation is possible for everyone, not just a few who are arbitrarily chosen by God, but not everyone will achieve that salvation because some will make poor choices and turn away from God's will.

Key terms

pardon: the forgiveness of sins offered by God to human beings when they repent

Five Articles of Remonstrance: a summary of a work called *The Remonstrance*, which was signed by followers of Arminius and debated at the Synod of Dort in 1618–1619

A Declaration of Sentiments: Arminius' writing that details his own views on free will and predestination

AO1 activity 1

a) Copy and complete the following table to compare the teachings of Augustine and the teachings of Pelagius. You will need to refer back to Chapter 7 to help you complete it.

	Augustine	Pelagius		Augustine	Pelagius
Original sin			Personal sin		
The role of Adam			The role of Jesus		
Grace			Free will		
Human nature			Predestination		

b) Highlight the similarities between the teachings of Augustine and Pelagius in one colour, and highlight the differences in another colour.

Arminius

Jacobus Arminius was a Dutch theologian and minister in the Dutch Reformed Church. He originally supported Calvinism, but came to object to the teaching of limited atonement. It seemed too harsh: if Christ's death and atonement for our sins was for the Elect only, then there appeared to be no place for human free will in the process of salvation. It is common for Arminius to be studied through the writings of his followers, the Arminians. However, what Arminius himself taught and the teachings that are attributed to him are not identical. 'The Remonstrance' was a theological document written in support of Arminius by Johannes Uyttenbogaert, and a summary of this work – the **Five Articles of Remonstrance** – was signed by Arminius' followers after Arminius died in 1609. It was this document that was debated at the Synod of Dort in 1618–1619. However, Arminius' own explanation of his teachings is found in **A Declaration of Sentiments**.

Synoptic link

Link to *Chapter 7: Determinism and free will: Determinism*. Refer back to the teachings of Calvin on predestination to help you remember what the Arminians objected to.

The Five Articles of Remonstrance covered the following main points:

- **Article 1** – Before the creation of the world, God predetermined that through Christ, he would save those who believe and condemn those who do not.
- **Article 2** – Jesus died for everyone, but only the believer will benefit from his death.
- **Article 3** – Humanity cannot save themselves. They need the help of Christ and the Holy Spirit. God can and will renew human understanding so that they can choose to believe.
- **Article 4** – Without prevenient grace (see page 310), humans can do nothing good. But God's grace can be resisted.
- **Article 5** – Through the help of the Holy Spirit, people can remain faithful provided they choose to cooperate. This means that God's grace can be resisted. However, the fifth article remains undecided over whether a believer can fall away from God.

The Synod of Dort subsequently rejected Arminianism, declared it an error and affirmed what they considered to be the five central principles of Calvinism.

At the beginning of his own Declaration of Sentiments, Arminius retells a story in which he was given five articles that were considered to be his own sentiments on several points of religion, including predestination, the fall, free will, original sin, and the salvation of infants. Arminius believed that he knew the author who, when challenged, claimed that the five articles were created from a summary of objections to Arminius' teaching made by his students. Arminius felt this to be misleading as they did not all accord with his teaching at all. He publicly renounced these articles and was challenged to explain his position for himself. The Declaration of Sentiments is Arminius' explanation of his actual teachings.

Denial of the Calvinist view of predestination

It is important to understand that Arminius did not reject the idea of predestination completely. Like the other scholars we have studied who debated the issue of free will and predestination, Arminius saw a place for both free will and predestination in his thinking. However, Arminius did reject the Calvinist understanding of predestination, because he felt that it was not consistent with the gospels. He claimed that Calvinism requires no faith, virtue, or effort from people before they are saved and was never approved in any early Church doctrine, even by those who dealt with Pelagius and his errors.

In Arminius' view, scripture clearly taught that salvation was through grace, faith, and Christ alone. The gospels tell people to repent and have faith so that their sins will be forgiven. Therefore, salvation is reserved for those who have faith in Christ, who died for everyone and not just the Elect. According to Arminius, a merciful, loving God cannot decree evil by creating individuals just for the pleasure of eternally condemning them.

> *God therefore has not, from his own absolute decree, without any consideration or regard whatever to faith and obedience, appointed to any man, or determined to appoint to him, life eternal. … God, therefore, has not, by any absolute decree without respect to sin and disobedience, prepared Eternal Death for any person.*
>
> Jacobus Arminius, 'A Declaration of the Sentiments of James Arminius'

Arminius gives around twenty reasons why the Calvinist doctrine of predestination should be rejected. Several of these reasons focus on Arminius' belief that scripture clearly requires a decision of faith from an individual before they are saved, and makes it clear that reward or punishment in the afterlife depends on the choices that an individual makes in this life. Arminius said this becomes impossible if God has predestined an individual to salvation or damnation without regard to the personal choices they make.

Arminius pointed out that the concept of sin requires someone to disobey or rebel against God. If a person has been decreed sinful, and can do nothing else but be sinful, such behaviour is not actually sin. In fact, it makes God the only sinner, because God causes the person to act in in this way. It is as though God has given human beings a law and then made it impossible for them to fulfil it.

According to Arminius, Calvinism makes prayer, baptism, sermons, and the work of ministers pointless. God has already decided who will be saved and there is nothing anyone can do to alter this decision. Arminius felt that Calvinistic predestination set everything back to front. Scripture requires a decision of repentance first, in return for the promise of salvation. Calvinism decides in advance who is saved or condemned, and then forces repentance afterwards.

> *The constitution of this doctrine is such, as very easily to render pastors and teachers slothful and negligent in the exercise of their ministry: Because, from this doctrine it appears to them as though it were impossible for all their diligence to be useful to any persons*
>
> Jacobus Arminius, 'A Declaration of the Sentiments of James Arminius'

The effect of original sin on free will

God's providence is the care and guidance of God over the whole of creation. Arminius understood God as supervising the whole world and everything in it, sustaining it, preserving it, and governing it. However, he did not hold God responsible for the existence of evil or sin. Arminius argued that when God created, heaven and earth were perfectly good. It is impossible, Arminius said, that God should create anything with the express purpose of condemning it as evil. Adam was free not to sin, because he was created perfect and holy, *imago dei*. He could, and should, have resisted the temptation to sin. God did not cause or dictate that Adam should sin, but instead allowed him the freedom to sin through **divine concurrence**. God permitted Adam to choose sinful acts, while at the same time disapproving of his choice. Through God's providence, Adam's sin was possible but it was just as possible that Adam could have avoided that first sin.

> **Key term**
>
> **divine concurrence:** God permitting human sin, while at the same time disapproving of it

Arminius viewed original sin as a terrible thing, which was transmitted to the rest of humanity, but which was performed freely. The effects of original sin are both physical (pain and death was introduced into the world) and spiritual (humanity can no longer think, will, or do anything truly good by themselves). Humanity is now deprived of that original ability to freely choose what is good and so they are now inclined towards further sin.

The result of original sin is the absence of the Holy Spirit at work in an individual. Humanity, after the fall, possesses a strong inclination to sin. Every part of the soul is negatively affected. There is no aspect of human nature that is unaffected, and no one can merit salvation through good deeds. This is the penalty for sin. Any remaining freedom, after the fall, is insufficient by itself to turn to God. However, according to Arminius, human beings continue to perform individual sin not because God causes them to do so, or because he has abandoned them to their sin, but because they are permitted to sin through divine concurrence. Original sin produces a tendency towards personal sin that God permits. God does not cause or will personal sin, and does not approve of personal sin, but allows it to proceed.

God's prevenient grace

As a sinner, a human cannot do good alone. To be capable of good, a person must receive God's grace, so that they can be renewed by God, in Christ, through the Holy Spirit. Arminius refers to two kinds of grace: **prevenient grace** and **subsequent grace**.

Prevenient grace precedes each moral decision, and is the work of the Holy Spirit, outside of the human being. It is offered to everyone and is sufficient alone for each person to receive Christ's salvation. Subsequent grace is the work of the Holy Spirit inside the person, aiding and assisting believers to accept the gift of faith. It is the cooperation of the Holy Spirit and the individual's will.

Arminius likens prevenient grace to Christ, through the Holy Spirit, knocking on a door, and subsequent grace to the Holy Spirit assisting the sinner to open the door and let Christ in.

Prevenient grace is compared to Christ, through the Holy Spirit, knocking at the door to be let in.

Key terms

prevenient grace: the grace given by God that precedes the act of a sinner choosing faith in Jesus Christ

subsequent grace: the grace given by God that helps a sinner by cooperating with them so that they can make a free choice of saving faith in Jesus Christ

> Here I am! I stand at the door and knock. If anyone hears my voice and opens the door, I will come in and eat with that person, and they with me. "
>
> Revelations 3:20, *Holy Bible (NIV)*

Without God's grace, no one can do good because original sin has deprived them of the working of the Holy Spirit, but with God's grace, individuals have the ability to be regenerated, that deprivation of the Holy Spirit is corrected, and they can freely choose faith.

The Elect and the possibility of rejecting God's grace

Arminius is clear that God requires people to use their free will to respond to the Holy Spirit, who will help them. The Holy Spirit balances the impulse to sin, but is not forced upon a human being; the Holy Spirit is God's guidance and not God's coercion. As a result, Arminius taught that it is possible for a person to reject God's gift of grace at any time.

> *Because the representations of grace that the scriptures contain, are such as describe it capable of 'being resisted', (Acts 7:51) and 'received in vain' (2 Corinthians 6:1) and that it is possible for man to avoid yielding his assent to it and refuse all cooperation with it.*
>
> Jacobus Arminius, 'A Declaration of the Sentiments of James Arminius'

The grace of God does not destroy a person's free will. It corrects a person's tendency towards sin and gives them the ability to understand the good. Sin is only possible if this is true because if sin is to exist, people must be able to rebel against and reject God. A Christian can commit apostasy and turn away from their faith, and they can choose to return to God. These choices are free acts of human will. According to Arminius, the Elect are therefore those who freely choose faith in God, who repent of their sins, and who accept the help of the Holy Spirit to live a good life.

Arminius affirms that through God's providence, or guiding of the world, God has complete foreknowledge, but he denies that human faith is determined by anything outside of human control. God knows who, by God's grace, will believe and who, by their own fault, will not. God does not coerce people into believing; they can resist faith and salvation if they choose to. This requires what Arminius describes as the doctrine of **middle knowledge**. This is God's knowledge of the full range of possible events that could occur and the full range of possible actions a person could choose from in response. God knows whether an individual will have faith in any given situation. God has given everyone enough grace in their unique circumstances so that they can freely choose faith if they wish, and knows who will accept or resist this assistance. God predestines them to salvation or damnation on that basis.

> **Key term**
>
> **middle knowledge:** God's knowledge of the full range of possible events that could occur and the full range of actions that a person could choose from in response

For Arminius, this does not damage the omnipotent character of God. God is omnipotent because God can do anything that is logically possible for an omnibenevolent being to do. In accordance with scripture, God cannot force a person to will something freely, and he cannot rightly cause them to do evil; to do otherwise is illogical. Arminius even appears to allow that true believers can possibly fall away from God and can be brought back. Just as a beggar, Arminius said, can reach out their hand for charity and can accept or refuse it, people can accept or reject God's grace. The gift is resistible at every step along the way, but is still a gift regardless of how it is received or even if it is rejected at any point.

Being a member of the Elect is conditional upon faith

Arminius argued that Calvinism is an inversion of the Gospel. He cited John 3:16 as evidence that God will save those who have first chosen to have faith.

> *For God so loved the world that he gave his one and only Son, that whoever believes in him shall not perish but have eternal life.*
>
> John 3:16, *Holy Bible (NIV)*

In contrast, Calvinists believe that God has promised eternal life, in advance, only to those who God will then force into faith by God's own irresistible will. According to Arminius, Calvinism gets everything backwards: it says that God has predetermined people so that they will believe, rather than saving people who have chosen to believe.

Arminius thought Calvinism was at odds with God's love. For Arminius, the foundation of the gospel is God's love for justice and God's love for people. This love is demonstrated by giving eternal life to the faithful. This is only possible for the faithful because of the salvation of Christ. Arminius does not accept that God's love is demonstrated by predestining any human being to salvation or destruction without regard to their will.

Arminius' approach is known as **conditional predestination** (or conditional election). Having faith is a condition of being elected. God, in his omniscience, knows in advance who will choose faith and be saved, and God helps the Elect choose faith with prevenient grace and the gift of salvation through the death of Christ. In this way, predestination and free will are compatible for Arminius.

Concepts of Libertarianism

It is important to be able to distinguish between religious concepts of free will that require a divine being and philosophical concepts of free will that do not. The concepts of Libertarianism that will be discussed offer arguments in support of a moral agent having control over their own actions and being free to make their own choices, without reference to an external cause such as a divine being that gifts free will to humanity.

Libertarianism is an incompatibilist approach: it is impossible for a libertarian to reconcile human moral action with any form of Determinism. This also distinguishes it from religious concepts of free will, which seek to reconcile some understanding of human free will with God's omnipotence. Libertarians argue that Determinism is false and that humans are free to make moral decisions. However, libertarians cannot claim that free actions are uncaused. An event that is uncaused is random, and a random or chance event is not one for which someone can be held morally responsible because they did not cause it. It is no more than chance.

Philosophical concepts of Libertarianism: Jean-Paul Sartre

Moral philosophers argue that reason demonstrates that for there to be any kind of human responsibility for moral actions, an agent must have moral autonomy to act other than the way that they do. Soft Determinism argues that the liberty of spontaneity is enough for moral responsibility. Libertarians argue that this is not enough. Compatibilist freedom still allows those actions to be caused by something outside the agent, and this is not what we mean by freedom. Some libertarians argue that a free agent must also have the liberty of indifference (the ability to do otherwise). Others argue that a free moral action must be caused by the agent to deserve any praise or blame that is given to them.

> **Key term**
>
> **conditional predestination:** the election of those who have first chosen to have faith in Christ; also known as conditional election

> **AO1 activity 2**
> Divide a large piece of paper into half. Give each half a name: Calvin, Pelagius. Then summarise, in ten bullet points or fewer, the main ideas of each scholar. Add images to help you to remember them. Emphasise significant differences by highlighting them in a bold colour.

Jean-Paul Sartre was a twentieth-century atheist, **existentialist** scholar who argued that human beings are free to make their own choices. Traditional religious doctrine states that human beings were created by a divine power who made them with a preconceived purpose in mind. Sartre disagreed, and used the example of a paper knife to explain that humans begin to exist before they acquire a purpose. Paper knives were invented to separate the pages of books, which used to be sold with the printed pages joined at the edges. They were also used to open letters. The paper knife was designed with these purposes in mind and so had an essence before it was even manufactured. In contrast, human beings were not created by any kind of higher being with any purpose in mind. Instead, Sartre said that when it comes to humanity, existence precedes essence.

> *What do we mean here by 'existence precedes essence'? We mean that man first exists: he materialises in the world, encounters himself, and only afterward defines himself.*
>
> Jean-Paul Sartre, *Existentialism is a Humanism*

Human beings come into the world and then begin to create their own essence as they make free decisions in the world. Each decision that is made helps to shape a person and construct their essence through their free choices.

Determinists claim that all decisions are pre-determined by prior causes, and that our genes and psychological conditioning govern how we behave in any given situation. Sartre acknowledged that there is a **facticity** about our lives that we have not chosen. We are physical creatures who live in a specific time and place and in specific conditions, and this determines facts about us. However, Sartre argued that Determinism is mistaken because it treats a person as if these facts are all the information to be known about them; it objectifies them. Sartre argued that an object within the world is **être-en-soi** (a being-in-itself). To exist *en soi* is to be a fact. A paper knife is *en soi*; it is an object that exists and is subject to the operation of cause and effect.

However, human beings are not simply objects. A human being is **être-pour-soi** (a being-for-itself). Their identity is not bound up in a preconceived and fixed label. An *être-en-soi* is fixed and can be nothing else, and when we treat a human being as an *être-en-soi* (as determinists do), we imply that a person's essence is fixed. On the other hand, *être-pour-soi* is what makes a being into a person rather than a thing. It is consciousness, subjective desires, and individual experiences. *Etre-pour-soi* arises out of the *être-en-soi*, and makes itself through the process of living.

For example, the statement, 'Safi is a student, therefore she made notes in a lesson', treats Safi as an *être-en-soi*. This is backwards because it implies that Safi's identity as a student is fixed and dictates her actions. Instead, actions show the essence of the person that we are. It is more accurate to say, 'Safi made notes in a lesson, therefore she is a student'. Free actions are not the consequence of a fixed identity; they are the

Key terms

existentialist: a philosophical idea that human existence is without a set purpose in an uncaring universe; it emphasises human responsibility for actions

facticity: the facts of a situation or circumstance

être-en-soi: (French) being-in-itself; an object that has no conscious awareness

être-pour-soi: (French) being-for-itself; a free agent who can make themselves through free, conscious choices

Synoptic link

Link to *A Level Religious Studies for Eduqas: Philosophy of Religion*, Chapter 1: Arguments for the existence of God: inductive. Look back at the design argument for the existence of God. It suggests that God has designed humans before creating them. Sartre rejects not only this argument for God's existence, but also the idea that humanity came into being with a pre-conceived purpose.

foundation of an identity. Freedom allows a person to re-create their identity in any way they like. If Safi decided to put down her pen, leave the room, and climb a mountain, she could re-create her identity as a mountain climber. Safi's identity is not a straight-jacket that dictates her future. Just because she is a student now, does not mean she cannot be a climber in the future. We are not enslaved by a divine creator that fixes the course of our existence.

Some people embrace objectification but to act as an *être-en-soi* is to act in **bad faith**, to deceive yourself that your life is determined when in reality you are free. Sartre gives the example of a waiter. The waiter acts in a pretentious way as he serves his customers and behaves as though his role as a waiter is all that he is. The waiter is lying to himself. He acts according to his label of 'waiter' because he believes that he has no choice but to play this part. He makes himself into a waiter-thing. He must know the reality of the situation but disguises it from himself carefully. This is bad faith because, in fact, the waiter can be anything that he wants to be. He is free to put down his cloth and tray and leave the café if he wishes. This might mean he is fired, but he is free to be fired! Acting in bad faith is a tempting way to live because it is less scary. It is easier to live in ignorance and play act as though there is no other choice. But it is a dishonest way to live.

> ## Key term
>
> **bad faith:** self-deception; refusing to accept the fact of personal freedom and acting as though Determinism is true

It is inevitable that a person will sometimes come up against facticity that will prevent certain actions. We cannot choose to fly or remain underwater unaided. But a free choice is not the ability to do anything one wishes. It is the ability to decide how to act. For example, a prisoner is not free to leave prison, but they are free to try to escape. Furthermore, while facticity can limit what a person can do, the limitations arise primarily because of the choices the person makes. For example, a person is free to choose to scale a cliff but may fail because it is too hard. This means that they cannot do what they chose, but the limitation only arises because of their original choice to scale the cliff. The cliff is not the limitation; it is just a cliff. The limitation came about because the person decided to try to see what was at the top of the cliff, and this limitation vanishes if the person makes a different decision. Bad faith treats humans as nothing more than facticity, and does not understand that people can transcend this aspect of their nature.

Sartre wrote a play called *No Exit* about three people who had died and are sent to hell. They expected to be tortured but, instead, they are placed in a room together with no possibility of escape. Each character labels themselves or is subject to the labels of others. Their hell is their judgement of, and interaction with, each other. One man, Garcin, is tortured by being labelled by the others as a coward. He labels himself as courageous, although he never took the opportunity to make courageous choices in his life. He limited his options by blaming his environment and the actions of other people. He behaved as a *être-en-soi*, determined and fixed by circumstances, and was, therefore, living in bad faith. He had failed to make the choices that would have allowed him to be courageous, and so he did not life authentically.

> INEZ: … For thirty years you dreamt you were a hero, and
>   condoned a thousand petty lapses—because a hero, of
>   course, can do no wrong. An easy method, obviously. Then
>   a day came when you were up against it, the red light of
>   real danger—and you took the train to Mexico.
>
> GARCIN: I died too soon. I wasn't allowed time to—to do my deeds.
>
> INEZ: One always dies too soon—or too late. And yet one's whole
>   life is complete at that moment, with a line drawn neatly
>   under it, ready for the summing up. You are—your life,
>   and nothing else.
>
> Jean-Paul Sartre, *No Exit*

Sartre argued that rather than having a fixed nature that dictates our actions, a human being makes themselves. They are the sum of their actions, and their essence can only be known at the end of their life. If they believe there are rules or laws that restrict their freedom, they are making excuses and not living authentically. There are unlimited possibilities and, to avoid bad faith, one must make authentic choices.

Those who understand the reality of their situation, accept they are *être-pour-soi* and radically free to make any decision they choose, are struck by the huge responsibility that this brings. This means, Sartre pointed out, that we are responsible for making ethical decisions in 'abandonment'. This means there is no God to help us and so we are on our own. We also experience anguish in our decision making when we understand the weight of that responsibility.

The terror of realisation that we can only blame ourselves for our poor decisions is a horrible thing. Sartre likened it to a feeling of vertigo. He considered the analogy of a walker negotiating a narrow cliff path with a drop on one side. Loose rocks could cause the walker to stumble; the narrow, crumbling pathway could give way; and the facticity includes the knowledge that the walker is subject to gravity if something goes wrong. Yet, the real fear does not come from these practical difficulties. The real fear comes because the walker knows they could choose 'negative conduct' and not take care, or worse still, they could choose 'opposite conduct' and choose to throw themselves off. They know that they alone are responsible if their life comes to an end and the feeling is horrifying. It produces anguish because plummeting to their death is a real possibility, and the only thing standing in the way of it happening is the walker's free choices. This is what people feel when they accept their freedom to make any decision that they like.

A walker on a cliff path can experience vertigo when they look down, just as people can experience existential dread when they realise they are solely responsible for the choices they make and the life they live.

We may act without anguish in our day-to-day lives and perform acts without much reflection. But, at any moment, there is the possibility that we can act in any number of ways. The realisation that we are radically free, and the sense of responsibility that comes with that realisation, is what makes acts truly human. Sartre says that, ironically, we are determined to make free decisions. We can choose to take responsibility, or we can hide from that responsibility, but we cannot *not* choose. We are condemned to be free.

> *I am condemned to exist forever beyond my essence, beyond the causes and motives of my act. I am condemned to be free. This means that no limits to my freedom can be found except freedom itself or, if you prefer, that we are not free to cease being free.* **"**
>
> Jean-Paul Sartre, *Being and Nothingness: An Essay on Phenomenological Ontology*

Scientific concepts of Libertarianism: Angela Sirigu

Any scientific account of free will must focus on the empirical world, and so must involve the human brain as a physical object. There is substantial evidence from science that is used to support universal causation – the idea that everything, even the brain, is subject to external causes. However, cause and effect is not demonstrated by science to be universal. The work of quantum mechanics shows that Determinism may be false. Quantum mechanics is the investigation of matter on a very small scale, and shows unpredictability and randomness within nature at this level. This might demonstrate that material cause and effect does not apply universally, and therefore that it is possible that not everything is subject to causation.

As human beings, we experience the conscious sensation of making choices. This sensation gives us a sense of control over our actions, and is an important part of developing a sense of personal identity. Modern neuroscience is interested in explaining what this sensation is and how it occurs within a person's brain.

Experiments by Benjamin Libet in the 1980s monitored the brain activity associated with a decision to move a wrist, using electrodes placed on the subject's scalp. Libet discovered that unconscious brain activity could be detected before the participant made a conscious decision to move. These findings were damaging to the concept of free will and to Libertarianism, because movement was triggered by unconscious brain activity before the participant had knowingly willed it. They can be used to suggest that our apparent choice-making is just a link in a chain of cause and effect.

In 2003, Angela Sirigu led a team of neuroscientists who repeated and refined Libet's experiments to consider the origin of willed action. Their study of patients with damage in the parietal cortex (a region towards the back of the brain that is involved in decision making) showed that the sensation of deciding occurred at the same time as the movement itself. The damage meant there was no interval between the awareness of making a choice and performing the action. The team proposed that unconscious planning and awareness of a decision to act occur as part of a processing loop that involves the parietal cortex.

AO1 activity 3

The television series *The Good Place* is based upon Sartre's play *No Exit*. Pick any episode, or part of an episode, and identify the ways in which the characters act in bad faith. Remember: bad faith is about self-deception rather than lying to others.

In 2009 another team, which included Sirigu and Michel Desmurget, studied the part of the brain where intentions are formed to try to understand the connection between intention to act and awareness that an action has been performed. They performed experiments on seven patients who were undergoing brain surgery to remove tumours that were not in regions of the brain the team wanted to test. The patients were all awake during the surgery and could answer questions. In each case, different regions of the brain were stimulated with an electrical current and the results were observed.

When the premotor cortex (an area towards the front of the brain that sends messages directly to the spinal cord and plays a role in controlling behaviour) was stimulated, it resulted in real, complex, multi-joint movements, such as flexion and rotation of the hand, arm and wrist, or movements of the mouth. However, patients had made no prior decision to move and were unaware of what had happened, even denying that they had moved. The stronger the electrical current, the more pronounced or complex the movements, but the patients were never conscious of the movements.

Stimulation of the parietal cortex caused the patients to desire to move and, when the strength of the electrical current was increased, they actually told the researchers that they had moved even though they had not; no motor responses were detected by the team at all. Some patients reported that they wanted to move their mouths or roll their tongues, others reported having spoken and asked to be told what they had said, but no one had spoken and no one had moved. When no current was applied, the patients reported no intention to move. All the patients used terms such as 'will' or 'desire', without any prompting by the team.

> Without prompting by the examiner, all three patients spontaneously used terms such as 'will', 'desire', and 'wanting to', which convey the voluntary character of the movement intention and its attribution to an internal source, that is, located within the self.
>
> M. Desmurget, K. T. Reilly, N. Richard, A. Szathmari, C. Mottolese, A. Sirigu, 'Movement Intention After Parietal Cortex Stimulation in Humans'

These experiments tell us that there are two brain regions involved in making decisions to act, and both must work in concert for humans to create an intention to move, to actually move, and then check that the movement has been performed. It is speculated that the parietal cortex makes predictions about future movements and sends instructions to the premotor cortex; the premotor cortex controls the movement and then returns the outcome of the movement to the parietal cortex, and the parietal cortex confirms that movement has taken place. This tells us that the desire or will to perform an action originates in the parietal cortex and occurs before the movement itself. The awareness that a person has of performing an action also occurs in the parietal cortex, and appears to function independently of sensory evidence. This helps to account for the feeling people have that they are the authors of their own movements.

AO1 activity 4

Produce an information sheet on the libertarian interpretation of Sirigu's work. Include:

- a list of important terms and definitions
- a flow diagram to show the series of events that take place in the brain between intention and the completion of an action
- the libertarian interpretation of Sirigu's findings.

> *Our study suggests that motor intention and awareness are emerging consequences of increased parietal activity before movement execution. The subjective (and potentially illusory) feeling that we are executing a movement does not arise from movement itself, but it is generated by prior conscious intention and its predicted consequences.*
>
> M. Desmurget, K. T. Reilly, N. Richard, A. Szathmari, C. Mottolese, A. Sirigu, 'Movement Intention After Parietal Cortex Stimulation in Humans'

So how does this research help to support Libertarianism? Headlines at the time of the report's publication suggested that the site of free will had been discovered. Yet, it was not the goal of Sirigu's team to produce evidence in support of free will, and the report draws no conclusions on this issue. The study can, in reality, be interpreted in a range of different ways by contributors to the free will debate, depending upon which side of the argument they prefer, but since this research is based on an understanding of causes that operate on the brain, it seems likely that these findings are more useful for determinists than libertarians. However, some writers for popular science magazines have chosen to see this research as support for the concept of free will. The research has identified the area of the brain in which decision making occurs. This shows that the experience of decision making is a real brain event, not an illusion, and could therefore imply that an individual can be held morally responsible for their actions if both their parietal cortex and premotor cortex are functioning normally.

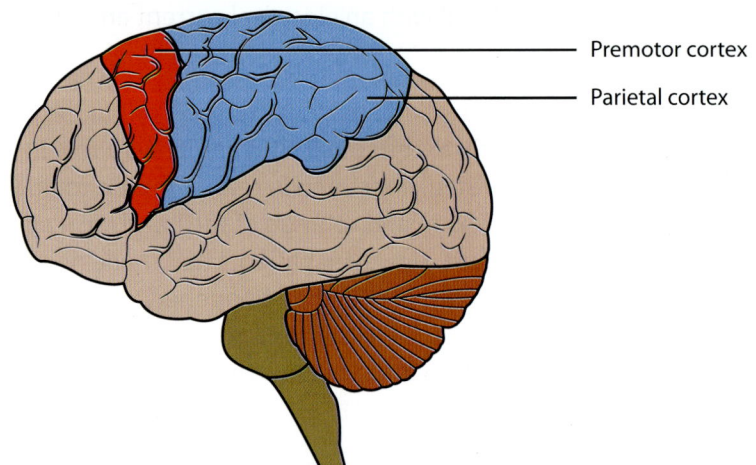

Premotor cortex

Parietal cortex

The parietal cortex and premotor cortex must work together for a movement to be intended, performed, and consciously experienced.

Psychological concepts of Libertarianism: Carl Rogers

To argue that human behaviour is free requires the belief that humans can make real choices for themselves from a range of possible options that can all be chosen. Psychological support for Libertarianism must challenge the findings of behaviourism, which explains all human behaviour in terms of external forces that control the apparent choices people make. However, psychology itself has developed out of a belief that psychological states are caused, and can be changed with treatment.

Carl Rogers was a twentieth-century humanistic psychologist. This means that he took a holistic approach to treating his patients, believing that each was a unique individual, and seeking to work with the whole person and not just their symptoms. As a practising psychologist, his writings are primarily about the effective treatment of patients rather than an extensive discussion of free will and Determinism. However, his writings acknowledged that the implications of his therapeutic approach were that an individual in good mental health could be considered to have complete free will.

Rogers rejected Freud's approach to psychotherapy, which focused on diagnosing a problem and applying fixed, pre-defined methodology to bring about a 'cure' within a 'patient'. This approach to psychotherapy involves a therapist–patient relationship whereby the patient is directed towards goals that have been chosen for them by their therapist. Rogers argued that this approach treated the client as an object rather than an individual.

> *The relationship is manufactured but limited. It confirms a person as an object – a basically mechanical, manipulatable object.*
>
> Carl Rogers, *On Becoming a Person: A Therapist's View of Psychotherapy*

Rogers took a more holistic approach to therapy, whereby the client sets personal goals for themselves, in keeping with their own personality, aided by a therapist who assists the process rather than controlling it. Rogers did not deny that behaviourism was possible and recognised the ability of scholars, such as Skinner, in developing operant conditioning to lead, control, and predict behaviour. However, just because it is possible to control a patient, does not mean it is desirable. Using behaviourist approaches produces a patient who has been moulded to conform to an image that the therapist determines. They disintegrate personality and control the individual.

> *I would remark that colossal rigidity, whether in dinosaurs or dictatorships, has a very poor record of evolutionary survival.*
>
> Carl Rogers, *On Becoming a Person: A Therapist's View of Psychotherapy*

Skinner had argued that these techniques could be used to create a utopian society, in which the whole population is controlled in every area of their lives so that they live in happiness. However, Rogers pointed out that these ideas were played out in Aldous Huxley's novel *Brave New World* and George Orwell's novel *1984*, and the outcome was horrifying: the governing powers use this kind of science to manipulate people to such an extent that even their thoughts are controlled. According to Rogers, controlling clients is undesirable because it turns people into robots, destroying the essential qualities that make a person who they are.

> *To me this kind of world would destroy the human person as I have come to know him in the deepest moments of psychotherapy. In such moments I am in a relationship with a person who is spontaneous, who is responsibly free, that is, aware of this freedom to choose who he will be, and aware also of the consequences of his choice.*
>
> Carl Rogers, *On Becoming a Person: A Therapist's View of Psychotherapy*

Rogers pointed out that the goal of controlling human behaviour, while possible, is a subjective preference. There is no reason why a different subjective preference could not be selected, and then the scientific method successfully applied to achieve it. Rogers gives the example of education. If someone thinks that the primary value of education is to achieve academic skills, then science can explore how best to realise this goal and then put it into practice. If someone else believes that the goal of education is problem solving, citizenship or something else, then science can explore these goals instead. However, the goals themselves are subjectively valued, and science is not equipped to judge which goal has the highest value or decide on the value of new goals.

Rogers valued the individual person as unique and free. He used the scientific method to record and analyse his therapy sessions to measure their effectiveness in enabling clients to develop their own unique potential in a continually changing world, to live as **fully functioning people** with healthy personalities and fulfilling, 'good' lives. He compared results with the more theory-laden therapist–patient models of psychotherapy and concluded that his approach – which he called Client-Centred Therapy – was successful in allowing humans to make free, unpredictable decisions. This is in contrast to Skinner who had argued that with the right conditioning, behaviour was utterly predictable.

Rogers developed a form of therapy in which the individual was self-directing. The process involved treating each person as an individual, listening to their feelings and emotions, and reflecting these back to the client rather than directing them to behave in a particular way.

In Rogers' view, each person has an image of their **ideal self**. This is the person who, in their minds, they would like to be. They also have an image of their **actual self**. This is who they see themselves to be in the present moment, based upon their previous life experiences. A person whose two ideas of self coincide is in a state of **congruence**. However, many people struggle to achieve this state of harmony, because their understanding of who they are and who they would like to be is quite different. People who are incongruent become constrained, conflicted, and incapable of fulfilling their true potential.

According to Rogers, a person gets their ideas about themselves from their childhood experiences and the feedback they receive from others. When a person receives **unconditional positive regard** from others, when they are accepted and loved for who they are no matter what they do, they find it easier to achieve congruence. These people feel free to make their own choices because they are not worried that people will stop loving them if they make a mistake. Someone who does not receive unconditional positive regard has limited freedom to make their own choices, because they are worried about what people think of them.

Humans, Rogers argued, have an in-built tendency to want to **self-actualise**. They are motivated to develop their individual potential to become their own ideal selves. People who are in a state of congruence are capable of self-actualisation because they can set their own goals, accept their own feelings, and freely choose the behaviour that will be the most satisfying to them. When a person is self-actualised, they are open to new experiences even if they are sometimes negative, they live in the moment and can adapt, and they trust their own abilities rather than complying with a rigid code of conduct imposed on them.

Key terms

fully functioning person: a person with a healthy personality who lives a fulfilling 'good' life

ideal self: the person that an individual wishes they were

actual self: the person that an individual sees themselves as being in reality, based upon their previous life experiences

congruence: the state in which a person's ideal self and actual self are very similar

unconditional positive regard: acceptance and support no matter what a person does

self-actualise: the realisation of a person's individual potential

Rogers said that to help a client self-actualise, a therapist must:

- be congruent and attentive to the client with no emotional distance
- communicate unconditional positive regard for the client's uniqueness
- express genuine empathy for the client, imaging what it is like to be in their position.

If a therapist does these three things, the consequences are predictable in the sense that we know that the client will become more self-directing, less rigid, more open to their own senses, and more congruent. However, the exact decisions and actions of the individual client are unpredictable because Client-Centred Therapy results in more freedom, more self-direction, and flexible adaptiveness. With Client-Centred Therapy, the scientific method is used to achieve the goal of free will. None of this appears to mean that a person's decisions become random or chaotic (and therefore beyond human responsibility). Instead, the fully functioning person orders their responses in a creative way towards the achievement of their own values and purpose.

Some thinkers point out that Rogers is a compatibilist rather than a libertarian because he does not deny the truth of Determinism. The application of scientific principles within the field of psychology makes cause and effect undeniable. However, Rogers considers it an equally important truth that a fully functioning person can make spontaneous and voluntary choices that are free from psychological or emotional constraints.

Rogers argued that conditioning – the dystopian consequences of which can be seen in novels such as Huxley's Brave New World *– destroys the essence of a human being.*

> *We will recognise that behaviour, when examined scientifically, is surely best understood as determined by prior causation. This is the great fact of science. But responsible personal choice, which is the most essential element in being a person … is an equally prominent fact in our lives. We will have to live with the realisation that to deny the reality of the experience of responsible personal choice is as stultifying, as closed-minded, as to deny the possibility of a behavioural science.*
>
> Carl Rogers, *On Becoming a Person: A Therapist's View of Psychotherapy*

The implications of Libertarianism and free will

The implications of Libertarianism on moral responsibility

Libertarian views about the nature of free will have implications for moral responsibility. For a human being to be morally responsible for their actions, they must be able to act as they choose and have been able to act differently if they had wanted to. Libertarianism states that a person's actions are within their control and, consequently, the responsibility for those actions lies with them alone.

A.J. Ayer pointed out that uncaused actions are of no value when it comes to moral responsibility. An action that is uncaused is random, chaotic, and has little or no connection with the moral agent who is performing the action. Therefore, Ayer, a soft determinist rather than a libertarian, argues that Libertarianism does not leave room for moral responsibility. The research by Sirigu and her team is of little help in resolving the question of moral responsibility, because it tells us only that the area of the brain in which decisions are made has been identified. Sirigu's research implies that choice making is caused by brain events but it does not indicate whether humans have any freedom in their choices, and cannot indicate whether an agent has moral responsibility.

Sartre and Rogers do not deny that cause and effect operate upon a person, but Sartre believed that human beings are inherently responsible for their actions because individuals create themselves through their choices. Each choice that a person makes causes them to shape their character and their sense of morality. There is no such thing, for Sartre, as an external guiding force or an objective moral standard, and so moral responsibility lies solely with the moral agent as the cause of their own personality. Rogers embraced the knowledge that we are subject to causation, but argued that a self-actualised person can make free decisions. While the ability to act in a certain way is caused, the specifics of an individual action can be called free because they are unpredictable and chosen by the moral agent. This means that the moral agent is morally responsible for their actions.

For both Sartre and Rogers, freedom to act is more than just a lack of constraint. A person who has been subjected to conditioning may still act as they choose, but their ability to choose is constrained by outside forces. This means that they cannot be held morally responsible for the choices that they make. Moral agents must be capable of acting independently of outside forces to have moral responsibility. Sartre can accept that this is possible for the moral agent who makes themselves, since they come into the world with no fixed essence or nature and then create themselves through their own free choices. The causes that operate upon them are of their own making.

Moral responsibility requires that a moral agent could have acted in a different way than they did. Both Sartre and Rogers argue that this is possible. To deny it is, for Sartre, to act in bad faith. The determinist attempts to escape moral responsibility by denying that other options were available to them, but they are lying to themselves to escape the dread that comes with taking responsibility for their actions. Sartre claimed that taking moral responsibility is a frightening prospect because it means a moral agent has no one to blame but themselves. Rogers was not an existentialist like Sartre. He did not deny the power of external causes that operate upon a person. However, he believed that a moral agent can act without fear with freedom and creativity. This moral responsibility is the very definition of a fully functioning person.

The worth of human ideas of rightness, wrongness, and moral value

Moral responsibility implies that there are some actions that are right or wrong, or good or bad. This implies that one should act in a certain way. Libertarians can argue that ideas of right and wrong are worthwhile because they act as a guide to help us understand the value of a person or their choices. Alternatively, libertarians might describe them as subjective measures of behaviour, which are valuable if they help a person make decisions that give them the best chance of living a fulfilling life.

Sartre dismissed the idea of a divine law maker who can guide people with their life choices. For him, the only morality is the morality that an individual devises for themselves as an *être-pour-soi* (a being-for-itself). This has led to the accusation that Sartre's philosophy results in an abandonment of moral values. However, Sartre argued that when we choose one action over another, we choose as if we are defining the whole of humanity. This is because my freedom to choose depends upon reciprocal freedom: I must allow others to make free choices so that they allow me to make free choices. Therefore, Sartre rejects behaviour that deliberately exploits or oppresses others. Authenticity involves freedom for everyone, and so there can never be an authentic oppressor. The ideas of right and wrong that moral agents create for themselves are worthwhile to the people who create them, helping them to construct their own essence, but the only use they have in providing a universal understanding of how a person ought to behave is in their acceptance of freedom for everyone to create themselves.

As a humanistic psychologist, Rogers saw the application of fixed, theory-based approaches to the client–therapist relationship as unhelpful. Rogers did not focus on ethical philosophy or morality in his writings, but his rejection of theory-based approaches to treatment could be used by a libertarian to argue that a fixed system of morality is worthless if it leads to poor mental health. The therapist, according to Rogers, must have unconditional positive regard for their client. It is essential that the client feels understood and accepted without judgement for the client to have free will and to self-actualise. Rogers was not an existentialist, so he did not claim that we make ourselves from scratch, but he saw a fully functioning person as someone who is creative and prepared to take risks. A libertarian might then infer that a person is free to select moral principles that best fit their view of themselves as they work towards congruence. Rogers argued that science was unable to comment on the worth of things like morality, since the scientific method is not concerned with values; values are imposed upon it from the outside.

The value in blaming moral agents for immoral acts

Praise and blame are responses to moral actions. Praise is given to those who perform good or right actions; blame is given to those who perform bad or wrong actions. Praise implies reward; blame implies punishment. But is there any value in praise or blame if human beings are free to do what they choose? Praise and blame are methods of controlling human action. If human actions are determined by external causes, it may be useful to blame someone who performs an undesirable action because it may prevent them acting in a similar way in the future, or it may restore balance if the person's actions have brought about unfairness.

It is not possible for science to determine the value of blame unless science is given a subjective measure against which it can weigh blame. If the value of blame is that it can control people's behaviour, science can and does study the extent to which blame and punishment change the behaviour of a subject. Sirigu and her team were not involved in a study like this, and her research has raised no conclusions or arguments concerning this issue. Ayer argued that moral agents can only be praised or blamed if they are the cause of their own actions, whereas an uncaused action is random and chaotic, so blame cannot have any effect.

In regard to his therapeutic relationships with clients, Rogers saw no value in blaming the moral agent for the actions they performed. The relationship between the client and the therapist should be one that is emotionally present, positive, and empathetic. This means that judgement of a client's mistakes or choices could be damaging to their progress as they work towards self-actualisation. While Rogers did not discuss the moral implications of praise or blame, a libertarian might observe that developing productive relationships with other moral agents might require the same absence of judgement, to ensure that individuals are free to be creative in their moral lives and make positive decisions that best reflect their ideal self.

For Sartre, while humans create their own essence, they do so in relation to other people, and so they may experience praise or blame. In Sartre's play *No Exit*, the characters have no mirrors. They can only see or understand themselves through the eyes of the other characters and, in doing so, they feel shame. Some might argue that when a person does something that causes them to feel shame, the punishment is having to live with that shame. There is no need to add blame from other people. If the person feels no shame, then no amount of blame is going to alter how the person feels about what they have done and what they do in the future. In other words, the only person who can administer meaningful blame is the moral agent themselves.

The usefulness of normative ethics

A normative approach to ethics is concerned with formulating actual rules for human behaviour. Normative ethical theories do not necessarily imply that a person is caused, compelled, or restricted in any way, because for a person to be morally responsible for their actions, they must be able to choose to act in accordance with a system of values or to act against them. A normative ethical system acts, therefore, as a benchmark against which moral actions can be measured, as moral agents freely choose to obey or ignore the rules. However, a normative ethical system can be restrictive if it includes an authority or punishments that prevent moral agents from making a free choice.

For Sartre, rigid obedience to a normative ethical system could be an example of bad faith. If a person obeys the rules in such a way that they convince themselves that they have no other choice, then they are lying to themselves. Just as the waiter in Sartre's analogy behaves as though he is an object, merely a waiter and nothing else, a moral agent who obeys a rigid normative ethical system as though they are merely a vessel for obedience acts in bad faith, and denies their own nature as an *être-pour-soi*.

Sartre argued that there is no divine source of normative ethics, and so we make our moral choices on our own and have sole responsibility for them. There is, therefore, no objective value in any single normative ethical system. People should consider themselves free in the moral choices that they make. There is subjective value in these self-created choices, and it is up to us to take responsibility for the choices that we make. However, Sartre did not reject normative ethics entirely. He believed that we should act as though our moral choices are for the whole of humanity because our behaviour does impact upon other people, but he rejected the idea that there was a set of inflexible moral commandments that can govern every situation.

As Rogers did not discuss the value of normative systems of ethics, it is not possible to know what he thought of them. However, since he dismissed any theory-laden system of therapy as unhelpful to a client's self-actualisation and potentially harmful to their self-image, a libertarian could argue that normative ethical systems are unhelpful for free moral agents who are faced with unique moral situations. Rogers argued that an individual should be able to make their choices in a way that is consistent with their ideal selves, and it therefore seems unlikely that he would have seen much value in a rigid, restrictive ethical system.

The implications of free will on religious belief

The teachings of Pelagius and Arminius on predestination are intrinsically linked with, and arise from, their beliefs about the nature of God and God's relationship with humanity. They developed their ideas because they objected to the implications for God's nature arising from the Augustinian and Calvinist views of predestination. For teaching about free will to be acceptable within Christianity, it must not compromise the belief that God is omnipotent, omnibenevolent, and omniscient, or the doctrine of Christ's salvation.

The link between God and evil

It is a fundamental Christian belief that God is good. Therefore, the commands that God gives are good, and God is utterly without sin. A concern for scholars like Pelagius and Arminius was that the doctrine of predestination appears to make God the author of sin and evil. God created

Sartre's play, No Exit, contained the famous line 'Hell is other people.' He said that when we see ourselves as others see us, that is when we feel shame.

AO1 activity 6

Imagine you have been given an exam question that asks you to give details of the implications of Libertarianism on moral responsibility.

Create a chart with three columns and label as follows:

1. Human ideas of right and wrong
2. Praise and blame
3. Normative ethics

Summarise in each column three ideas that draw on libertarian scholars to explain the possible significance of believing that human beings have free will.

the world *ex nihilo* and is, therefore, responsible for everything that exists in the world. Yet, evil exists in the world, both in nature and in human actions. Furthermore, if God has predestined all human actions, then one could conclude that God is responsible for the sins of Adam and for each individual sin committed by humanity. Both Pelagius and Arminius sought to avoid holding God responsible for evil and sin in this way.

Pelagius argued that God created everything in a perfect state, but that Adam, in the beginning, needed to eat from the tree of knowledge to gain free will. Adam's sin was not, as a result, a wholly terrible thing. God, who is omniscient, gave Adam a choice. By choosing to eat the forbidden fruit – something God knew Adam would do – Adam was granted the opportunity to mature into God's image. Adam would not have had this opportunity had sin been impossible. Similarly, when humans are born, they are sinless and they can choose freely whether to sin or to do their duty, and God knows which choice they will make. Pelagius' approach spares God the responsibility for creating evil. God created only good; it is humans who are responsible for evil actions that go against God's law. God allows sin and evil to remain in the world because it is the rejection of sin and evil that enables humans to grow to become perfect, in God's image.

> 'Sin is not a substance but a wicked act. And because it is not natural, therefore the law was given against it, and because it proceeds from the liberty of our will.' **99**
>
> Pelagius, as quoted in Augustine, *On Nature and Grace*

The difficulty with Pelagius' view is that, although he believed in God's grace, when human beings take the burden of responsibility for the existence of evil, there is less dependency upon God. It is vital to Christian doctrine that God has no equal. No being can be more powerful than God, God's will cannot be overturned, and humans are fundamentally dependent upon God for their existence. Yet, if humanity has free will, then it seems as though they can make decisions over which God has no control. If humans can choose evil, they can resist God's will. If they can choose to be good, then there is no need for Christ's salvation on the cross.

Arminius solved this problem to some extent. He was also concerned that if predestination is true, then God is responsible for creating sin and evil. God would have directly created some souls for the pleasure of reprobating them and would, therefore, have caused the sinfulness that is evident in the whole of creation. God would have not only made it impossible for these souls to do good, but would have actively brought about their sinful actions. This seems wholly inconsistent with God's goodness, and was abhorrent to Arminius.

Arminius believed, therefore, that humans are responsible for their own evil choices, but God provides everyone with everything they need to do good. Humanity cannot do good without God's prevenient grace and subsequent grace, but they can resist. God provides them with all they need, and they are free to cooperate with or to resist God. Aminius sought to ensure that evil was the responsibility of humans, but that humans must look to God for good.

The implications for God's omnipotence and omnibenevolence

Arminius' approach to predestination was seen, by his opponents, as challenging the sovereignty of God. Arminius suggested that humans can resist God, and this implies that events that are outside God's will can occur, something which is unacceptable in Christian doctrine. However, Arminius maintained that God's power is limited by God's own nature. God is the highest good and can only act in accordance with God's good nature; God cannot, therefore, command evil. It is impossible for God to will that some people are damned and incapable of goodness. Yet, God's power is not lacking; God permits sin through divine concurrence without ever actually approving of it.

Arminius' understanding of prevenient grace and subsequent grace means that the Holy Spirit is required for a person to be capable of choosing good, maintaining God's omnipotence in accordance with scripture and tradition. Yet, God does not force humans to perform any action against their will, and they are free to resist this gift. The implication is that God's will can be thwarted. God may will a person to be saved, but they may not share that desire, and so God's plan for them will not come to fruition. This appears to imply that God is not omnipotent because God cannot override the will of a human being. Calvinists objected to the idea that God's grace was resistible, because God has power over all creation and there is, therefore, nothing that can resist the will of God. To allow human beings control over their own destiny is, the Calvinists argued, like putting humans on an equal footing with God.

Arminius aimed to solve this difficulty by treating predestination as related more to God's omniscience than his omnipotence. God's middle knowledge means that God knows the full range of possible events, and predestines some for election or reprobation based on what God knows they will freely choose. This avoids the possibility that someone can act outside of God's providence (God's attentive care and guidance of the world) because God provides them with everything they need to help them have faith in their own unique situation. Yet, God is not responsible for evil, since humans are responsible for their own free choices; they are not compelled or caused to act in a particular way. Arminius' opponents were not, however, satisfied and thought he was in error. They continued to argue that if humanity can resist the will of God, God's omnipotence over the whole of creation is damaged.

This same error is certainly seen in the work of Pelagius. While Pelagius was able to maintain God's goodness by giving humanity responsibility for their evil choices and allowing infants to be born without the stain of original sin, there seemed to be little room for the salvation of Christ if humanity could save themselves through their good deeds. Augustine felt this was not in

Synoptic link

Link to *Chapter 1: Ethical though (part one)*. Remind yourself of the principles of Divine Command Theory and the Euthyphro dilemma. Are God's commands good just because they are God's? If so, this would allow God to condemn people regardless of their behaviour and that command would be good.

accordance with scripture, which emphasises the importance of faith for salvation. The gospels tell humanity to repent and have faith in order to be forgiven for their sins, so good works are insufficient for salvation.
In addition, God's sovereignty is limited if salvation seems to be achievable without God.

In Pelagius' defence, he felt that God's grace is still essential if humans are to make the right choices. He argued that through the gift of grace and the guidance of scripture, humans can freely make rational moral decisions, and are forgiven by God when they make mistakes. This approach, Pelagius believed, maintained human dependence upon God and God's goodness.

The use of prayer

Prayer is central to Christianity, taught and practised by Jesus and others throughout the Bible. It is not, however, unique to Christianity; it is embraced by most world religions. Pelagius argued that to ensure salvation, a human must find out God's will. God's will can be found in scripture by looking at the teaching and example of Jesus. Praying for guidance when faced with a complex moral choice also helps a believer to understand God's will for them in their unique situation so that they know what to do. It also helps to provide them with the strength required to keep to a difficult path when that is what God's will requires.

> *In order to love and please God, we must find out what he wants … we can talk to God, asking him to guide our thoughts. We can be sure that, if we consider every choice carefully, and if we seek divine guidance, our decisions will please God.*
>
> Pelagius, 'Letter of Pelagius to Demetrias, AD 385'

Arminius pointed out that although Calvin encouraged the Elect and Reprobates to pray, it is futile if we are predestined for salvation or damnation regardless of anything we do in this life. This is also true of any commands for moral behaviour and of the work and sermons of ministers. There is little motivation for anyone to spend their time trying to develop a relationship with God if it will make no difference to their life after death.

> *It [the Calvinist teaching on predestination] extinguishes the zeal for prayer, which yet is an efficacious means instituted by God for asking and obtaining all kinds of blessings from him, but principally, the great one of salvation.*
>
> Jacobus Arminius, 'A Declaration of the Sentiments of James Arminius'

Prayer is considered useful for petition, thanksgiving, praise, and confession. However, prayer as a way of petitioning God, asking God to respond to human will, is problematic because it requires God's divine will to change to fall in line with human will. If the Augustinian or Calvinistic understanding of predestination is applied, it is difficult to see how prayer can be considered as a way to influence God, since human destiny has already been decided in accordance with divine will. However, if God has middle knowledge, as Arminius taught, then God knows in advance what an

Synoptic link

Link to *A Level Religious Studies for Eduqas: Philosophy of Religion, Chapter 5: Religious experience (part one)*. Look at religious believers' experience of prayer. How might prayer be useful if humans are free to accept or reject God's salvation for themselves?

individual will pray and has already decided whether or not to respond to the petition. Instead of petition to affect God's will, prayer may be used to bring a believer's will in alignment with God, and so it has a clear purpose. According to Arminius, prevenient grace and subsequent grace enable the Holy Spirit to help people to cooperate with God through prayer and to receive salvation.

The existence of miracles

The idea of God intervening in the world if humanity has free will is a difficult one. The events of creation and Christ's salvation are considered miraculous to Christians, and the purpose of these miracles was to first establish and then repair God's relationship with humanity. However, one can argue that God miraculously interfering in the natural world risks interfering with human free will. If Pelagius or Arminius are correct, then salvation requires human beings to respond to God with faith, even though they are uncertain whether they will be saved or damned. But, if God performs miracles, people no longer need faith. God becomes a self-evident truth and our free will to believe or not to believe in God is removed. Yet Arminius clearly placed scripture at the heart of his theology, making belief in miracles an essential part of the Christian faith.

> *To deny the existence of those great and admirable miracles which are related to have really happened, when they also have the testimony of both Jews and gentiles, who were the enemies of the true doctrine, is an evident token of bare-faced impudence and execrable stupidity.* **"**
>
> Jacobus Arminius, *The Works of James Arminius, Volume 1*

Arminius believed that miracles confirm Christ's doctrine and demonstrate God's authority. For Arminius, miracles do not detract from our ability to freely decide whether to have faith in God or not. Instead, they support Christian doctrine and teaching, and encourage a person to make a decision of faith.

Christ's death on the cross and subsequent resurrection was a miracle performed by God to reconcile God and humanity.

Synoptic link

Link to *A Level Religious Studies for Eduqas: Philosophy of Religion*, Chapter 6: Religious experience (part two). Look at the different ways different scholars have defined miracles, and consider the reasons why religious believers might accept that miracles occur. Do any of these reasons require a suspension of human free will?

AO1 activity 7

Write the following headings onto the top of some index cards:

- The link between God and evil
- The implications for God's omnipotence and omnibenevolence
- The use of prayer
- The existence of miracles.

On the reverse side of each card, divine it in half down the centre and summarise each point from the text that maintains a Christian understanding of God on one side, and the points that show problems for a Christian understanding of God on the other side.

This section of the chapter will enhance your ability to **analyse** and **evaluate** the topic and help you develop your AO2 skills. For each question, think about the different positions you might take, and decide which you find most persuasive and why. It is not enough to memorise a list of 'for and against' points; you need to develop an argument.

How convincing are religious views on free will?

This question focuses upon the beliefs of those who are religious. It expects you to consider whether or not religious ideas about free will are logical, persuasive, or morally acceptable. You might consider whether or not they are convincing to the non-believer, but it is probably more productive to consider whether or not they are convincing to a religious believer. The scholars we have studied are Christian, but they could easily be related to another religion you have studied.

The view that religious views on free will are convincing

Christians believe that God is all-loving, and it is more convincing to argue that a loving God has given humanity the gift of free will. It is more loving for God to allow humans to decide for themselves whether or not they are saved, by choosing whether or not to have faith in God and obey God's commands, than it is to predestine people to salvation or damnation regardless of what they do. It is unreasonable to believe that a loving God would coerce someone into a relationship with God. An atheist, who not only does not believe in God but also does not want fellowship with any god, has made a choice that they do not want eternal life in heaven after death. A loving God would respect such a choice, and not force someone into submission against their will.

Justice requires fair punishment or reward in the afterlife for the life lived on Earth. It does not make sense that a faithful believer could be eternally damned when they have worked to be in fellowship with God, or that a person who has turned away from God could be one of the Elect. Calvin did suggest that a person without faith would never be one of the Elect because God's grace is irresistible. However, Calvin's predestination is unjust because it means that no one is deserving of punishment or reward, since either their actions have no real consequences, or they could not be the author of their own behaviour.

Free will is a fundamental belief, teaching, and assumption that underpins the whole of traditional Christian thought. The doctrine of the fall is dependent upon the teaching that humans were created as free beings who chose to disobey God. The practices of evangelism and preaching sermons are dependent upon the idea that human beings are free to decide to believe in God, and that it is in their best interests to do so.

The view that religious views on free will are not convincing

Roger Haight argues that Pelagius' emphasis on humanity's freedom to obey or reject God's law is unconvincing, because it appears to make God a tyrant who will condemn people to eternal damnation if they make a mistake and choose not to obey God's law. Pelagius' asceticism demanded nothing less than perfection, and forced religious believers to follow a rigid legalism that may be unrealistic or inhumane on the basis that it demands a standard of moral perfection that could drastically reduce a person's quality of life.

Haight goes on to suggest that Pelagianism risks becoming elitist. Pelagius wanted everyone to live ascetic lives, like monks or nuns, and this would make the Christian Church an exclusive society that puts up barriers between the Elect, who are living this perfect lifestyle, and everyone else. This is not consistent with the narrative of the gospels. Jesus' preaching appealed directly to the marginalised and the weak. It directly challenged those who judged others by their ability to follow intricate moral laws, and instead valued those who had faith as they went about their different and difficult lives.

The reward or punishment of eternal salvation or damnation are unjust and therefore unconvincing because they are disproportionate to the finite lives that people have lived on Earth. This seems to be an overreaction to the limited actions of human beings. God is supposed to be a supremely just being, but this cannot be the case if God punishes the unbeliever for eternity for freely choosing not to have faith. This is a kind of deception that appears to offer a free choice and yet then ultimately forbids one of the options.

The view that religious views on free will are partially convincing

The idea that God has given humanity free will is partially convincing because while it absolves God of moral responsibility for creating evil, it fails to answer questions about why God would allow evil to exist. It seems unacceptable to argue that evil gives humans the ability to make genuinely free choices because of the unfair way in which suffering is distributed. People who are born into difficult circumstances can experience significantly more suffering than others, and can sometimes find themselves in circumstances where 'good' choices are much more challenging to make. It does not seem reasonable to argue that those who experience evil or suffering are somehow 'more free' than those who are comfortable, any more than it is reasonable to argue that suffering is in any way a just consequence of human sin.

Haight points out that Pelagius' understanding of free will must be appreciated in the context of the time in which he lived. Pelagius was preaching in Rome in the early-fourth and late-fifth centuries, to aristocrats who had been influenced by pagan morality. Converting to Christianity was seen as fashionable or a convenient way to make social progress, and Pelagius was trying to ensure his listeners understood that Christianity required them to change their lifestyles. Therefore, while Pelagius' understanding of free will might have been convincing to the people he was preaching to, it is not convincing for people today.

The idea that infants are sinful and condemned to eternal damnation unless they are baptised appears to be insulting to God. Pelagius objected to the idea that new-born babies who die are condemned to hell, because it is inconsistent with a God of love and justice. Many people today also object on similar grounds. It is, therefore, more attractive to accept that free human choices dictate who is saved and who is damned at the end of their lives. However, a child who dies at a young age has not had the chance to freely do anything worthy of God's election or damnation either. Therefore, the view of free will does not satisfactorily account for God's judgement of them.

To what extent does an individual have free choice?

This question asks you to consider whether, when a moral agent makes a decision, they can be considered to have made a choice that is fully their own and not fixed by external causes over which they have no control. You may want to draw on ideas from Chapter 7 in a response to this question. You may also feel it is not simply a case of deciding whether or not we are free, and that there is no way it is possible to know the answer to the question.

The view that an individual has complete free choice

A significant libertarian argument is based upon simple intuition. Humans experience the sensation of choice making. We feel free. We experience deliberating over moral questions and weighing up our reasons for acting. We experience indecision, we reason, and we ask for advice when we are unsure. Humans also experience being coerced or restricted, and the sensation of making a free choice is quite different from the experience of acting when there is only one option available to us. Therefore, it is reasonable to argue that humans have complete free choice.

Roderick Chisholm argued that humans have contra-causal freedom. This is the ability to choose a different course of action from the one that is chosen. For individuals to have free choice, human actions cannot be caused by external events in the same way as the rest of the physical world. However, we cannot argue that human actions are uncaused, because

AO2 activity 1

Make a list of statements about whether religious views on free will are convincing, just as you might find in an AO2 question. Try to create as many variations as possible.

Set a timer for five minutes, choose one of your statements at random, and make a list of as many points as you can that you could raise in a response.

people have no control over random events. Instead, we must accept that a free action is caused by the person doing the action. This is called agent causation, and it allows for a moral agent to have freely chosen a different course of action if they had wanted to.

When people make moral decisions, they reason; they think about alternative options and choose one over another for specific reasons. The word 'reason' can be used in different ways, and we should not conflate 'reason' as referring to this logical thinking process, with 'reason' as referring to the fixed cause of an event. A characteristic of an ethical action is that it has been thought through and chosen for a reason, but this does not mean that it is a fixed, unalterable action. To give the reasoning behind a decision implies that the person acted for a purpose and would have chosen differently if they had felt that their purpose would have been achieved more effectively by doing so. This is the sign of a free action.

The view that an individual has no free choice

The feeling of being free is a weak argument for the existence of free will. Arthur Schopenhauer joked that appealing to the sensation of choice making is like a puddle of water exclaiming that it can make waves or rush down a hill but is choosing, currently, to sit still in a pond. The experience of free will is illusory and offers no convincing evidence for real free will.

The libertarian argument that humans can have contra-causal freedom is unconvincing. It requires us to accept that there is a part of a moral agent that is not subject to empirical forces, which transcends the physical world, such as a soul or a mind. If the libertarian denies this, they are left trying to justify how a physical being is exempt from physical laws. If an event takes place inside a moral agent that causes an act, it is the same as any other event, and brings us back to the chain of cause and effect that is Determinism.

Harry Frankfurt distinguishes between free actions and free will. Free actions involve doing what one wants to do, but free will involves being able to will what one wills (to choose your own desires). He argues that the will we have is either a direct result of causality or is a result of chance and is, therefore, outside of our control. Galen Strawson agrees that this understanding of free will is illogical. To will what we will would require us to pre-exist ourselves, so that we can determine our own personality and, therefore, our own will. This would ultimately lead to an infinite regress of 'self' that is illogical.

The view that it is impossible to know if an individual has free choice

The scientific experiments on the phenomenon of human decision making involve such trivial decisions that they do not tell us if people have the free will needed to make moral decisions. People do not reason before they decide to tap a button or raise an arm, but people do go through a reasoning process before they decide to steal or give to charity.

In addition, the experiments seem to involve the patient being commanded to demonstrate free will, which is rather paradoxical. Free will, by definition, cannot be controlled by anyone other than the moral agent, and so scientists cannot analyse it.

Anthony Flew argued that libertarians tend to resort to the principle of indeterminacy (Heisenberg's uncertainty principle) in quantum mechanics in a kind of 'desperate clutching' challenge to Determinism. The principle states that the speed and position of a particle cannot be known with complete accuracy, and libertarians hope that this will help to prove, or give weight to, their argument that not all effects are caused. Yet, it tells us nothing about moral responsibility.

T.H. Huxley argued that we must be cautious not to confuse descriptive laws of nature with prescriptive laws that tell us what to do. A law of nature is statistical in that it describes events as they usually take place. For example, an unsupported stone usually falls to the ground. However, this law does not command that an unsupported stone must fall to the ground. It is this confusion that makes us think that science demonstrates that all events are necessary ones, but neither free will nor necessity are demonstrated in scientific investigation. Science can only tell us what has occurred in the past and give suggestions about what we can expect in the future. It cannot tell us whether we are free or determined.

To what extent do concepts of Libertarianism inevitably lead people to accept Libertarianism?

This question requires you to consider whether the libertarian arguments that we have considered are so convincing that, once you have heard them, you cannot avoid accepting that humans have free will. There is an interesting paradox in the question, in the sense that it implies that we have no choice but to accept that we have a choice!

The view that concepts of Libertarianism make acceptance of free will inevitable

Immanuel Kant argued that philosophical reason demonstrates that we must be free. Practical reason shows us that moral laws that we have a duty to obey exist. Moral laws only make any sense if we are free to choose to obey them. It makes no sense for us to have a duty to do something that we have no choice but to do. Therefore, freedom is an essential assumption based on the rational evidence of moral duty.

Sartre's claim that we make ourselves through our own conscious choices is attractive because it reflects the experience of the individual, who feels that they make free choices, and it gives a person positive ownership over their actions. Although Sartre's liberty is rather gloomy in its proclamation that we are 'condemned to be free', he means that, ultimately, the only thing we have no option but to accept is our freedom to choose. Therefore, we must accept that we are free, and begin to take responsibility for that freedom.

Rogers' psychological approach to the issue of free will means that clients of Client-Centred Therapy practitioners will inevitably accept their freedom to make choices that are consistent with their own personalities. By achieving a congruent state, they will be released from the mental struggles that come from a poor self-image and an inability to self-actualise. The client whose therapist empathises with and positively supports them through Client-Centred Therapy has been determined by this process to inevitably accept their freedom.

The view that concepts of Libertarianism make acceptance of free will unlikely

Rogers did not give sufficient evidence for human free will. He presented an explanation of human free will that involves an acceptance that while human beings are subject to causality, they can be considered free under the right circumstances because their behaviour can be unpredictable and spontaneous. However, it is not enough to say that a person's behaviour is free because we have not conditioned it ourselves or traced backwards in time to work out how it was conditioned. Not knowing the causes that lead to a specific action does not mean it is not determined or theoretically predictable.

Paul-Henri Thiry d'Holbach argued that we think we are free because we consent to what we are, in reality, caused to do. He gave the example of a swimmer who is swept along in the current of a river but thinks he is free because sometimes he chooses to glide with the stream that carries him along. Holbach claimed that this belief that our mental state has power over the course of our lives is illusory. This means that the libertarian belief that the experience of choosing demonstrates free will is founded on weak evidence; it may be mistaken.

There is nothing in science that brings us to inevitably accept a libertarian position. While quantum mechanics shows that not all things are caused, the level at which it operates is so small that it has very little meaning when applied to human action. Furthermore, the work of Sirigu and other neuroscientists does not indicate very much about the reality of free will. If anything, it demonstrates that much of our decision making is actually outside our conscious control. The headlines, when the 2009 study was released, made too strong a connection between free will and the brain events that Sirigu's team identified. In fact, the study builds on the earlier work of Libet, and provides much stronger scientific evidence to suggest that conscious choices are really caused by external or unconscious forces.

The view that concepts of Libertarianism make acceptance of free will possible

Roger Scruton argued that the idea that all future human actions are the unstoppable consequences of factors beyond human control, stretching back to the beginning of time, is almost certainly false. Scruton argued that the laws of the universe are statistical, and explain the likelihood of certain events given the existence of certain causes, but they do not dictate the future in such a way that makes any other course of event completely impossible or inevitable. Elizabeth Anscombe developed this argument with an analogy. She asked us to imagine that a lump of radioactive matter is placed next to a Geiger counter and wired to a bomb. Things are arranged so that if an alpha particle strikes the counter, the bomb will explode. When the bomb explodes, we know that it was caused by the positioning of the Geiger counter in relation to the radioactive matter. However, the laws of nature do not predict that the bomb will definitely explode. Even if no particle is emitted, it is still true that an alpha particle striking the Geiger counter will cause the bomb to explode. There is a causal connection, but the cause does not determine the effect.

Scruton also claimed that the findings of quantum mechanics show that there is a limit to what can be known about a particle when we consider it on a sub-atomic scale. Heisenberg's uncertainty principle says that there is an unpredictability in nature, and Scruton claimed that this does not simply describe isolated events of no general significance. It means that there is a systematic uncertainty in nature that is not simply a result of human ignorance. To say that every event is determined by a cause is, therefore, refuted by physics.

Kant argued that we cannot reconcile free will with our position in the universe as a part of nature and causal laws. We can only transcend this conflict. Both Libertarianism and Determinism offer a complete description of the world, but their descriptions come from rival viewpoints. If I raise my arm, the viewpoint of understanding tells us about the natural process that took place (synapses fired, muscles contracted and so on). And the viewpoint of practical reason talks about reasons rather than causes: I raised my arm to get someone's attention. We can view an event from the perspective of practical reason because we are rational creatures with rights, duties, and values, not just objects to be observed.

AO2 activity 3

a) Divide a sheet of paper in two. On one side, summarise the arguments that you feel are persuasive in favour of Libertarianism. On the other side, summarise the arguments that you feel are persuasive in favour of Hard Determinism.

b) Look at your sheet of paper. Do you feel there is sufficiently compelling evidence that makes it possible to argue that free will is likely?

c) Is there any one argument in support of Libertarianism that you feel is stronger than all the other arguments on the sheet of paper? If yes, why is that argument so compelling to you?

To what extent should free moral agents follow a normative ethic?

This question asks you to consider whether someone who is free has a moral obligation to follow a normative ethical theory of moral behaviour, such as Natural Law or Situation Ethics. If a moral agent is free, then there is no reason to assume that following a normative ethical theory damages that freedom. Following the theory would be a free choice and, at any time, the moral agent could choose to abandon it. However, a person following the theory could find their choices restricted to behaviour that is consistent with the theory regardless of their own wishes in the moment.

The view that free moral agents should follow a normative ethic

Both Sartre and Max Stirner, while arguing that a moral agent should be completely free, did acknowledge the importance of relationships with other people. A human being rarely exists outside of any relationships with other people, and cooperation and respect are at the heart of the vast majority of normative ethical theories. For example, for Stirner, joining a Union of Egoists to achieve a goal is in a free moral agent's self-interest, and they can freely choose to join or not. Sartre acknowledged the importance of behaving authentically and recognising the freedom of other beings-for-themselves.

Libertarians argue that unless an individual is the ultimate cause of an action, it is not appropriate to punish them or hold them morally responsible. This means that normative ethical theories only make sense if moral agents are free beings. A free moral agent can make choices with the guidance of a normative ethical theory and can, legitimately, be praised for following it closely or blamed for ignoring its principles. Without freedom, such a system is meaningless, because the praise and blame have not been earned by the agent.

Normative ethical theories are vital for a healthy society. Free moral agents need a normative ethical theory to help them make consistent judgements and adjust their attitudes and behaviours to the people around them. This ensures their actions are not random or arbitrary. For example, Fletcher's Situation Ethics ensures that moral decisions are not *ad hoc* and are guided by *agape* (selfless love for others) and T.M. Scanlon's Contractualism requires free agents to create social contracts that respect the freedom, rationality, and equality of everyone involved.

The view that free moral agents should not follow a normative ethic

Sartre appeared to reject the idea that a moral agent should follow a normative ethical theory as they negotiate moral dilemmas. This is because he considered the free person should make their choices in abandonment. He meant that there is no guiding force, such as God, who will rescue us or instruct us in our moral behaviour. Instead, free people must make themselves through their own decisions, moulding their personalities as they become beings-for-themselves. This *ad-hoc* approach to morality suggests that allowing oneself to be bound by a set system of ethics would be to act in bad faith.

Rogers' assessment of what makes for a mentally healthy person could imply that following a normative ethical theory is unnecessary or even damaging to a person's ability to self-actualise. Rogers did not comment on such a question, but his instruction that clients require unconditional positive regard in order to make free, creative decisions, implies that a free person is one who can create their own ethical solutions when faced with dilemmas. A person with good mental health is not constrained by fixed laws or judgemental attitudes. Instead, they are free to make decisions that are consistent with their own sense of self.

Stirner argued that the free moral agent should certainly not follow a normative ethical theory unless, in a particular moment, it is in their own self-interest to do so. For Stirner, to be bound by normative ethical theories is to allow oneself to be shackled by duty or obligation to an illusion or 'spook', and to become little more than a sheep. The moral agent ends up striving to satisfy the requirements of the theory, and is never totally free to act in their own self-interest.

The view that free moral agents could follow a normative ethic

While it is possible that a free moral agent could see the value in following a normative ethical theory of some kind, there is no objective way that a free moral agent can choose which normative ethical theory they are going to live by. Even more rigid, legalistic systems, such as Natural Law, assume that a moral agent is free to choose their moral actions, so it is not as simple as selecting a system that most clearly allows for freedom. All normative ethical theories that involve praise or blame also assume people have freedom to make choices.

Rogers' approach to free will did not rule out the possibility that a moral agent could select a normative ethical theory that is consistent with their concept of self. An individual could use a normative ethical theory as a guide to help them make their actual self and their ideal self more congruent. Rogers may have been suspicious of theories that are restrictive or judgemental, such as more absolutist religious theories, if they prevented a client from being creative in their decision making. However, his Client-Centred Therapy was all about accepting people regardless of any mistakes they might make, and experimentation with normative ethical theories could be part of a person's journey towards self-actualisation.

Normative ethical theories imply a set of rules or duties that a moral agent is obliged to fulfil. This does not necessarily restrict a moral agent's freedom; a theory can act as a guide to help an individual reason a moral course of action. However, some normative ethical theories are more restrictive in their nature, including systems of authority or punishment that could be interpreted as limiting a person's free will. There is nothing to prevent a person from suspending their own moral autonomy in response

> **Synoptic link**
>
> Link to *Chapter 1: Ethical thought (part one)*. Remind yourself about Ethical Egoism and Max Stirner.

to a more restrictive theory; it could be an act of free will to do so. However, from that moment onward, it is difficult to see how that person can be understood as a free agent.

Does free will make the use of prayer irrelevant?

This question brings you back to religious notions of free will. It expects you to consider the role and purpose of prayer for religious believers, and evaluate whether that purpose can be fully achieved if believers accept that human beings have free will. It is worth looking back at Chapter 7 to help you answer a question like this, because that chapter considers whether or not prayer has any purpose if we are predestined.

The view that free will makes the use of prayer irrelevant

One of the traditional purposes of prayer is petition. When someone petitions God, they ask God to help them or to grant them certain requests. This can be seen in the Lord's prayer, which states:

> *Give us today our daily bread.* **"**
>
> Matthew 6:11, *Holy Bible (NIV)*

In this type of prayer, the believer is asking God to get involved in day-to-day life on the Earth, to change the course of events to ensure that an individual gets what they request. This clearly is incompatible with teachings about free will because it involves God interfering with the natural course of events and therefore compromising free will. For instance, if a believer prays that their bus arrives on time when they know the traffic is particularly bad, God would have to interfere in the natural order of things to make it happen: God would have to clear the traffic, finding ways to ensure people get out of the way of the bus or leave the roads the bus is traveling along, and remove the long queues waiting at earlier bus stops. God would have to interfere in the free will of lots of other people to answer the prayer of one individual.

If human beings have free will, then prayers of thanksgiving seem rather redundant. If God does not suspend free will to answer prayers, then there seems to be little that God can do that might require thanks. If God does suspend free will, then humans are required to thank God for setting aside the one gift that is supposed to bring meaning and purpose to human existence.

Prayers that ask for God's intervention treat freedom as though it is a toy, something to play with and then give back to God when it no longer suits your purpose. If God is expected to step in and fix human problems when asked, then free will only operates on a temporary basis. Real freedom requires God not to intervene directly to answer individual prayers, and not to change the course of nature or interfere in the affairs of the world.

AO2 activity 4

Look back at the normative ethical theories covered in this book: Divine Command Theory, Virtue Theory, Ethical Egoism, Natural Law, Situation Ethics, and Utilitarianism. What do each of these theories say about free will? Do any of these theories make it difficult for people to be considered free moral agents? Do any of them appear to curtail free will in the way that they are applied?

Richard Swinburne has argued that free will requires human responsibility where actions matter and consequences count. Therefore, we can argue that God must not intervene to rescue humanity, even if asked to do so in a prayer; God must allow people to live with the consequences of their human actions.

The view that free will does not make the use of prayer irrelevant

Prayer is relevant even if humans have free will. Prayer is traditionally used to praise God, to petition God, to confess, and to offer God thanks. Even if God is unable or unwilling to answer, prayer has a purpose. It is an active demonstration that a believer has made the free choice to have faith in God.

Free will makes the use of prayer more relevant than predestation does. If humans are predestined then prayer is useless because, whatever they do, they cannot change the will of God or affect their own future. Prayer becomes pointless because nothing can be achieved by it. However, if humans are free, prayer is a way for people to decide their own destiny, helping them to alter their thoughts to focus more on God. The value of prayer is not in whether or not it affects God, but in its effect on the believer.

Prayer is about communicating and developing a relationship with a personal God. Human relationships are not limited to asking for things, saying sorry or thank you. They are multi-faceted, and communication is complex. Just as friends will reflect on events that have occurred and make decisions together, prayer enables a believer to do this in the presence of God so that they can make decisions in cooperation with God, with God's will at the centre of their decision-making process. This kind of communication can only take place if people are free.

The view that free will makes it difficult to see the use of prayer

Free will does not make prayer completely irrelevant, but it is reduced to little more than the secular practice of mindfulness. It is no longer about perfecting a relationship with a divine being who interacts with humanity, because that would compromise human free will. Prayer becomes simply about focusing the individual mind on being aligned with God's will. There can be no expectation that God will respond, and some may ask whether there is anything more to be gained through prayer than can be gained by the secular practice of mindfulness.

John Hick suggested that in Irenaean-type theodicies, humans are at an epistemic distance from God. This means that we are distant in knowledge or awareness of God, so that our choices can be absolutely free. Just as it would be difficult to freely choose whether or not to obey the speed limit if the chief constable was sitting beside us in the car, it is difficult for people to make real choices if they are completely certain of God's presence. The freedom to sin is dependent upon human uncertainty in God's existence.

But if God is truly at this distance, it is difficult to see how effective prayer can be. It cannot be for the traditional purpose of communicating with God, because God's distance from human knowledge requires that there can be no concrete communication.

The Lord's Prayer becomes rather redundant if humanity has free will. The Lord's Prayer demonstrates that prayer is for praise, petition, thanksgiving, and confession. Yet, these purposes seem pointless if humans have free will, since God cannot intervene in the world without damaging free will. The best that humanity can do is to freely suspend their free will during prayer, giving back the gift of free will they have been given so they can be guided by God.

Synoptic link

Link to *A Level Religious Studies for Eduqas: Philosophy of Religion*, Chapter 3: Challenges to religious belief: the problem of evil and suffering. Remind yourself of the Irenaean type theodicy and the role of free will.

AO2 activity 5

Decide whether you think that prayer is irrelevant if humans have free will.

Practise structuring a paragraph to support your view:

- State your argument and give a reason for it.
- Find a quotation, example, or point from a scholar that agrees with your view.
- Summarise a direct challenge that someone might give to oppose your point of view.
- Find a quotation, example, or point from a scholar that would support their opposing view.
- Make a judgement about which is the stronger argument.
- Give a reason or additional evidence to support your judgement.

Try writing these ideas into a full paragraph, rather than a simple bullet point list.

To what extent can beliefs in free will and predestination be reconciled?

This question is asking if it is possible to believe in both free will and predestination at the same time. All four scholars that we have studied – Augustine and Pelagius, and Calvin and Arminius – seem to think that it is possible, because they all refer to both free will and predestination. However, you need to establish whether this is a reasonable approach, or whether the two ideas are entirely incompatible.

The view that beliefs in free will and predestination can be reconciled

Augustine reconciled the concepts of free will and predestination by allowing people the freedom to choose individual actions within the confines of our human nature. Our human nature is free, but it has been compromised by original sin. This means that we are free only to sin. Augustine's explanation reflects human experience of the real world. Human beings are limited by their nature; for example, they cannot flap their arms and fly away, but they are free to move and travel within the limits of their humanity. Under Augustine's thinking, human nature is limited by sin, so humans are free only to the extent that they can sin. God then chooses some from all those limited beings, thereby predestining some for salvation. God saves some out of mercy, even though justice does not allow everyone to be saved.

Karl Rahner argued that human beings consist of two elements. The first, 'person', is the part of us that is able to make real choices that bring about effects in the world and impact our own personalities. The second, 'nature', is the element that is constrained by biology, psychology, and society. These two elements make us who we are, and so we are never completely free of them. They also interact so we cannot be completely free or completely determined. Humanity can make free choices, but within the constraints of what we have made of ourselves through our choices and who we are. Paul Tillich argued that human action is part of a tension between freedom and unfreedom. We are not machines that are entirely predictable, but we are not a series of arbitrary acts either. Freedom exists within a context of systems and powers that impact upon us and restrict us.

Arminius reconciles free will and predestination by arguing that God cooperates with humanity so that God's will can be freely chosen, but only with the help and support of God's grace. In this way, God's grace enables human freedom rather than destroying it, and God's sovereignty over all things is upheld.

The view that beliefs in free will and predestination cannot be reconciled

It is a paradox to suggest that Adam freely committed the original sin if God preordained that he would do so. Calvin's doctrine of predestination suggests that God decided, before creation, that Adam would fall, and so God is the author of sin and should be held responsible for evil in the world; Adam is the victim, predestined, never free.

Arminius' suggestion that predestination results from God's knowledge rather than God's direct action is not predestination at all. There is a big difference between knowing what someone will choose to do and actively directing them to do something. Knowing what someone will choose to do suggests uncertainty, because there was a real alternative that the individual could equally have chosen. John Feinberg pointed out that if God really is certain about what a person will choose, then they have not made a free choice at all. One cannot have complete certainty about what someone will do in advance of them performing a truly free action; if one is certain, then other options were not possible and the action was never really free.

Holding a belief in free will and predestination at the same time involves redefining 'free will' very narrowly so that it becomes freedom only to sin, or redefining 'predestination' very broadly so that it becomes knowing all possible events in all possible circumstances. Either way, the terms cease to mean what we usually expect them to mean; in their usual sense they are not, therefore, reconcilable. This is akin to the challenge that Flew made regarding the falsification principle: eventually free will and predestination are redefined until one of them simply does not exist anymore.

The view that beliefs in free will and predestination can be partially reconciled

It is not correct to see humanity as completely free in the way that Pelagius did. There are aspects of our lives that we are not in control of. We are influenced by society; for instance, Freud pointed out that our morality is shaped by our nurture, or upbringing in our family, and society, until it becomes part of our unconscious mind. We are also influenced by our genetic inheritance since our nature influences what we desire. While this is not quite the same as the seminal presence described by Augustine, where the sin of Adam is passed on to the rest of humanity as they were present in his semen, human personalities are determined by our nature and our nurture, and therefore give us some predisposition to certain acts that religious believers would class as sin.

According to Arminius, Calvin's understanding of predestination is inspired by Satan, and is utterly incompatible with the Christian doctrine of free will. However, Arminius' understanding of predestination requires God's middle knowledge of all the possible choices people may make and who will be saved, without God causing the choices people make. God's tolerance of our decisions allows human freedom without damaging God's sovereignty, and this appears to be a way that free will and predestination can be reconciled.

Augustine's doctrine of predestination allows for humanity to be free, even if it is in a restricted way. Our freedom to sin is freedom within the boundaries of sin. This means that we can choose what we desire, but what we desire is sinful because of our fallen nature. For Augustine, God's grace collaborates with sinners, and those who have been liberated from sin through God's grace can do good works and can grow in holiness. So, while humans can do nothing good without God, they do have free will to choose their sins.

AO2 activity 6

Consider whether you agree or disagree that beliefs about free will can be reconciled with beliefs about predestination. Answer the following questions:

- Do I like the idea from Augustine, Calvin, Pelagius, or Arminius about whether we are both free and predestined?
- Do any of these ideas make sense?
- Do their ideas conflict with or complement Christian teaching?
- Which are simpler or more complicated options?
- How do the ideas make any difference to my life or the lives of others?

Give reasons for each of your answers.

Practising AO1 questions

You now know the kinds of AO1 command words that you might face, and have seen many common essay writing mistakes that students make and how to avoid them. Now it would be useful to consider how to put all these features together.

Read the past paper question below and the example paragraph written in response before completing the activity on page 345.

> *Examine Arminius' concept of free will.*
>
> (Eduqas A Level Religious Studies, Summer 2019, Component 3: Religion and Ethics, Question 5a)

Example

Arminius[6] thought scripture was clear that people have[1] free will[2]. For example, in Luke 24:47, Jesus commands the disciples to tell everyone they should repent so their sins can be forgiven.[4] This means that people must have the[1] free will[2] to obey or rebel[1] because a loving God would surely not command evil by condemning people to hell no matter what they choose[3]. Arminius[6] thought the Calvinistic doctrine of[1] limited atonement[7], that God elects some people based on nothing but his own will, was[1] 'repugnant to the nature of God'[6]. Instead, he taught that Jesus died for everyone's sin, but that only those who use their[1] free will[2] to accept God will be saved.[1] Arminius[6] acknowledged that human beings cannot make this kind of good choice without the help of God's[1] grace[7], but that God does not force faith upon people.[1] Arminius[6] refers to[1] prevenient grace[7], which is the work of the Holy Spirit. This is offered to everyone and gives them the ability to receive Christ's[1] salvation[7]. God also gives[1] subsequent grace[7], which is the help of the Holy Spirit inside the person to help them accept the gift. Therefore,[1] Arminius[6] taught that the Holy Spirit cooperates with individual human[1] free will[2] so that people can choose faith.[1]

What went well

1. This paragraph is thorough and accurate in its explanation of some of the aspects of Arminius' concept of free will.

2. This paragraph makes regular reference to the question by using the term 'free will' and the name 'Arminius' throughout the response.

3. The paragraph uses an example to explain why God's character must demand humans have free will.

4. There is an example of a source of wisdom. While it is not directly quoted, the student shows clear knowledge and understanding of the contents of the quotation and its relevance to Arminius.

5. This response has not made any connections with other approaches. This is not a problem in this paragraph since connections should not be forced.

6. In this paragraph, the only scholar who is necessary is Arminius, and the paragraph refers to his teaching throughout.

7. The student has used specialist vocabulary appropriately and in context.

Activity

a) Read the example paragraph on page 344 and identify three things that this student did successfully in their response.

b) Make a list of things that must be added to complete the entire essay and ensure that it fully addresses the question.

AO1 practice question 1

Now it is your turn. Have a go at answering the following question. There are some points to remember underneath to help you if you are not sure how to start.

> *Explain the arguments of the philosopher Jean-Paul Sartre and the psychologist Carl Rogers in support of Libertarianism.*
>
> (WJEC A Level Religious Studies, Summer 2019, A2 Unit 4: Religion and Ethics, Question 2)

Points to remember

- Make sure that you include every aspect of the question in your answer: Jean-Paul Sartre, Carl Rogers, and Libertarianism.
- Use the key vocabulary that is relevant to each of the scholars, such as 'bad faith' or 'self-actualising'.
- Make sure that you give plenty of examples to demonstrate the scholarly arguments. Sartre gives a wealth of examples for you to choose from.

AO1 practice question 2

Now try this question by yourself.

> *Explain Libertarianism with reference to philosophical, scientific and psychological concepts.*
>
> (Eduqas A Level Religious Studies, Summer 2018, Component 3: Religion and Ethics, Question 2a)

Practising AO2 questions

As you now know, AO2 questions always require analysis and evaluation. You now know how to pick apart the details of any issues that you raise and to weigh up the quality of any arguments that you present. You have also seen the importance of making sure that you answer the question carefully and you know how to plan an effective answer. Now it would be useful to consider how to put all these features together.

Read the past paper question below and the example paragraphs written in response before completing the activity on page 348.

> 'The libertarian concept of psychology inevitably leads to the belief that we are totally free.' Evaluate this view.
>
> (Eduqas A Level Religious Studies, Summer 2018, Component 3: Religion and Ethics, Question 2b)

Example 1

The question presents us with a[1] paradox[6]. If adopting the belief we are[1] free is inevitable[2], then we have no choice to believe anything else. We are[1] determined to believe that we are free[2] as soon as we hear[1] Rogers'[4] psychological explanations of human behaviour. However[1], Rogers[4] does not necessarily lead us to believe in[1] total free will[2]. He accepted the[1] behaviourist[6] approach of scholars like[1] Skinner[4] do lead clients to be programmed by the therapist. He said that 'behaviour, when examined scientifically, is surely best understood as determined by prior causation'[3]. This is[1] Determinism[6] not free will. In addition, he claimed that his approach actually caused patients to make less predictable choices when in receipt of[1] unconditional positive regard[6], implying Determinism. Yet, it does seem that as a result of undergoing[1] Roger's[4] Client-Centred[6] Therapy, a[1] fully-functioning[6] individual should necessarily[1] believe that they are totally free[2], even if they are not.[1] He said freedom is 'an important condition of the relationship' because that is the only way that such individuals can achieve[3] congruence[6] and therefore, the belief in free will does appear to be inevitable[2].

What went well

1 There is a substantial amount of confident critical analysis as the student has engaged with the question perceptively and analysed it.

2 The paragraph addresses the question all the way through, noticing subtleties such as the 'belief' in 'total' freedom rather than simply weighing up whether we have free will.

3 There are no specific examples given in this paragraph. However, as evidence, the student has given two quotations from Rogers to back up their points.

4 There is a great deal of focus on the work of Rogers. There is also mention of Skinner and behaviourism.

5 There is no attempt to make connections with other areas of the course. There is no need to force a connection, however it is possible that there could be links to Freud from the Philosophy paper if this supported a relevant point.

6 There is significant use of specialist vocabulary that is relevant to the work of Rogers.

Example 2

Rogers'[4] approach to free will was a psychological[2] one. He acknowledged that psychology could determine and predict human behaviour through[1] operant conditioning[6] or[1] applying fixed methodology like a mechanic fixing a car[3], but he did not consider it desirable.[1] He argued that 'colossal rigidity… has a very poor record of evolutional survival'[3] because he thought that such methods were damaging for the personality[1]. This means that it is not inevitable that we should consider ourselves to have free will[2] because free will depends upon the type of therapy or experiences that a person receives. However[1], Rogers[4] felt that a possible goal of psychology could be to enable people to have freedom to live as[1] fully functioning[6] people[1]. Client Centred therapy functioning[6] can allow humans to have unpredictable freedom in their decision making[1]. Yet, this is not the same as free will being inevitable[2]. It simply means that free will is possible. Evaluation type therapies will always be[1] 'threatening'[4] to free will according to[1] Rogers[4] and so they are undesirable, but this does not mean we[1] must believe in free will[2]. Free will cannot ever really be known through psychological investigation because, by definition, it is unpredictable and therefore unanalysable.[1]

What went well

1. This paragraph contains arguments on both sides of the question statement. This student has not engaged with the question in the same way as example 1, but has still produced clear analysis and evaluation.

2. This paragraph contains regular reference to the wording of the question throughout.

3. The paragraph contains a brief example to illustrate a point, and includes a quotation from Rogers to support the idea that conditioning is not beneficial.

4. The student has included reference to Rogers, and has mentioned operant conditioning, but without reference to any other scholar.

5. There are no connections made to any other part of the course. This is not a problem as these connections should not be forced, but there could be a reference to the methodology of Freud from the Philosophy paper, which Rogers rejected.

6. There is accurate use of specialist language in context.

Activity

a) Read Example 1 on page 346 and Example 2 on page 347. Find five differences between the two responses. Which example do you think is better and why?

b) Make a list of four things you could do to write an effective conclusion to an essay on this question.

AO2 practice question 1

Now it is your turn. Have a go at answering the following question. There are some points to remember underneath to help you if you are not sure how to start.

> *'Free will means that God is not responsible for evil.' Evaluate this view.*
>
> (WJEC A Level Religious Studies, Summer 2018, Unit 4: Religion and Ethics, Question 6)

Points to remember

- There is a good opportunity here for you to include some connections from the Philosophy paper by including reference to the problem of evil.
- Make use of scholars such as Arminius and Pelagius, but also draw from the scholars in Chapter 7 by using Augustine and Calvin. If relevant to a point that is answering the question, you can even use scholars like Irenaeus.
- Remember to think about both natural and moral evil when considering God's responsibility for evil. You might also consider the nature of God as a creator, and whether he can be held responsible for the existence of hell.

AO2 practice question 2

Now try this question by yourself.

> *'Arminius' concept of free will is totally unconvincing.' Evaluate this view.*
>
> (Eduqas A Level Religious Studies, 2019, Component 3: Religion and Ethics, Question 5b)

Mark schemes for all exam questions can be found at www.eduqas.co.uk and www.wjec.co.uk.

Glossary

A Declaration of Sentiments: Arminius' writing that details his own views on free will and predestination

absolutist: the belief that there are universal moral principles or acts that are intrinsically right or wrong

Act Utilitarianism: a form of Utilitarianism associated with Bentham that treats each moral situation as unique, and each 'act' is deemed to be right or wrong based on the consequences it produces; Bentham presumed that happiness should be sought and pain avoided

actual self: the person that an individual sees themselves as being in reality, based upon their previous life experiences

agape: (Greek) the 'selfless love' principle which is the foundation of Fletcher's Situation Ethics

altruism: actions that are motivated by a desire for the well-being of another person, even at one's own personal cost

antecedent causes: causes that happened before an event that occurs later

antinomianism: 'against law'; the idea that people are under no obligation to obey the laws of ethics or morality as presented by religious authorities

apostasy: give up, or fall away from, one's faith

apparent good: Aquinas viewed an apparent good as an act that seems to be in accordance with right reason but is not; instead it moves us further away from the ideal human nature that God had planned for us

arbitrariness problem: the criticism of Divine Command Theory that morality must be determined by a whim of God if it is based upon God's commands

arete: (Greek) excellence, goodness, or virtue

asceticism: self-disciplined avoidance of sensual pleasure

asylum seeker: someone who crosses an international border to find safety from war or persecution; they are referred to as a refugee once their claim for asylum, for safety, has been accepted

atonement: the reconciliation of God and humanity through the redemptive life and death of Jesus

bad faith: self-deception; refusing to accept the fact of personal freedom and acting as though Determinism is true

basic human good: Finnis' Natural Law identifies seven basic human goods as the basis for morality: life, knowledge, friendship, play, aesthetic experience, practical reasonableness, and religion

beatific vision: a right relationship or fellowship with God that is sought through reason in this life and fully achieved in eternal life with God in heaven after death

Beatitudes: blessedness; the complete happiness that comes from being blessed by God; the blessings recounted by Jesus in the Sermon on the Mount

capital punishment: the legally authorised killing of someone as a punishment for a crime

cardinal virtues: virtues identified by Plato, developed by Aristotle and recognised as key virtues by Aquinas: prudence, justice, fortitude, and temperance; they are believed to form the basis of a moral life

casuistry: the application of general ethical principles to particular cases of conduct (as in Natural Law)

cognitive: connected with thinking or mental processes relating to knowledge; a cognitive statement is a statement that can be known to be true or false

commensurate: measuring or weighing up in relation to something else

compatibilist: the view that free will and Determinism are not contradictory but, rather, are entirely compatible

concrete universal: the realisation of the self as an integrated part of the society that has constructed it

concupiscence: the desire for earthly pleasures

conditional predestination: the election of those who have first chosen to have faith in Christ; also known as conditional election

congruence: the state in which a person's ideal self and actual self are very similar

consequentialist: a theory that judges the goodness or badness of a moral action based on its outcome

controlled immigration: where laws limit the number of people who can immigrate to a country, or restrict the circumstances in which immigration can take place

deduction: reasoning in which the premises of an argument lead to one possible conclusion

deontological: from the Greek, *déon*, for duty; deontological ethical theories are normative ethical theories that focus on duty and rules that govern how a person 'ought' to behave

Determinism: the philosophical idea that all events are necessarily the effect of antecedent causes

direct action: the immediate action that was intentionally performed

disvalue: lack of moral importance or worth; of negative value or worth

Divine Command Theory: an ethical theory that believes morality is dependent upon God; moral goodness occurs when moral agents are obedient to God's commands

divine concurrence: God permitting human sin, while at the same time disapproving of it

Doctrine of Election: the Calvinist teaching of predestination: God's unchangeable command that from before the creation of the world, God would save some (the Elect) for eternal life, while others (the Reprobates) would be sentenced to 'eternal damnation'

dogma: a fixed set of rigid principles or beliefs that must be accepted without question

double predestination: God has selected, in advance, some souls for damnation and others for salvation

economic migrant: sometimes referred to as a migrant worker; someone who chooses to live in another country to improve their standard of living

eigenheit: (German) ownness; Max Stirner's word for complete moral control over one's own decisions

Elect: also sometimes called Saints; those chosen by God, before the creation of the world, to receive salvation

embryo: a new organism in an early stage of development, between the second and eighth week after fertilisation

Emotivism: an ethical theory which argues that ethical decisions are expressions of feelings and emotions rather than meaningful rational argument; also known as ethical non-cognitivism

empirical: based on, and verifiable, using our five senses; empirical knowledge comes from things that can be experienced or observed

empiricist: someone who states that knowledge can only be found through experience of the material world

ensoulment: the dualist idea that a body is animated with a distinct and separate soul at a particular moment in time

Ethical Egoism: an ethical theory that claims moral agents should do what is in their own self-interest; an action is morally right if it maximises one's self-interest

être-en-soi: (French) being-in-itself; an object that has no conscious awareness

être-pour-soi: (French) being-for-itself; a free agent who can make themselves through free, conscious choices

eudaimonia: human flourishing or living well (sometimes translated as happiness)

Euthyphro dilemma: a dilemma originally found in Plato's dialogue *Euthyphro*, asking if goodness is dependent or independent of, God

existentialist: a philosophical idea that human existence is without a set purpose in an uncaring universe; it emphasises human responsibility for actions

ex nihilo: (Latin) out of nothing

external act (exterior act): the physical act itself

external cause: a cause that exists outside the control of a moral agent, e.g. being locked in a room

facticity: the facts of a situation or circumstance

fallacy: a false or mistaken idea

Five Articles of Remonstrance: a summary of a work called *The Remonstrance*, which was signed by followers of Arminius and debated at the Synod of Dort in 1618–1619

five primary precepts: the five main purposes of humankind's existence (given by God) according to Aquinas' Natural Law Theory

foetus: an unborn young, beyond the eighth week after fertilisation

four levels of law: Aquinas believed there was a hierarchy of law, with four levels: Eternal Law, Divine Law, Natural Law, and Human Law

four working principles: one of two sets of guiding principles of Situation Ethics to help people assess the most loving action in any given situation; they are Pragmatism, Relativism, Positivism, and Personalism

free will: the belief that God allows humanity the ability to choose between different courses of action

fully functioning person: a person with a healthy personality who lives a fulfilling 'good' life

general thinking: using empirical evidence and reasoning to determine the facts and relationships involved in a situation

genes: units of DNA that control the development or function of characteristics in an organism

genetic inheritance: characteristics are passed from parents to their offspring through DNA

Golden Rule: the principle of treating others as you would like to be treated, which appears in one form or another in most religions and cultures

grace: for Augustine, the gift of mercy shown to humanity that rescues some from sin through Jesus' death on the cross

greatest happiness principle: according to Utilitarianism, an action is right if it produces the greatest happiness for the greatest number

Hard Determinism: the proposition that all actions are caused and therefore determined, meaning that there is no such thing as a 'free' choice

harm principle: a principle created by Mill that argues the only reason power can be rightfully exercised over another person, against their will, is to prevent harm to others

hedonic calculus: the seven criteria by which Bentham attempts to measure happiness and determine whether or not an act is right

hedonism: valuing or seeking pleasure as the highest good

hedonistic: concerned with maximising happiness or pleasure

higher pleasures: a term used by John Stuart Mill to identify superior pleasures of the mind

Hume's Law: Hume argued that there is a significant difference between descriptive statements (what is) and prescriptive statements (what one ought to do), so you cannot derive what should be done from what is the case; also known as 'Hume's Guillotine'

ideal self: the person that an individual wishes they were

imago dei: (Latin) in the image of God

immigration: the act of migrating to another country, usually for permanent residence

incompatibilist: the view that free will and Determinism cannot co-exist

indirect action: understood differently by different thinkers, as an accidental effect of an action or as an immediate but unintended, known aspect or by-product of an act

induction: reasoning in which the premises of an argument lead towards one possible conclusion

inerrant: without error; cannot be wrong

instrumental knowledge: knowledge that is sought to achieve a further objective, such as money or popularity

internal act (interior act): the intention for performing an act

internal cause: a cause that exists within or originates from the mind of the moral agent, e.g. a desire for food

Intuitionism: an ethical theory which argues that intuition forms the foundation of ethical knowledge; also known as Ethical Non-Naturalism

irresistible grace: the Elect cannot resist the calling of God

justified: saved by the death of Jesus Christ on the cross

legalism: conformity to law or to a strict religious or moral code

libertas: (Latin) liberty

Libertarianism: a philosophy that holds that human beings are free, have free will, and concepts of Determinism are false

liberum arbitrium: (Latin) free will to choose

licit: permissible or legal

limited atonement: Christ's death and atonement for humanity's sins was for the Elect only

lower pleasures: a term used by John Stuart Mill to identify inferior pleasures of the body

massa peccati: (Latin) a lump of sin

meta ethics: a branch of ethics that is concerned with the meaning of ethical terms, the nature of moral statements and the foundations of moral principles

meta-ethical: concerning the meaning of ethical terms, the nature of moral statements, and the foundations of moral principles

metaphysical: relating to existence or knowledge that are non-physical, supernatural and beyond purely sensory description, such as love, truth, and God

middle knowledge: God's knowledge of the full range of possible events that could occur and the full range of actions that a person could choose from in response

miracle: an act of wonder; variously defined, for example, as a violation of the laws of nature (Hume) and an unusual and striking event that evokes and mediates a vivid awareness of God (Hick)

moral evil act: an act that is defined as bad because it breaks a religious rule and is therefore immoral; includes evil intent as part of the action

Moral Rationalism (Ethical Rationalism): the meta-ethical view that moral principles are knowable through a process of philosophical reasoning

moral realism: ethical statements can be shown to have an objective reality or be objectively true; they are not just a matter of opinion or feelings

moral thinking: coming to an intuitive understanding of our obligations

moral virtues: Aristotle established 12 moral virtues that need to be developed by identifying and practising the mean between the two vices of deficiency and excess

mortal sin: a grave sin that involves deliberately and knowingly turning away from God and his grace; a mortal sin requires repentance before death or there will be punishment in the afterlife

natural grace: the gifts of reason and free will that are an essential part of the human nature created by God

Naturalism: an ethical theory which argues that objective moral principles can be derived from empirical, naturalistic facts; also known as Ethical Naturalism or Naturalistic Ethics

Naturalistic Fallacy: an argument associated with G.E. Moore which states that moral facts cannot be reduced to natural properties

Nine Requirements of Practical Reason: nine principles developed by Finnis that create the optimum conditions to attain the basic goods

non-cognitive: a proposition that is not concerned with facts about the world and cannot, therefore, be known as true or false

non-natural property: a term Moore uses to refer to an ethical property that is not discoverable by empirical investigation

normative: concerning the rules or principles that determine ethical attitudes and behaviour

nutritive: relating to nutrition or nourishment; characteristic of all living things

objective: a truth or reality that is independent from the mind of the individual who perceives it

omnibenevolent: all-loving, perfectly good

omnipotence: an attribute of God that states God has an infinite level of power

omnipotent: all-powerful

Open Question Argument: an argument associated with G.E. Moore and his Naturalistic Fallacy; terms like 'good' cannot be defined according to natural qualities because any attempt to do so results in an open question

original sin: the condition of sinfulness and guilt that all humans are born into, caused by the first sin of Adam and Eve, and passed down through the generations

pardon: the forgiveness of sins offered by God to human beings when they repent

perseverance of the Elect: the Elect cannot commit apostasy (give up their faith); the Holy Spirit ensures this

Philosophical Determinism: the 'hard determinist' philosophical position which argues that all events are necessarily the effect of prior events and conditions subject to the laws of nature

phronesis: using practical wisdom or prudence to work out how to be virtuous in a given situation

pluralism objection: an objection to Divine Command Theory that refers to the contradictory nature of God's commands as claimed by different religions

polyamorous relationship: a romantic and intimate, sometimes sexual, relationship between more than two people, which all the participating parties are aware of and fully consent to

polygamy: being legally married to more than one person at the same time

posits: suggests something is true

practical reason: a specific form of reasoning that we use to determine what 'ought' to be done; can be contrasted with theoretical reason

prayer: a devout petition to God or to an object of worship

pre-determined: something decided in advance

pre-embryo: a fertilised egg in the first 14 days of development, before implantation in the uterus

pre-moral: prior to the formulation of a moral code or law

pre-moral (or ontic) evil: for proportionalists this is an unavoidable lack of perfection that is present in all human actions. Pre-moral/ontic evil includes natural disasters, which are a result of living in a fallen world, as well as the unintended evil that is part of any decision we make.

precepts: guiding principles, rules, or commands

predestination: the belief that God has already decided what will happen and, specifically, has already elected certain souls for salvation

preliminaries: the initial facts about a situation that will help an intuition to be formed

prevenient grace: the grace given by God that precedes the act of a sinner choosing faith in Jesus Christ

principle of discrimination: the principle that determines who are appropriate targets in war and who should be immune from attack

principle of double effect: a principle to manage situations where precepts conflict; where one action will produce two effects, one of which violates a precept, the action that was intended will be judged

principle of the lesser of two evils: a principle that allows a moral agent to choose the lesser evil of two evil options when there is no other choice available

principle of totality: the principle that parts are ordered for the good of the whole; e.g. organs are useful for the whole body, but have no moral significance outside of the body

principle of utility: Bentham developed the principle of utility which states that an action is right if it promotes pleasure and reduces pain

Proportionalism: a twentieth-century development of Natural Law, centred around a debate about proportionate reason as identified by Aquinas in the principle of double effect

proposition: a statement or proposal that requires proof or demonstration

pseudo-concept: having the appearance of a concept but falsely categorised as a concept

Psychological Determinism: a form of Hard Determinism based on the study of human behaviour; all actions, thoughts, and feelings are the inevitable outcome of complex psychological processes

Psychological Egoism: a descriptive theory that proposes that people naturally act out of self-interest

puritanical: rigid adherence to strict rules of moral behaviour that forbid pleasure

qualitative: a measure of the standard or value of an item, experience, or situation

quantitative: a term applied to Bentham's assessment of happiness – concerning amount (of happiness, as opposed to quality)

real good: Aquinas viewed a real good as an act that is in accordance with right reason, which helps us become nearer to the ideal human nature that God had planned for us

recta ratio: (Latin) right reason

reductionist: an attempt to explain something complex in an over-simplified way

refugee: someone who crosses an international border to find safety from war or persecution; a refugee is an asylum seeker who has had their claim for asylum, for safety, accepted

relativist: the view that 'right' or 'wrong' are not absolute, fixed, objective, or unchanging, but are to be judged in relation to something else, such as how much love they produce or the culture that someone is based in; it means morality can be understood differently by different people

Reprobates: those not chosen by God as one of the Elect are predestined to receive just punishment for their sinful nature

revelation: the gift of God's law and the example of Jesus' life on Earth, given to humanity through scripture

revisionists: another name for proportionalists, who are concerned with a revision of the traditional understanding of Natural Law

Rule Utilitarianism: a view associated with John Stuart Mill; rule utilitarians believe that by using the principle of utility, one can draw up general rules, based on past experiences, which would help to keep this principle and so should be obeyed

sanctified: given the ability to obey God's will

Scientific Determinism: a form of Hard Determinism based on the theory of causation; for every physical event there is a physical cause, and this causal chain can be traced back to the Big Bang

secular: having no connection with religion

self-actualise: the realisation of a person's individual potential

self-evident: containing within itself the evidence or justification for itself; no external proof is required

self-realisation: identifying one's place in society and the role or function that one plays in society, and the duties associated with that role

sensitive: concerning the senses and features of a being that are shared with all animals, such as feeling and movement

single predestination: God has selected, in advance, some souls for salvation

six fundamental principles: one of two sets of guiding principles of Situation Ethics to help people assess the most loving action in any given situation; they are: love is the only good, love is the ruling norm of Christianity, love equals justice, love for all, loving ends justify the means, and love decides situationally

Soft Determinism: the proposition that all actions have elements of free will within causally-determined boundaries

special revelation: the knowledge that God reveals directly to humanity through supernatural means (e.g. via the Bible)

speciesism: a prejudice or attitude of bias in favour of the interests of members of one's own species and against those of members of other species

speculative knowledge: theoretical, intellectual knowledge that seeks truth

spook: an illusion or an abstract idea that people treat as reality

subsequent grace: the grace given by God that helps a sinner by cooperating with them so that they can make a free choice of saving faith in Jesus Christ

sui generis: (Latin) of its own kind; unique; in a class of its own

station: our place within society; the role that we play in society

synderesis rule: the natural desire of humans to do good and avoid evil

tabula rasa: (Latin) blank slate; the idea that at birth there is no part of our character that is predetermined or fixed

tautology: repeating an idea within a statement, maybe with different words, but giving no new information about the idea

teleological: from the Greek, *telos;* to do with end goals or outcomes

telos: (Greek) end, purpose, or goal

theists: people who believe in a personal, creator God who can and does interact with humanity; Christians, Muslims and Jews are theists

theocentric: focused on God as the central or ultimate concern

Theological Naturalism: using reason, based on human experience or natural phenomenon, to arrive at religious beliefs

Theological Positivism: starting with faith, rather than reason, to arrive at religious beliefs

theoretical reason: reasoning that concerns factual, descriptive matters; can be contrasted with practical reason

three revealed virtues: the three virtues of faith, hope and charity, revealed or disclosed through Scripture in 1 Corinthians 13

unconditional election: the Elect are chosen purely through God's will

unconditional positive regard: acceptance and support no matter what a person does

uncontrolled immigration: when there are no restrictions on the number of people who can immigrate to a country

underivative: original, not having been brought about by, or based upon, other things

universal causation: the laws of cause and effect occur to everything that exists in the universe, without exception

unreflective consciousness: an awareness in the mind of our moral obligations, which is independent of general thinking

utility: how useful an act or object is in bringing about pleasure or happiness

value maximisation: an approach to Proportionalism proposed by Hallett that involves balancing the moral values in any action to maximise value as fully or nearly as fully as any alternative action

Virtue Theory: a broad term for a range of moral theories that focus on the role of character and virtue rather than specific actions; also known as Virtue Ethics

Index

Acknowledgements

The publisher would like to thank the following for permission to use copyright material:

Scripture quotations [marked NIV] are taken from the **Holy Bible, New International Version®**, NIV®. Copyright © 1973, 1978, 1984, 2011 by Biblica, Inc.™ Used by permission of Zondervan. All rights reserved worldwide. www.zondervan.com
The "NIV" and "New International Version" are trademarks registered in the United States Patent and Trademark Office by Biblica, Inc.™
Excerpts from **Catechism of the Catholic Church**, http://www.vatican.va/archive/ccc_css/archive/catechism/ccc_toc.htm (Strathfield, NSW: St Pauls, 2000). Reproduced with permission from The Vatican. © Libreria Editrice Vaticana
Excerpts from *Eduqas A Level Religious Studies, 2019, Component 3: Religion and Ethics; Eduqas A Level Religious Studies, Autumn 2020, Component 3: Religion and Ethics; Eduqas A Level Religious Studies, Sample Assessment Materials, Component 3: Religion and Ethics; Eduqas A Level Religious Studies, Summer 2018, Component 3: Religion and Ethics; Eduqas A Level Religious Studies, Summer 2019, Component 3: Religion and Ethics; Eduqas AS Level Religious Studies, Summer 2017, Component 3: An Introduction to Religion and Ethics; Eduqas AS Level Religious Studies, Summer 2019, Component 3: An Introduction to Religion and Ethics; WJEC A Level Religious Studies, Sample Assessment Material, A2 Unit 4: Religion and Ethics; WJEC A Level Religious Studies, Summer 2018, A2 Unit 4: Religion and Ethics; WJEC A Level Religious Studies, Summer 2019, A2 Unit 4: Religion and Ethics; WJEC AS Level Religious Studies, Summer 2018, AS Unit 2: An Introduction to Religion and Ethics*. Used under licence from WJEC CBAC Ltd. WJEC bears no responsibility for the example answers to questions taken from its past question papers which are contained in this publication.
R. M. Adams: *A Modified Divine Command Theory of Ethical Wrongness*, from G. Outka and J. R. Reeder (eds.), Religion and Morality, (Anchor Press, 1975). Reproduced with permission from R. M. Adams.
Augustine: *The Spirit and the Letter*, from Later Works, John Burnaby (ed.) (Westminster, John Knox Press, 1955). Reproduced with permission.
A. J. Ayer: *Philosophical Essays*, (Macmillan and Co., 1959). Reproduced with permission from Macmillan through PLSclear.
W. Barclay: *Ethics in a Permissive Society*, (Collins Fount Paperbacks, 1971). Reproduced with permission from the trustees for the Estate of William Barclay.
Cicero: *Volume XVI: On the Republic. On the Laws*, translated by Clinton W. Keyes, Loeb Classical Library Volume 213, (Harvard University Press, 1928). Loeb Classical Library ® is a registered trademark of the President and Fellows of Harvard College. Used by permission. All rights reserved.
M. Desmurget, et al.: *Movement Intention After Parietal Cortex Stimulation in Humans*, Science, volume 324, pp. 811–813 ww.science.sciencemag.org/content/324/5928/811.full (AAAS, 2009). Reproduced with permission from The American Association for the Advancement of Science.
Epicurus: *Letter to Menoeceus*, from The Extant Remains, translated by Cyril Bailey (Oxford University Press, 1926). Reproduced with permission from Oxford University Press.
J. Feinberg: *Predestination and Free will: Four views of Divine Sovereignty and Human Freedom*, (Downers Grove Intervarsity Press, 1986). Reproduced with permission.
J. Finnis: *H. L. A. Hart: A Twentieth-Century Oxford Political Philosopher: Reflections by a Former Student and Colleague*, The American Journal of Jurisprudence, Volume 54, Issue 1, pages 161–185, (Oxford University Press, 2009). Reproduced with permission from Oxford University Press.
J. Finnis: *Natural Law and Natural Rights*, (Oxford University Press, 2011). Reproduced with permission from Oxford University Press through PLSclear.
J. Finnis: *The Church Could Teach that Capital Punishment is Inherently Wrong*, Public Discourse, (Public Discourse, 2018). Reproduced with permission from Public Discourse.
J. Fletcher: *Situation Ethics: The New Morality*, (Westminster, John Knox Press, 1966). Reproduced with permission.
J. Fletcher: *Moral Responsibility: Situation Ethics at Work,* (Westminster, John Knox Press, 1967). Reproduced with permission.
G. Hallett: *Greater Good: The Case for Proportionalism*, (University of Notre Dame Press, 1983). Reproduced with permission from University of Notre Dame Press.
B. Hoose: *The Punishment of Criminals*, from Christian Ethics: An Introduction, Bernard Hoose (ed.), (Cassell, 1998). © B. Hoose. Continuum, an imprint of Bloomsbury Publishing Plc. Reproduced with permission.
B. Hoose: *Proportionalism: The American Debate and its European Roots*, (Georgetown University Press, 1987). Reproduced with permission from Georgetown University Press.

G. E. Moore: *Principia Ethica*, (Cambridge University Press, 1903). Reproduced with permission from T. Baldwin for the Estate of G. E. Moore.
William of Ockham: *Opera Theologica V*, version by Sharon Kaye, www.iep.utm.edu (Internet Encyclopedia of Philosophy, 2022). Reproduced with permission.
Pelagius: *Letter of Pelagius to Demetrias, AD 385*, from The Letters of Pelagius, Robert Van de Weyer (ed.), (Arthur James Ltd, 1996). Reproduced with permission from Fr Robert Van de Weyer
Pope Francis: *Fratelli Tutti*, October 3rd 2020 (The Vatican, 2). © Libreria Editrice Vaticana. Reproduced with permission from The Vatican.
Pope John Paul II: *Humanae Vitae*, July 25th 1968 (The Vatican, 1968). © Libreria Editrice Vaticana. Reproduced with permission from The Vatican.
Pope John Paul II: *Veritatis Splendor*, August 6th 1993, (The Vatican, 1993). © Libreria Editrice Vaticana. Reproduced with permission from The Vatican.
Pope John Paul II: *Evangelium Vitae*, March 25th 1995 (The Vatican, 1995). © Libreria Editrice Vaticana. Reproduced with permission from The Vatican.
H. A. Prichard: *Does Moral Philosophy rest on a Mistake?*, Mind, volume 21, issue 81 (Oxford University Press, 1912). Reproduced with permission from Oxford University Press.
C. Rogers: *On Becoming a Person: A Therapist's View of Psychotherapy*, (Houghton Mifflin, 1961). Reproduced with permission from HMH Co.
Sacred Congregation for the Doctrine of the Faith: *Declaration on Euthanasia*, May 5th 1980 (The Vatican, 1980). © Libreria Editrice Vaticana. Reproduced with permission from The Vatican.
J.-P. Sartre: *Being and Nothingness: An Essay on Phenomenological Ontology*, (Routledge, 1956). Reproduced with permission from Routledge through PLSclear.
J. A Selling: *The Problem of Reinterpreting the Principle of Double Effect*, Louvain Studies, Volume 8, pages 47—62. (Louvain Studies, 1980). Reproduced with permission from Pr J. A. Selling.
P. Singer: *Animal Liberation*, (Bodley Head, 2015). Reproduced with permission from Random House Group Ltd.
M. Stirner: *The Ego and His Own*, translated by Steven T. Byinton, (Verso Books, 2014). Reproduced with permission of Verso Books through PLSclear.

Cover photo: elodea.proteus/Shutterstock. **Photos: p11:** PX Media/Shutterstock; **p13:** Inked Pixels/Shutterstock; **p14:** Stephen Bisgrove / Alamy Stock Photo; **p16:** Marilyn McCord Adams; **p18:** Ververidis Vasilis/Shutterstock; **p23:** Chris Jackson/Getty Images; **p25:** public domain; **p28:** CoraMax / Shutterstock; **p47:** ChristianChan / Shutterstock; **p49:** View Apart / Shutterstock; **p52:** Lebrecht Music & Arts / Alamy Stock Photo; **p57:** Stocksnapper / Shutterstock; **p58:** © National Portrait Gallery, London; **p64:** Rawpixel.com / Shutterstock; **p66:** Popperfoto/Getty Images; **p68:** UK Parliament/Mark Duffy (CC BY 3.0); **p88:** Panchenko Vladimir / Shutterstock; **p91:** jorisvo / Shutterstock; **p93:** Radachynskyi Serhii / Shutterstock; **p94:** Onchira Wongsiri / Shutterstock; **p95:** Ringo Chiu / Shutterstock; **p104:** David Pereiras / Shutterstock; **p108:** meunierd / Shutterstock; **p126:** fizkes / Shutterstock; **p127:** Faculty of Law, Oxford University; **p134:** Matt Gush / Shutterstock; **p139:** megaflopp / Shutterstock; **p146:** Nicolas Economou / Shutterstock; **p152:** Alexander Chaikin / Shutterstock; **p175:** Ink Drop / Shutterstock; **p183:** Followtheflow / Shutterstock; **p186:** Claude Moore Health Sciences Library at the University of Virginia; **p188:** Fine Art Images/Heritage Images/Getty Images; **p193:** LightField Studios / Shutterstock; **p197:** Pressmaster / Shutterstock; **p216:** Pressmaster / Shutterstock; **p221:** Nick Harrison / Alamy Stock Photo; **p222:** Zolnierek / Shutterstock; **p223:** Everett Collection / Shutterstock; **p232:** unoL / Shutterstock; **p235:** Kev Gregory / Shutterstock; **p254:** SvetaZi / Shutterstock; **p257:** Miglena Boneva / Shutterstock; **p258:** GL Archive / Alamy Stock Photo; **p261:** The Granger Collection / Alamy Stock Photo; **p266:** GL Archive / Alamy Stock Photo; **p269:** vitstudio / Shutterstock; **p270:** Pictorial Press Ltd / Alamy Stock Photo; **p277:** Tatyana Dzemileva / Shutterstock; **p283:** Doidam 10 / Shutterstock; **p302:** MIA Studio / Shutterstock; **p305:** PVDE / Bridgeman Images; **p310:** Angelo Hornak / Alamy Stock Photo; **p315:** Dan Tautan / Shutterstock; **p321:** Pixel-Shot / Shutterstock; **p325:** LeventeGyori / Shutterstock; **p329:** Maciej Wojtkowiak / Alamy Stock Photo. **Artwork** by Integra Software Services.